SYRIA AND THE
DOCTRINE OF ARAB
NEUTRALISM

For My Children
Yoav, Mia and Oliver

SYRIA AND THE DOCTRINE OF ARAB NEUTRALISM

From Independence to Dependence

Rami Ginat

sussex
ACADEMIC
PRESS

BRIGHTON • PORTLAND

#55124329

4-26-06

2 4 6 8 10 9 7 5 3 1

First published 2005 in Great Britain by
SUSSEX ACADEMIC PRESS
PO Box 2950
Brighton BN2 5SP

and in the United States of America by
SUSSEX ACADEMIC PRESS
920 NE 58th Ave   Suite 300
Portland, Oregon 97213–3786

British Library Cataloguing in Publication Data
A CIP catalogue record for this book is available from the British Library.

Library of Congress Cataloging-in-Publication Data
Ginat, Rami.
 Syria and the doctrine of Arab neutralism : from independence to dependence / Rami Ginat.
    p. cm.
 Includes bibliographical references and index.
 ISBN 1-84519-008-4 (hardcover : alk. paper)
 1. Syria—Politics and government—20th century.
 2. Neutrality—Syria. 3. Arab nationalism—Syria. 4. Syria—Foreign relations. I. Title.
DS98.2.G56 2005
327.5691′009—dc22
                                                          2004010991
                                                          CIP

Typeset and designed by G&G Editorial, Brighton
Printed by MPG Books, Ltd, Bodmin, Cornwall
This book is printed on acid-free paper.

Contents

Illustrations

Jacket picture: Anti-Western demonstration in Damascus. The title of the banner is: "The purpose of the [Four Powers] collective defense [proposal] is the bringing in of foreign and Jewish armies into our country," *al-Musawwar*, 23 November 1951.

Illustrations between pages 137 and 143: All pictures courtsey of the Dayan Archive, Tel Aviv University.

Signing the formation of the United Arab Republic: Presidents Shukri al-Quwatli (Syria) and Gamal Abdel Nasser (Egypt), *al-Musawwar*, 7 February 1958.

Discussing the future of the union: Sabri al-'Asali, the Syrian Prime Minister (left), Akram al-Hawrani, a Ba'thist leader (second left), Egyptian President Nasser (second right) and the Syrian President al-Quwatli (right), *al-Musawwar*, 28 February 1958.

Greeting an old friend: Tito, the Yugoslav leader, and Nasser, the President of the UAR at the opening ceremony of the Belgrade Conference of non-aligned countries, *al-Musawwar*, 15 September 1961.

A post-Bandung meeting: Nehru, the Indian leader and his new ally Nasser, the Egyptian leader, Cairo, *al-Musawwar*, 15 July 1955.

Changing shifts: Shukri al-Quwatli, the newly elected Syrian President, at a meeting with his predecessor, Hashim al-Atasi (right), Damascus, *al-Musawwar*, 27 August 1955.

Spreading smiles in Cairo: Sa'id al-Ghazzi, the Syrian Prime Minister (white suit, left), Nasser (center), and the Saudi Crown Prince, Emir Faysal bin 'Abd al-'Aziz (right), satisfied with their consent to conclude a mutual military pact, *al-Musawwar*, 14 October 1955.

Following the formation of the UAR: Nasser and Nehru among the world's great leaders, a caricature in *al-Musawwar*, 7 March 1958.

Whither is Syria heading? One of many demonstrations in Damascus calling to object Western military defense arrangements and to adhere to a policy of neutralism, *al-Musawwar*, 17 December 1954.

A demonstration of Syrian women in the streets of Damascus remonstrating against the Four Powers' proposal to the Arabs to participate in the formation of a MEC, *al-Musawwar*, 15 November 1951.

The Cairo Conference of Arab leaders in response to the imminent Turco-Iraqi mutual defense pact. Faris al-Khuri, the Syrian Prime Minister, is in the middle between Nasser (left) and the Saudi Crown Prince, Emir Faysal bin 'Abd al-'Aziz (right), *Akhir Sa'ah*, 26 January 1955.

The opening speech of the Bandung Conference by Ahmad Sukarno, the Indonesian leader, *Akhir Sa'ah*, 27 April 1955.

Abbreviations

AMSZ	Arkhivum Ministerstva Sprav Zagranitshnykh [Archives of the Ministry of Foreign Affairs, Poland]
CENTO	Central Treaty Organization
CIA	Central Intelligence Agency
CPSU	Communist Party of the Soviet Union
FO	Foreign Office [Britain]
FRUS	Foreign Relations of the United States
ISA	Israel State Archive
KDP	Kurdish Democratic Party
MEC	Middle East Command
MEDO	Middle East Defense Organization
NA	National Archives of the USA
NAI	National Archives of India
NATO	North Atlantic Treaty Organization
NKVD	Narodni Komitet Venutrenix Dyel [People's Commissariat of Internal Affairs]
NMM&L	Nehru Memorial Museum & Library
NSC	National Security Council (US)
RGANI	Rossiiskii goasudarstvennyi arkhiv Noveishei Istorii [Russian Governmental Archive of Contemporary History]
PRO	Public Record Office
RCC	Revolutionary Command Council
RG 59	General Records of the Department of State
RG 84	Foreign Office Posts of the Department of State
RGASPI	Rossiskii goasudarstvennyi arkhiv sotsial'no-politicheskoi istorii [Russian governmental Archive of Social-Political History]
SAWPY	Socialist Alliance of Working People of Yugoslavia
SCP	Syrian Communist Party
SCUN	Security Council of the United Nations
SEATO	South East Asian Treaty Organization
SOAS	School of Oriental and Asian Studies

SPP	Syrian Partisans of Peace
SSNP	Syrian Social National Party
SWB	Summary of World Broadcast
UAR	United Arab Republic
UNO	United Nations Organization
WPM	World Peace Movement

Preface

This book deals with the modern history of post-mandatory Syria. It also deals, peripherally, with Third World and Arab countries such as India, Indonesia, Yugoslavia, and Egypt—the pioneering states of neutralism. The main concern is Syria's foreign policy, the chief feature of which was the reliance on the doctrine of Arab neutralism, a doctrine whose multi-faceted character is in keeping with its historical evolution. The effects that Arab neutralism had on shaping Syria's foreign policy and its national identity are examined. This study also charts the evolution of the ideology and policy of neutralism in Syria, from the early 1940s—the first days of the Cold War, when many Asian and Arab countries were still under the influence and hegemony of Western powers—through the 1950s and early 1960s, when revolutionary Arab countries such as Egypt and Syria (the two were united from 1958 to 1961) played a leading role in the newly established movement of non-aligned countries—the largest group of countries in the international arena. Although the focus is on Syria's foreign policy, it has many references to pre- and post-revolutionary Egypt, which exercised an enormous influence over Syria's foreign policy, in particular after the downfall of Adib al-Shishakli in 1954.

Following the end of World War II, Arab governments, in particular those in Syria and Egypt, began to wonder whether their close ties with the West served their national interests. Britain and France were considered by most Arab countries as imperialist powers whose aim was still to exploit the Arab world and to bring it under their control. Arab manifestations and expressions of goodwill toward the United States gradually changed to bitterness and disappointment. This was a result of three major factors: US policies toward the Arab–Israeli conflict; America's ambiguous stand during the years of intense struggle with Britain, particularly in the case of the Anglo-Egyptian conflict; and pressure to establish a Middle East Command, which would have meant allying the Arab nations themselves with the West in case of conflict with Eastern bloc countries.

In contrast to the Western powers, the USSR, while not necessarily considered trustworthy, was viewed by the Arabs as a power that did not share links with Western imperialism and did not have an imperialist record in the Middle East. The Soviets consistently, and without reservation, gave full support to the Arabs in their respective struggles to liberate their countries from foreign powers. Despite Soviet support, however, Arab leaders continued to suspect Soviet motives and emphasized their dislike of Soviet communism, preferring to conduct independent foreign policies that would coincide with their own interests. This approach was explained by Muhammad Salah al-Din, the then Egyptian Foreign Minister and formulator of Egypt's neutralism, in a statement he made on 11 July 1950:

> Egypt, which combats imperialism and considers it one of the causes of international disturbances and of wars, is equally anxious to combat the hidden imperialism implicit in communist methods. Like the Western powers, Soviet Russia seeks to exercise domination by conquering other nations from within and submitting them to dictatorship. Egypt wishes to spare weaker nations and the whole world the ambitions of domination, imperialism, and exploitation.

Although not defined by name, neutralism in practice had already emerged in some Arab countries by the end of World War II. This neutralism, which aimed at achieving full independence, was based on national interests and utilitarian purposes, and can be considered as a "calculative/pragmatic nationalist neutralism."

Since the late 1940s and early 1950s, India had gradually taken the leading role of the newly emerged post-colonial Asian and Arab states. India's third way of neutralism suited many of these new states that gradually embraced the doctrine. Relations between Arab countries and India had greatly improved since the latter had taken the Arab side throughout the debate over the future of Palestine in the late 1940s. By the early 1950s, India had managed to lay the initial foundations for the consolidation of the Asio-Arab camp in the UN. Following the successful outcome of the Bandung Conference of Afro-Asian states in 1955, Nehru, along with Nasser and Tito, became a co-leader of this camp. By the late 1950s–early 1960s, they had formed the movement of non-aligned states in reaction to the East–West Cold War conflict.

The phenomenon of Arab neutralism has been raised by many scholars, but has hitherto never been comprehensively investigated. Several studies have dealt with the Afro-Asian movement and the non-aligned movement, referring to Arab neutralism and Arab non-alignment within the framework of a wider Third World movement, and focusing mainly on Nasser's Egypt and the leading role it played in the non-aligned camp.[1] One such study is David Kimche's *The Afro-Asian Movement*,[2] which describes the historical process that led to the emergence of the Afro-Asian movement, starting with the initial stages of consolidating the Asio-Arab bloc and delineating the causes for its rise and decline. Kimche's references to the policy of Arab neutralism are only in relation to the Bandung Conference of 1955 and its aftermath, where he focuses on Nasser's Egypt. Kimche asserts that, in the post-Bandung years, Nasser was the one who transformed the policy of non-alignment "into the dominant trend in Asia and Africa . . . [he] set the pace of militancy and . . . gave birth to the new concept of positive neutralism."[3]

Bahgat Korany's interdisciplinary study *Social Change, Charisma and International Behaviour* deals with the Third World foreign policy of non-alignment. His objective was to unravel

> relevant foreign policy variables or determinants and establish linkages that might not appear at first glance. This conceptual mapping would be even more useful when the variables are drawn from different conceptual islands . . . and from the home territories of other academic disciplines (e.g., sociology, social psychology, anthropology); for in this case, interdisciplinary integration can be consolidated and bridges can be extended toward the work of theory-oriented researchers in other areas . . . Though the work is interdisciplinary, it is not limited to the mere borrowing of "foreign" concepts from other social sciences but, more importantly, it is concerned with how to transform rather than transfer, and adapt rather than adopt, these imported concepts to the concerns of International Relations analysts.[4]

Korany argues that the foreign policy of non-alignment is better discovered by studying the actual mode of practice employed by the Third World countries themselves, rather than by focusing on the global level. He also suggests that non-alignment was not only a foreign policy orientation or subsystem, but was also the behavior of individual actors, such as Nasser's Egypt. Korany examines the process of social change in Egypt and the pattern of Egypt's non-aligned behavior. He also draws a comparison between two pioneering non-aligned actors—Nasser and Nehru—in order to show how and why two close Third World pioneers could differ in their foreign policy behavior.

In his comprehensive, pioneering and illuminating study *The Struggle for Syria*,[5] Patrick Seale alluded to the fact that neutralism in the Arab world preceded Nasser's era. Seale correctly pinpoints some of the main explanations for Syria's neutralism of the period 1950–1. However, his main concern is for inter-Arab politics and less on inter-bloc issues and the Arab stance toward them.

The most profound study to be written on this subject was Fayez al-Sayegh's *The Dynamic of Neutralism in the Arab World*,[6] a collection of articles to which he contributed an introduction dealing with the term "neutralism" from the view of the political sciences. Sayegh was one of the first scholars to show that neutralism had many faces, and that countries that adhered to neutralism developed and consolidated their own patterns, which were derived from their special conditions, circumstances, and requirements. Sayegh's book, as well as those of Kimche, Korany, and Seale, may be placed within the framework of contemporary studies that are traditionally challenged by three obstructive factors: "inadequate sources, excessive subjectivity, and stunted perspective,"[7] to use Gordon Wright's phrase. Sayegh's book was published in 1964 when Arab neutralism was at its peak. The contributors dealt with a historical process of which they were a part; their "stunted perspective" colored their attempt to present an accurate historical picture. They were not able to pinpoint the beginning of the process, nor the appropriate dynamics of its evolution. None of the aforementioned studies were exposed to a variety of archival material from various countries, much of which has only recently been declassified and made accessible to scholars, nor to the large volume of literature in Arabic, including political memoirs and biographies, issued after the publication of many of these earlier studies.

Sayegh's introduction to his book correctly suggested that there were many faces of neutralism; some of his definitions and classifications of the term "neutralism" are to be relevant and supportive of the present historical analysis. Those definitions that fitted the historical cases treated in this study have been borrowed, with some modifications and adjustment where necessary. In addition to Sayegh's classifications, my own definitions form a vital, necessary aspect of the theory of neutralism.[8]

The current belief among contemporary Middle East scholars suggests that the formulation and realization of the policy of neutralism only began during Nasser's first years in power. In contrast, my research shows that the roots of neutralism were already sown in Arab soil in the early 1940s. The Syrian and Egyptian governments had begun to carve out a policy of neutralism in international affairs from the final stages of World War II and throughout the outset of the 1950s. Moreover, their decisions in 1943 (Egypt) and 1944 (Syria) to establish diplomatic relations with the USSR were based on utilitarian considerations—the Soviet Union's central role during World War II made it, internationally, a highly influential country, in European as well as in Eastern affairs. Syrian and Egyptian policy-makers held the view that, in the postwar peace talks, their countries would need as much international support as possible. The USSR, with its new international role, could certainly provide this if diplomatic relations with Moscow were established. They also expected that such a move would promote economic and commercial relations between their countries and the Soviet Union, from which both could benefit.

Arab leaders had been making declarations on the advantages of pursuing a policy of neutralism from the mid-1940s onward. The official formulation and implementation of such a policy, however, began in Syria in 1950 under the government of Khalid al-'Azm (1949–50), as well as in Egypt under the reign of the Wafd (1950–2), but Arab intellectuals had already created the ideological conditions in the early 1940s for the rise of neutralism. This book aims to expose the ideological sources of neutralism in Syria and Arab countries throughout the 1940s, analyzing the process of infiltration into political elites of neutralist ideas and the gradual process by Arab policymakers of implementing them. The focus is on the special contribution made by Syrian Ba'thist ideologues to the formulation and consolidation of the pattern of "ideological/doctrinaire neutralism" in the mid-1940s, and emphasis is placed on the factors behind the shifting of that paradigm to the new form of "positive neutralism." There were many modes and faces of neutralism, which were shaped in various countries to conform to their national interests. Neutralism was a doctrine that emerged out of the inter-bloc conflict. Those countries that refused to be fully allied or identified with one of the two international blocs chose their own form of neutralism, based on their local conditions, political heritage and tradition, and special needs. There were several patterns of neutralism specially relevant to this analysis, and, in the case of Syria, some of their adherents, who were vying for power, did everything they could to ensure victory for their mode of neutralism.

Methodologically, careful attention is paid to the mutual feedback between political history and the history of ideas. It examines the question of the dynamic between ideology and policy: to what extent is policy the implementation of ideology, or, conversely, how far is ideology an *ad hoc* realization of *realpolitik*? The sources of the various themes in neutralism, and Arab neutralism in particular, are located. Considerable use is made of theories and definitions drawn from the disciplines of political science and political sociology in order to pinpoint the origins of neutralism and to comprehend its ideological foundations. This was made possible by developing a conceptual framework wherein patterns such as "passive neutralism," "ideological/doctrinaire neutralism," "pragmatic/calculative nationalist neutralism," "positive neutralism," "negative neutralism" and "anti-western neutralism" feature prominently.

Primary sources, studied in the original Arabic, consisting of books, essays, and articles by Arab intellectuals and policymakers were utilized in order to elucidate the internal discourse on ideological concerns among targeted Arab countries. Source material gleaned from Syrian state archives, as well as Egyptian and other Arab archives, could have helped my research work, yet unfortunately, these archives are, at the present time, not accessible and one can only look forward to the day when Arab states will open their archives to scholars and public (including Israelis).

In order to describe and analyze the evolution of neutralism from the inarticulate and inconsistent ideology of the 1940s to the detailed and systematic policy practiced in the 1950s and 1960s, much of the source material was also gleaned from archives in Britain, the United States, India,

Israel, the former USSR, and Poland. Most of these sources give a clear picture of the political processes as made by and seen through the eyes of higher-level policymakers; however, they do not always provide the small details which reveal policymaking at its lower level. The advantages and disadvantages of consulting archives from Western and former Eastern bloc countries lay in the fact that both blocs' interests in the Middle East, at the time, were inextricably bound to the Cold War context. Both blocs were vying for increasing their political influence and safeguarding and strengthening their strategic strongholds in the Middle East; what made the task of their diplomats in the area more complex was that they were making huge efforts to get both official and clandestine information concerning each other's moves in the region. These nations closely monitored the political developments in Arab Middle Eastern countries—particularly Syria and Egypt; both countries joined the neutralist camp and often manipulated the inter-bloc rivalry in order to advance their interests.

Poland, a prominent member state within the Eastern bloc and a provider of arms to Arab countries, opened its archives following the conclusion of the Cold War. In the period under review, its embassies in Damascus and Cairo were very active and Polish diplomats developed a rapport with policymakers in both countries and were kept informed of local current affairs. Their reports and analyses were accurate and based on reliable sources. Access to documents in the Soviet archives is very selective. The researcher has to inform the archivist of the research topic in advance and the latter decides what documents will be made available to the researcher. Different scholars, for various reasons, can end up getting access to different information. The key to understanding Soviet policy toward the Arab Middle East, which was mainly conducted through clandestine channels, lays somewhere deep in the basements of the archives of Soviet Military Intelligence (GRU) and the KGB. Unfortunately, these archives remain, in most cases, inaccessible. Both Eastern and Western archives are needed to ensure that the historical picture is not distorted. Use of a variety of archives—Eastern and Western—contributes significantly in getting a better view of the two major blocs' policies toward Syria and the Middle East, and receiving an inside panoramic view of Syrian and Arab politics.

Indian archives also proved to be of the utmost importance since India's relations with Syria and Egypt were close, particularly in the 1950s. Indian diplomats in both Cairo and Damascus enjoyed access to and were highly regarded by local ruling circles. Their correspondence with their superiors in New Delhi is illuminating, informative, and reliable.

The process of selecting the relevant source material drawn from all the abovementioned archives was careful and censorious. Many of the documents used are drawn from the British and US archives, and are classified as intelligence reports which generally derive their analyses from well informed Arab and non-Arab sources. The other documents can be classified as daily, weekly, monthly, and yearly reports and the correspondence of foreign diplomats stationed in Damascus and Cairo. Every effort has been made to cross-reference these reports with other sources.

Primary and secondary literature in various languages, including Russian, Hebrew, Arabic, and English have also been utilized.

This book is composed of eight units. The first is an introduction, which lays down the theoretical foundations. It defines the terms "neutralization," "neutrality," "neutralism," and "non-alignment." Various patterns of neutralism as practised by Middle Eastern and non-Middle Eastern countries are highlighted; some of them are used while dealing with the Syrian political arena.

Chapter 1 charts Syria's meandering road to independence, 1944–6, describing Syria's search for international support in calling for an end to French and British domination. This period marked the onset of the Cold War, and Syrian policymakers took advantage of this development, urging the USSR to establish diplomatic relations with Syria. They believed that the USSR, which had emerged as one of the two major powers following World War II, would be able to help them gain their independence and sovereignty. They also courted the goodwill of the United States—the second major power—which had, at the end of World War I, emerged as an anti-imperialist and anti-colonialist power. In this period, Syria employed a "pragmatic/calculative nationalist neutralism."

Chapter 2 covers the period 1947–54, Syria's first years as an independent state. In addition to internal political instability, Syria had to face regional developments that posed external threats to its independence; some of these developments were directly related to the spread of the Cold War to the Middle East. This period also saw the emergence of various neutralist trends in Syria, where neutralist currents gradually came to dominate. Although pro-Hashemite and pro-Western politicians representing the old traditional elites were still active within the Syrian political arena, their actual influence decreased significantly. In the case of Hasan al-Hakim's government, they were bound to promote the main principles of neutralism adhered to by their political rivals—a foreign policy which reflected the anti-Western atmosphere prevalent in Syria among the public and most political groups, including Syria's unofficial policymaker, Adib al-Shishakli.

Chapter 3 analyzes the major stages on the road to the establishment of the non-aligned movement, with special emphasis on the Arab perspective. Considerable attention is paid to India's motives and desire to play a leading role in Asia, as well as its special relations with Arab countries based on mutual interests and ideological affinities. It is now generally agreed that from the beginning Nehru and Nasser had close political relations and enjoyed a good rapport. The study argues in contrast that Nehru's initial image of Nasser was not positive; he doubted Nasser's intellectual abilities. It was clear from his writings that he respected and appreciated Muhammad Najib—Nasser's rival—with whom Nehru developed close ties. Nehru was therefore disappointed when Nasser removed Najib. Even in early 1955, when Nasser and Nehru were strengthening their ties, the latter doubted Nasser's motives in embracing neutralism. Nehru, who was the formulator of "ideological/doctrinaire neutralism," had a low regard for the principles of Nasser's "positive neutralism." The initial steps in the consolidation of Nasser's relations with Tito, and the growing ideological cooperation between the Syrian Ba'th Party and Yugoslav ideologues and theoreticians are discussed, and the chapter concludes with the implications and repercussions of the Bandung Conference on the Syrian and Arab political scenes.

Chapters 4 and **5** begin with the downfall of Adib al-Shishakli (1954) and conclude with the formation of the United Arab Republic (1958). This period saw the gradual takeover by the Syrian heterogeneous left, which was composed of three neutralist streams vying for domination: the Ba'th Party, the Communist Party, and Khalid al-'Azm's group of independents. Following the Bandung Conference, neutralism and non-alignment became established aspects of Syrian political life. At this stage, even old guard politicians, such as the President, Shukri al-Quwatli, embraced the doctrine of positive neutralism, which was shaped and implemented by Nasser. From the mid-1950s, and in particular throughout 1957, the so-called external threat expedited the search for foreign anchors in order to defend Syria's independence. Two of the major neutralist factors within Syria's ruling circles—the Ba'th Party, which was supported by the army and President al-Quwatli; and Khalid al-'Azm's group together with the communists—were trying to consolidate an alliance with two different foreign sources. The first maintained that union with Egypt would save Syria and would promote the idea of Arab unity. The positive neutralists were encouraged by Nasser, who had his own reasons for unification with Syria. Nasser wanted to manipulate the inter-bloc conflict in order to advance Egypt's foreign policy, and did not want to see the Soviets gain a stronghold in Syria—a scenario that could have weakened his position *vis-à-vis* the Soviets. He wanted to appear before the two blocs as both the leader of the Arabs and one of the leaders of the Third World. Nasser repressed communism within Egypt, despite the fact that he continued to maintain close relations with the USSR. He did not want to see the rise of communism in Syria and other Arab countries. For Nasser, the communists were foreign agents at the service of the USSR and international communism. The struggle for Syria was not between the two international blocs but between Egypt, a regional Arab power, and the USSR, the leader of the Eastern bloc. The Soviets had their own allies within Syria: al-'Azm's group and the communists. Al-'Azm was one of the key figures and most influential ministers inside the Syrian government. He strove to strengthen the USSR's stronghold in Syria and to prevent unification with Egypt.

This study concludes with the formation of the United Arab Republic (**Chapter 6**). It shows that the USSR and the Syrian communists coolly received the Syrian–Egyptian union, and the years 1958–61 saw a growing tension between the Soviet Union and the UAR, mainly because of ideological concerns following Nasser's oppressive campaign against communism in the UAR. These years may be regarded as the pinnacle of positive neutralism. Under Nasser's sole leadership, the UAR sought hegemony in the Arab world and the Afro-Asian movement. Nasser believed himself to be one of the main leaders of the newly emerged third bloc; he did not have an inferiority complex when it came to dealing with the two superpowers as equals—he looked at their leaders "at the height of their eyes." This positive neutralism was short-lived, however. With the collapse of the UAR in 1961, the neutralism of Nasser and Syria was no longer "positive"—it became anti-Western, pro-Soviet neutralism.

Following the Syrian Ba'th coup of March 1963, "pro-Soviet positive neutralism" became prominent. Moreover, Syria's defeat in the June 1967 conflict was to have an immediate effect on its inter-bloc policy—it became a Soviet satellite in international as well as in domestic affairs, even though it did not formally join the Soviet bloc. The demise of communism and the disintegration of the Soviet Union and the Eastern bloc marked the conclusion of the Cold War. At this point, neutralism lost its essence and significance; the demise of communism was also the demise of neutralism.

Acknowledgments

I wish to express my appreciation to the Elie Kedourie Memorial Fund and the British Academy for their generous research grant, which helped pursuing my study in India. I would also like to express my gratitude and appreciation to Professor Sasson Somekh, the then director of the Israeli Academic Center in Cairo, for providing me with a research grant while pursuing my study in Egypt.

I would like to acknowledge the assistance extended to me by the staff of the various archives and libraries.

Mr. Haim Gal, Mrs. Catherine Logan, Mr. Yezhi Burnshtein, Mr. Asaf Maliah, Mr. Meir Nuwama, and Mrs. Sisam Ditsa are to be congratulated for their help. Special thanks to Dr. Uri Bar-Noi for allowing me to utilize his collection of Eastern European archival material. My friend and colleague Dr Uzi Rabi provided me with constant help, encouragement, and inspiration throughout. I would like to include Professors Israel Gershoni and Haggai Erlich for their encouragement and knowledge. Finally, I would like to thank my wife Nicola, my children and family for their patience, ceaseless support, and love; this book is therefore dedicated to them.

Introduction

Neutralism in Retrospect: Definitions and Paradigms

This Introduction lays down the theoretical foundations of neutralism, beginning with the historical evolution and political science's definitions of the terms "neutralization," "neutrality," "neutralism," and "non-alignment." An analysis of the Middle Eastern scene demonstrates how the various patterns of neutralism fit in with each historical instance. The cases illustrate the gradual historical evolution of the political doctrine of neutralism in Middle Eastern countries. These patterns are used throughout the chapters while dealing with the Syrian political arena.

Neutrality, suggested Roderick Ogley,[1] can have four different categories. The first is termed "neutralization"—neutrality that is "imposed upon a state by international agreement." Ogley gave as an example the neutralization of Belgium following the Treaty of London in 1839, by which the European powers guaranteed that this state would be made a "perpetually Neutral State." The second category is defined as "traditional neutral": when a state becomes neutral by choice, but, theoretically, retains its right to participate in any war. Examples are Switzerland and Sweden, both of which followed the path of neutrality more as "a matter of principle and tradition" rather than a specific policy. Switzerland's neutrality was recognized by the participant states of the Vienna Congress of 1815, and since then it has, by tradition and choice, preserved its neutrality "attempting by its own efforts to uphold its neutrality, rather than that of a neutralized state, whose neutrality is imposed and in certain circumstances, [like the Belgian case], guaranteed by others."

The third category is that of *ad hoc* neutrality—when a state desires not to take part in a particular war, or when it has not consolidated its tradition of neutrality. This form of neutrality, Ogley emphasized, can be dangerous when a weak state is territorially adjacent to a conflict between two or more stronger states. An example is Cambodia during the Vietnam War, which found itself in the middle of a major ideological conflict: contrary to the first and second categories, Cambodia could have decided how to preserve its neutrality or, alternatively, whether it wanted to be neutral or not.

I

Ogley's fourth category is that of non-aligned or neutralist states. In his view, this is, a relatively new phenomenon that emerged following the conclusion of World War II, which also marked the beginning of the Cold War between the Eastern bloc, led by the USSR, and the Western bloc, led by the US. Formulation and implementation of this policy of non-alignment/neutralism was pioneered by India under then Prime Minister Pandit Jawaharlal Nehru. Many Asian and African states of the post-colonial era were gradually attracted by Nehru's formula. Non-alignment was an active policy "primarily aimed at averting a major war and settling minor ones" between the two major superpowers and their allies. The main concern of the other three categories of neutrality was to keep out of any future war, whereas non-aligned states could, at the same time, fight their own wars, as the cases of Nasser's Egypt and India's conflict with Pakistan over Kashmir demonstrate, and still remain non-aligned. A non-aligned state then, would cease to be considered as such once it decided to join one of the two contesting camps in the Cold War.

Ogley's classification of four categories is useful as a historical introduction to the various stages of the evolution of neutrality. The terms "neutrality," "neutralization," and "neutralism" (non-alignment), however, have still remained undefined as far as their international legal and political status are concerned.

The political definition of the term "neutrality" is dependent on social and political historical circumstances. The concept of neutralism, however, entered into mainstream international current affairs after World War II to indicate the position of those states that objected to political or diplomatic commitments to either side in the Cold War.[2] It is commonly accepted by most dictionaries and encyclopedias of the social and political sciences that "neutralism" and "neutrality" bear different meanings. The modern legal status of neutrality, suggests the *Encyclopedia of the Social Sciences,* implies "the impartiality of one state towards two or more belligerent states,"[3] while *A Dictionary of the Social Sciences* defines it as denoting "the condition of impartiality or non-belligerence in war or the rights and duties of states enjoying such a condition."[4] Neutrality has a precise meaning in international law:[5] non-participation in a state of war.

Neutralism "expresses detachment in relation, not to war or peace as historically understood, but to conflict, peaceful or violent between two organized power groupings."[6] According to *A Dictionary of Modern Politics,* it has no clear-cut meaning and is not a term recognized or defined by international law. Drawing its definition from the newly created post-colonial world—the post-World War II era—neutralism is the "status of many if not most of the Third World countries who have decided not to be formally involved in either of the two superpower alliances, and which take aid and support from either or both as offered."[7] According to this definition, neutralism and non-alignment bear the same meaning. A state of formal neutrality breaches the general duty all United Nations members have to support a UN mandate against aggressors; neutralism, on the other hand, allows active participation in international affairs, including full membership in the UN. Neutralism does not involve total neutrality, since membership in regional alliances and defense pacts which do not involve superpower relations are possible.[8] The *International Encyclopedia of the Social Sciences* maintains that the terms neutralism and non-alignment are used "loosely and interchangeably to refer to the desire of a majority of Afro-Asian nations to avoid military alliances with either side in the Cold War." Neutralism and non-alignment were associated with two major international developments: the emergence of independent nations in Asia and Africa (the end of Western colonialism and imperialism); and the emergence of a bipolar conflict between East and West (each possessing weapons of mass destruction). Aware that there was a wide range of policies encompassed by neutralism and non-alignment, the *International Encyclopedia of the Social Sciences* viewed both terms from three different perspectives: First, as a strategy for maximizing one's security in a bipolar world; second, as a foreign policy expression of domestic political, cultural, and psychological needs; and third, as a policy of newly independent countries for securing their regional interests.[9] Michael Brecher draws a distinction between neutralism and non-alignment; according to his analysis, non-alignment is a political status which refers to a state that declares itself separate from bloc conflicts. Non-alignment is not neutralism, but is, rather, the passive first stage of neutralism. Both neutralism and non-alignment have in common "an expressed desire to remain aloof from bloc conflict. But neutralism goes much further, for it involves a positive attitude towards bloc conflicts." Brecher's conclusion is that "non-alignment is the policy guide of the neutralist state, but neutralism represents an attitude and a policy which are much more activist than non-alignment as such." He cites India as an example of a neutralist state, and Sweden as an example of a non-aligned state.[10]

Neutrality is a relatively modern concept that only entered international political dictionaries in recent centuries. Black, Falk, Knorr, and Young suggested that "A neutralized state is one whose political independence and territorial integrity are guaranteed permanently by a collective agreement of great powers, subject to the conditions that the neutralized state will not take up arms against another state, except to defend itself, and will not assume treaty obligations which may compromise its neutralized status." That status "is often referred to as permanent neutrality to signify that it is valid in times of peace as well as war."[13] They noted, however, that from past experience, this definition does not cover all cases, and they offered a more general definition: "Neutralization is a special international status designed to restrict the intrusion of specified state actions in a specified area."[12]

Neutralism and neutralization are two different concepts. Being neutralist means dissociation from the post-World War II East–West conflict—to declare a policy of non-alignment in the Cold War. The neutralist states wanted to play a major role in international affairs—they simply refused to become neutralized. Only relevant in times of formal hostilities, neutralization, by contrast, means permanent neutrality—it is concerned with "preventing, moderating, or terminating interstate coercion." Like neutralism, neutrality is based on non-participation in wars and describes the posture of a state *vis-à-vis* a military or potential military conflict between other states. Unlike neutralism, and like neutralization, neutrality has international legal status.[13] While neutrality is isolationist, neutralism, as Brecher defines it, is interventionist.[14]

In *al-Qamus al-Siyasi*, a political dictionary, Ahmad 'Atiyyallah uses an Arabic word—*hiyad*—to describe neutrality, neutralization, and neutralism, classifying the term into several categories:[15] First, *al-hiyad al-taqlidi* [traditional neutrality], which is defined in line with Ogley's second category; second, *al-hiyad da'im* [enduring neutralism], as in the case of Switzerland; and third, *al-hiyad Amriki* [American neutrality] or *al-hiyad juz'i* [partial neutralism], that of the law pronounced by the US President Franklin Roosevelt on 4 November 1939. Roosevelt considered the US a non-belligerent state, which, however, should be allowed to support one of the belligerent states without being a participant in any fighting. The US would not sell arms to these countries except for hard currency, and American citizens would not be allowed to privately take part in economic or commercial transactions with these states. The underlying theme behind this law was to help Britain's military effort without being involved directly in the war; hence, a sort of partial neutrality. Finally, the dictionary listed *al-hiyad ijabi* [positive neutrality], whose adherents tend to strongly criticize the policy of *al-hiyad al-taqlidi* for its passivity. A state that follows *al-hiyad ijabi* cannot remain passive or indifferent to international occurrences, be they armed struggles or a Cold War [*al-harb al-barida*]. It must take a positive stand to ease tension in order to, first, protect its own independence and sovereignty and, second, act for the restoration of a durable peace.

The Bandung Conference of 1955 attended by independent Asian and African states laid the theoretical foundations of positive neutralism, and Nasser's Egypt played a major role in diffusing this concept as vital to the protection of international peace and security, and as a necessary measure to enable independent underdeveloped states to seek for appropriate channels to help them reach economic growth. As stated in *al-Qamus al-Siyasi*, positive neutralism was to change its name and content following the

Belgrade Conference of 1961, and was replaced with *'adam al-inhiyaz* [non-alignment], and the countries that adhered to it were called *duwal 'adam al-inhiyaz* [non-aligned states]. The principles of the "non-aligned countries," or "positive neutrality," which had common goals, were formulated at the Belgrade Conference. The adherent states of positive neutrality were required to accept the following principles:[16]

1.   Not to take part in military alliances and to avoid supporting any party involved in armed conflict.
2.   Not to dissociate themselves from international society because of the appearance of two world blocs, but to cooperate with all parties on the basis of political and economic independence. Ideological differences should not prevent the neutralist countries from receiving economic and technological aid, not as a gift, but through normal agreements between sovereign states.
3.   The positive neutralist states would act jointly or separately to seek solutions to every international conflict that posed a threat to world peace and security. Special emphasis should be put on conflicts in which Third World countries are involved.
4.   Positive neutralist states should not take negative stands or be non-aligned in regard to every international conflict, but must take the side of the just party. Accordingly, they should take part in any peacekeeping measures decided by the UN, including military aid.

This definition does not precisely correspond with the historical facts. Positive neutralism preceded the Bandung Conference, and non-alignment was also practised much earlier than the Belgrade Conference. As the following paradigm indicates, both positive neutralism and non-alignment were two different patterns of neutralism that had similarities and dissimilarities.

Fayez Sayegh suggests that, from "the stand point of its causes, its motivation, or the rational of its objection to the cold war" there are five types of neutralist policies: (a) "traditional, legal or universal neutralism" (e.g., Sweden or Switzerland); (b) "neutrality by virtue of neutralization," such as in post-1955 Austria and post-1962 Laos; (c) "aprioristic, doctrinaire, or dogmatic neutralism," with India as this type's model; (d) "ideological neutralism," e.g., in Ghana, Guinea, and Indonesia; and (e) "nationalist-pragmatic neutralism" (demonstrated by all Arab neutralist countries and by most neutralist states). Sayegh noted that neutralist policy may also be defined "from the standpoint of its orientation, or the forms of expression of its objection to the cold war." In this regard, he offers four types of neutralism: "passive," "negative, or non alignment," "positive," and "messianic."[17] The Indian model is important and relevant to the present discussion, and in this study the term "doctrinaire/dogmatic neutralism" has been altered to "doctrinaire/ideological neutralism" to emphasize that India's opposition to the Cold War was "augmented by opposition to its methods, stratagems, and general climate . . . [and that] at the roots of this opposition was the concept of non-violence."[18]

"Passive neutralism"—"a manifestation of general indifference to the cold war . . . an expression of disinterest in either the ideological or the political antagonism of outside powers and power groups,"[19] is also relevant to the discussion of Syria during the mid-1940s, as is "negative neutralism/non-alignment," which Sayegh describes as "the attainment of a state of freedom from all alien determinants of foreign policy. It is the achievement of the ability to judge every issue . . . on its own merits and in the light of one's national interests and principles, and not on the basis of commitments made in advance to other parties nor in the light of such extraneous considerations as alignment with power blocs."[20]

Sayegh draws a distinction between "negative" and "positive" neutralism. Whereas nations adhering to the first doctrine "lie outside the framework of the cold war," and "refuse to participate in its power arrangements or to take part in its antagonisms," the latter countries "conduct relations with other countries, including countries which are involved in the cold war, without reference to their cold-war positions: it is virtually to ignore their politico-military affiliations and their ideological complexions." "Negative neutralism," Sayegh stressed, "rejects self-embroilment in the cold war," and "positive neutralism" also rejects "the thesis that the cold war is the sole context within which a country lives and moves and has its being . . . to be free of the limitations imposed upon international conduct by cold-war discipline, or entailed by bloc membership."[21] "Positive neutralism," he concluded, "is nothing less than the revolt of non-aligned countries against the exercise of monopoly, by either party to the cold war, in the supply of goods, services or capital to underdeveloped lands. It is their protest against unfair practises, discrimination, and the attachment of politico-military conditions to trade, economic aid, or technical assistance . . . "[22]

Sayegh's final category is "messianic neutralism," which may be defined as "challenging neutralism." It differs from the others because, unlike them, it confronted the Cold War—"looking it in the face, as it were, and trying to do something curative and constructive about it." Unlike the other forms of neutralism, here the "pragmatic element is secondary" and "national self-interest, even where it does stimulate this neutralist policy, occupies a subordinate position." The promotion of world peace is vital, so that the weak neutralist states would be able to develop their national welfare.[23]

The historical examples used by Sayegh to support his analysis do not always fit in with the historical facts, as will be demonstrated in the following chapters. What he called "messianic neutralism" can easily be incorporated into the pattern of "doctrinaire/ideological neutralism." Some of the patterns presented by Fayez Sayegh are utilized in the present study, though the analysis of some of the historical cases referred to may require the introduction of minor changes or redefinitions of some of his paradigms. For example, the term "nationalist-pragmatic neutralism" was altered to "calculative/pragmatic nationalist neutralism", which refers to a country that was under the hegemony or influence of one of the traditional great powers—Britain or France—and was embroiled in a struggle for national independence. Some of the methods it employed to achieve that goal were to utilize the emerging inter-bloc conflict in order to advance these national aspirations. The idea was that the intentional improvement in relations with the Soviet bloc, in all fields, would definitely put pressure on the Western bloc, particularly, the USA, to alter their policies toward the Arabs. In order to prevent the falling of these countries into Soviet zones of influence, the US would exert enormous pressure on its allies to evacuate their troops from these countries. Based on national interests and utilitarian purposes, this pattern of neutralism was in fact exercised by Egypt and Syria in the mid-1940s and early 1950s.

In his book *The Afro-Asian Movement*, David Kimche elaborated on Sayegh's patterns of "doctrinaire/ideological neutralism" and "positive neutralism." Kimche wrote of two contrasting approaches to the Cold War among Afro-Asian countries. The first, which was developed to its extremes by India and Burma, viewed the "rivalry between the two power blocs as a constant threat to world peace. A Sword of Damocles hanging over the heads of humanity . . . [therefore] the cold war must be neutralized. An 'area of peace' must separate the two rivals, and the leaders of Afro-Asia must labour on the world scene in order to bring about a *détente* in the cold war." The second approach was that to which Afro-Asian countries such as Egypt adhered, by which the Cold War was viewed as:

> a triple blessing: as long as the cold war exists the countries of Africa and Asia are assured of outside support, as both world blocs seek to buy political gains in Afro-Asia by means of economic aid; as long as rivalry between the two blocs continues, the countries of Afro-Asia can ask for help from one of the blocs if they feel that the other is seeking to encroach on their independence—the existence of the cold war thus becomes a guarantee for their independence and solves the problem of a possible limitation on it through taking foreign aid; and thirdly, any *détente* in the cold war could lead to a dividing up of the world into spheres of influence between the two blocs, which is one of the possibilities most to be feared.[24]

The term "positive neutralism" as described above can be enriched by expanding it to incorporate into it another motive that Kimche ascribed to "non-alignment"—the attempt to play one bloc against the other while gaining aid and benefits from both, which proved to be more advantageous than being allies of one bloc alone.[25] This is a profound definition of positive neutralism and will be used in the examination of Nasser's positive neutralism of the period 1954–61. The two patterns put forward by Kimche fit the neutralist trends of the Syrian Ba'th Party. The first pattern, "ideological neutralism," was relevant to the period 1946–55. The second pattern reflects the later period from 1955 to 1966, in which the party was greatly influenced by Nasser's model of positive neutralism—a theory and practice that was welcomed by Ba'thism.

The term "non-alignment" is here employed as a general term identical with "neutralism," as suggested by Ogley. Unlike Sayegh and Brecher, it is used as a literal meaning—as Kimche put it, "no regular, permanent, and automatic taking of sides in the cold war, whether for reasons of ideology, benefit or pressure."[26]

By analyzing these paradigms of neutralism, we can clearly see that the Cold War period imposed upon the world a dichotomy of division—the Western and Eastern blocs. Countries that were not allied with either of the two blocs were neutralists. In the case of Syria, throughout the Cold War period, there emerged several neutralist currents that fit in with previous definitions. The prefix "positive" of the term "positive neutralism" can be misleading since it had not always been a balanced policy. In several periods it had shifted to "pro-Soviet positive neutralism." Examples of pro-Soviet policy can be found in the inter-bloc policies of Syria and Egypt for the period 1955–8. Jordan's foreign policies, except for a short period (1955–7), and the inter-bloc policies of Iraq over the period prior to the Baghdad Pact of 1955, are good examples of "pro-Western neutralism." In the case of Syria, during the period that followed the Ba'th coup of March 1963, pro-Soviet positive neutralism became prominent; the defeat in the June 1967 war turned Syria's neutralism into a pro-Soviet policy. Although there was no formal effort to join the Soviet Bloc, Syria became, to a great extent, a Soviet satellite, until the disintegration of the USSR in 1991. The same applies to Nasser's Egypt of the period of June 1967 up to Nasser's death in September 1970.

Nehru's India was the first country to formulate the theoretical foundations of neutralism—first as a political doctrine and later as an established policy. Nehru's decision to embark upon a neutralist path was determined by the particular global circumstances and conditions created at the conclusion of World War II—that is, the emergence of a bipolar world and the beginning of the Cold War. As early as 1941, several years before the outbreak of the Cold War, Nehru's views of communism were positive.

Nehru drew a clear-cut distinction between communism as a theory and the way Soviet Russia practised it. While declaring unequivocally his faith in communist theory, which he found to be sound and correct, Nehru cautioned that, "it was absurd to copy blindly what had taken place in Russia, for its application depended on the particular conditions prevailing in the country in question and the stage of its historical development." This approach may be considered a central element in the doctrine of neutralism, which he was to formulate and consolidate later on. Nehru suggested that India and any other state could extract positive aspects of the communist system and disregard those that held less appeal. Communism had to be molded to suit each country's own peculiarities. Marxism seemed to be a panacea for world problems, in particular those of India, even though the violence he believed inherent in Russian communism was abhorrent to him. But Nehru saw that, while the rest of the world was in the grip of depression, in Russia a great new world was being created.[27]

Nehru modestly dismissed the idea that he was the architect of non-alignment, suggesting that he had "not originated non-alignment; it is a policy inherent in the circumstances of India, in the conditioning of the Indian mind during the struggle for freedom, and inherent in the very circumstances of the world today."[28] India's inclination to dissociate itself from the inter-power international conflicts was translated into action during World War II, which it denounced as a war between imperialism and fascism. It opposed both and believed that, by not intervening, India would preserve its freedom and peace.[29]

In early 1944, while in prison, Nehru predicted that the USA and the USSR would emerge from World War II as the major new international powers, and that the nature of the future relations between them would have a powerful effect on the newly emergent world order. He sensed that the outcome of the deep ideological differences between them would lead to conflict, and that the attitude of the Afro-Asian nations toward that conflict should be determined by the questions:

> Did it help towards their own liberation? Did it end the domination of one country over another? Would it enable them to live freely the life of their choice in cooperation with others? Would it bring equality and equal opportunity for nations as well as for groups within each nation? Did it hold forth the promise of an early liquidation of poverty and illiteracy and the establishment of better living conditions?[30]

These ruminations embody in brief the main tenets of neutralism/non-alignment as they evolved over time.

Nehru, as Kimche noted, maintained that there was "room for a third ideology"—that "there is a third way which takes the best from all existing systems . . . and seeks to create something suited to one's own history and philosophy."[31]

Upon assuming his duties as Member of the External Affairs and Commonwealth Relations in the Government of India in September 1946, Nehru made his first official declaration of a policy of non-alignment, stating that his country would "keep away from power politics of groups aligned against one another, which have led in the past to world wars and which may again lead to disasters on an even vaster scale."[32] The Cold War, Nehru said, was a new expression of the traditional desire of the Great Powers to maintain the balance of power in their favor, and not an ideological conflict between communist and non-communist societies. Nehru argued that every conflict could be resolved rationally if it was removed from the context of the Cold War. The newly emerging Afro-Asian states, he believed, had nothing to gain out of that war.[33]

A short while before India gained its independence, Nehru elucidated the logic behind his country's policy of neutralism:

> We wish for peace. We do not want to fight any nation if we can help it. The only possible real objective that we, in common with other nations, can have is the objective of cooperating in building up some kind of world structure, call it one world, call it what you like. The beginnings of this world structure have been laid in the United Nations Organization. It is still feeble, it has many defects; nevertheless, it is the beginning of the world structure. And India has pledged herself to cooperation in its work. Now, if we think of that structure and our cooperation with other countries in achieving it, where does the question come of our being tied up with this group of nations or that group? Indeed, the more groups and blocs [that] are formed the weaker will that great structure become.[34]

Unlike Nehru, Josip Broz Tito, the Yugoslav communist leader who was also regarded as one of the pioneers and forefathers of the doctrine of non-alignment, saw and understood neutralism as less an ideological and more a practical, realistic concept—it derived from a need to fill the void created following his detachment from Soviet patronage. Tito's neutralism, according to the *International Encyclopedia of the Social Sciences*, was directed at deterring Soviet interference and dictation by seeking American assistance without a military alliance with the West (which might precipitate Soviet intervention).[35] Banerjee believes that two motives were behind Tito's decision to break away from the Cominform in June 1948: First, he did not want Yugoslavia to become a Soviet satellite state; and second, he was keen that his country would play "an independent and constructive role" in the international arena.[36] The years 1948–50 saw a gradual process of Yugoslavia's estrangement from the Soviet Union, on the one hand, and on the other, a limited coexistence with the West by means of mutual trade. By 1950, Yugoslavia's views on world affairs were well formulated:

> The policy of Yugoslavia cannot accept the assumption that mankind must today

choose between the domination of one Great Power or another. We consider that there is another path, the difficult but necessary path of democratic struggle for a world of free and equal nations for democratic relations among nations against foreign interference in the domestic affairs of the people and for the all round peaceful cooperation of nations on the basis of equality.[37]

Yugoslav theoreticians justified their country's decision to pursue a policy of non-alignment, implicitly rejecting Soviet hegemony over the socialist camp. The program of the League of Communists of Yugoslavia offered a rationale for the split with the USSR and for the attempts to build socialism in accordance with the conditions prevailing in each country. The program indirectly criticized the USSR for its insistence that the Soviet path to socialism was the only one possible, and for its refusal to accept the right of other peoples to build socialism in conformity with their own historical exigencies.[38]

There are points of similarity and disparity between Tito's and Nehru's roads to neutralism. Both leaders regarded communist theory in a positive light; however, while Nehru sympathized with communist theory as an outsider, Tito was a communist practitioner—the leader of the Yugoslav Communist Party—who had had close ties with Moscow and international communism until his expulsion by the Soviets in 1948. Both statesmen gave the nationalist factor an important place in their social and political doctrines and formulated their own version of socialism—a nationalist socialism contrary to Moscow's internationalist communism. Tito, who had many ideological and political disagreements with Stalin, was seeking for, and paving, a new way. Socio-economically he continued to adhere to communism, but his was a nationalistic interpretation, one based on the special conditions and circumstances of the Yugoslav Federation. Ideologically, it was closer to the Eastern camp. Politically, Tito was determined not to associate himself with any of the rival international blocs—he aspired to maintain correct relations with both major powers without succumbing to either. While Tito had been an integral part of the Soviet bloc in his first years in power, Nehru started his political prominence as an independent leader who was facing a new world order—a post-colonial era characterized by the demise of traditionalist world powers such as India's ruler, Britain, and the emergence of the USA and the USSR as the two superpowers. Nehru had to develop his country's position within the reality of these new tensions in world affairs. Whereas Tito may be regarded as one of the formulators and practitioners of negative neutralism, Nehru is viewed as the spiritual father of doctrinaire/ideological neutralism. The establishment of the non-aligned movement should therefore be attributed to both leaders. Their influence on the evolution of neutralism in the Arab world was highly important, in particular after the mid-1950s.

Since the late 1940s, the doctrine of neutralism was exercised by several countries on an individual basis. Israel, soon after it gained its independence, embraced neutralism—non-alignment with either Eastern or Western camps—as an ideology based on the special circumstances of the state. Israel was supported by both superpowers throughout its most crucial hours; both superpowers supported the UN partition resolution of November 1947, and both immediately recognized its independence in May 1948. During the 1948 War, the two superpowers supported Israel—the US economically and the USSR internationally and militarily. Under these circumstances, the Israeli government, as an expression of gratitude to both superpowers (and for other reasons of self-interest[39]) embarked on the path of non-alignment. Israel had the privilege, until late 1949, when it was accepted as a member state at the UN, of sitting on the international fence without having to take a stand on issues concerning the East–West conflict. This policy was short-lived, however, and from the early 1950s Israel sided with the West, although it never formally joined the Western camp in any sort of alignment until the 1980s. Uri Bialer analyzed the reasons behind Israel's adherence to the policy of non-identification in the period 1948–50:

> One was Israel's sense of responsibility for the fate and welfare of the entire Jewish people, which was dispersed throughout both major international blocs. Secondly, neither could Israelis ignore the historic fact that their state had been established with the agreement and support of both the Superpowers. Israel owed them a certain debt of gratitude and was interested in maintaining good relations with both in order to surmount the difficulties involved in the defense of her independence. The third motive was a sincere concern for peace in the world and the wish to refrain from encouraging inter-power rivalry or intensifying it by identifying with one side or the other . . . the desire to keep peace within the ranks of the labor movement in Israel, constituted a fourth reason . . . Finally, there was the immensely important factor of self-perception . . . the concept of "a people that shall dwell alone," a people with its own morality and responsibility, which aspired to liberate itself from all outside bonds so as to select its own path in accordance with its own ideas, principles and viewpoints.[40]

Until 1950, aspects of Israel's policy of non-alignment (in particular the third reason, as noted by Bialer), were closer to India's prototype of neutralism, although both arose from different reasons. The other reasons may be related to what Sayegh called "nationalist–pragmatic neutralism" and positive neutralism—to get the most out of the two blocs without being involved in the actual inter-bloc conflict. Israel's neutralism at this period was inevitable because of its unique conditions and particular circumstances. The change that took place in Israel's foreign orientation after the outbreak of the Korean War in mid-1950 requires us to define

Israel's neutralism differently: it had become less balanced, shifting gradually toward the West—becoming pro-Western positive neutralism.

The roots of neutralism were already sown in Arab soil in the early 1940s. It was Nahhas Pasha, the Egyptian Wafdist Prime Minister, who became, at the outset of the 1950s, the first Arab leader to carve out a policy of neutralism in international affairs. His decision in 1943 to establish diplomatic relations with the USSR against King Farouk's will was based on utilitarian considerations—the Soviet Union's central role during World War II made it an influential country internationally, in European as well as in Eastern affairs. Failure to form diplomatic relations with the USSR, he stated in a memorandum submitted to King Farouk on 13 March 1943, "might weaken Egypt's case in the forthcoming peace talks; Egypt would need as much international support as possible, and the USSR, with its new international role, could certainly provide this if diplomatic relations with Moscow were established." He also maintained that such a move would promote economic and commercial relations between the two countries from which both could benefit.[41] Although the motivating force behind him was his dynamic Deputy Foreign Minister Muhammad Salah al-Din, it would be historically correct to argue that Nahhas Pasha, who foresaw the coming East–West conflict, should be regarded as the formulator of the premature pragmatic/calculative nationalist neutralism in Egypt and the Arab world.

The period 1944–7 may be considered as the phase of passive neutralism, because, soon after the establishment of relations with the USSR, the Nahhas government was dismissed and the process of rapprochement between the two countries was halted. It was only during this short period that Egypt's successive governments were indifferent to the East–West conflict.

Since the dismissal in October 1944 of the Nahhas government by King Farouk, who objected to diplomatic relations with the Soviets, relations between the two countries had been practically at a standstill until 1947–8, when Mahmud Fahmi al-Nuqrashi, a former Wafdist, took power. In August 1947 he managed to persuade the Soviets to support Egypt's demand in the UN Security Council calling for the immediate withdrawal of British troops from Egypt. This Soviet move led Nuqrashi to declare that Egypt "would consider the possibility of neutrality in the international arena and that Egypt would seek the support of other powers in its struggle against Britain." In February 1948, he sent a military mission to purchase arms in Prague and on 3 March 1948, in a move possibly not unconnected to the opening of dialogue with the Eastern bloc to obtain arms, Egypt signed a large barter commercial agreement with the Soviet Union for the first time. Nevertheless, Nuqrashi's gradual drift toward neutralism was short-lived; he was assassinated in December of that year.[42] Although the years 1947–8 showed symptoms of pragmatic/calculative nationalist neutralism, the implementation of an active and systematic policy of such neutralism occurred in 1951 under the Wafdist government led by Mustafa al-Nahhas (1950–2).

The Wafdist government, however, embraced in its first months in power the policy of anti-Western neutralism. It derived mainly from the extended Anglo-Egyptian dispute, which frustrated many Egyptians and created anti-British feelings among most political circles in Egypt. These anti-British sentiments later expanded to include the US, which did not support Egypt's demands for British evacuation and acted against Arab interests with regard to the Palestine issue. In a press conference on 11 July 1950, Muhammad Salah al-Din (now the Egyptian Minister of Foreign Affairs), the motivating force behind Egypt's policy of neutralism, in interpreting Egypt's abstention on the Security Council resolution of 27 June 1950 on the Korean War,[43] emphasized Egypt's policy of non-alignment by criticizing both Eastern and Western blocs:

> Egypt, which combats imperialism and considers it one of the causes of international disturbances and of wars, is equally anxious to combat the hidden imperialism implicit in communist methods. Like the Western powers, Soviet Russia seeks to exercise domination by conquering other nations from within and submitting them to dictatorship. Egypt wishes to spare weaker nations and the whole world the ambitions of domination, imperialism and exploitation. All her acts are inspired by true democratic principles. This explains Egypt's refusal to recognize the Communist Government of China . . . Egypt desires that the UN should succeed in its mission and that the Western Powers should succeed in their attempts to stem the communist danger, but these powers must prove to the world that they are not out for imperialism and exploitation.[44]

The latter half of 1951 witnessed growing tension and events related to the inter-bloc conflict and a gradual shift toward a policy of calculative/pragmatic nationalist neutralism. The idea of concluding a non-aggression pact with the Soviets was translated into practical steps when, on 8 August, Salah al-Din met two Soviet diplomats who had arrived in Cairo on a twofold mission: First, to assess Egyptian reactions to the new Soviet peace offensive; and second, to find out whether Egypt would agree to lead the peace offensive in the Middle East by signing a non-aggression pact with the Soviet Union. The Soviets emphasized that opening negotiations with the USSR on such a pact would reaffirm Egypt's stand for neutrality between the two blocs. A point was also made that, "if Egypt were to conduct negotiations with the USSR, such negotiations would nullify the 1936 treaty and would be the first positive and sensational step towards real neutrality."[45] Salah al-Din was quoted as replying: "I am also a partisan of peace, of a well-balanced world peace, because peace is our goal and wars will only do good for the imperialistic states."[46] The meeting concluded with Salah al-Din's assurance that he would discuss the Soviet proposal with his colleagues. For Salah al-Din the idea of concluding a non-aggression pact with the USSR was an essential element in furthering the realization of the policy of calculative/pragmatic nationalist neutralism. He also believed that raising the issue of a non-aggression pact might also be used as a means of putting pressure on the Western powers to alter their policy with regard to the Anglo-Egyptian conflict. There is little historical evidence available to support the claim that a non-aggression pact was concluded between Egypt and the USSR; however, the meeting between Salah al-Din and the Soviet diplomats bore fruit several weeks later when the Egyptian government decided unilaterally to abrogate the 1936 treaty with Britain. This decision was made following a stormy debate within the Wafdist government between Salah al-Din's left-wing followers—who took pains to advance their policy of calculative/pragmatic nationalist neutralism, which was oriented toward the Soviet bloc, and were deter-mined to move ahead with the abrogation—and Fu'ad Siraj al-Din's right-wing faction, which also adhered to that pattern of calculative/prag-matic nationalist neutralism, but was less enthusiastic about nurturing relations with the Soviets. Siraj al-Din, Minister of the Interior, tried to prevent such a move. In this debate, Salah al-Din had the advantage: when he threatened his colleagues that he would resign and undertake a campaign against the government, Siraj al-Din's group surrendered, knowing that the resignation of Salah al-Din would be disastrous for the Wafd, since most political groups in Egypt supported abrogation.[47]

The Egyptian government's decision to abrogate the treaty of 1936 was considered by Britain and the US to be invalid; nevertheless, many Egyptians considered the presence of British troops in the Suez Canal area to be illegal, and anti-British guerrilla warfare was being conducted by radical young Egyptians in the Suez Canal Zone. The fact that the Egyptian government allowed such activities to take place is supported by Salah al-Din's description of these guerrilla fighters as "Egyptian patriots." British forces in Egypt reacted to these provocations by occupying the Suez Canal Zone, consequently losing the few sympathizers they had among Egypt's ruling circles (including King Farouk). British military activity in the Suez Canal area played into Salah al-Din's hands; he could now reiterate his belief that Egypt's main enemy was Britain and not the USSR, and that Egypt should rule out the idea of a military alliance with Britain. In its final months in power, the Wafd government sharpened its policy of calcula-tive/pragmatic nationalist neutralism; on the one hand, there was a general deterioration in Egypt's relations with the Western powers, in particular with Britain; and on the other, there was significant improvement in relations with Soviet bloc countries. Egypt rejected the Western proposal of October 1951 to join them in establishing a Middle East Command, which was to be a regional military alliance aimed at preventing the spread of communism and Soviet expansion into the Middle East. Disappointed with its failure to bring the Anglo-Egyptian conflict to an end, the Wafd government put pressure on the governments of Britain and the US to alter their policies toward Egypt. The shift toward neutralism and the strengthening of relations with the Soviet bloc was a tactical move—a means to pressure the West, and also a mode of revenge. This wave of Egyptian neutralism reached its conclusion following the dismissal of the Wafd government on 27 January 1952 following British military actions in Isma'ilia on 25 January and the Cairo riots (known as "the burning of Cairo") the next day.[48]

The downfall of the Wafdist government was only a temporary end to the policy of neutralism; the ideological elements of neutralism were still deeply rooted in Egypt. Neutralism in the period of 1950–2 did not remain theoretical, but became a practical doctrine. Nasser's decision to embrace neutralism soon after he established his hegemony was not an abrupt change or the product of original thought—it was actually the renewal of a policy that had been artificially terminated by self-motivated forces. Neutralism suited the social and political climate of post-World War II Egypt.

In contrast to the Wafd's neutralism, Nasser's revolutionary regime adopted, in his first year-and-a-half in power, a policy of pro-Western neutralism. Soon after the July coup, US influence in Egypt had significantly increased, and the new Egyptian leaders did not hide their sympathy toward the US. As they were opposed to communism and distrusted the British, the US became their favored alternative; they publicly declared their intentions to be affiliated with the West, under certain conditions.

The American–Egyptian honeymoon was, however, ephemeral. The efforts of the "Free Officers" (the name of the group of young officers who took over Egypt in July 1952) to persuade the US to prove its good intentions by supplying Egypt with military and economic aid did not meet with success. Truman refused, stating that selling military equipment to Egypt would create pressure from Israel and other Arab countries for similar assistance. Britain's refusal to evacuate its troops and to buy Egyptian cotton led Egypt's rulers to seek other sources of supply and export.[49] In the second half of 1953, owing to the Free Officers' inability to implement their political credo—the liberation of Egypt—Nasser adopted and sharpened Salah al-Din's policy of calculative/pragmatic nationalist neutralism in order to manipulate both American and Soviet interests, which he would then use to his own advantage in furthering Egypt's foreign policy. In December 1953 Nasser sent Deputy War Minister Hasan Rajab on a tentative tour of the Soviet bloc countries in order to bring the West to heel. The tour had two goals: First, to widen economic relations with the Eastern bloc; and second, to seek alternative sources of arms. Nasser calculated that the dialogue with the Soviets would expedite British evacuation, enabling broader ties with the West, which Nasser declared was his preferred partner in trade, aid, and arms supplies. Nasser's two-faced policy was too shrewd for US Secretary of State John Foster Dulles to appreciate, however; especially in light of his covert flirtation with the Soviets in the winter of 1953–4, which paved the way for arms deals with the Soviet bloc.[50]

Despite the American–Egyptian row over the Baghdad Pact of February 1955, Nasser contacted Dulles again in April 1955 with the intention of concluding a major arms deal. In February, only two months earlier, Nasser had concluded an arms deal with Czechoslovakia, and discussions were well under way for a major arms deal with the Soviets. This latter deal, which was concluded in July and announced on 20 September 1955, upset the entire Middle East military balance.[51] One month earlier, in August 1955, Dulles had approved the Egyptian request, only to be rebuffed by Nasser. His negotiations with the Soviets, which had begun as a tactical ploy, had netted him a much better deal, based on an easy repayment package, a large quantity and high quality of weapons, and a "no-strings" concession or compulsory membership in a military alliance—terms that the West was unwilling to offer. In a letter to Nasser, Dulles seemed more nonplused than angered: "We have placed full confidence in your repeated assurances regarding Egypt's identification with the West . . . our economic assistance programs . . . approval of arms purchases, and my statement on August 26, on the Arab–Israel situation are all based on that same general thought."[52] Nasser did not allow his early Western orientation to influence his military or economic considerations, an example of the irrelevance of ideology to the regime in its first years.

The plan to construct the Aswan High Dam was another example of Nasser's policy of playing the US off against the USSR and vice versa. In their efforts to fill the economic void created in Egypt's relations with the West, the Soviets had already made an attractive offer to the Rajab delegation while visiting Moscow in the winter of 1953–4, to assist in constructing the Dam. The Soviets made another tempting offer in June 1955, this time offering to supply equipment for the project together with financial assistance and engineering services, as well as a thirty-year loan of an unspecified amount at 2 percent interest, repayable in Egyptian cotton and rice;[53] but nothing came of the Soviet offers of 1955. In December, the US offered to help finance the project together with the British government and the World Bank. On 19 July 1956, however, Dulles announced that the US was withdrawing its offer owing to disagreements with Nasser. Soon after, Nasser decided to conclude the deal with the USSR.[54]

Nasser's success in settling the Anglo-Egyptian dispute and concluding arms deals with the Eastern bloc, however, as well as his meetings with Nehru and Tito before and after the Bandung Conference of April 1955, brought him closer to Nehru's and Tito's concepts of neutralism. Since late 1954, following the conclusion of the Anglo-Egyptian agreement of July 1954, which marked the complete liberation of Egypt, Nasser reformulated and modified the pattern of calculative/pragmatic nationalist neutralism to positive neutralism. The latter form of neutralism refers only to independent states that wish to play a major role in the international arena by manipulating the inter-bloc conflict and the Cold War for the furthering of their national interests.

Following the Bandung conference, Nasser became one of the major leaders and the co-founder of the new movement of non-aligned countries. Nasser's policy of positive neutralism was to change significantly in the mid-1960s, when he became fully oriented with the Soviet bloc, a process that reached its peak in 1968, when he supported, in contrast to the Bandung spirit, the Soviet invasion of Czechoslovakia. This created indignation among his close allies of the non-aligned movement—in particular, Tito. This policy change was expressed in Nasser's official statements and in practical measures.

Nasser's positive neutralism was directed "at reducing Western influence in the Middle East by delicately flirting with, but not inviting, Soviet intervention,"[55] until his defeat in the June 1967 war. His neutralism was not a policy of opposing both sides in the Cold War, but, rather, of using each of the two superpowers in an effort to further Egyptian goals.[56] Nasser did all he could in the 1950s and early 1960s to terminate Western influence in the region, such as his extended efforts to dissolve the Baghdad Pact. He also combated Soviet and communist influence in Syria in the latter half of 1950s in order to establish his hegemony there. Nasser tried to repeat this feat in Iraq following the demise of the Hashemite monarchy in 1958.

Other Arab countries that refused to ally themselves with either of the two world camps included Lebanon, Jordan, Iraq, and Saudi Arabia. Iraq was the only Arab country to formally join the Western camp in 1955 with the formation of the Baghdad Pact. This alliance did not last long, however; a military coup overthrew the Hashemite monarchy in July 1958 and installed an anti-Western regime, which gradually leaned toward the Soviet Union. From the outbreak of the Cold War until the formation of the Baghdad Pact, Iraq, despite its pro-Western stance, did not formally ally itself with the West; it instead tried to persuade Arab countries to follow its inter-bloc policy, without success. The Iraqi government's inter-bloc policy until 1955 may be defined as pro-Western neutralism. There were, however, neutralist political figures in Iraq who advocated the employment of a non-aligned doctrine. At the onset of 1950s, the main opposition party, *al-Hizb al-Watani al-Dimuqrati* [the National Democratic Party] expressed its objection to military alliances with any of the rival blocs. In the fourth conference of the party held in November 1950, it was declared that the party condemned propaganda activity by either of the two blocs, and "we don't want that our country should become a scene for total war, which would impose upon our people an inescapable destructive fate. This view falls in line with the idea of neutralism, which prevails among popular Arab circles—this is the correct view [to be held] by every Arab country, regardless of the argument put forth by [those] who want to see us yielding to the accomplished fact."[57] On 19 March 1950, the main Iraqi opposition parties issued a manifesto of neutralism [*Bayan al-hiyad*] which advocated, for the sake of peace, Arab objection to Middle East defense plans and the neutrality of the Iraqi and Arab peoples toward the East–West conflict. Special emphasis was placed on the need to be freed of imperialism and to be able to pursue an independent policy toward the Cold War, because the Iraqi people, unlike the imperialists, "have no interest in it." The Iraqi people were willing to cooperate with all countries that sought world peace and took a stand of complete neutralism [*al-hiyad al-tamm*].[58] The neutralism presented in this manifesto may be called "negative neutralism."

An attempt to draw Jordan into the Syrian–Egyptian–Saudi camp was made by these countries in the period 1955–7 with scant success.[59] King Hussein of Jordan, who was exposed to domestic and external pressure by radical anti-Western forces, decided to call an end to the British patronage of his army and dismissed Glubb Pasha, the Commander-in-Chief of the Arab Legion, installing a government led by neutralist figures such as Abdullah Rimawi, the Ba'th Party leader, and Prime Minister Sulayman Nabulsi. The newly appointed government of Jordan wanted to establish diplomatic relations with the USSR, refused to join the Baghdad Pact, and, for a short period of time, followed a policy of anti-Western neutralism. In 1957, King Hussein dismissed the government and declared his acceptance of the Eisenhower Doctrine, which was intended to check the spread of Soviet communism and Nasserite expansionist plans in the Middle East.

I
Syria's Road to Independence

The Emergence of "Pragmatic/Calculative Nationalist Neutralism"

Great Power Interests in the Middle East to 1945

"For Britain and France, control over the Arab countries was important not only because of their interests in the region itself, but because it strengthened their position in the world," declared Albert Hawrani.[1] Indeed, British and French interests in the Middle East were based on two different considerations—European and imperial. The European interest can be classified as strategic and political, resulting from the wish to maintain a balance of power in the Middle East. As a result, Britain and France found themselves involved in Eastern Mediterranean affairs, including the consolidation of a clear policy toward the gradual demise of the Ottoman Empire and its neighbors, in particular Russia. From the imperial viewpoint, France and Britain's presence in the Middle East helped to maintain their position as Mediterranean and world powers.

British imperial considerations primarily centered on the fact that the main sea-route to India and the Far East ran through the Suez Canal. Britain had developed air-routes across the Middle East during the interwar period and protected its interests by establishing a series of military bases, airfields, and ports situated at strategic points throughout the British zones of influence and control in the Middle East. The economic aspect was another consideration of the utmost importance for Britain: the British textile industry for example, depended on Middle Eastern cotton; Britain was deeply involved in developing the oil industry in the Persian Gulf; and the Middle Eastern countries were excellent markets for exported goods from Britain. Britain also invested extensively in those countries, particularly in Egypt.[2]

French interests in the Middle East were limited compared to the importance they attached to the Maghrib area in their imperial system. First, there were political and strategic imperial considerations. France's military presence in Syria and Lebanon strengthened its position as a Mediterranean and global power. The French army and navy used the land and ports of Syria and Lebanon and established a military air-route from Lebanon to France's empire in Indo-China. Second, France had extensive economic interests in the Levant and invested considerably in the Ottoman Empire, the Mount Lebanon area, and Palestine and Egypt before World War I. French companies in the Levant area had almost total control of the railway system and had vast interests in ports, gas, and electricity companies. Third, there were the humanitarian and cultural aspects, namely, "the French civilizing mission," which required the development of education systems, the nurturing of health services, and teaching the French language and culture. France also claimed to be protectors of the Christians, particularly, the Catholic Maronites in the Levant.[3]

American interests in this part of the world were very limited. The US joined the Allies in World War I only in the final stages of the war (April 1917), but nevertheless contributed significantly to the Allies' victory. The US was not party to any of the secret agreements concluded between its allies during the war and took an anti-imperialist approach. On 8 January 1918, while the war was still going on, US President Woodrow Wilson made his declaration on self-determination for the peoples who were still under Ottoman rule and called for the abolition of secret diplomacy. At the end of the war, he became concerned with the political future of the Asian territories of the Ottoman Empire as part of the general peace settlement. Unlike Britain and France, the US had no special interest of its own to advance in the Middle East. For a short period of time the US was involved in Middle Eastern affairs. In June 1919, Wilson, who was suspicious of British and French intentions in the Middle East, appointed the King–Crane Commission to ascertain the desires of the native populations. The recommendations of the King–Crane Commission, however, became irrelevant when the US Senate decided not to endorse Wilson's international affairs policy. With the failure of Wilsonian internationalism and the return to isolationism, the US lost interest in the political future of the Middle East. US economic interests, however, had grown vastly in the area—mainly in the oil fields—since the conclusion of World War I. As early as 1920, US oil concerns had appealed to the American government to secure for them equal opportunity in Middle Eastern countries that were under French and British hegemony. The US Department of State responded positively to their request and secured an open-door policy without discrimination against private American oil companies and businesses.[4]

In the interwar period US interests in the Middle East were marginal. In the 1930s and early 1940s, US policy toward the area was influenced to a great extent by the British view of the area. Elie Kedourie explains:

This view was that British interests in the area could be preserved precisely by working with what was believed to be the emerging dominant force of [Arab] nationalism. Hence reliance on a deal with the Wafd for the preservation of British interests in Egypt, hence the stance adopted towards the French in the Levant, and the encouragement of Pan-Arabism. This was a very recent line of policy, but it happened to be the dominant one in the 1935–1945 decade . . . another feature of United States policy in this period . . . was to ensure free and equal access for US oil companies in the Middle East. This was only to uphold a long-standing policy of insisting on the open door in international economic enterprise.[5]

The Middle East has always attracted the attention of Russia in its various historical phases—Tsarist Russia, the Soviet Union, or the present Russian Federation—because the region is the southern gateway to Russia. The eighteenth and nineteenth centuries saw the expansion of Tsarist Russia southward as a result of colonial conflict with the Ottoman Empire and Persia. Tsarist Russia, along with Britain, France, and Italy, were involved in the negotiations during World War I that dealt with the division of the Ottoman Empire between the Four Powers should the Empire be defeated. According to these treaties, Russia was to annex the Western coast of the Bosphorus, the Sea of Marmara, the Dardanelles, Constantinople, and other Ottoman areas creating a direct sea-route to the Mediterranean.[6] Following the Bolshevik revolution in 1917, Russia opted out of the war and its new leaders publicly revealed and condemned the secret treaties. The new Soviet leaders repeatedly declared that they had no territorial claims over Ottoman territories. In 1919 Lenin declared "pre-war frontiers will be respected, no Turkish territory will be given to Armenia, the Dardanelles will remain Turkish and Constantinople will remain the capital of the Muslim world".[7]

In the 1920s and 1930s, the Soviet leaders showed only a mild interest in the Arab region. Soviet relations with Arab countries were limited to two independent Arab states: Saudi Arabia and Yemen. In the late 1930s, the attention of Soviet policymakers was focused on Central European and Far Eastern danger zones, and less attention was paid to Middle Eastern affairs, ideological or political. The Soviets did not and could not hold any contacts with other Arab countries, since their foreign relations were controlled by France and Britain, thus preventing any relationship with Moscow. Nevertheless, toward the end of World War II and thereafter, Soviet interests and political activity in the Middle East grew extensively, resulting in a deep Soviet penetration into the heart of the Arab world.[8]

Syria, Lebanon, and the Great Powers
following World War I

The British and their allies, reinforced by regiments of the Northern Arab army, captured Damascus on 1 October 1918, thus putting an end to four centuries of Ottoman control. Emir Faysal, the military leader of the so-called Arab revolt, entered the city and became its head of government.[9] General Sir Edmund Allenby, the Commander of the British and Allied forces, allowed him to proclaim a provisional independent Arab government in the areas designated A and B under the Sykes–Picot Agreement, with Damascus being its central city.[10] This arrangement was later rejected by France. At the San Remo Conference of April 1920 the Allied Supreme Council granted France the mandate over the Levant area (territory presently covering Syria and Lebanon). This development was met, on the one hand, with strong protests from Damascus and, on the other, with great satisfaction by most Christians in Lebanon.[11] The French were determined to exercise their full control over the entire mandated territory. On 22 July 1920 French forces defeated Faysal's army at the Maysalun Pass and proceeded to occupy Damascus. On 27 July, Faysal was asked to leave Damascus.[12] On 1 September, Greater Lebanon was established by annexing the coastal area and the Biqa' Valley up to Mount Lebanon.[13] The French divided the mandated territory into three distinct areas: the state of Damascus (including the Jebel Druze district); the state of Aleppo (including Alexandretta); and the territory of Latakia. Each area was ruled by a French governor who was instructed by the office of high commissioner stationed in Beirut.[14]

French policy toward the Levant, declared George Lenczowski, "tended to follow the pattern of administration in the French colonies. It was centralized rule *par excellence*, with little or no regard for local autonomy." Philip Khoury holds a different view regarding the character of French rule in the Levant. According to Khoury, the mandate system was not a direct system of rule; the French, like the Ottomans before them, needed a partner from within the native society in order to govern. Khoury concluded that France could not afford direct rule in the Levant for two main reasons: first, it was obliged by the League of nations to prepare Syria and Lebanon for independence; second, its postwar economy was fragile.[15]

The French mandatory regime, whether direct or indirect, was negatively perceived by nationalist circles in Syria. The prevailing belief among Arab propagandists and English writers and scholars, according to Elie Kedourie, is that the actions of Britain and France after World War I "twisted and deformed the political development of the Arab countries. There were then upright, moderate Arab nationalists who were prepared to cooperate with the West and to set up modern, enlightened and progressive policies. They were thwarted, betrayed, and driven to violence and extreme courses. Britain conspired with France and the Zionists, to deny the Arabs their just claims and to bring ruin to them."[16]

The French mandatory regime in the Levant states dramatically changed following France's defeat by the Third Reich in June 1940. On 14 June, Paris was conquered by the Germans. French officials controlling Syria and Lebanon were now subordinated by the Nazi-controlled Vichy government. This development did not last long. On 8 June 1941, British and Free France forces invaded Syria from Palestine, Iraq, and Transjordan, and by 14 July, after a month of fighting, the entire Levant area was now controlled by the British Middle East Command.[17]

Kamal Salibi argues that the French Mandate in Syria and Lebanon came to an end on 8 June 1941 with the Free French general proclamation of the independence of the two countries. General Charles de Gaulle appointed on 24 June General Georges Catroux "Delegate General and Plenipotentiary of Free France in the Levant". Catroux was instructed by de Gaulle to negotiate treaties with Syria and Lebanon as soon as possible.[18] He formally proclaimed the independence of Syria and Lebanon on 27 September and 26 November 1941, respectively.[19] According to Catroux's declaration, Syria, was about to enjoy: "the rights and prerogatives of an independent and sovereign state . . . [and] would have the power to appoint diplomatic representatives abroad; [Syria] would have the right to organize her national forces . . . [and] would be obliged to accord France and her allies necessary aid and facilities during the war . . ."[20]

In February 1942, when the situation on the battlefield, particularly on the Northern African front, did not look promising for the Allies, Britain recognized *de jure* the independence of both Syria and Lebanon, an act of recognition followed by the appointment of General Edward Spears as Britain's first Minister to Syria and Lebanon. Despite this positive development, France was not enthusiastic about translating Catroux's declaration into practice. This led to growing discontent and anti-French feelings among nationalist political circles in both Syria and Lebanon. The pressure exerted on the French authorities by the nationalist movements and by the British, in both Syria and Lebanon, finally bore fruit when, in March 1943, the French decided to reestablish the suspended constitution in the two Levantine states. As a result, elections took place in the summer in both countries.[21]

The elections resulted in the defeat of French-appointed leaders and victory for the nationalists in both countries. The year 1944 saw the gradual handing over of nearly the entire mandatory prerogatives and functions of the French Delegate-General to the Syrian and Lebanese governments. Nevertheless, the French insisted on retaining the locally recruited *Troupes*

Speciales[22] under French local command. France was also still pursuing the conclusion of two special treaties with the governments of Syria and Lebanon to safeguard French cultural establishments. France wanted Syria, Lebanon, and the Allies to recognize its economic rights and strategic interests in the Levant; Syria and Lebanon, supported by strong opposition from Britain and the Allies, particularly the USA and the USSR, remained hostile to any French demands.[23] It was only in early 1946 that French and British troops evacuated both Syria and Lebanon, following a resolution passed by the Security Council of the United Nations on 15 February 1946.[24]

Since June 1941, Syria and Lebanon had been, to a great extent, dominated by the two prewar Western powers in the Middle East, Britain and France. The presence of a majority of British forces in these countries up to the end of the war, however, had put the British into a superior position *vis-à-vis* France, which was, at that point, fully dependent upon British generosity. France was soon to realize that the British were not that generous when French activities and interests in the Levant did not serve their long- and short-term ends in the Middle East. The German invasion of the Soviet Union and the consolidation of the Anglo-Soviet alliance in mid-1941 were also to have significant implications for policies of both powers toward the region. The Anglo-Soviet joint military occupation of Iran in the latter part of 1941 and the impressive Soviet victory over Nazi Germany in Stalingrad in February 1943 gave the Soviets significant entrée into the Middle East.[25]

A widespread belief among many contemporary Middle Eastern scholars is that Soviet interests and political activity in the Middle East throughout Stalin's rule were marginal. Stalin, it is claimed, was doctrinaire and paid great attention to ideological concerns—the global spread of the communist revolution. Stalin therefore focused his efforts, as far as the Middle East was concerned, on building and nurturing communist organizations in the region, which he believed would, when strong enough, be able to take over their countries and subsequently ally them with the Soviet Union. Accordingly, Stalin refused to establish any contacts or develop relations with non-communist Middle Eastern ruling elites. These scholars argue that only after Stalin's death in 1953 did Soviet policy toward the Middle East change dramatically.

Stalin's Middle Eastern policy can be divided into two main periods: 1922 to the early 1940s; and the 1940s to 1953. True, in the first period Stalin's interests in the Middle East were limited. In contrast, the second period saw a remarkable change in Soviet interests and activities in the Middle East. Being fully aware of the USSR's growing international influence and prestige toward the end of World War II, Soviet policymakers appealed to Middle East nationalist groups to concentrate on the task of putting an end to Western influence in the region. To achieve that end, the Soviets nurtured relations with governments that were already pursuing anti-Western policies. The place of ideology—that is, the export of the principles of the worldwide communist revolution—were relegated to secondary importance. Stalin began to follow the line of *realpolitik* in his international affairs program. Foreign policy was, first and foremost, based on utilitarian considerations derived from the USSR's growing interests in certain parts of the world. This policy shift included the Middle East. Stalin was able to overlook the fact that some of the Middle Eastern governments with which he was trying to tighten relations were in fact anti-communist; what mattered more to him was that they pursued anti-Western policies. The gradual process of creating a dialogue with Middle Eastern nations first paid off in Egypt when the two countries established diplomatic relations in August 1943—a development that enabled future Soviet penetration into that country. This approach also met with success in Syria and Lebanon, where the Soviets later managed to gain diplomatic strongholds in these countries following the establishment of formal relations in July 1944. From this stage onward, Soviet political activity in the Levant significantly increased.

This chapter shows that the Syrian government's decision to establish diplomatic relations with the USSR was a calculated move intended to advance Syria's struggle for national liberation. Syrian policymakers believed that the newly emerged anti-imperialist superpower would fully support their demand, internationally, without political strings attached, for a speedy and complete evacuation of foreign domination from their country. Like Egypt before, they embraced a premature neutralist policy based on the pattern of "calculative/pragmatic nationalist neutralism." This pattern was derived from utilitarian considerations and national interests—the Soviet Union's central role during World War II made it a very influential country internationally, in European as well as in Eastern affairs. In the forthcoming postwar peace talks Syria would need as much international support as possible, and the USSR, with its new international role, could certainly provide this if diplomatic relations with Moscow were established.

The Establishment of Diplomatic Relations between the USSR, Syria, and Lebanon

On 26 August 1943, Egypt and the Soviet Union established diplomatic relations, and the first Soviet minister to Egypt, Nikolai Novikov, presented his credentials at an audience with King Farouk on 25 December.[26] The establishment of formal relations between both countries was a bilateral decision in which economic and political considerations on both sides played a major role.[27]

The USSR, led by Stalin, was emerging toward the end of World War II as one of the two major superpowers. The Soviets, encouraged by their success in Egypt, were making great efforts to establish diplomatic relations with other Middle Eastern countries.

As early as June 1944, the Syrian and Lebanese governments were notified by the French about the Soviets' preliminary soundings in Algiers, with a view to recognizing the independence of the Levantine states. According to Sir Edward Spears, the British Minister to Syria and Lebanon (based in Beirut), Syria and Lebanon realized that the "establishment of relations [with the USSR] is inevitable at some stage."[28] Spears was informed by the Syrian government that it had already sent an envoy to Cairo to meet Novikov, in order to establish direct contacts with the USSR and to confirm Soviet intentions to recognize the independence of the Syrian Republic. The meeting with Novikov turned out to be very confusing for the Syrian envoy, since Novikov remained quite obscure and could not provide the Syrian envoy with the necessary information. According to the Syrian envoy he was either ill-informed or not anxious to impart information. In the course of their conversation, Novikov expressed doubt as to what the international position of Syria was and asked whether Syria had already been recognized by any other state. Novikov claimed he did not imagine the USSR had intended to do more than send some consuls to Syria, without however, considering reciprocity. The envoy replied that "this would be totally unacceptable to the Syrian government."[29]

It may be concluded that Novikov had not been informed of the Soviet–French dialogue in Algiers. It would seem that Soviet activities in the Middle East were at that stage conducted through several channels. The Soviet approach to Iraq, with an offer to establish diplomatic relations, was made through the Soviet ambassador at Tehran, and not through Novikov.[30] Spears reported to his superiors that the Syrian government, following its dialogue with Novikov, concluded that "the project of the so-called recognition was purely a French idea to plant the Soviet representatives in the Levant, where, it was thought, they might further French interests."[31] The Syrians believed that France was aware of the growing international position of the USSR as a result of its achievements during World War II. They believed that, by promoting the idea of Soviet recognition of the independence of the Levantine states, they could gain two advantages: First, Syria and Lebanon would see that France was helping them gain international recognition by major international powers, thus anti-French feelings might change in its favor; and second, the USSR would express its gratitude to France for its initiative in persuading Syria and Lebanon to form relations with the Soviets who would therefore acknowledge French interests in the Levant. That, in turn, could enhance the French stance in any future disagreements with Britain over the future of safeguarding French interests in the Levant.

Novikov's confusion, as reflected in his conversation with the Syrian envoy, was soon to change significantly. A few days later, after receiving instructions from his superiors in Moscow, he informed the Syrian government that the USSR "has favourably reacted to the suggestion of establishing direct contact with the Syrian government." He also expressed his wish to visit Syria for this purpose, to which the Syrian Minister of Foreign Affairs promptly reciprocated with an invitation.[32]

The Syrian Minister of Foreign Affairs approached Spears to discuss Novikov's visit,[33] and Spears, after consulting the British Foreign Office, answered that Britain had no objection to the Soviet recognition of Syria. The Levantine states had been occupied mainly by British forces after a short period of domination by the Vichy government; Britain still retained an impressive presence in the area, showing sensitivity to the French position and their special interests in the area. At this stage Britain did not want to confuse or embarrass the French—this was particularly true regarding the establishment of diplomatic relations between Syria and the USSR, which as an emerging superpower, might challenge and jeopardize French interests in the future. The Foreign Office's sole interest was to keep the French representatives informed of any information the British received or held regarding Soviet–Levantine relations.[34]

On 10 July 1944, Novikov traveled to Syria and Lebanon via Palestine on what he described as a "clandestine" mission. He wrote later that the British Embassy in Cairo and Egypt's Deputy Minister for Foreign Affairs Muhammad Salah al-Din—who was one of the key figures behind the establishment of Soviet–Egyptian diplomatic relations—were the only ones who were informed of his plan.[35] The details of Novikov's subsequent discussions with his Syrian hosts found their way in due course to the British Consulate in Damascus, which on 10 July 1944, received a request from the Syrian Minister for Foreign Affairs Jamil Mardam Bey, to arrange a meeting between Novikov and the British authorities in Haifa, after which he should continue his journey to Damascus by car and not by train, as first planned. The British agreed to assist in this matter and suggested that the Syrian government send a representative to Haifa and a car "to meet so distinguished a person who was, after all, coming to establish contact with the Syrian government."[36] Haydar Rikabi Bey, *Chef de Bureau* of the Syrian Ministry of Foreign Affairs, was accordingly sent to Haifa the following day. Ricabi met Francis H. O. Fuller, the British Acting District Commissioner, in Haifa, and the latter accompanied him to greet Novikov. On 11 July, Novikov arrived in Damascus, accompanied by Rikabi, the Second Secretary, and an Attaché of the Soviet Legation in Cairo.[37]

Novikov's discussions with Jamil Mardam took place on 12 July. Novikov expressed his government's desire to recognize Syria's independence and establish diplomatic relations between the two countries, making it clear that these relations were to be based on "acceptable principles according to international law and recognizing the principle of equality between both parties."[38] He made a point of stating that the USSR should not be considered an imperial power meeting with a small inferior country; rather, he stressed his government's endorsement of equality between peoples and nations. Mardam replied that the fact that the USSR expressed its willingness to establish diplomatic relations with Syria was a significant event, which could contribute to Syria's future development.[39] Satisfied with the progress he had made so far in his talks with his Syrian hosts, Novikov sent a ciphered telegram to his government recommending that the USSR recognize Syria's independence and subsequently establish formal diplomatic relations.[40]

Another issue that came up during the Mardam–Novikov talks was the possibility of Soviet recognition of Lebanon's independence and the establishment of diplomatic relations between the two countries. It was Mardam who suggested to Novikov that the "Soviet government might care to recognize Lebanese independence simultaneously." Novikov showed interest, saying that he "would be pleased to do so if a member of the Lebanese government would discuss the matter with him."[41] The Syrians acted promptly, organizing a meeting between Novikov and Salim Taqla, the Lebanese Minister for Foreign Affairs, for the very next day. The meeting took place in Bludan with Mardam participating. Upon the conclusion of their talks, Novikov dispatched another ciphered telegram to his government recommending the recognition of Lebanese independence as well.[42]

On 19 July, while still in Syria, Novikov received a telegram from his government recognizing Syrian independence in principle. The Soviet government also added their willingness to favorably consider a similar request for recognition from the Lebanese government. Consequently, Salim Taqla expressed his agreement and sent a telegram, through Novikov, to the Soviet government proposing an exchange of diplomatic missions.[43]

On his way to Lebanon on 23 July 1944, Novikov received a telegram from Molotov, the Soviet Commissar for Foreign Affairs. Molotov agreed to establish diplomatic relations with Syria and to open a diplomatic legation in Damascus.[44] The Syrian government received Molotov's decision warmly, and on 25 July all Soviet papers published the telegrams exchanged between Molotov and Mardam on the issue of diplomatic relations.[45]

Soon after the Soviets agreed to exchange diplomatic representatives

with Syria, Novikov, at a banquet given in his honor by the Syrian government on 31 July, explained to Gilbert Mackereth, a British diplomat, the
Soviet government's policy, which favored the integral restoration of
French government in France, but opposed French sovereignty in colonial
territories as well as its other "imperial" designs.[46] The day before the
banquet Novikov had assured the Syrian Prime Minister Sa'dallah al-
Jabiri that the USSR would oppose any attempt by France to re-establish
its mandate over Syria.[47]

The British Foreign Office was surprised by Novikov's disclosures,
public and private, about his government's intentions. The Foreign Office
stressed that Novikov's statement clearly applied to the French Empire as
a whole and not just to its mandates over Syria and Lebanon. This statement was "clearly of considerable importance. Soviet diplomats do not
usually make this kind of statements without authority."[48]

Reacting to the news on Soviet–Syrian diplomatic relations, Nuri al-
Sa'id, the pro-British Iraqi leader, told Mackereth on 30 July that he felt
the "Syrians had stolen a march on them with Russia." Al-Sa'id expressed
his anxiety concerning Soviet political penetration of Kurdistan, which he
believed might "have uncomfortable repercussions on Iraq."[49]

In an analysis of these developments on the relations between the Soviet
Union, Syria, and Lebanon, based on discussions with Soviet, Syrian, and
Lebanese statesmen, Mackereth provided the Foreign Office with additional detailed information on the motives behind these countries'
decisions to establish diplomatic relations with the USSR. The Syrian
leaders, he noted, were motivated by their anxiety to protect Syria's independence; thus they refused to be tied solely to one great power. They
wanted to achieve complete sovereign independence and favored the idea
that the United Nations Council would appoint a commissioner to Syria
to protect it from aggression. The Syrians made it clear, however, that the
commissioner should not come from one of the great powers, for fear of
his being biased. The Syrians, stressed Mackereth, "are just as alive to the
danger on that score from Russia as they are to similar dangers from Great
Britain or France." The establishment of relations with the Soviets, he
continued, rose out of "a purely fortuitous circumstance, i.e., French intervention at an early stage with a view to the appointment of Russian Consuls
in the Levant States."[50] The Syrians distrusted French motives and decided
to take the initiative by forging direct contacts with the Soviet Legation in
Cairo. They offered Novikov "the more alluring prospect of diplomatic
representation direct to the states rather than Consular representation,
which might be effected through the agency of the French Delegation
Generale."[51] Upon his arrival in Damascus, Novikov was greeted warmly
in a demonstration of Syria's respect for the USSR. In response, Novikov
assured his hosts of his government's reluctance to acknowledge the

predominance of any power in the Levant. He also told Mackereth that the Soviet government would not subscribe to Britain's respect for the French position in the Levant. There was a feeling among Syrian statesmen, wrote Mackereth, that, with the Soviets on their side, Britain and France would find it impossible to concoct a deal whereby France would endorse Britain's interests in Palestine and Britain would reinstall the French in the Levant states.[52]

The Syrians were pleased with the Soviet attitude, and satisfied with the Soviet agreement (mentioned in Molotov's telegram of 22 July) to abolish the capitulations and other privileges and immunities enjoyed by Tsarist Russia. The Syrian government felt it would thereby be prepared for any future negotiations on the abolition of "such vestiges of the capitulatory regime as still remained," and that Soviet recognition of its independence would help to protect Syria against any future territorial colonizing designs, in particular of the French.[53]

The French and the Syrians both suggested that the USSR recognize the independence of the Levant states. The French were the first to raise the issue of Soviet recognition, with the goal, as Jamil Mardam believed, of luring the Soviets to their side "as the champions of the Greek Orthodox and the Roman Greek Catholic minorities in this country [Syria] . . . " reported W. Weld-Forester of the British Consulate in Damascus. The categorical confirmation by the Soviet government that "they will consider any privileges enjoyed by Tsarist Russia as abolished, lays for the Syrian government the chimerical spectre thus conjured up."[54]

Encouraged by the successful Syrian initiative to win Soviet recognition and establish diplomatic relations, the Lebanese government followed suit, and approached the Soviet government with a proposal for official recognition. On 31 July, Salim Taqla, the Lebanese Minister for Foreign Affairs, sent a telegram to Molotov similar to Mardam's telegram of 21 July.[55] Molotov, on behalf of the Soviet government, thanked Taqla briefly for the sentiments he expressed regarding the heroism of the peoples of the USSR in their battle against Nazi Germany and the Axis. The Soviet government, stated Molotov, "accepts with satisfaction the suggestion of the government of the Republic of Lebanon concerning the establishment of friendly diplomatic relations between the USSR and Lebanon."[56] Both governments agreed on the level of their diplomatic relations being that of legations, namely, each country would be represented by a minister—a diplomatic rank below ambassador.

At a luncheon given in honor of Novikov by the diplomatic corps in Beirut on 9 August, Mackereth, who was one of the invitees, took the opportunity to exchange views with Novikov. The latter explicitly reiterated that the Soviet Union, unlike Britain, would not recognize France's privileged status in Syria and Lebanon. He remained mute, however, when Mackereth referred again to other French colonial territories.[57] Novikov also promised his Lebanese hosts that the USSR would not allow the French to re-establish their hegemony over Lebanon and Syria.[58]

On 19 September 1944, the first two Soviet designated diplomats held a meeting with the Lebanese Minister for Foreign Affairs. These were M. Tcherniev, who was appointed by his government as the Soviet *Chargé d'Affaires* for Syria and Lebanon, and M. Maliarov, who was appointed as Secretary of the Soviet Legation for Lebanon. Tcherniev arrived in Beirut from Algiers to open up the Soviet Legation and prepare for the arrival of the new Soviet minister, Daniil' Solod, who at the time served as Soviet Counselor in Cairo.[59] Tcherniev informed a member of the British Consulate in Beirut about Solod's arrival on 3 October, and that he would be accredited the same position as Spears, the British Minister to Syria and Lebanon. The Soviets planned to form separate missions, each including a First Secretary, two Second Secretaries and two Attachés. The *Chargé d'Affaires*, who held the rank of Counselor, would be stationed in Damascus. According to a reliable Soviet source, the number of staff members of the Soviet Legation in Beirut was to be sixty.[60] On 26 October, Daniil' Solod presented the letter accrediting him as Envoy Extraordinary and Plenipotentiary to the Syrian President.[61]

The British Legation in Beirut prepared a well-detailed and interesting memorandum describing, analyzing, and evaluating Soviet policy toward Syria and Lebanon. The memorandum noted that, less than half a year since the USSR established diplomatic relations with Syria and Lebanon, the prestige of the Soviet Union had rapidly increased. The Soviets had only began to show an interest in the two Levantine countries some time after France, Britain, and the US were diplomatically represented, but a British report noted that their influence was already such as to put them on the same footing as the other powers. The memorandum attributed part of this Soviet success to geographical proximity, as well as to the deep impression the victories of the Soviet army in World War II had made upon public opinion in the area.[62] The report noted that there were also certain important elements in the population of Syria and Lebanon that, by their readiness to support the Soviet Union, gave the Soviets a stronger position in these countries. The most important of these was the Greek Orthodox Church—second only to the Maronites in size, and possibly wealthier—which had played an important part in the political scene. Greek Orthodox ecclesiastical authorities spoke openly of enlisting Soviet support in their efforts to enhance their position of prestige and to accord their communities the official protection of the USSR. The minorities of Northern Syria also viewed the Soviets with much the same feelings. They lived in the periphery and felt that they need the protection of a strong power. They had little favor for the French and British, who had done little in the past for them; therefore they were inclined to turn for support to the Soviet Union—geographically the nearest of the Great Powers. According to the memorandum, both the Armenians and the Kurds had connections with the USSR through their resident compatriots. The Kurds entertained the idea that the Soviets would support the formation of a Kurdish Republic within the framework of the Soviet Union composed of those parts of Turkey, Persia, and Iraq inhabited by Kurds. The Armenians, persecuted in the early years of the twentieth century, also looked to the Soviets as their protector against Turkey.

Another element in the Levant that attracted support for the Soviets were the left-wing organizations, among them the Communist Party. These organizations, although somewhat restricted, had an extremely active and influential following in the Levant, including the intelligentsia and the working class in Beirut and Damascus. Since early 1943, membership of left-wing parties had more than doubled, with a similar increase in the number of adherents. These left-wing organizations were in touch with the Soviet diplomats in the Levant.[63]

The memorandum also revealed that the Soviet Union gained wide sympathy amongst the population of Syria and Lebanon for its official policy *vis-à-vis* the French, in particular the negative stance the USSR had adopted toward French claims for a predominant position in its former mandated areas. Daniil' Solod had also continually reiterated Soviet support for the complete and untrammeled independence of Syria and Lebanon; the Soviets would not countenance any contrary policy in the Levant. These Soviet assurances had given the Syrian and Lebanese governments considerable encouragement. Moreover, Britain had made it clear that it favored the conclusion of treaties with a provisional French government. It was therefore largely upon Soviet and US support that the governments of Syria and Lebanon were counting in their refusal to conclude any agreement enabling France to retain predominant influence in the Levant. However, the two Levantine governments, the report concluded, were doubtful of the extent to which they could depend on US support because of the American-British intimate alliance on world affairs.[64]

The British memorandum also noted that, since the establishment of the Soviet legations in Beirut and Damascus, there had been a marked increase in the dissemination of Soviet propaganda. This coincided with the appointment of a Tass agency representative who frequently kept in touch with the editors of the local newspapers and the local communist leaders. To quote the memorandum:

Some indications of the immense amount of propaganda material which is being supplied from the Soviet government to the local press is provided by the fact that, while last summer the Soviet *Soupresse* service was averaging about 8,000 words a day, it has now risen to over 12,000 words a day. Large quantities of books, newspapers and propaganda pamphlets in the Russian language are being imported, and recent issues of *Pravda* and *Izvestiia* figure prominently among the copies of the *Sphere* or *Life* on bookstalls. To all this should be added the propaganda pamphlets in Arabic extolling the life and social conditions obtaining in the Soviet Union, which the friends of the Soviet Union . . . are engaged in printing and distributing. They are, furthermore, organizing a large exhibition in Beirut covering Soviet activities in cultural, artistic, scientific and industrial spheres, which has received considerable publicity. This increased interest is also confirmed by the little information available of the activities of Soviet agents in these two countries . . . while up to the end of 1943 the majority of NKVD (*Narodni Komitet Venutrenix Dyel*) agents here appeared to be acting as passive observers engaged primarily in collecting information, they are now taking a more active line.[65]

The British memorandum warned that the Soviets were relying on a method of infiltration based on their propaganda and the active support of pro-Soviet elements within the country, and that the process "might have gone too far before the Syrian and Lebanese governments awoke to the realization of the danger by which they were encompassed."[66] As future events were to demonstrate, this warning was correct. The memorandum concluded that it was in Britain's interest to pursue a policy that would do everything possible to discourage and resist the increase of Soviet influence and position in Syria and Lebanon. The USSR should be prevented from having free access to the Mediterranean because such a development might jeopardize British strategic interests in the Middle East.

The policies of Britain and France toward the Middle East were severely criticized by the official organs of the Communist Party of Syria and Lebanon. The Soviet Legation could be satisfied with the anti-Western line expressed by these organs, and indeed, it was fully aware of the direction of the party's newspaper policy.[67] Khalid Bakdash, the leader of the Syrian and Lebanese Communist Party, found a direct connection between the project of Greater Syria mooted by King Abdullah of Jordan and British imperialist plans in the region. In his party's organ *Jhoghovourti Tzain*, published in Armenian, he declared:

Those who conceived the project of Greater Syria want to create a bigger zone of imperialistic influence. They want to create a capitalist stronghold out of a Zionist Palestine, and in this way they try to divide the Arabs. Syria does not want a change of masters. We want complete independence, without any foreign interference. The Syrian people refuses any foreign influence. Any power that recognizes our independence without any back [ulterior] thoughts is our friend. That is why we welcome the friendship of the Soviet Union.[68]

Several days later, in a joint statement made by the Central Committees of the Communist Parties of Syria and Lebanon, the project of a Greater Syria was declared to be the work of the agents of foreign imperialism in accord with Zionist leaders. This project, the communists stressed, aimed to create a new zone of imperialistic influence.[69] The communists continued with their harsh attacks on Zionism and the idea of dividing Palestine into two independent states, Jewish and Arab. They did so even after the USSR had declared in summer 1947 of its intention to support the partition of Palestine. A joint manifesto of the central committees of the Lebanese and Syrian communist parties issued on 17 October 1947 declared that the two parties

> firmly believe that . . . the settlement of the Palestine problem is: [British] evac-
> uation, independence, abolition of the Mandate and definite rejection of the
> partition scheme. They also believe in the possibility of Arabs and Jews living in
> Palestine under one independent democratic state in peace . . . the Arab struggle
> for Palestine is first of all a nationalist struggle against colonization . . . [70]

The communists considered the Palestine question an Arab nationalist issue. They had consolidated an independent stand, not in line with Moscow, but rather in line with the Arab national consensus. Indeed, there appeared to be a broad consensus among all Arab political circles from left to right regarding an appropriate solution to the Palestine question. They were particularly united in their rejection of the Zionist aspirations. The Syrian communists, of whom many were also Arab nationalists, embraced the pattern of "pro-Soviet neutralism." Meaning, they wanted Syria to maintain close relations with Moscow, in all fields, but not to formally ally itself with the Soviet Union as far as the emerging inter-bloc conflict was concerned.

The Communist Party organ *Sawt al-Sha'b*, published in Arabic, largely referred to traditional Anglo-French rivalry in the Eastern part of the Mediterranean. France, the organ declared, wished to guard its privileged position in Syria and Lebanon, while Britain regarded them as vital strategic areas in relation to its Empire. The interests of the Syrians and Lebanese could not lay with France or Britain; they were not and could not be, under any circumstances, identical with the interests of "a foreign power defending us because we are a 'vital area' for its great empire, a bridge for it, or a defensive line . . . Syria and Lebanon . . . cannot accept, nor is it in their interest to accept, any sacrifice [of their sovereignty], nor tolerate any foreign ascendancy or guaranteeing a privileged position for any nation, or making a 'vital area' or means of communication secure with respect to any empire."[71] *Sawt al-Sha'b* praised the USSR for the support it had given Syria and Lebanon in their struggle for national liberation "with all sincerity, without asking for a 'privileged position' for a particular state or a 'vital pathway' for a particular empire."[72]

On 18 June 1945, a lecture that dealt with events in Syria and Lebanon was delivered by V. F. Putski, a Candidate of Historical Sciences in the Polytechnic Museum in Moscow. Putski drew the audience's attention to the fact that the US, like Britain and France, had interests in the Levant. The US, Putski said, desired an open door in the Middle East (though it had no colonies in that area), and wanted to keep for itself the possibility of establishing bases there. The US therefore supported the tendency of the Arab states to independence, as it would then be able to apply its own policy to independent Arab states. The Americans had acted in the Levant directly and not through the intermediary of France or Britain. Unlike the Western powers, the USSR, Putski declared, was not following any imperialistic policy and had no claims on territories in the Middle East. The Soviets did not seek special privileges in this area, and wanted all colonial and dependent peoples to become independent. The Soviet Union recognized the right of Syria and Lebanon to independence, and desired that other nations should respect this right.[73]

The Deepening of Soviet Involvement in the Levant Area

Jamil Mardam, the Syrian Minister for Foreign Affairs, encouraged by Soviet and American recognition of Syria's independence and by their opposition to granting special privileges to France in the Levant, made the following points in a letter he addressed on 19 September 1944 to the Foreign Ministers of the US, Britain, and the USSR:

> The British Minister and the French representative in Syria have suggested that the Syrian government enter into negotiations with the French representative for the conclusion of a treaty under which France should obtain . . . a privileged position in Syria. Such an arrangement . . contradicts both the principles of the Atlantic Charter, on the basis of which the United Nations is to be established, and the independent and sovereign status of Syria, which has been recognized by the three allied powers.[74]

The French, however, had a different agenda with regard to their future presence in Syria and Lebanon. On 17 May 1945, ten days after VE Day, French troops (of African origin) arrived in Beirut in order to "reinforce the French army in Syria and Lebanon."[75] A day later, French Representative General P. E. M. Beynet dispatched a memorandum to the Syrian and Lebanese governments demanding "economic, cultural and military privileges for the French."[76] These French demands displeased both the Syrians and the Lebanese, who reacted violently: a wave of anti-French feeling swept over Syria and Lebanon, and strikes, riots, and assaults against French citizens and property erupted. The Syrian and the

Lebanese governments vehemently demanded the unconditional and immediate withdrawal of all French and British troops from their lands. This aggressive reaction reached its peak on 29 May with the French bombardment of Damascus. The British now took the initiative to stop the violence by siding with Syria and Lebanon. At the end of May, the British Prime Minister, Winston Churchill, called General Charles de Gaulle to order the French troops to ceasefire and withdraw to their barracks. Aware of his inferior position *vis-à-vis* British forces in the Levant, De Gaulle complied with Churchill's demands and the British redeployed their forces between the French and the local forces.[77] The British maneuvers and their manipulative methods against France in the early 1940s are described and analyzed by Kedourie, who explained how the British would eventually lose most of their Middle Eastern strategic assets:

> Anti-French prejudices, which colored so much of British political attitudes between the wars, made it seem, therefore, safe, reasonable and attractive to edge the French out of the Levant, so that Britain would remain the sole dominant power. In the event, this led to the undoing not only of the French position but of the British position as well. The very same arguments that were used, with British encouragement and applause, against the French, were later turned against Britain with equal effect.[78]

In early June 1945, the Soviet government dispatched letters to the governments of the other powers calling for "urgent measures . . . for the cessation of [French] military actions . . . and settlement of the arisen conflict by peaceful means."[79] An analysis and evaluation of the political situation in Syria and Lebanon by the Department of International Information of the Central Committee of the Communist Party in the USSR in late June, praised the two countries as having "the most advanced governments in the Middle East." Pro-Soviet sentiment in both countries was, the report noted, widespread and openly expressed. One notable group that advocated closer relations with the Soviet Union was the League of Friends of the Soviet Union in Syria and Lebanon, which was headed by prominent scientists and intellectuals.[80]

At the Potsdam Conference that opened on 17 July 1945, the USSR, represented by Stalin, after a Syrian request for the USSR's intervention, demanded that the Syrian–Lebanese issue be included on the agenda. Stalin was quoted as saying, "we do not propose the removal of troops from any country." However, he pointed out that both the Syrian and Lebanese governments were reluctant to award the French any privileged status. President Truman reinforced Stalin's view, stating that the US "stood for equal rights for all."[81] Churchill, on his behalf, explained to Stalin and Truman why British troops were still stationed in the Levant area. On 22 July, he declared that his government was discussing how to withdraw its forces as soon as conditions allowed, though at that moment such a move was impossible because "immediate withdrawal would mean the massacre of the French."[82]

Constant pressure exerted by both the USSR and the US on Britain and France to respect the uncompromising demands of the Syrian and Lebanese for an immediate evacuation of all foreign troops from their lands began to bear fruit. On 13 December, both France and Britain expressed their willingness to discuss evacuation on the condition that there be "the maintenance in the Levant of sufficient forces to guarantee security, until such time as the United Nations Organization has decided on the organization of collective security in this zone."[83] The two powers still rejected the idea of an immediate and unconditional withdrawal. The USSR decided to use the situation to their own ends in view of the troubled relations of the Syrians and Lebanese with France and Britain, in order to increase Soviet influence in the Levant and subsequently in other parts of the Middle East. On 10 January 1946, Daniil' Solod, acting as Soviet negotiator and signatory, approached Bishara al-Khuri, the President of Lebanon, and proposed that the Soviet, Lebanese, and Syrian governments sign a secret treaty. Following negotiations, both Lebanese and Syrian governments agreed to accept the first formal treaty proposal from the USSR. On 1 February 1946, the secret Soviet–Syrian treaty was signed in Beirut. Two days later, an identical treaty was signed in Beirut between Lebanon and the USSR. Both treaties included, *inter alia*, the following clauses:[84]

a. The Soviet Union agrees to support the Syrian and Lebanese governments in all steps that the two countries may initiate to establish complete independence. The Soviet Union will back Syrian and Lebanese demands for immediate evacuation of all French and British troops;

b. The Soviet Union agrees to assist in the cultural development of Syria and Lebanon. A considerable number of teachers would be sent from the Soviet Union to assist the Syrians and Lebanese to organize a Syrian/Lebanese educational system, free of foreign influence;

c. The Soviet Union recognizes the need for signing a comprehensive treaty with Syria and Lebanon as soon as possible, including provisions for economic, commercial, and navigational interests. The Soviet Union agrees to send a sufficient number of military personnel to Syria and Lebanon composed of military instructors and high-ranking officers, to help them build a national army as rapidly as possible;

d. The Syrian and Lebanese governments agree to award the Soviet Union the highest status as a favored nation.

A day after the signing of the Lebanese–Soviet treaty, the governments of Syria and Lebanon addressed a note to Trygve Lie, the Secretary-General of the United Nations, asking him to bring their dispute with France and Britain "to the attention of the Security Council and request it to adopt a decision recommending the total and simultaneous evacuation of the foreign troops from the territories of Syria and Lebanon."[85] The presentation of the Syrian–Lebanese issue before the Security Council began on 14 February 1946. The USSR exercised its commitment to Syria and Lebanon following the agreement in clause "a" of the secret treaties. At the Security Council meeting on 15 February, the Soviet Union supported the demands of the governments of Syria and Lebanon calling for a speedy and complete removal of British and French troops from both countries. In his speech before the Security Council, Andrei Vyshinskii, Soviet Vice-Commissar for Foreign Affairs and Head of the Soviet Delegation to the UN, attacked Britain and France on their past and present policies in the Levant. The British, he said, declared that they and the French "must not be held responsible for peace and order in Syria and Lebanon." The Soviet government, stated Vyshinskii, "will readily and immediately release France and Great Britain from this responsibility, especially since no one has ever saddled them with such responsibility." Syria and Lebanon would gladly release Britain and France from this responsibility too; only Syria and Lebanon, as sovereign states, were responsible for the security and peacekeeping in their own countries. The Security Council, Vyshinskii concluded, should respect the demands of Syria and Lebanon by adopting a decision calling for "the general, immediate, and simultaneous evacuation of French and British troops from Syria and Lebanon." The Soviet government would fully support such a decision.[86]

The anti-French and British climax that prevailed in the Security Council regarding the presence of their forces in Syria and Lebanon led the two powers to declare their intention to comply with the Security Council's resolution calling for the evacuation of their forces. The evacuation process from Syria began at the end of April 1946 and was completed in Lebanon on 31 December 1946 when the last foreign troops left the Levant.[87]

The Soviet Union also fulfilled its part of the military clause of the secret treaties with Syria and Lebanon. Following the recent declassification of intelligence files in Western archives, we now know that before and during the 1948 Palestine War, large shipments of arms arrived in Syria and Lebanon from the Eastern Bloc.[88] According to an Israeli source, toward the end of 1947 a Syrian military mission purchased 8,000 rifles and six million cartridges from Czechoslovakia. The arms were to be given to the Arab troops that were about to take part in the invasion of Palestine.[89]

Realization of clause "b", dealing with the development and promotion of cultural relations, was also fulfilled soon after independence was declared by Syria and Lebanon. A lengthy, official combined Lebanese–Syrian cultural expedition to the USSR began on 15 February 1947. The visit, which stretched out over a period of almost five weeks, included visits to many industrial and cultural centers. Efforts made by the Soviet hosts to present their country's positive aspects proved successful: a statement made by Dr. Kamil Ayyad, a member of the Syrian Board of Education, at the conclusion of the visit, reflected that success. Ayyad declared that his expedition was fortunate to be given the pleasure of touring the USSR—"that new state which is considered to be in the fore-most ranks of world states," adding that, in spite of all the obstacles in their way, the Soviets had been able to make "great strides towards the realiza-tion of a comprehensive culture . . . a culture which does not recognize the distinction of origin and race, which repudiates the expansionist and impe-rialist ideology . . . and which believes in peace and independence for all the nations of the world." Ayyad concluded by expressing the hope that the visit would lead to "a wider reciprocation of cultural and mutual relations" between Syria, Lebanon, and the Soviet Union, which he called a "great state."[90]

Syria's foreign policy in the period 1944–6 was intended to achieve a single goal—full independence. Since, at that point, Syrian territory was controlled by French and British forces, Syrian leaders employed a tactical move intended to win the support of the postwar superpowers—the USSR and the US—hoping that, since neither had an imperialist record in the Middle East and were opposed to the principles of imperialism, they would provide the necessary support Syria needed to gain its independence. Syria's policy toward the powers at the time may therefore be character-ized as "pragmatic/calculative nationalist neutralism."

1946–9: The Years of "Passive Neutralism" in Syria

After it gained its independence with the support of both the USSR and the USA, Syria was ruled until early 1949 by the old traditional elite, which was embroiled in personal domestic rivalries, and it was also split on inter-Arab affairs. In this period the Syrian government remained indifferent to the newly emerged inter-bloc conflict. It expressed disinterest in either the ideological or the political antagonism of outside powers and power groups. The Soviet Union's relations with Syria and Lebanon came to a standstill in the late 1940s. Shortly after gaining full independence, and following a vehement struggle, Syria and Lebanon chose two different routes in their foreign policy. Lebanon focused its efforts on building a new state, despite all the internal obstacles, and oriented itself with the West in the inter-bloc conflict. Syria had its own unique domestic problems: the old traditionalist ruling elite found itself challenged by new social and political streams that were attempting to turn the newly established democratic parliamentary system to their own advantage. In the period 1946–9 Syria was comparatively stable, though the standard of administration was low and gradually deteriorating.

The years 1946–9 were characterized by domestic power struggles concerning Syria's future relations with its neighbors. The Arab unity issue gained considerable momentum, bringing in its wake the dilemma of who to unite with—Iraq, or King 'Abdullah and his scheme for a Greater Syria. In addition, the Syrian army's defeat in the War of Palestine led to growing discontent, bitterness, and hatred directed toward the "corrupt" old traditionalist elite. All this culminated in 1949, when three military coups reflected Syria's political instability. In that year, the chart of Syria's relations with the Arab states was extraordinarily unpredictable and reflected Syria's constant internal problems.

Syria's relations with the Hashemites, particularly Iraq, suffered most. The third military coup of December 1949 had appeared to put a stop to ideas of union between Syria and Iraq. In 1949, in addition to the coups, Syria had experienced six different governments and was now in an unstable situation, the worst in Syria's short period of independence. Syria's relations in 1949 with Britain, France, and the US at this time reflected the trend of its relations with the Hashemite kingdoms, Egypt and Saudi Arabia. Syria's relations with the Western powers throughout the year is well-described in a British report:[91]

> Relations with Britain were at the outset good and the Syrian government in February approached H.M.G. with a vaguely defined object of reaching agreement on defense and other matters. Under [Husni] Za'im, France and the United States became Syria's chief friends. British stock tended to fall thanks to Za'im's loathing of Hashemites, in particular Iraq. Britain's apparent unwillingness to give him substantial supplies of arms, unlike France, only strengthened Za'im's suspicions that Britain was secretly in favour of the Fertile Crescent scheme. In fairness to Za'im, however, it must be said that he made a tentative suggestion of offering Britain air bases in Syria in time of war. The overthrow of Za'im reversed the situation. Britain became the favoured one at the expense of the United States and particularly France . . . [the two] were blamed for encouraging the opponents of the scheme. A few months later, however, the situation had changed again and Syro-Iraqi union was out of the picture. In the popular mind the army's intervention was interpreted as a definite set-back to Britain's relations with Syria.

The irony was that the British report failed to foresee the anti-Western nature of Khalid al-'Azm's government (December 1949–May 1950). It was al-'Azm's government that was the first to officially practise the policy of neutralism. The same British report states: "the present Prime Minister is a sensible statesman and as long as he remains in power he will certainly not wish to drive a wedge between the [three] Big Powers in their relations with Syria."[92]

Soviet–Syrian relations embarked on a new stage in early 1950 following the formation of Khalid al-'Azm's government. His government's inter-bloc policy embraced a doctrine of "anti-Western neutralism," one that was highly unbalanced. It maintained that Syria should strengthen its links with the Soviet Union and, by so doing, Syria would position itself out of the Western camp should a third world war occur. Moreover, there was a strong will to humiliate the West for all the injustices and evils it had caused the Arabs.

The government took a very anti-Western stance, objecting to the idea of unification suggested by the two pro-British Hashemite monarchies, and went about removing the final vestiges of French influence over Syria, including breaking economic ties with France. Syria also condemned the US for its pro-Israeli attitude in the Arab–Israeli conflict,[93] and, in the early months of 1950, statements advocating a policy of neutralism and calls to improve relations with the Soviet Union were made by senior officials in the Syrian government.

2

The Rise of "Anti-Western Neutralism" in Post-Mandatory Syria

It is generally agreed among scholars that the years 1955–8 were characterized by a growing Soviet influence in Egypt and Syria and a process of tightening relations between these countries and the USSR. This development was a result of decisions made by the policymakers of Syria and Egypt to instrumentally embrace neutralism as a political doctrine intended to manipulate the inter-bloc conflict between the East and West, in order to advance their own interests. Indeed, 1955 was characterized by a strong shift to the left in the Syrian political scene and a gradual takeover of key governmental positions by leftist elements.

In order to comprehend the shift in Syrian policy toward the Soviet Union, one has to first expose and examine the roots of Syria's neutralism—a broad political phenomenon that characterized many newly emerged political parties and organizations in post-mandatory Syria. Common wisdom among political scientists holds that neutralism emerged following the conclusion of World War II, which also marked the beginning of the Cold War between the Eastern bloc, led by the USSR, and the Western bloc, led by the US. India, under Nehru's leadership, pioneered the formulation and implementation of the policy of neutralism. Many Asian and African states of the post-colonial era were subsequently attracted to Nehru's brand of ideological/doctrinaire neutralism. This formula was an active policy "primarily aimed at averting a major war, and settling minor ones" between the two major superpowers and their allies— a war that, if it ever became an open all out conflict, threatened world stability and security .[1] Although this may be the most common definition of the term "neutralism," many post-colonial countries interpreted it in different ways, each motivated by its own interests. Neutralism, as a new phenomenon, was characterized by its many nationalist models.

As for Syria and many other Arab countries, their decision to embark on the voyage of neutralism in the late 1940s and early 1950s was mainly a result of their disappointment with the West. France and Britain, with their links to the Middle East were considered by the Arabs to be imperialist powers whose primary interest was to exploit and dominate the Arab world. Arab hopes and expectations that the US, as the new leader of the Western camp, would support their struggle to achieve liberation and full independence gradually changed to bitterness and disappointment. There were three main reasons for this: First, US policy toward the Arab–Israeli conflict and its commitment to the existence of the Jewish State; second, the ambiguous stand taken by the US during the years of the Arabs' bitter struggle against Britain, particularly during the Anglo-Egyptian dispute; and third, pressure from the US for Arab countries to take part in the establishment of a Middle East Command as a frontline defense against the Soviets. Khalid al-'Azm's motivation for adopting a policy of neutralism seems, mainly, to have been the issue of Israel,[2] whereas the Ba'th Party's decision to embark on a policy of neutralism was based on the Arab–Israeli conflict and hostility toward the Middle East Command concept. There was also the ideological element in the Ba'th doctrine that ruled out both communism and capitalism.

The purpose of this chapter is to expose, describe, and analyze the various stages of the gradual rise of neutralism after the end of World War II. The timeframe for discussion is from the mid-1940s to November 1951. These dates may be divided into two periods. The first, which may be defined as ideological, began with the outbreak of the East–West conflict and concluded in December 1949 when a military coup initiated by Adib Shishakli (who preferred to control Syria from behind the scenes until November 1951) inaugurated a new political phase in Syria's history. During this period, neutralist ideas had begun to sprout in Syria, and the vanguard of these ideas were Ba'thists; their mode of neutralism had its own character. The second period began in December 1949 with the formation of Khalid al-'Azm's government and continued until November 1951, when Shishakli performed his second coup and officially became Syria's Head of State. Al-'Azm's government[3] was the first to practise the formula of "anti-western neutralism," a policy aimed at strengthening links with the Soviet Union for the purpose of positioning Syria out of the Western camp should a third world war occur. It was also motivated by a strong desire to humiliate the West for all the injustices and evils it had caused the Arabs. Although short-lived, the al-'Azm government's policy of anti-Western neutralism was embraced and implemented by most successive Syrian governments. In fact, neutralism was by now institutionalized and deeply-rooted in Syria, a development that paralleled what was happening in Egypt.

The second period of the rise of Syrian neutralism saw three major occurrences in the international arena that also had direct (and indirect) relevance to Syria: the Tripartite Declaration of May 1950, the Korean

War (1950–1), and the Four Powers' proposal to the Arabs to participate in the establishment of a Middle East Command (October–November 1951). We shall examine how, on the one hand, official Syria dealt with these issues; and on the other, how the Syrian public, as indicated through a wide range of Syrian newspapers representing a variety of political views, reacted to these developments and to the way its governments conducted these issues. The result was that the groundwork for the Soviet penetration of Syria of the mid-1950s had already been laid by the outset of the 1950s.

Ideological Ba'thist Neutralism and the Emergence of Neutralist Thought

Ideas of neutralism were put forward by the ideological fathers and founders of the Arab Ba'th Party [*Hizb al-Ba'th al-'Arabi*] after the outbreak of the East–West conflict in the mid-1940s. In its formative years (1940s to the early 1950s), the Ba'th advocated a policy of doctrinaire/ideological neutralism, which had its theoretical foundations in Nehru's neutralism. When the party became prominent in the Syrian political scene in the mid-1950s, it embraced the Egyptian mode of "positive neutralism." In articles 22–25 of the Constitution of the new Party (1947), it was stated with regard to foreign affairs that:[4]

> The foreign policy of the Arab state will be inspired by the Arab national interest and the eternal Arab mission, and it will be aimed at cooperation with other nations in improving the harmony, freedom, faith, and righteousness of the world and its continuous progress . . . The Arabs will struggle with all their power to undermine the supports of colonialism and foreign occupation and all foreign political or economic influence in their country . . . The Arab foreign policy will be revealed to have received its correct form from the will of the Arabs to live in freedom, and from their desire to see all other nations similarly enjoying freedom.

Michel 'Aflaq,[5] founder of the Ba'th Party, placed great emphasis on ideological and doctrinal concerns. From the beginning his party expressed their objection to international communism as a philosophy and as an internal force within the Arab nation. In June 1944, 'Aflaq and Salah al-Din al-Bitar[6] declared that "communism triumphs where there is muddled and weakness of national spirit. But the well-informed Arab cannot be a communist without giving up Arabism. The two are mutually exclusive. Communism is alien and foreign to everything Arab. It will remain the greatest danger to Arab nationalism so long as the latter is unable to give a systematic, coherent and overall definition of its aims . . ."[7] The Ba'th Party thinkers considered communism a product of European thought and of social historical circumstances relevant only in Europe.[8] It emerged in the more developed part of Europe, which went through the industrial revolution and lengthy processes of national unification before entering the new phase of imperialist expansionism. Those early nineteenth-century conditions in Europe did not exist in the Arab world even in the first half of the twentieth century. Communism, then, was foreign to the Arab ethos and to Arab historical conditioning and bore no organic connection to the Arab way of life or thought.[9]

Nevertheless, the Ba'th theoreticians had learned to draw a clear-cut distinction between the Soviet Union as a newly emerged superpower that had begun to play a major role in world affairs, and communism as a theory and the way it had been introduced by local communist parties, which were vying for influence in the Arab world. Also in June 1944 'Aflaq and Bitar declared:

> We are not against the Soviet Union . . . We make a sharp distinction between the Soviet Union as a state and the local Syrian Communist Party. The Arabs see no necessity to oppose a great state like the Soviet Union, which from its inception, has shown sympathy for countries fighting for their independence. Our aim is to establish friendly relations with the Soviet Union by means of official inter-governmental treaties and not through the medium of the local Communist Party.[10]

Two significant developments took place in the period 1944–6 in terms of Soviet–Syrian relations. First, both countries established diplomatic relations in July 1944, and from this point on, the USSR firmly supported Syria's demands for full independence. Second, in February 1946, the two countries signed a secret agreement. Several days later, in accordance with the terms of that agreement, the Soviets supported the demands of Syria and Lebanon in the Security Council of the UN (15 February 1946) for a speedy and unconditional withdrawal of French and British troops from the two Levantine countries.[11] The Ba'th had employed a utilitarian approach regarding the need to nurture good relations with the USSR. 'Aflaq elucidated this point: "The Arabs hope that the intentions of the Soviet state will have a good and practical impact on international politics." He continued, "their friendship with her [the USSR] will be strengthened to the extent that they feel the sincerity of these intentions and their harmony with their [Arab] national interests."[12]

The leaders of the Ba'th Party severely attacked the Anglo-French agreement of December 1945. The agreement, they protested, was designed to protect the interests of both powers at the expense of the Arab people. These imperialist powers had wounded the dignity of the Arab people, exploited their national resources and their rights, and confiscated land for military installations. The withdrawal of French and British troops from

Syria and Lebanon, stressed the Ba'th leadership, was not mentioned at all in the December 1945 agreement; the French and British still maintained a threat to the security and freedom of the Arab people. There was little difference between this agreement and the Sykes–Picot Agreement—the root of the problems that the Arabs had been suffering from for the past three decades.[13] On 10 July 1946, in the early stages of the Cold War, 'Aflaq declared that Syria should not fear the Western threat. Syria, he said, could now manipulate the East–West rivalry for the purpose of furthering its own national goals. The policy that weighed most heavily on the affairs of the Arabs was that of the two Anglo-Saxon states, Britain and the USA. In 'Aflaq's view, nothing could equal this policy in impact and force or counter-balance its danger except the policy of a great country that had always been on guard against the designs of British and American imperialism: the Soviet Union. One of the simplest political rules, and the first national duty of governments that were conscious of the interests of their own countries—governments that were free to take their stands internationally—was, according to 'Aflaq, to fight their enemies with the help of their enemies' enemies, or to use them as a threat. Attention could therefore be concentrated on fighting the occupying enemy—the enemy that attacked Syrian nationality.[14]

After the emergence of his party in the early 1940s, Michel 'Aflaq inaugurated the discourse on what Syria's inter-bloc policy should be. The discourse gathered momentum with the outbreak of the Cold War in the mid-1940s and the development of events in the Arab arena, particularly the displacement of the Palestinians, which placed Arab nationalism in opposition to both the Western and Eastern camps because of their support for the establishment of Israel. On 21 January 1948, several weeks after the partition resolution was approved by the General Assembly, Michel 'Aflaq elaborated his view on neutralism:[15]

> If the Arabs were free today from colonialism, foreign occupation, Zionist threat, and dismemberment and had to take a stand in the global struggle, a stand, which would be closest to their ideas and national interest, they would take the side of the Western democracies rather than that of the Eastern dictatorships. They would choose this course because they know so very well that freedom has been, is, and will remain the very essence of their existence and the best guarantee for the development of their personalities. The present status of the Arab world, however, and the inimical policies of the West regarding Palestine and other Arab issues dictates that the Arabs' interest can in no way be served by alliances with the Western bloc or any of its members.

The Ba'th attacked both the Soviets and the Western powers for their unfavorable policies toward the Arabs. The former were accused of committing a grave mistake with their decision to support the partition of Palestine—a decision "based on ignorance." The Soviet decision to vote for partition, stated the Ba'th, was an expression of their disappointment with Arab governments such as the Syrian, Lebanese, Egyptian, Jordanian, Saudi and Iraqi, which did not pursue an independent policy in international affairs. They instead systematically surrendered to Western pressure. What the Soviets failed to take into account was the fact that the Arab people, in contrast to their rulers, were no longer willing to cooperate with, or yield to, the West. The same applied to the Western powers: they did not anticipate that the reactionary regimes they had established in the region would eventually collapse and all the agreements signed with these fallen or deposed regimes would be nullified. Should the West wish to develop friendly relations with the Arabs, it would first have to win the sympathy of the Arab people—the determinant factor. The Ba'th Party established that the interests of the Arab countries were not to side with the Western bloc, but, rather, to be neutralist as far as the inter-bloc conflict was concerned. Neutralism would serve their interests better than identification with one of the two world blocs.[16] The Arab states, stressed the Ba'th Party, must remain neutral in the struggle between the Western and Eastern blocs. The party opposed the conclusion of agreements with any foreign powers.[17]

There were striking similarities of aims and principles between 'Aflaq's Arab Ba'th Party and Akram al-Hawrani's Arab Socialist Party. Amalgamation between the two parties therefore seemed a natural next step. Indeed, at the end of 1953, the process of unification was completed with the establishment of the Arab Socialist Resurrection Party [*Hizb al-Ba'th al-'Arabi al-Ishtiraki*]. The combination of nationalist and socialist ideas, asserts Itamar Rabinovich, "attracted younger radical elements, and the forceful simplicity of its slogans ('Unity, Freedom, Socialism' or 'one Arab nation with an eternal mission') appealed to humbler adherents. Armed with this doctrine and with the political muscle of al-Hawrani, the party seemed ready to play a crucial role in the last half of the 1950s."[18]

The year 1951 witnessed growing Western pressure on Syria and other Arab countries to take part in the formation of a military alliance aimed at blocking the danger of "Soviet expansionist plans" to the Middle East. The Ba'th, however, continued to adhere to its traditional ideological neutralism. In early 1951 it declared that the people wanted to exercise veracious neutralism [*hiyadan haqiqiyan*] toward the East–West conflict. The Ba'th warned the Arab League to avoid joining the imperialist Western bloc [*al-Kutla al-gharbiyya al-isti'amariyya*], stating that, at that point in world history, the conflict between the two international camps had reached its peak. It was the duty of every camp to act in order to defend its interests. At this delicate and sensitive stage, the policy of the West, led by the US and Britain, was to put great pressure on the Arabs to ally themselves with the Western bloc in its battle against the Eastern bloc. The Western powers exerted enormous pressure upon the Arab League and the "ruling feudal class" of the Arab countries to take part in advancing the plans of the imperialist camp. The Western political and strategic stranglehold on the Arab countries, including economic control of the oil resources, may be understood by the Eastern bloc as an already-existing alliance between the Arabs and the West. With the outbreak of another world war, the Arab countries might become a war zone and could be attacked by the Eastern bloc. This grave situation required an immediate Arab declaration in favor of a policy of neutralism. The Arabs, stressed the Ba'th, had no common ideological basis with either of the two blocs. Their main concern was to exercise full Arab sovereignty over their lands, to achieve independence coupled with socialism.[19]

The early 1950s saw considerable willingness in Arab countries to embark upon policies of neutralism. In the first half of 1950, senior Arab politicians in both Syria and Egypt made statements advocating neutralism and calling for the improvement of relations with the USSR.[20] The Arab–Israeli dispute, Seale claimed, seemed in danger of breaking out once more into armed conflict. There was a feeling among many political circles in Syria that the Western powers would put pressure on the Arabs to settle their conflict with Israel peacefully, a scenario that was opposed by all Arab political circles. A bitter chorus arose, declared Seale, "that the Arabs would a thousand times prefer to fall into the arms of Russia than a prey to Israel."[21] Mustafa al-Siba'i,[22] one of the leaders of the Islamic Socialist Front, who was not pro-communist, was one of the first to explain the logic behind Syria's tilt toward neutralism: "we are resolved to turn toward the Eastern camp if the democracies do not give us justice . . . To those who say that the Eastern camp is our enemy we would answer: when has the Western camp been our friend? . . . We will bind ourselves to Russia were she the very devil."[23] The Islamic Socialist Front was one of the main advocates on the Syrian political scene for a rapprochement with the Soviet Union. Although al-Siba'i was an ardent Muslim and declared himself to be anti-communist, the articles in his newspaper *al-Manar* were dichotomist—ideologically and domestically anti-communist, anti-Western, and pro-Soviet in foreign affairs.

Although a large percentage of Syrian newspapers supported Siba'i's statement, a number of daily newspapers did not remain indifferent to statements made in religious circles advocating an alliance with communist Russia. Some of them criticized the hypocritical nature of such statements, placing great emphasis on the contradiction between Islam and communism. On 23 May, the paper of the Nationalist Party, *al-Qabas*, wrote: "religious dignitaries are advocating Marxist communism and associating the teachings of religion with the teachings of Lenin and Stalin in complete disregard of the fact that communism is based on the principle of overthrowing religion together with all spiritual values. Religion is being prostituted to serve personal ambitions and local and international politics."[24] According to *al-Qabas*, political circles in Syria learned to draw a distinction between Soviet communism as an ideology, and the USSR as a superpower. On the one hand, the highest authoritative figures in Syria detested communism and persecuted communists, while, on the other hand, few cabinet ministers and Islamist politicians were "making declarations in the streets and in Parliament attacking the western powers and advocating alignment with the east."

On 5 January 1950, the Arab Socialist Party [*al-Hizb al-Ishtiraki al-'Arabi*] founded by Akram al-Hawrani, the then Minister of Defense, preceded Siba'i's party in bearing the new banner of neutralism. The party defined itself as a "national, popular, progressive, socialist, and revolutionary organization." The party, whose dislike of the West was noticeable, paid considerable attention to Arab nationalist concerns, particularly the Palestine problem. Chapter I of its platform provided that the party considered all territory forcibly taken from the Arabs as still part of the Arab homeland and that the Arab socialists were determined to fight with all means available to them against Zionism in an effort to restore Palestine to the motherland. Chapter V of the constitution dealt with foreign affairs and was a clear statement of the new party's adherence to neutralism:

> The foreign policy of the Arabs should be independent of any foreign direction. It should be solely concerned with national interests and should help the Arabs occupy their historical place in the group of the nations of the world . . . Arab policy advocates peace inside and outside the Arab nation . . . Imperialism obstructs the progress and development of civilization. Consequently, Arab policy should fight imperialism in whatever shape it may appear.[25]

In a conversation between al-Hawrani and the reporting officer of the US Legation in Damascus, which took place in al-Hawrani's house on 12 September 1950, al-Hawrani strongly advised the US to regain the Arab goodwill that it had enjoyed in the 1920s. The US, he argued, had frequently viewed Syria "through the eyes of the British and French reactionaries who had supported Syrian reactionaries."[26] The West had not bothered to understand the peasants and their leaders, "but had supported the same old gangs and played one gang against the other." Throughout their conversation, al-Hawrani repeated his sincere belief that there was an urgent need for socio-economic reforms in Syria, and he voiced his disapproval of communism: "the spread of communism in the Near East makes it even more urgent to find solutions to Syria's problems." In his view, the Syrian government was to be blamed for the rise of communism in Syria because the government had done nothing to improve the socio-economic chaos.[27]

Another new political party advocating similar ideas was the Democratic

Republican Party, founded in early 1950 by 'Arif Ghamyan and 'Abd al-Karim Dandashi. A considerable number of its members were businessmen. The party's platform was center-left,[28] standing for an independent republican Syria; support of the Arab League as a step forward toward Arab unity, which the party felt should be the goal of all the Arab states; adherence to the United Nations charter; the principle that the sovereignty of the state rested with the people; basic human freedoms; and the strengthening of the army. With regard to foreign policy, its platform stated that:

> The Party shall oppose all projects, treaties, and agreements that are inconsistent with the independence of any Arab state or that provides [any] opportunity for foreign intervention and imperialist influence to infiltrate into the Arab countries ... The Party advocates a foreign policy based on national interest and jointly followed by the Arab states. The Party maintains that the country should adhere to the United Nations Charter and cooperate with those states that respect this charter on a basis of equality, mutual interests, and respect for a country's sovereignty and independence.[29]

The rise of neutralism in Syria also found its expression when news arrived at the end of January 1950 of US President Truman's decision to order the production of the hydrogen bomb (H-bomb), which was condemned as an act that would increase the possibility of war with the Soviets. On 1 February, the headline of the independent paper *al-Balad* proclaimed, "The Road to War." *Al-Nasr*, another independent paper, also blamed the US for taking further steps toward world destruction, declaring that the reports regarding the production of the H-bomb were intended to intimidate and exert pressure on the Soviets, "now that Russia has discarded the secrets of the atomic bomb, into a rapprochement with the United States."[30]

Anti-Western Neutralism in Action:
Al-Dawalibi's Statement and its Repercussions

These manifestations of neutralism should be seen as the prelude to what may be described as a "political bomb" thrown by Ma'ruf al-Dawalibi,[31] the Syrian Minister of National Economy, during the Arab League session held in Cairo in April 1950. On 9 April, al-Dawalibi proposed that the Arabs conclude a non-aggression pact with the USSR. Al-Dawalibi was opposed to reliance on policies of the Western powers.[32] He attacked the American ruling circles, suggesting that they were ruled by Zionist and Jewish pressure groups: "If the American government continues to exert pressure on the Arab states in an endeavor to persuade them to follow a policy that would eventually make the Arab peoples subservient to the Zionists, I hope that a plebiscite will be held in the Arab countries so that the world may know whether or not the Arabs prefer a thousand-fold to become a Soviet republic rather than to become prey to world Jewry."[33] On 12 April, he stressed that such a pact would "protect the Arab states in case a third world war should break out." 'Abd al-Rahman 'Azzam, the Arab League's Secretary-General, endorsed al-Dawalibi's view and stated that he believed many Arabs had had enough of US pro-Jewish policy and supported the Minister's remarks.[34]

Al-Dawalibi's statement was strongly supported by the Syrian press, which concentrated on castigating "American pressure on the Arabs to make peace with Israel."[35] The immediate response of the Muslim Brothers' paper *al-Manar* illustrates the bitterness and anger directed toward the Western powers: "Along with their milk our children have been suckled on hatred of England and America." *Al-Manar* cynically claimed that Syrians would align with Russia just to see "blood gush from the wounds of our treacherous enemies."[36] A similar anti-Western tone was expressed by the independent daily *al-Barada*: "We should stain the faces of their [the Western powers] representatives with our blood so that they may get acquainted with the smell of free men and not of slaves who are sold in the slave markets in return for a handful of dollars."[37]

Al-Dawalibi's statement, understood by Western officials as a "tactical move," sparked a wave of speculation throughout Syria and the Arab world about a new diplomacy of seeking favor with the USSR. Much of the comment was surprisingly favorable and enthusiastic. There had been reports, some considered highly reliable, of Syrian–Soviet discussions about the possible conclusion of a non-aggression pact and an economic agreement, as well as possible shipment of Soviet arms to Syria.[38] Colonel 'Abbara, Chief of the Syrian Army's Armored Section, confirmed that Syria was "verging on the point of leaning toward Russia" in order to obtain military assistance. Although Syria was opposed to communism, 'Abbara said he could foresee where ideological reasons would be cast aside for Soviet material aid.[39] In reference to these reports and actions, the US State Department held the view that they were probably originally intended "more as a pressure on the United States in respect to its Palestine policy than as a concrete intention to align with the Soviet Union." However, the State Department did not overlook or disregard this development, stating that it "does not detract from the seriousness of the situation," which was symptomatic of bitter resentment against the US. The State Department's conclusion was that it was not "inconceivable that the Syrians will impulsively rush so far down this dangerous path that it will be impossible to return."[40] To strengthen the US position *vis-à-vis* Syria, it was necessary to emphasize "our friendship for and desire to cooperate with the Syrians." It was also of the utmost importance to point out the dangers of "such flirtations with a country which eventually demands as an absolute condition that its allies forego all independent action in complete devotion to the interests of the Soviet Union and Marxist dogma." Syria should also be warned that an alignment with the Soviet Union would inevitably bring to power in Syria the Communist Party and other "irresponsible political elements."[41]

Khalid al-'Azm, the then Syrian Prime Minister who also attended the Arab League session, stressed that he knew nothing of al-Dawalibi's motives and that his own statements had been coordinated with Muhammad Salah al-Din, the Egyptian Foreign Minister.[42] The al-Dawalibi move marked one of the initial phases in the gradual but consistent growth of Egyptian influence in Syria. It was also a coordinated move under Egyptian inspiration that was intended to indicate to the Western powers—which were engaged, at the time, in the formulation of the Tripartite Declaration (announced on 25 May 1950)—that a pro-Israeli declaration would push the Arabs into the open arms of Moscow. Al-'Azm wrote in his memoirs that, although he was not enthusiastic about al-Dawalibi's Cairo statements, he eventually realized that the Arabs should make full use of the effect of his statements during clandestine talks between the Arabs and the Western powers regarding the forthcoming Tripartite Declaration. Al-'Azm expected that the Americans would protest against al-Dawalibi's move and prepared his reply to the Americans in advance. His words reflected how deep his hatred of Israel was, and it threw new light on the motives behind Syria's new wave of anti-Westernism:

> You Americans support the Jews, and there is no wonder that the Arab leaders arrive at statements such as that of al-Dawalibi. How can you ask us to see the Russians as [our] enemies, while at the same time you act against us and support the Jews? I and the vast majority of my countrymen do not consider communism as a right policy, but also, we do not see it as a more severe danger than the Zionist epidemic . . . Is there any wonder that a Syrian citizen prefers to share his property with the rest of his people, like communism preaches, [rather than] being deported from his homeland and see his property being taken by a foreign and hated Jew? . . . If you do not want the Eastern countries to fall like ripened fruit into Russian hands, there is only one way for you: gain the sympathy of the Arabs and contain the aspirations of the Jews; otherwise, it will be impossible to alter the underlying tendency behind al-Dawalibi's words and [consequently] the Russians will take over all of the oil resources of the region.[43]

On 17 April 1950, Khalid al-'Azm and the US Minister to Syria, James H. Keeley, held talks in Damascus. These were initiated by Al-'Azm, who wanted to acquaint Keeley with the general content of the decisions at the Arab League meeting at Cairo earlier in April. Keeley seized the opportunity to ask the Prime Minister about the genesis and purport of the pro-Soviet statement made by al-Dawalibi. Al-'Azm responded that the statement was made without consulting him; that "the first he knew of it being when he read it in the Egyptian newspapers the following morning." Al-Dawalibi, explained 'Azm, expressed his own feelings, "and he was himself surprised to find how widespread the feeling seemed to be that it represented, judging from the congratulations that had poured in to Minister al-Dawalibi from every quarter."[44] Although al-'Azm pretended to be unfavorable to al-Dawalibi's declaration, he took advantage of the indignation and shock it created in the West to put forward his argument that anti-Westernism in Syria and the Arab world was mainly a result of the pro-Israeli stance taken by the US over the Arab–Israeli dispute. Al-'Azm indicated that the people of Syria had become disillusioned to the point of desperation with respect to the continued support given to Israel by the US; al-Dawalibi's statement should be interpreted in this context.[45] The statement did not mean that Syria was as willing to align itself on the side of Russia as on the side of America, or even desired to do so; it was not a question of choosing between two friends; it was a question of deciding between the devil and a friend who had let one down.

Keeley listened to al-'Azm talk about how opposed communism was to Islam, and that the West "might better understand the depth of Syrian disappointment over our manifest partisanship for Israel . . ."[46] The conversation between the two concluded with al-'Azm expressing his hope that the US would realize the extent of disillusionment and despair which its support of Israel had engendered in the Syrian people and the wish that it would not continue thus to exacerbate Syrian feelings. He asked that, in order to improve the US image in Syria and the Arab world, the US become truly impartial and cease trying to influence Syrian opinion in favor of Israel. Keeley concluded from his conversation that "al-Dawalibi's statement was intended as a plea not as a threat."[47]As we have already seen—and as future events would demonstrate—Keeley's conclusion was only partly correct. Although it had a strong impact on the anti-Western feelings of the Arabs, the Arab–Israeli issue was only one of a complex set of factors.

During April and May 1950, many reports (some of which were considered reliable) claimed that the Soviets had offered arms to Syria and Egypt by way of new barter agreements. On 27 April, the CIA reported to President Truman that, based on information from a senior Syrian official, Syria had signed a secret non-aggression and economic agreement with the USSR, by which Syria was to receive Soviet arms via the port of Latakia.[48]

Al-Dawalibi confirmed that the USSR offered arms to Syria and that talks about a treaty of friendship and commerce were taking place between Farid Zain al-Din, Syrian Minister to Moscow, and Vyshinskii, the Soviet

Foreign Minister. According to al-Dawalibi, the Syrian government had not reached any conclusive decision regarding the Soviet offer to supply all Syria's requirements with arms manufactured in the USSR or Czechoslovakia. Prime Minister Khalid al-'Azm stated at that time that Syria would obtain its arms from any available source.[49]

Alarmed by al-Dawalibi's statement and the recent reports that Syria was leaning toward the Soviet Union, the British Foreign Office opined that it was all designed "as a crude form of political blackmail on the Western Powers, and that the Syrian press, which for the most part welcomed them, recognized this intention. The real danger was that the Syrians, and perhaps other Arab hotheads, might be foolish enough to commit themselves irretrievably to Russia—not for any love of Russia or communism, but merely in order to bring pressure on the Western Powers in regard to Israel."[50]

According to the British Foreign Office, there were several reasons for the spread of Soviet and communist influence in Syria: First, continuous political instability and the absence of any effective Western influence; second, a failure to realize the menace that the Soviet Union and communism represented; third, the negative effect of the existence of Israel. The case was not lost, the British Foreign Office decided, but it suggested employing certain counter-measures to check this development:[51]

1. To intensify Western overt and covert anti-Soviet and anti-communist propaganda;
2. To establish the closest possible relations with Syrians in all walks of life, "in order that our representatives may be able to take advantage of the contacts thus established to educate the Syrians on the dangers of Russia and communism";
3. To exhaust all possible avenues for the promotion of better relations between the Arab states and Israel.

Aware of the potential danger in the Soviets' offer of arms to Syria and other Arab countries—and in light of the recent Soviet–Arab rapprochement, which could lead to an acceleration of the arms race in the Middle East—the Western powers acted swiftly. They realized that if they failed to lift the arms embargo imposed on Middle Eastern countries after the Palestine 1948 war, the Soviets would quickly sell arms to the region, thus improving their position in Arab countries and accelerating the arms race between Israel and its Arab neighbors.[52] On 25 May 1950, the US, Britain, and France announced the Tripartite Declaration, which recognized the right of Middle Eastern countries to purchase arms to ensure their security and "their legitimate self-defense and to permit them to play their part in the area as a whole." The three powers agreed that arms were to be provided only to those countries that abstained from aggression. In case of violation of frontiers or armistice lines by any country, the three powers would "immediately take action, both within and outside the UN, to prevent such violation."[53] On 21 June, Arab governments informed the three powers of their acceptance of the declaration (with some reservations), a move which was coolly received by Moscow.

Al-'Azm appreciated that al-Dawalibi's move was to have considerable influence on the formulation of the Tripartite Declaration, which he considered to be, despite several disadvantages, relatively positive and a good change compared to the previous Western stands on the Arab–Israeli dispute. In a letter he sent to the Egyptian Foreign Minister, Muhammad Salah al-Din—the chief advocate of neutralism and the key figure behind al-Dawalibi's move—he wrote: "what happened is what we had already predicted—the foreign ministers of the three powers (the USA, the UK, and France) are examining the issues of the region in light of the newly emerged trend among Arab public opinion, which is manifesting goodwill toward Russia."[54]

Inspired by al-Dawalibi's statement, the Syrian press continued its anti-American and anti-Western tone. Special emphasis was placed on American support for Israel. In reference to the East–West conflict, the general approach was to regard the Western camp as provocative and destructive. Soviet propaganda, declared *al-Nasr*, was gaining ground not by the force of its principles, but because people had started to feel annoyed with the US and its exploitation of weak nations, especially the people of the Middle East. The US could not win the favor of the Arabs, stated *al-Nasr*, by "expelling thousands of innocent people and wresting their lands and property [away] to hand them over to Israel, which represents American capitalism and its strategic base for future military operations against the Soviet Union."[55] *Al-Masa'*, the Muslim Brothers' newspaper, wrote that the US—"the first champion of peace!!"—had, on several occasions, betrayed the cause of peace and sacrificed the cause of justice "on the altar of its never-ceasing attempt to extend the scope of its ugly capitalism and spread its imperialistic influence." *Al-Masa'* referred to Truman's speech of 19 April in which the US President stated that communist propaganda was false, crude, and blatant, and wondered how any person could be swayed by it.[56] *Al-Masa'* claimed its intention was not to defend communism, whose propaganda was indeed false; however, the US could not be regarded as a state that was worthy enough to voice such accusations because it had violated the freedom of other peoples by depriving them of their right of self-determination and forcibly removing them from their land, as with the Jews, who took over Palestine.[57]

In contrast to the Syrian and Arab governments, which eventually accepted the Tripartite Declaration, the reaction of the Syrian press to the

Declaration was almost wholly unfavorable. Most papers interpreted the Western move as an attempt to divide the Middle East into zones of influence in order to consolidate the position of Israel.[58] *Al-Manar* described the Tripartite Declaration as a flagrant intervention in Arab affairs.[59] *Al-Nasr* interpreted the Declaration "as disposing of the Palestine problem on the basis of the status quo, as transforming the Middle East, including Israel, into a coordinated military unit, and as returning French influence to Syria and Lebanon."[60] *Al-Shabab*, the National Party's daily, described the declaration as worse than the Sykes–Picot Agreement—a Western plan that had divided the Middle East during World War I into spheres of influence.[61] The independent daily *al-Kifah* explained why the Arabs abandoned the West and paved their route to neutralism: the Arabs, it declared, agreed with the West on the necessity of combating communism, but, because of US policy toward Palestine, the Tripartite Declaration was considered by the Arabs to be an American ruse designed to consolidate the position of the Jews at the expense of the Arabs.[62] *Al-Kifah* was not pleased with the Arab League's response to the Tripartite Declaration, and expressed astonishment that the statement was not rejected outright. A firm Arab rejection would have taught the Great Powers a lesson on how to respect the rights of small countries, and not to take for granted the fact that the West's strength and international position could guarantee the subordination of small and weaker countries to their will and plans.[63]

When the Korean War broke out on 25 June 1950, Syria and Egypt exploited the substantial opportunities created by the needs of the US and the West for international support to put pressure on the West over its pro-Israeli policy. On 27 June 1950, Mahmud Fawzi, the Egyptian member of the Security Council, abstained on the American resolution that recommended collective action to defend South Korea.[64] The Korean crisis had no positive or tangible effect on the diminishing prestige of the US and the West in countries such as Egypt and Syria. Although, generally, the initial Syrian reaction was that it was time for the West to stand up to communist expansion, many in Syria took the opportunity to make a pointed contrast between the willingness of the UN to go to war in Korea and its failure to carry out decisions on Palestine. Many editorial articles asserted that this showed clearly that the West was willing to carry out UN decisions only when they furthered its own aims.[65] Most of Syria's papers favored Syria remaining neutral in the conflict. Their espousal of anti-Western neutralism was based more on resentment against what they considered the pro-Israeli stand of the US and the UN in the Palestine War than on a careful appraisal of what policy would best serve Syria's interests.[66] In the first week of July 1950, Damascus' leading independent paper, *al-Nasr*, stated:

As a matter of fact, we believe that, if the Korean War involves any aggression, such an aggression is reflected in the Security Council's illegal decision permitting the United States to intervene with its fleet and air force against a weak people who are apparently resisting the separation and division of their country into spheres of influence. The Syrian people condemn the attitude of the Security Council, which has proven to the entire world that it is a submissive tool in the hands of America.[67]

In the second week of July, the press published the reply of the Syrian government to the UN resolution on Korea. The reply was interpreted by the media as ambiguous and weak. *Al-Nasr*, which had followed a pro-Soviet line from the outset of the Korean conflict, thought the Syrian reply implied:

a negative attitude toward both parties, including the United States, which is seriously and unaccountably striving to thwart every attempt to effect the unification of the Korean nation. In other words, Syria is not bound by its reply to give even moral support to the United States' aggressive actions in the Far East.[68]

Toward the end of 1950, *al-Nasr*'s neutralism became more balanced. According to the paper, there was not much difference between the US and the USSR—both were aggressive and employed forceful measures in order to achieve their goals. Force alone, the paper stated, now ruled the world and dominated international political developments. It was by force, declared *al-Nasr*, that the Soviet Union "succeeded in controlling half [of] Europe, three quarters of Asia, and half the human race. It is by force that the US succeeded in directing world policy and the United Nations, in gaining the votes of the majority of the governments of the world, and in exploiting the natural resources of the Middle East. [And] it is by force that the US invaded Korea, destroyed its cities and civilization, and spread destruction in it. It is also by force that Red China succeeded in defeating the international forces [in Korea] . . ."[69] *Al-Nasr* concluded that the Arabs should act in the same way, resorting to force: "The Arabs should reinforce themselves and demand respect from the world."[70]

The pro-Labor Damascus paper *al-'Alam* attacked President Truman's decision to send forces to Korea "where neither he nor his armies can overcome the determination of a people to struggle for their independence, unity, bread and happiness." According to the paper, Truman interfered with the affairs of small nations with the object of colonizing them, irrespective of their wish to liberate themselves, and in complete disregard for concepts of freedom.[71]

The pro-Nationalist Party paper, *al-Qabas*, saw no difference between the USSR, which stood behind North Korea in the Far East, and the US, which defended Israel in the Middle East. Why had the UN singled out the USSR's attempts to extend aid to free nations, and accused it of imperiling world peace because it was arming the Koreans and Chinese? asked *al-*

Qabas. Moreover, why were similar accusations not made against the US, since it supplied Israel with arms, ammunition, and influence, protected and saved them from Security Council sanctions, and did not force them to abide by UN resolutions? The US, which invented the principles of both the UN and the Security Council, and was also the first to violate them, should not be surprised to see similar behavior in other nations such as the Soviet Union, whose actions in Korea were no worse than what the Americans had done in Palestine—ignoring and overlooking all UN resolutions. The Arabs and Islam, concluded *al-Qabas*, should realize that those who had attacked them and violated the sacredness of their holy land were the Americans, who used the name of Israel.[72]

Syria was ruled during the Korean crisis by Nazim al-Qudsi's weak government (4 June 1950–9 March 1951), which, in contrast to al-'Azm's anti-Western government, was not hostile to the West and developed close relations with Hashemite Iraq. Al-Qudsi supported the actions taken by the US and the UN in Korea. On 7 July, several days after Egypt's abstention in the Security Council, al-Qudsi initiated a conversation with Morgan C. G. Man, the British First Secretary in Damascus, asking for his advice. Al-Qudsi informed the British that there was a strong inclination among all Syrian political groups to follow Egypt's lead of neutralism. He stressed, however, that his own view, with which many Syrians agreed, was that Syria must support the Security Council resolution and come out in favor of the West. He felt that his government might be able to take the Western side, "with slight reservations," but if it did, he wanted to make it clear that Syria would expect military and economic assistance from the Western powers in return. In addition, the Western powers would have to change their policy toward Syria by showing willingness to help it. Man replied that both Britain and the US were already willing to help Syria in many ways; if Syria declared itself neutralist, however, public opinion in Britain, France, and the US would certainly "not be in favor of continuing assistance to Syria."[73]

Al-Qudsi's inclination toward the West was later raised again during a conversation he had in Cairo on 6 December with Paul Parker, US Treasury Representative in the Middle East. In the course of their conversation, al-Qudsi considered the situation in the Far East, arising from the military developments in Korea, as extremely grave, and he identified himself with the Western powers.[74] He criticized Arab governments as not being as seriously concerned with developments in the Far East as they should be. In al-Qudsi's opinion, this was a result of the policy of Western powers to restrict arms procurement by Arab countries since the outbreak of the 1948 war with Israel. "So long as the Arab countries are deprived of the means of defending themselves against Russia," warned al-Qudsi, they would be forced "to deal with the Russian threat by amelioration or conciliation, rather than by taking a strong stand." He went further, saying that the kind of future he wanted for Syria would not be attained "in a world situation dominated by Russia." His objectives in Syria "could eventually be achieved within the political framework envisaged by the Western Powers as embodied in the United Nations." Although he considered the conflict with Israel to be a serious political issue, he was more concerned with threats of domination from outside the Middle East, and he therefore attached the utmost importance to the development of a defensive Arab alliance to protect the Arab states. Al-Qudsi made a connection between Israel and the communist menace; communist activity in the Middle East, he declared, was "directed from Tel Aviv, where the principal agents had their headquarters."[75]

Official Syria, concluded US diplomats in Damascus, approved of the UN and US position on Korea. While discussing the Anglo-Egyptian question with the British Press Attaché, Colonel Adib Shishakli, the true ruler behind the scenes, asked: "Why do you worry about bases to protect the Suez Canal in time of peace? In time of war the Arabs will be with the West, and you can have bases anywhere you like."[76]

Nevertheless, according to these same diplomats, many Syrians resented the contrast between UN action in Korea and UN failure to apply its decisions in Palestine; the UN seemed disposed to attach itself "to the victor's star, whether in Korea or in other areas of conflict between communist and Western democratic forces and ideas . . . the indirect effect of the Korean crisis had been to contribute to the Syrian desire to carry out previous UN decisions on Palestine, particularly those favorable to the Arab position."[77]

US diplomats concluded, incorrectly, that the Korean crisis "appears to have had no effect on the policies of the Syrian government or the attitude of the Syrian people toward communism and the USSR."[78] They were misled by the internal anti-communist campaign led by the Syrian authorities. Most political groups in Syria disliked and disapproved of communism within their country. At the outset of 1951, most of Syria's political groups were almost unanimous in their opinion that the Syrian government should not align itself internationally with either the West or the East, but should follow the same policy of neutralism that had distinguished its more recent policy in the Arab League: promoting the idea of political blackmail and manipulation of the two international blocs. Even inside the largest political group, the People's Party, there existed a strong left wing composed of figures such as Ma'aruf al-Dawalibi, 'Abd al-Wahab Hawmad, and Ahmad Qanbar, who were all strong neutralists. These leftists succeeded in keeping their party and the government out of the Western camp.[79] Prime Minister al-Qudsi, when asked during an interview he gave to the Egyptian paper *al-Misri*, whether the Tripartite Declaration precluded the purchase of arms from Russia, replied that, "If Russia were to offer us any arms which we consider necessary, we will buy them."[80] On 17 January 1951 al-Qudsi held a conversation with W. H. Montagu-Pollock, the British Minister to Damascus, during which the two discussed the implications of the Korean crisis on Syria's relations with the Western powers. Al-Qudsi maintained that the West could not expect Syria "to support any resolution which may lead to war, so long as you refuse to provide her with arms and so long as the USA provides Israel with funds to enable her to prepare for another attack on the Arab world."[81] The British diplomat reported to the Foreign Office that the Korean crisis had created a situation whereby the Syrian government and public opinion were both in an "extremely difficult mood."[82]

The more influential leftist political organizations, however—such as the Ba'th Party, the Arab Socialist Party, and the Islamic Socialist Front—drew a clear distinction between the USSR as a friendly power, and internal communism, which, in their view, represented foreign interests and was anti-nationalist. The strongest support for neutralism came from those political groups which had shown themselves to be distinctly anti-Western and which represented the hardcore of neutralist sentiment in Syria. For the Islamic Front, neutralism was their best lever for manipulating a redressing of the situation in Palestine, concerning which they remained completely irreconcilable.[83] The development of events around the Korean War and the Arab League meetings of January 1951 led the Ba'th Party to distribute a tract on 25 January 1951 manifesting the party's vigorous rejection of efforts made by "the Western Bloc's imperialist policy directed by America and Britain" to compel the Arabs to join them in their war against the communist bloc—a war in which the Arabs' cause would be neglected. The Ba'th warned the Arab League against joining any of the two camps and against adopting a policy that was not real neutralism:[84]

We demand real neutralism preventing the cruel forces of Western imperialism from making our country [into] military bases and from using our petroleum and wealth in its war. We urge the mobilization of all national forces to ensure this neutralism and to overcome the plots of imperialism and its agents.

The neutralist groups in Syria continued to be a thorn in the side of any Syrian politicians who favored a pro-Western alignment for Syria. These same neutralist political organizations were to determine many political decisions for Syria in the mid-1950s. Montagu-Pollock, British Minister to Damascus, said in January 1951 that "Syria is drifting at the moment like a ship without a rudder. Public opinion, impressed by communist successes in the Far East and at the same time apathetic regarding their dangers for Syria, is in an ugly mood, and neutrality is the most popular catchword."[85]

Anti-Western feelings and adherence to neutralism were translated into action when, in early 1951, the Western powers announced their plans to establish defense arrangements in the Arab world as part of their global policy of preventing Soviet expansionism. A few weeks before General Robertson, the Commander of the British Land Forces in the Middle East, arrived in Damascus on 7 February, the three leftist political organizations called for "a policy of full neutralism" toward the two international blocs.[86] Their fear of Western intentions to promote the establishment of a Middle East Command (MEC) increased when the Four Powers' (the US, Britain, France, and Turkey) proposal was submitted to Egypt on 13 October, and several weeks later, on 10 November, to other Arab countries. The formation of a Middle East Command, the US claimed, was intended to protect the Middle East against outside aggression. The proposal stated that the MEC was a defense agreement aimed at preventing penetration of the region by communism in peacetime and to prepare the defense of the region against Soviet military power in wartime. These proposals were rejected first by Egypt and later by the other Arab states. Although not ruling out the proposals in principle, the Arab states refused to consider them before the Anglo-Egyptian conflict had been settled.[87] The fact that the Syrian and other Arab governments—unlike Egypt, whose rejection was total—left room for possible participation led Syria's neutralists to attack "these quarters [which] urge us to use a treacherous and stupid logic to accept the joint defense project on the false pretext that we are threatened with Russian imperialism."[88] On 27 March 1952, Akram al-Hawrani's Arab Socialist Party paper *al-Ishtirakiyya* attacked the idea of military defense arrangements under Western auspices. The paper reiterated the Arab Socialist Party's commitment to neutralism, emphasizing that Soviet Russia was not the enemy of Syria and the Arabs:

> Is not Russia far from us, while we are in the laps of Anglo-American imperialism? . . . We believe in neutralism because we do not feel the danger of Russian imperialism. If we believe in the fable that communism is a menace to our country and if we do not admit the presence of Anglo-American Jewish imperialism, we are crazy. We still believe that the question of joint defense, the settlement of the refugees, and peace with Israel is one project aimed at colonizing and eliminating the Arab people.[89]

Al-Ishtirakiyya criticized those who argued that it was impossible for Syria to refuse the joint defense project, and claimed that neutralism was a fable: "They deceived us, by saying that [the imperialist powers would] provide Syria with arms and military equipment should we submit our [national interests] to imperialism."[90]

The bearers of neutralism in Syria often asserted that, since the Syrians had nothing to expect from the US and the West but support of Israel, Syria's best policy would be to stand neutral *vis-à-vis* both blocs. They argued that Syria and the Arabs should use the present unsettled international situation as a lever to maneuver a proper settlement of the Palestine problem. An American report evaluating neutralism in Syria argued that US support of Israel was not the exclusive cause of Syrian neutralism. The report pointed at "many other important historical, geographical, and psychological factors" which had also influenced the development of neutralism:[91]

> Starting with a characteristic tendency toward rationalization of unpleasant realities, involving an admixture of pacifism, Syrian neutralism seems to draw strength from the average Syrian's ultra-nationalistic appraisal of his country's past experience with the Great Powers. Moreover, living at one of the world's great crossroads, the average Syrian politician is attracted by what he imagines to be a good international bargaining position.

The report stressed that several occurrences had combined to give added stimulation to the neutralist sentiment, which already existed in Syria: "The bitterness regarding Palestine, the recent turn of events in Korea, the unfortunate conjuncture of circumstances at the time of the announcement of the 35 million [US] dollar Export-Import Bank loan and rumors of a billion dollar loan to come to Israel, the propaganda of the Partisans of Peace in Syria, the general public's ignorance of international politics, and the politically naïve, but dangerous, propensity of the Syrians to play international blackmail."[92] The report noted few positive pro-Soviet elements in contemporary pronouncement on neutralism. There were indications that the Muslim Brotherhood, the Islamic Socialist Front, and the Ba'th Party, who represented the hardcore of Syrian neutralism, might be re-examining the basis for relationships with the Soviet Union. There were reports that Mustafa al-Siba'i and the Ba'thist Jalal al-Sayyid, as well as other Ba'thists and Islamic Socialists, were calling at the Soviet Legation. The report concluded, "There is a distinct possibility that if neutralism gains ground in Syria it may be increasingly exploited for Soviet purposes."[93]

Indeed, in the first half of 1951, Soviet propaganda in Syria had attempted to exploit Arab enmity toward Israel. The Soviets often declared that the Anglo-American imperialists were employing the State of Israel to realize their imperialist aims in the Arab states. Considerable use was made by the Soviets of Israel's alleged expansionist ambitions directed against Arab territory. The Soviets used the services of the organization of the Syrian Partisans of Peace (SPP)—a group that associated itself with the World Movement for Peace, which had been formed and was supported by the Soviet Union. The SPP presented a petition to the Syrian government on 12 April 1951 asserting that Zionist aggression in Palestine was another example of imperialist pressure on the Arabs and the outcome of recent visits of Anglo-American personalities to Israel and the Arab states.[94]

The winds of neutralism continued to blow in the Syrian political arena throughout 1951. On 23 June 1951, the neutralist Ma'aruf al-Dawalibi was elected by the Syrian Chamber of Deputies to be its President—one of the highest political positions in Syria. His party (the People's Party), the Islamic Socialists with whom he maintained close alignment, the Ba'thists, and several independents supported al-Dawalibi's candidacy.[95] The Prime Minister at the time of al-Dawalibi's election was Khalid al-'Azm (March–July 1951); al-Dawalibi's election and al-'Azm's premiership may be seen as further proof that neutralist ideas were gaining a solid stronghold in Syria in the early 1950s. The politicians who influenced Syria's tilt toward neutralism in the first half of 1950 were back in power. Western diplomats in Damascus were concerned by al-Dawalibi's election, which they interpreted as:

> a vindication of if not a reward for his neutralism and anti-Western attitudes of the past. In the ear of the more undisciplined disciples of Syrian nationalism his election sets a tone of endorsement of neutralism, and many less courageous Syrian politicians though disagreeing with al-Dawalibi are still afraid publicly to denounce him. In the circumstances his election is somewhat discouraging. Even if he should abide by the promise of his Party that he would not use his new position for partisan purposes, the implication that he succeeds in Syrian politics despite, or possibly because of, his neutralistic attitude remains.[96]

The foreign policy of al-'Azm's government reflected al-Shishakli's views on Arab affairs. Al-Shishakli, who feared and opposed the extension of Hashemite influence at the expense of Syria, had turned to Egypt and Saudi Arabia for aid. Both Arab countries opposed the Hashemite union plans, as did al-Shishakli and al-'Azm, who firmly objected to the People's Party's plans for union with Iraq. Inter-Arab relations and their effects on Syria's foreign policy is well described by an American evaluation of al-'Azm's short-lived cabinet:

> Many aspects of 'Azm's policy can be traced to Egyptian influence and to the results of al-Shishakli's having led Syria into the Saudi-Egyptian fold . . . On the basis of this al-Shishakli–Egyptian relationship, Syria in essence has agreed that the present fragmentation of the Arab East (which enables Egypt by means of the Arab League to dominate the region and to exercise thereby considerable influence over six clamorous nationalistic voices in the UN, and which is so much to the liking of Ibn Sa'ud [King of Saudi Arabia] because of the restrictions it places on the expansion ideas of his Hashemite enemies) must be preserved. The states concerned still believe in Arab unity, but in the form of Egyptian domination (the Arab League) and not in the form of a unified Arab State, or a federation, or a confederation (Qudsi's "union" plan), which could ever rival Egypt. This is the essentially Egyptian doctrine to which al-Shishakli has tied Syria and which Khalid al-'Azm apparently had no qualms about carrying out.[97]

The rapprochement and alignment of Syria with those countries were to reinforce the popular anti-Hashemite, anti-British, and anti-American trends prevalent in Syrian politics. Like Egypt's neutralism of the early 1950s, which had been formulated and implemented by its Wafdist Foreign Minister Muhammad Salah al-Din (1950–2), Syria's neutralism was characterized by its anti-Westernism, on the one hand, and on the other by its manipulative use of the Eastern bloc option as a tactical and opportunistic move intended to put pressure on the Western powers to change their overall policies in the Middle East in favor of the Arabs. As an American diplomat in Syria put it, "If the British and Americans were [to be] displeased by neutralism, Syria like Egypt would find it well to be neutralistic."[98] Al-'Azm's foreign policy was not challenged by strong opposition elements in the Parliament, yet they did strike at him, both in Parliament and in the press, over his domestic misgovernment. These opposition elements worked covertly to bring together the army and anti-'Azm factions with the aim of making a populist government possible again. The pretext to act was given when al-'Azm's cabinet presented the budget for the fiscal year 1951–2. Following the government's failure to pass the budget in Parliament after three attempts, al-'Azm resigned on 30 July 1951.[99]

Following the collapse of al-'Azm's anti-Western and neutralist cabinet, a new government was formed by the independent Hasan al-Hakim (9 August 1951–10 November 1951), who was known for his pro-Hashemite and pro-Western disposition. This marked the end of the existing harmony between the army and the previous government in collaborating to shape Syria's foreign policy.

In the first days of August, prior to the formation of al-Hakim's cabinet, Adib al-Shishakli visited King Ibn Sa'ud to discuss financial issues arising from Saudi Arabia's economic aid to Syria and the development of events in the Arab world following the assassination of 'Abdullah, the King of Jordan.[100] Shortly after he returned to Damascus he released a statement in the Egyptian paper *al-Ahram* reassuring the paper's readers that Syria's policies were oriented generally toward Egypt and Saudi Arabia—"two countries that are anxious to safeguard Syrian interests."[101] At the same time, he also denounced Iraqi expansionist plans, and the tone of his observations on foreign affairs was anti-British. He reiterated his commitment to neutralism, stressing that "we have an independent country and we have fought and sacrificed much to win our independence and to liberate ourselves from every foreign influence. It is impossible for us to accept the return of any foreign influence, regardless of its nature, to our country."[102] Al-Shishakli explained that he did not oppose the idea of an organized communist party, "which believes in a specific social doctrine similar to other parties that advocate social and political doctrines, provided that this party be purely national with local objectives and not related to a foreign power, a case which I will not accept, since it would be a traitorous cause directed at the country. I do not in any way accept the principle that our citizens be permitted to pay the way for infiltration of any foreign influence into their free country."[103] Al-Shishakli was not against the idea of internal communist activity, as long as the advocates and activists were Syrian nationalists who were acting purely for, and on behalf of, Syria's interests. He would not tolerate the existence of a Communist Party connected to, and associated with, international Soviet communism. He made it clear that Syria did not have any plans to ally itself politically, militarily, or economically with either the Eastern or Western blocs.[104]

Al-Shishakli's statement was formulated in such way to make it clear that, although there was a Prime Minister whose personal views on foreign affairs were not in line with those of his own government and the army, the true leaders of Syria—al-Shishakli and the Syrian army—fully controlled Syria's fundamental policies. As future events were to demonstrate, the army closely monitored al-Hakim's government, and its ability to independently conduct Syria's foreign policy was highly restricted. It was obvious from the beginning that al-Hakim's government would not last very long. Dominated by the People's Party, which held both the foreign and internal affairs ministries, its first political steps were divisive.

Al-Hakim had made his personal views on Syrian foreign policy obvious from the moment he took office. For several reasons he believed that Syria's best interests were to favor the Western camp over communism. First, the Arabs could not face the dangers of the present world situation alone and, despite the fact that they had been treated badly by the West, notably in the Palestine affair, they should not allow their resentment to lead them into anti-Western neutralism, which meant hostility to the Western bloc and would lead to negative repercussions for the Arabs. He believed neutralism to be imaginary "as long as we are weak, and as long as strong countries do not respect the neutrality of weak countries if war exigencies so require, especially in the case of a ferocious war in which most of the world would participate."[105] Second, he expressed his pro-Hashemite disposition by declaring that the Arabs should unite themselves; and, if a Hashemite union had proved impossible in the past, then at least Syria, Iraq, Jordan, and Lebanon should join together. And third, Syria should draw closer to Turkey in every way, notably through a defensive pact.[106] Al-Hakim was careful to point out that these were his own personal views, not his government's official policy. The government's views, he argued, were to be determined not by him, but by the whole cabinet.

Indeed, Syria's foreign policy, as outlined by Foreign Minister Faydi al-Atasi, was in utter contrast to al-Hakim's personal views based as it was on the general guidelines laid down by Shishakli and the army. In its first weeks in power, however, al-Hakim's government looked as though it was making an attempt to moderate the deeply rooted anti-Western feelings that prevailed on the Syrian political scene. This was an impossible mission, since Syria's foreign policy was influenced to a great extent by Egypt and by the wave of anti-Westernism prevalent in many parts of the Arab world. On his return on 10 September from a meeting of the Arab League Political Committee in Alexandria, Faydi al-Atasi held a press conference at the Ministry of Foreign Affairs that was intended to cover the transactions of that meeting. One of the main items to be discussed by al-Atasi was the condemnation of Egypt by the UN Security Council on 1 September, following complaints against Egypt by Israel and Britain over its long-term policy of imposing restrictions on Suez Canal traffic to Israel.[107] Despite the inflammatory diatribes in the Syrian press and Parliament on that subject, al-Atasi was not forced into making any wild remarks. He moderately supported the Egyptian action, stressing that it was approved by the other Arab states. Al-Atasi preferred to rely on the reference to this subject of the Political Committee of the Arab League, saying that the "Security Council has denied to Egypt and the other Arab countries a right which the UN Charter has admitted to all countries, namely the right to take, within their sovereignty and internal powers, all measures considered necessary for their safety and security. In attempting to prevent the flow of oil to Israel, the Arab states [are] taking an action that is similar to that taken by other known states . . . The same countries that complained of Egypt's action have made themselves the judges when they participated in the voting."[108] Al-Atasi also spoke in a conciliatory tone with regard to Turkey's policy toward the Arab–Israeli conflict. Although Turkey aligned itself with the Western camp, it also maintained close ties with Hashemite Iraq. Turkey's policy toward the Arabs, said al-Atasi, was inspired by the fact that it was a Mediterranean country and a natural friend of the Arabs. Syria sincerely appreciated Turkey's attitude with respect to the partition of Palestine and the "Huleh question" (Syria's recent controversy with Israel). "Although we did not expect the attitude with respect to navigation in the Suez Canal" he said of Turkey's decision not to take the Arab side, "we still hope that in future international events her attitude will be dictated by the exigencies of mutual interests resulting from neighborhood, and by history and old amicable ties."[109]

A few weeks later, in response to the Four Powers' proposal for the MEC, al-Atasi's relatively moderate tone with respect to foreign affairs abruptly changed to sharp criticism and condemnation of Western military plans in the Middle East. On 23 October, during a statement he made on the MEC before Parliament, al-Atasi took the opportunity to attack the proposal. He said, *inter alia*, that "association in a defensive group should be justified by a clear and definite national interest. I honestly . . . searched for such interests and, despite exhausting efforts, I could not find them. I still see no such justification . . . Who is our enemy? . . . Does this enemy threaten us, and what harm has he done to us?"[110] After a long process of analysis, al-Atasi concluded that he had discovered that the only anti-Arab move taken by the Soviets in the past was their vote for the partition of Palestine. Nevertheless, if one compared policies of the Eastern and Western blocs toward the Arabs, it was clear to al-Atasi that the Western powers had taken a graver course of action against the Arabs on the Palestine question—they had, after all, established Israel and "attended to it, and extended to it open and hidden aids to such a degree that its aggressive strength gives us neither sleep nor rest." The Western powers, said al-Atasi cynically, maintained that the Tripartite Declaration should put the Arabs at peace. He responded to this argument by asking the Western powers:[111]

> Who would guarantee that the tripartite statement—with respect to your observance of it and your living up to its contents—is not one more of your old statements and decisions? . . . What happened to your decisions issued by the UN General Assembly with respect to Palestine? Have you not pledged yourself in 1948, 1949, and 1950 that the [Palestinian] refugees should return to their homes? . . . You established Israel by force and in open and hidden twisted ways in the heart of the Arab countries . . . Is it not with your aid that it [Israel] has acquired a navy and air power, commercial and military? Is it not with your aid that it possesses now your most modern and destructive weapons? You [Western powers] may say: Have we not offered you the same aid? Good God! You give Israel yards and you give us inches! Do you not realize that your unequal aid has a negative effect? Would you leave Israel and us to our private means? What do you think of the stream of immigration to Israel, you who have placed yourselves as guardians of peace? Why do you not take into consideration the explosive factors from this huge immigration? Do you think that Palestine can hold all these creatures? What have you done vis-à-vis these questions other than demonstrating your support for Israel? They [Western powers] say they cannot use force and compel Israel . . . [We say] you can do it simply by ceasing your aid . . . Will you do it?

In al-Atasi's view, both the Western powers and the Arabs faced tangible threats—the fears of the former were centered on Russia, whereas for the latter, the real menace was Israel. Under these circumstances, it was impossible to ask both the Arabs and Israel to side with the West. "Do you not see the contradiction of your policy?" al-Atasi asked the Western powers. He accused them of stating that they were seeking peace, order, and stability in the Middle East, and they wanted to protect the Middle East from communism by raising the standard of living of its peoples. At the same time, al-Atasi noted, the West established Israel in the heart of the Middle East, and by doing so nullified their objective, because Israel, with its expansionist ambitions and its aggressive preparations, was a source of disturbance and trouble. This led the Arab countries to seek any means of preventing trouble: "Had the appropriations for defense in the budgets of the neighboring countries been spent for improving the condition of these countries and for increasing their production, there would not be anyone to complain about poverty," stressed al-Atasi.[112]

Al-Atasi concluded his statement by declining the "joint defense" proposal of the Western powers and called upon the West to redress their mistakes and return to doing right: "ask yourselves what harm you have done to the Arabs and what injustice you have done." He justified Egypt's adverse attitude toward the Four Powers' proposal: "These proposals were unreasonable in their phrasing as well as their content, and they were presented as if the Western Powers wanted the proposals to be answered without delay."[113]

Al-Atasi's statement led to strife within Syria's government and the subsequent resignation of Prime Minister al-Hakim. In an interview given to the Lebanese newspaper *al-Hayat* a week before his resignation, on 3 November 1951, al-Hakim expressed his determination not to give in to populist trends when deciding Syria's foreign policy: "I will not be influenced in the conduct of Syria's foreign policy by street politics which were responsible for [the] ruin of Faysal[114] and the loss of Alexandretta and Palestine.[115] I will not speculate on [the] future of [our] nation in an atmosphere of emotion . . . I believe we should take [this] opportunity of replacing foreign treaties by this defense plan [the Four Powers' proposal]."[116] On 10 November, however, al-Hakim presented his letter of resignation to President Hashim al-Atasi. In his letter, he blamed his Foreign Minister for not consulting the Cabinet with respect to the contents and details of his statement concerning Syria's stand on the MEC. Faydi al-Atasi, stressed al-Hakim, created "a critical situation for the government which was studying the subject carefully and consulting [other] Arab governments for the purpose of arriving at a unified decision in its respect."[117]

Al-Hakim's reasons for resigning were explained in a letter he sent to the Parliament on the same day. In comparison to al-Atasi's statement, this letter reflects a different view with regard to al-Hakim's approach to the Four Powers' proposal for the MEC. Al-Hakim advocated collaboration with the Western powers in the MEC and the tying of this move to a concrete change of the West's policies toward the Arabs generally, and the Arab–Israeli conflict in particular:

> Today we live in a world in which fear and anxiety prevail and the danger of war is drawing near us. It is wise to consider consequences instead of marching with emotions . . . Events and catastrophes followed but we did not learn from our experiences . . . exaggerations on our side led us to lose our causes and our friends and left us alone in the field . . . Moderation is brave and we must all be moderate. It is the way that we should follow if we are seeking the security and

deliverance of our country . . . I recommend the acceptance of the joint defense scheme as a good opportunity for the Arabs to reinforce themselves militarily and economically and to withstand the evil of Israel. In the meantime, I believe that [our] acceptance should be accompanied by [the West] meeting their [the Arabs'] national aspirations and the settlement of their pending questions.[118]

Al-Hakim's letter displayed a certain degree of criticism of the way Egypt conducted its rejection of the Four Powers' proposal. Although he accepted Egypt's leadership of the Arab world and supported its national aspirations and desire to attain full sovereignty, al-Hakim did not hesitate to make it clear that Syria had the right to expect Egypt not to separately say "no" to the MEC proposal without consulting "by virtue of the Arab League Charter, the Arab countries concerned and considering their opinion." Al-Hakim expressed his belief that a reasonable and appropriate response by the Arabs to the joint defense scheme and the employment of the correct approaches for them to take in their negotiations with the Western powers might consequently help in finding a just solution to the Palestine question.[119]

The downfall of al-Hakim's short-lived government was inevitable. It was a government that spoke in two voices: one moderately pro-Western, the other tending toward neutralism. Failing to persuade his cabinet of the need to side with the West, as well as his moderate criticism of Egypt's unilateral rejection of the Four Powers' proposal, left al-Hakim without political support. The fact that neither his government nor the Parliament or the President were willing to endorse his policy was a clear victory for the Syrian neutralist forces and a reflection of the anti-Western feelings prevalent among the vast majority of Syrian political circles and institutions. All parties of the Syrian left, including the left-wing People's Party, which was dominated by al-Dawalibi, viciously attacked al-Hakim's approach toward the Four Powers' proposal for the MEC. They organized daily demonstrations of students and town vagrants intended to destabilize the political situation in the country.[120] These anti-Western manifestations found expression in the Syrian press, which declared unanimous support for Egypt's decision of 8 October 1951 to unilaterally abrogate its treaty of 1936 with Britain. The following day, the anti-People's Party paper al-Fayha' praised the Egyptian government for its move and concluded that this development clearly showed that the British stronghold in the rest of the Middle East would soon come to an end:

It has thus been the will of the almighty that such be the end of British influence in the East, a terrible defeat in the face of a mighty will of emancipation glowing in the hearts of these lovers of freedom. Britain was ousted from India and Pakistan, then yesterday from Iran, today from Egypt, and tomorrow from Iraq by abrogation of the 1930 [Anglo-Iraqi] treaty. Eventually every other place which yearns for liberty and freedom will do the same.[121]

Words in the same spirit were expressed by the independent and anti-People's Party paper *al-Barada*, which called on every Arab "to prepare to meet whatever is coming as the fading of imperialism in the Nile Valley is a sign of diminishing imperialism in the lands of all Arabs." *Al-Barada* called on the Iraqi government to follow the Egyptian example by abrogating the Anglo-Iraqi treaty of 1930.[122]

The Muslim Brothers, through their paper *al-Manar*, hailed the Egyptian government for its anti-British action, promising that "every Arab throughout the world is prepared to support Egypt in her struggle to the last drop of his blood."[123] Even *al-Sha'b*, the organ of the People's Party and known for its pro-Iraqi orientation, supported the Egyptian move. Moreover, it advised Egypt and the Arab states not to get involved in the Middle East Command, since such involvement could possibly lead them "to bloody wars."[124]

The Syrian stand on the question of the MEC and the issue of Egypt's abrogation of the treaty of 1936 led to a great deal of concern in the US Legation in Damascus. The question was raised of what could be done to prevent an increase in the anti-Western tendency in Syria and to halt the drift toward neutralism. One of the ideas suggested was to provide Syria with arms, some of which would be given on a grant basis, which would benefit the US, since records of the previous two years proved that Syria would procure arms whatever the cost to constitutional ideals and development, and that it would also accord internal leadership to whom ever could procure them and friendship to any country that supplied them. The selling of arms, the Legation reasoned, would put the US in a position of influence which currently it did not occupy. If the US were skillful in the matter, it might be able to use its new position to bring about an improvement in Syro-Israeli relations, reducing Syrian fears of a Israeli attack.[125] The US Legation's proposals were ignored. President Truman, who was supported by the Joint Chiefs of Staff, refused to grant military equipment to Arab countries adjacent to Israel, believing this would create pressure from Israel for similar assistance, which in turn might accelerate the arms race. Such a development would run counter to the principles of the Tripartite Declaration of May 1950.[126]

On 28 November, Ma'aruf al-Dawalibi formed a new cabinet, replacing Hasan al-Hakim as Syria's new Prime Minister with the support of his Peoples' Party, the Independents, and the Islamic Socialist Front. Al-Dawalibi also took for himself the portfolio of Defense Minister, a matter that, the following day, provoked Syria's fourth military *coup d'état* led by al-Shishakli, who, until then, had been ruling Syria unofficially. Al-Dawalibi's cabinet was one of the shortest-lived in Syria's history. Al-Shishakli announced that the army had taken over because the old political parties were no longer to be trusted—particularly the People's Party, which together with some of the Independents, were plotting a union with Iraq.[127]

The first wave of Syrian anti-Western neutralism, when politics was still conducted with a certain degree of independence by the Syrian traditional elite, ended on 29 November 1951 when al-Shishakli decided to overthrow the old guard politicians and established his own direct rule. Since December 1949, he had closely monitored and controlled Syrian politics from behind the scenes; al-Shishakli, however, gave the politicians wide latitude for political action. His period in power (November 1951–February 1954) saw no significant developments as far as Syria's inter-bloc policy was concerned. Relations with the Western powers—Britain and the USA—remained at a low ebb. In contrast, relations with France had improved and French influence within the Syrian army increased for two reasons: First, France supplied large shipments of arms to Syria; and second, senior Syrian officers were trained by the French military. The French also exerted much influence through the *Banque de Syrie* and there were many French schools in Syria. The French were not popular, a British report declared, but they were "well dug-in and will fight any attempt by the US or ourselves [Britain] to dislodge them. They suspected any offer of cooperation as an attempt to dislodge them."[128] Two faces characterized relations of the Western powers and Syria: closer relations with France, and denunciations of British and US imperialism. Al-Shishakli distrusted the British because they were allied with his Arab enemies, Iraq and Jordan. As for the Americans, "their responsibility for Israeli misdeeds remained great in Syrian eyes," noted the British report.[129] There were no noticeable changes in Syria's relations with the Soviet bloc. Al-Shishakli was known for his lack of tolerance for any political action in Syria directed from abroad, and that included internal communist activity directed from the USSR. His inter-bloc policy may have fitted in with the pattern of "passive neutralism," that is, he showed not much interest in the Cold War, in either the ideological or the political antagonism of outside powers and power groups.

In the period 1950–1 the successive Syrian governments adhered to "anti-Western neutralism" focusing mainly on one main theme, its hostility toward the West, which was considered to be Israel's chief ally and therefore acting against Arab interests. Syria maintained that the Arabs should punish and humiliate the West.

The Syrian Partisans of Peace (SPP)—A Soviet-Communist Vehicle to Promote Anti-Westernism

The diverse neutralist trends which rose in Syria and the Arab world in the post-World War II period gained clarity and direction among Syrian communists. The warm welcome and popularity this new phenomenon had received from many Syrians required, as far as the communists were concerned, the formulation of an accommodative approach—one that, on one hand, would not deny the basic tenets of neutralism, and, on the other, would portray the Soviet Union as a peace-loving country whose main concern was to support unconditionally, weak and needy countries. In the late 1940s and early 1950s, the Syrian communists embraced, in line with Moscow, a type of neutralism that incorporated some tenets drawn from Nehru's doctrinaire/ideological neutralism: world peace, non-violence, the prevention of a third world war, and an emphasis on the likelihood that such a war would lead to the annihilation of mankind.

The SPP was a very prominent organization in Syria between 1949 and 1952. This period was characterized by the emergence of neutralist groups that had not always shared similar views regarding the appropriate approach to be taken toward the Cold War. During that period, the US had made intensive efforts to organize Middle Eastern countries together into a military alliance with the West for the purpose of preventing the expansion of the Soviets and communism to the region. At the same time, the USSR was doing everything it could to neutralize the Middle East, exploiting the existence of anti-Western feelings by offering unconditional diplomatic, economic, and military aid to Arab countries. In order to market the USSR as a peaceful country, the Soviets initiated the formation of the World Peace Movement (WPM), which had branches all over the world. The SPP acted as the Syrian branch of the movement, which was disguised as a universal peace organization.

Yusuf Ibrahim Yazbek, Fu'ad al-Shamali, and others organized the Communist Party of Syria and Lebanon in the period 1924–5.[130] Khalid Bakdash took over the party in 1932 and, after that time, controlled the party until the decision to split the party in two was made in 1943 by the party's national congress in Beirut (31 December 1943–2 January 1944). Bakdash ran the party in a centralized and rigid manner.[131] Up to al-Shishakli's coup of 1949, the Syrian Communist Party acted only semi-legally. After al-Shishakli's takeover, and until he was overthrown, however, the communists were persecuted ruthlessly. The SCP's reaction to this development, stated Tareq and Jacqueline Ismael in *The Communist Movement*, "was to close its ranks and withdraw into a more sectarian and doctrinaire ideological position. This reaction was intensified by the simultaneous eruption of the Cold War and worldwide ideological struggle and political tension between the Soviet Union and the western powers."[132] Declared illegal and persecuted by the state, the SCP needed to form legal satellite organizations or act within existing socio-political frameworks. In a report presented before the central committee of the SCP in January 1951, Khalid Bakdash did not hide the fact that there were direct links between the SCP, the Syrian Partisans of Peace (SPP), and other labor and social organizations. The SCP, he declared, "was charged with the direction and control of all other types of social organizations, including ones such as trade unions, peasants committees, the peace movement, and women's organizations . . . our party [SCP] supports and participates in the Partisans of Peace activities . . . this [however] does not mean that our views and positions on every question are the same as those of the Partisans of Peace."[133]

Table 2.1 Estimated Number of Communist Party Members in Syria, 1950

Town or Section	Number
Aleppo	6,200
Damascus District	4,600
Jazirah	3,100
Homs	3,000
Latakia	1,000
Suwayda	400
Hauran	100
Total	18,400

Further proof of connections between the SCP and the SPP was provided by the Lebanese Communist Party in its organ *People's Struggle* [*kifah al-Sha'b*] of 1 January 1951. The accusations against the Partisans of Peace as being communists were not correct, declared the *People's Struggle*, because supporters in both Syria and Lebanon came from various political creeds. It was, however, "natural and taken for granted, that the communists should give this movement their wholehearted support."[134]

The year 1950 saw an increasing number of communist organizations in Syria, and the scope of their activities had broadened. The Syrian Communist Party (SCP) grew numerically, although its growth did not alarm outside observers. Western reports from Damascus estimated that its membership was around 18,400 men and women (see table 2.1).[135]

Some reports from Damascus maintained that the SCP was purposefully maintaining a small but highly disciplined force. There was, however, a consensus that the SCP was more powerful than before, "especially since the Korean War, and that it is capable of causing considerable trouble in Syria when and if the Soviets give the word."[136] Following the outbreak of the hostilities in Korea, the activities of the SCP increased considerably in terms of demonstrations, petitions, and protests. The communists appealed for peace and for outlawing the atomic bomb, and they concentrated their attack on "Anglo-American imperialism." Despite the fact that the SCP was officially illegal, important Syrian communists were able to freely move about and carry out their activities. The political climate in Syria at the time was ripe for communist activity. Reports from Damascus revealed that the Syrian police and other authoritative bodies were unwilling to offend major communist leaders "perhaps as insurance so that in case of war or occupation by the Soviets they will not be branded as 'reactionary' or anti-communist." These reports suggested that "certain statements" that were made during 1950 by Syrian politicians—such as the al-Dawalibi statement and other public utterances by various cabinet ministers—"must certainly have heartened communists and fellow-travelers alike."[137] The SCP had been receiving orders from Moscow, whose Legation in Beirut had continued to be active in the conduct of local communist affairs, both in Syria and Lebanon. Daniil' Solod, the Soviet Minister to Syria and Lebanon, resided in Beirut until his mission ended in late 1950, from where he had occasionally visited Damascus. His successor, Vassily Belyayev, was due to reside in Damascus, a development that caused the Syrian authorities and Western diplomats to express concern that the Soviet Legation in Damascus would now assume a more active role in guiding local communist affairs.[138]

The SPP was perhaps the most successful and prominent of the Communist Party-oriented groups in Syria. A communist front organization dedicated to propagating and disseminating pro-Soviet propaganda and indirectly engaged in recruiting communists and carrying out the Soviet organizational program for Syria,[138] the SPP had been an important vehicle for furthering Soviet interests in Syria. The movement supported and adopted the decisions made in Warsaw at the Second World Congress held from 16 to 22 November 1950.[140] The SPP, according to the Soviets, were striving to prevent the realization of Anglo-American plots to ring the Arab states with an aggressive Israeli–Turkish military alliance.[141]

The Syrian Partisans of Peace succeeded in persuading prominent Syrian politicians to sign the Stockholm Appeal in the summer of 1950. Among those who signed were: Ma'aruf al-Dawalibi; Akram al-Hawrani; Ahmad Qanbar; Rushdi al-Kikhya; Farhan al Jandali; and Hasan al-Hakim. The Stockholm Appeal was formulated and issued by the World Movement for Peace and included a call for world peace and opposition to the atomic bomb.[142] The precise number of Syrians who signed the Stockholm Appeal is not really known; according to the SPP's claim, the total number was 150,000. Western sources considered this number somewhat exaggerated, but agreed that a sizable number of Syrians, including many intellectuals, did sign the Appeal and "might sign the Appeal even today if they were approached."[143] Those Syrians who put their signatures to the Appeal knew of the political and ideological connection between the World Movement for Peace and the Soviet Union. They decided to sign because, for them, the choice was between the East and the West, or neutralism. Many Syrian intellectuals recognized neutralism as being occasioned by Syria's geographical and strategic position and by the threat of world conflict, which they believed was implicit in the present international situation. Many of them had also accepted the Palestine issue as an example of "Western bad faith." Western denunciations of the Appeal and attempts to expose it as Soviet propaganda were regarded by these Syrians as hypocritical.[144]

The SPP was developed around a hardcore group of members of the SCP and dependable fellow-travelers. This nucleus carried out the orders of the SCP, and was responsible for the recruitment of members, the planning of operations, and propaganda. The SPP received its direction from, and was linked to, international communist groups. Evidence of its close relations with the Soviets is shown by the fact that several prominent members of the SPP often called at the Soviet Legation in Damascus and were received by the Soviet Second Secretary, who was thought to be the MVD (Ministry of Internal Affairs) representative for Syria and Lebanon.[145] Mustafa Amin, a prominent member of the SCP, and one of the chief organizers of the SPP, attended the First World Peace Congress of the WPM in Rome in October 1949. Amin and his communist colleague, Falak Tarazi, were part of a large Syrian delegation[146] that represented the SPP in the Second World Peace Congress of the WPM. It is worth noting that most of the delegates received a free trip.[147] The movement supported and adopted the decisions made in Warsaw; the return of its delegates received considerable publicity, and thereafter the organization became markedly more active in Syria.

According to information provided by the SPP, the organization extended its influence into Syrian villages and towns. The Partisans stated that they intended to create "committees in every quarter, factory, village, and school . . . assembling all elements supporting peace, without other considerations and in spite of political or ideological differences of opinion."[148] The first months of 1951 saw a considerable increase in the number of committees of the Partisans of Peace throughout the area. Satisfied with this development, the Central Committee of the Syrian and Lebanese Communist Parties had instructed its members to concentrate their attention on the creation of other front organizations.[149]

The SPP was involved in organizing public demonstrations, which were forbidden by the police; however, the demonstrations, although spectacular, were only minor disturbances. In late November the police arrested twenty-nine people whom the SPP described in the press as "martyrs to the cause of peace." In reaction to their arrest, al-Nasr, an independent paper,[150] wrote that these people were arrested "not for committing any crime against the state but for holding a conference in which they declared their love for peace." The newspaper argued that they were not communists for a simple reason: "if they are, [then] the delegation which represented Syria at Warsaw should be labeled communist." Could anyone call Shaykh Muhammad al-Ashmar and Shaykh Salah al-Za'im communists? All the Syrian people advocated peace, *al-Nasr* stated: "it is illogical to brand the whole country as communists."[151] The last months of 1950 saw a considerable intensification of the SPP's activities. They carried the slogan of peace as the sole item of their campaign believing that such a marketable concept would be warmly welcomed by many Syrians.

In late November 1950, the Central Committees of the Syrian and Lebanese Communist Parties jointly issued a tract that attacked the Middle Eastern and global policies of the Western powers.[152] The tract placed special emphasis on the need for the unity of all Syrian "patriots of various political and idealistic tendencies" to withstand the common danger, Anglo-American imperialism, which was trying to provoke a third world war. These powers, it was argued, were planning to use Syria and Lebanon as military bases for their aggressive designs. In case of total war, the imperialist powers might use the atomic bomb, which "will not differentiate between citizens of this or that creed or political tendency." By employing these slogans, designed to appeal to Syrian nationalism, the tract called upon all patriotic Syrian citizens to contribute to the cause of peace by participating with other peoples of the world in the struggle against the outbreak of a third world war. The communists blamed the Western powers for hiding their "aggressive designs and their imperialist policy under the disguise of 'struggle against communism' or the necessity of withstanding an alleged Soviet danger." However, Western claims were false and misleading—both Syrians and Lebanese could find daily "irrevocable proofs of the peaceful policy of the Soviet Union." It was not the Soviets or the communists that issued the Tripartite Declaration, but the Western powers, "which gave themselves the right of military interference in the internal affairs of the Arab countries."[153]

The tract blamed the Syrian government for yielding to Western pressure by spending the country's wealth and increasing taxes "to meet the military demands of the Anglo-American colonizers while constructive projects relating to the daily life of the people . . . are being neglected."[154] The Lebanese Communist Party's organ *People's Struggle* [*kifah al-Sha'b*] declared on 1 January that the peoples of Syria and Lebanon condemned the policy of their retrogressive rulers, saying, "we will not allow you to tie us up with the war-risking adventures of the American imperialists and their Anglo-French accomplices. We stand for peace . . . we follow the course that is guided by the Soviet Union, the first land of socialism."[155]

The shift in the Soviet attitude toward Israel began at the outset of 1950 as a result of Israel's inter-bloc policy, which did not suit Moscow. The new policy found its expression in the communist tract. To advance their anti-Western propaganda, the communists exploited, for the first time, Arab enmity for Israel by asserting, first, that the Anglo-American imperialists "are striving to have the Arab states join aggressive blocs, which will include Turkey and Israel"; and second, by stating that the "imperialist pressure on the Arab countries to conclude a final peace and later a military pact with Israel is being increased." The imperialist powers, the tract noted, also endeavored to promote the project of a Greater Syria by seeking union between Syria and Iraq, so that the imperialists would be able to maintain their economic and military stronghold in the region.[156]

The SPP preceded its Egyptian sister and on the occasion of the formation of the preparation committee of Egypt's Partisans of Peace, sent a congratulatory cable on behalf of the national committee of SPP. The Egyptians expressed their intention to execute the decisions reached at the second congress of the WPM. During January 1951, through their various organizations (but mainly through the SPP), the communists instigated organized anti-Western demonstrations and issued appeals and protests against Western policies toward the Arab world. They also advocated the implementation of a policy of neutralism. These activities took place in the principal Syrian towns on 5 and 6 February. Some of the actions were organized to protest against General Robertson's visit to persuade Syria to ally itself with the Western powers. Anti-Western sentiments over the Korean War, the alleged anti-Arab policies of the West in the UN, and the alleged Western plan for occupation of Syria, all figured as reasons for the protests. A number of communists were subsequently arrested. The SPP, promoting the need to embrace a policy of neutralism at every opportunity in the major Syrian cities, had sent out a number of appeals to Arab leaders urging them not to deviate from a policy of strict neutralism. Since her return from Warsaw where she attended the Second World Peace Congress, Falak Tarazi had been particularly active in propagating and agitating for peace and neutralism. The press published an open letter from Tarazi in which she appealed to the "cultured" in Syria to use their influence for the cause of peace. She also regularly attended parliamentary meetings aimed at persuading members of Parliament to support the peace campaign of the SPP.[157]

Western reports from Damascus indicated that the communists had taken advantage of a shortage in Syria of available newsprint in order to get their propaganda into the Syrian press. The US legation in Damascus considered assertions that the Soviets—through the SPP—had provided newspapers such as *al-Nasr*, *al-Manar*, and *al-Hawadith*, with newsprint and, in return, these papers agreed to publish articles given to them by the communists. As far as relations between local communists and the Soviet Legation were concerned, US diplomats in Damascus noted that the officers of the Soviet Legation did not directly occupy themselves with running the local communist movement. Soviet diplomats in Damascus assumed that "the legation was under close surveillance and realized that the work of the local communists would be more difficult if guided by the legation." The Soviet Legation in Damascus was mainly engaged in press and propaganda work, largely through the Tass representative in the area.[158] Newspapers such as *al-Nasr*, a Damascus daily with the largest circulation in Syria, had been faithfully reproducing the communist point of view for some time. The US Legation in Damascus reported in July 1951 that now, more than ever before, it was convinced that the editor of *al-Nasr* maintained close liaison with a Soviet representative and that he probably "receives some sort of subsidy from the Soviets for his endeavors."[159]

Efforts made by the SPP in July 1951 to interest Syrians, mainly noncommunists, to go to the Berlin Peace Festival, and to convince the Syrian government to grant the required travel documents for the trip, were met with scant success. Since mid-1951, the Syrian government seemed to have taken a more aggressive stand on restricting communist activity; there were several instances in July in which activities of the SPP were curtailed and, on the occasions when the SPP was in the process of distributing communist pamphlets, the Syrian police seized the SPP members and imprisoned them. Eventually, only nine persons left for Germany to attend the festival, which took place in Berlin in August; a small number, much smaller than what the SPP had expected.[160]

On 10 August, a day after the formation of al-Hakim's cabinet, the communists, through the SPP and the SCP, organized two large demonstrations which turned violent. Several policemen and demonstrators were injured, and the police detained twenty-five protesters for questioning.[161] These demonstrations were intended to show the new government that the communists and their sympathizers were still a forceful factor in Syria and that they would not tolerate the same policy of the previous government, which denied travel documents to Syrians attending conferences under the aegis of the WPM. The communists, who expected more Soviet-sponsored and Soviet-inspired conferences to take place in Europe in the near future, hoped to exert pressure on the new government to allow members of the SPP to leave the country to attend these future events. In addition, the communists wanted to warn al-Hakim's government against any alignment with the West.[162]

In July 1951, the SPP inaugurated the publication of their new weekly organ, *al-Salam*, which devoted a great deal of space in its July issues to the Berlin Peace Festival.[163] Through *al-Salam*, the movement attempted to disseminate as much pro-Soviet, anti-Western propaganda as possible. In August 1951, *al-Salam* published a copy of an appeal to hold a "convention of the Peoples" of the Middle East and North Africa. The appeal stressed that the political, social, and economic conditions of the peoples of the Middle East and North Africa were extremely bad because of the domination of imperialism in these areas. In recent years, it was noted, the international situation had become aggravated and the danger of a new world war had increased. There had been constant efforts to

make of our countries military bases and subsequently a field of terrible, destructive and annihilating fighting . . . Our peoples face joint conditions. On one side, they suffer from the pressure of imperialism and face the danger of war, and on the other, they look for their independence and the security of their countries and wish to live safely, freely, and sovereign in their homelands. Therefore, collaboration for the purpose of unifying efforts and strength is basic and essential to these peoples in this decisive, serious stage of their history . . . We the signatories of this appeal . . . are aiming at unifying efforts and forces for following a joint way which would avoid for our countries the horrors of wars and realize national sovereignty for every one of our peoples.[164]

In late August, *al-Salam* published an article criticizing the Anglo-American designs for the Middle East. The paper emphasized that Britain was striving to improve relations between Saudi Arabia and the Hashemites. Moreover, the Western powers took pains to conclude peace between the Arabs and Israel for the purpose of advancing their plans to establish Middle East Defense organizations under Western domination. The Western powers, stated *al-Salam*, made efforts to have Egypt, Syria, Lebanon, Turkey, and Israel join in the Mediterranean bloc "in order to permit the free circulation of foreign troops in this area. The SPP calls on the Arab peoples to combat all war projects, which are designed to eliminate our independence, [facilitate] the re-occupation of our countries by foreign troops, and the destruction of our cities and towns."[165]

The fact that the SPP was a Soviet tool and associated with the Syrian communists may be seen by examining the content of the articles of *al-Salam*'s issue of 1 September. The paper's front page widely reported the support given by the Soviet Union to Egypt at the Security Council during deliberations on complaints against Egypt from Israel and Britain. *Al-Salam* also reported extensively the unity, brotherhood, and friendship that had prevailed among the participants of the Berlin Youth Festival. This showed, the paper stated, that the youth of the world were a guarantee for the rescue of international peace. Special emphasis was given to the Soviet contribution to the festival's success.[166] There were also non-communist figures who were involved in the activities of the SPP, such as Ma'aruf al-Dawalibi, who often expressed his neutralist views in *al-Salam* and in public statements. On 1 September, he declared in *al-Salam*, "it is the duty of the peoples of the Middle East to meet and oppose war and imperialism."[167] Officers of the British and US legations met with Syrian government officials to discuss the connection between *al-Salam* and the communists and expressed their hope that "some action might be taken to revoke the license of the magazine." The Syrian officials agreed that the magazine was "obviously communist and probably subsidized by covert communist sources," but they politely declined the request, saying that *al-Salam*'s activity was within the framework of the "freedom of the press" and did not suggest taking this case any further.

Although the peace campaign conducted in Syria by the SPP and the SCP on behalf of the Soviets and international communism was received with sympathy by many Syrians who embraced neutralism in its various forms, there were also voices that criticized the growth of communist and pro-Soviet trends. On 24 August, *al-Jil al-Jadid*, the organ of the Syrian Social National Party [SSNP—*al-Hizb al-Qawmi al-Suri al-Ijtima'i*], launched a series of anti-communist articles that interpreted various aspects of communist history, describing the Soviet campaign for peace as "a destructive communist maneuver."[168] *Al-Jil al-Jadid* made an association between communism and Zionism, calling the former "this ferocious monster, or this communism composed of Zionism and destructive apostasy." According to the principles of "Marx, the Jew," and the teachings of Lenin and Stalin, the objective of communism was to expand across the world by means of armed aggression and "not through the force of conviction and argument."[169] *Al-Jil al-Jadid* pointed at the clear contradictions between the objectives of communism and those of the "campaign for 'peace' undertaken today by the communists themselves—the disciples of Marx, Lenin, [and] Stalin—who advocate revolutions, wars, and bloodletting against the non-communist inhabitants of the world." This "peace campaign" by the communists in Syria and other countries had undertaken "to obtain the greatest possible number of signatures for the 'peace appeal' known as the Stockholm appeal." But this was a communist tactic and trick inspired by the *Cominform* some years earlier. Moscow had exploited freedom of thought and speech, which was enjoyed by the individual in democratic states, and had instructed its agents to plead and demonstrate for peace and to attack the capitalist states as warmongers. Moscow had invented many names for a number of imaginary organizations, which, in fact, were only fronts for the Communist Party itself. *Al-Jil al-Jadid*, considering *al-Salam* to be published by the communists, argued that the paper was entrusted with the task of "championing peace on behalf of the 'World Peace Conference.'" One may derive from the reading of *al-Salam* that "every item of news, events, or analyses published therein is influenced by Soviet propaganda."

Al-Jil al-Jadid concluded that the peace campaign was in fact "a communist plot which conforms with destructive Zionist designs and totally agrees with the general rule of Zionism and communism; namely, that the end justifies the means." Syria was in a state of war with Israel, and this war could not end "except by victory for the Syrian nation, the defeat of Israel, and eviction of the Jews from our country." Under these circumstances, advocating peace during a state of war was "certainly a betrayal of the interest of the nation and can be termed as high treason."[170]

The US Legation in Damascus considered *al-Jil al-Jadid* to be one of the four most influential papers in Syria with considerable impact on intellectual and minority groups. The Legation also noted that the circulation of the organ had steadily grown since publication began in August 1950.[171]

Several months earlier, *al-Jil al-Jadid* published five detailed, analytical articles, all entitled "Communism." The articles, written under the pseudonym of Ghaddub Khazzaf, a member of the SSNP who, at the time of publication, was incarcerated in Lebanon for "unlicensed party activity in the Lebanon,"[172] suggested that communism was an imperialist movement that posed a direct threat to the Arab world. The first article, which was published on 23 April 1951, described the imperialist and expansionist nature of Soviet communism. Communism attracted followers in order to destroy the spirit of nationalism among other nations; communism "is like a poison which is intended to break the good and beautiful Syrian spirit and to confuse Syrian thought." It was argued that, out of Syria's many problems, communism was the most outstanding danger, "considering it is coated with a radiance designed to deceive simple persons who look only superficially at things surrounding them."[173] The author suggested four categories of persons who were attracted by communism: a paid agent acting on behalf of international communism; a poor person who looks forward to a communist victory hoping it will improve their standard of living; an opportunistic, influential figure who believes that a communist takeover would put them in a better position; and a naïve person who is deceived by communist propaganda.[174] The writer concluded that the majority of communists belonged to the second category. These individuals were not interested in the communist doctrine but in the material gain which they expected to derive from it. The article stated that these people needed to be persuaded that what they imagined as paradise was only "a deceptive mirage in a desert soaked with the blood of innocents and paved with the skulls of liberals during the last thirty-three years . . . Communism which Marx, the Jew dreamed about under the British flag . . . (and which Lenin, another Jew,[175] adopted later as the basis of a revolution after introducing many changes and explanations into it), was full of basic mistakes and numerous philosophical contradictions which time and the revolution in Russia has revealed."[176] The third article categorically established that communism, which aimed at "the presentation of a comprehensive, progressive, and reformative creed," had failed completely because it was not based on real foundations, "since it relies only on substance for the sake of reforming humanity which is composed of substance and spirit." The communist solutions, stressed *al-Jil al-Jadid*, were completely incorrect, distorted, and incomplete. It warned "those deceived communist Syrians" not to be mislead by the impressive propaganda of the communists and Soviets, which would lead them "to the destruction of human civilization, the foundation of which was first set up by the Syrians."[177] The SSNP, which maintained the existence of an ethnic "Syrian Nation," thus set forth its philosophical and political principles designed to combat communism. They first stirred up feelings of national dignity within the individual, and did away with individual selfishness, which was "the cause of social diseases and the source of defect and disorder in our small Syrian country." Second, they displayed the talents of the Syrian nation and revealed its ancient history, "showing to the world its true face, namely that it is the source of present civilization. The latter fact was twisted in the past by the Jews and obliterated by Greek and Roman historians who were the bitter enemies of [the] Syrians and who inherited Syrian glory and adopted their civilization." Third, they fostered a comprehensive economic movement based on the principle of the abolition of feudalism, organized the national economy based on production and equitable treatment of workers, and protected the interests of the state and the people. Fourth, they defined "the boundaries of the Syrian country on a correct and scientific basis, drawing attention to the importance of allegiance to this Syrian country, and indicating the serious consequence of partitions and their fruitlessness." The reading of all five articles reveals the anti-Semitic nature of the SSNP. In the party's political philosophy, Jews and communism were inextricably bound, and the party exploited the fact that many Syrians feared and hated Zionism by associating it with communism. The SSNP employed the reverse of the successful tactics used by the communists, who associated Zionism with US policy in the Middle East. The Jews, the SSNP claimed, were the creators of communism and did so for the purpose of serving their "criminal" Zionist objectives. The Jews were aware of the fact that their "debased objectives cannot be realized unless everybody disbelieves in his own nationalism. Only then will nationalism collapse, and the Zionist Jewish idea which is supported by God—as they claim—will move everybody in the direction it dictates for the realization of its destructive aims."[178]

Al-Jil al-Jadid concluded this series of articles on communism with a warning that the great danger which at the time confronted humanity was communist internationalism, which the USSR was attempting to implant in the minds of individuals in other countries of the world while it encouraged the spirit of nationalism in Russia with a view to enabling the Soviet Union to crush, at the proper time, all the forces of the world outside the Soviet zone.[179] *Al-Jil al-Jadid* called on the US to provide Syria with arms for defense, begging the US government to stop yielding to Jewish pressure, which had so far prevented Syria from receiving American arms. The strategic importance of arming Syria, in the view of the SSNP, would be greater than the present importance of arming individual European members of the Atlantic Pact. The US was warned not to repeat "her mistake in China and not to go any further in supporting Israel against us lest the day come when the Syrian people fall into the hands of their enemies [the Soviets] who are America's enemies also."[180]

Unlike the main political streams in Syria, which adhered to anti-Western neutralism, and showed more sympathy toward the Soviets, the SSNP adhered to anti-Soviet neutralism. The SSNP advocated closer relations between Syria and the Western powers, the US in particular. They rejected both communism as an ideology and the Soviet Union as an imperialist power planning to take over Syria and subsequently dominate it. However, it did not want to take part in the Cold War by siding with the West—it wished to see Syria remaining neutralist.

3

Neutralism in Practice

Syria and the Consolidation of the Arab-Asian Group

India, Egypt, and the Arabs:
The Rise of Nehru's Influence in the Arab World

The Initial Steps in the Emergence of the Arab-Asian Camp

India's desire to play a leading role in international affairs had already been expressed by Nehru before the UN was established:

> India is going to be inevitably one of the leadership of all the smaller countries of Asia. We should cooperate with them and seek their support . . . India should play a much more independent role in foreign affairs. That role should, of course, be a friendly role to other countries, but it should be made clear that our policy is our own and not determined by other people.[1]

In 1946, India made its decision to side with the Arabs on the Palestine question. This decision was intended to facilitate the initial stages of a consolidation of an Asio-Arab bloc in the UN that would be guided by principles of *entente cordiale* in international affairs. On 7 September 1946, Nehru declared,[2]

> We are of Asia and the peoples of Asia are nearer and closer to us than others. India is so situated that she is the pivot of Western, Southern and South-East Asia. In the past her culture flowed to all these countries and they came to her in many ways. Those contacts are being renewed and the future is bound to see a closer union between India and South-East Asia on the one side, and Afghanistan, Iran, and the Arab world on the other. To the furtherance of that close association of free countries we must devote ourselves . . .[3]

Nehru had always been interested in Egypt and he developed useful links with the Wafd Party, Egypt's most influential nationalist party. In 1931, he held meetings in Cairo with Mustafa al-Nahhas, the Wafdist leader, who arranged for him to meet with Egyptian nationalists in order to discuss national issues related to the struggle of both countries for independence.[4]

India's interest in the future of Palestine had grown since April 1947 after Britain's decision to refer the problem to the UN. On 23 April, the Indian government outlined the main principles of its policy with regard to the Palestine question, but although an effort was made to present a more balanced view, there was an inclination to side with the Arabs. The Indian government declared that it had sympathy with the Arab cause and regarded Palestine "as primarily an Arab country." At the same time, however, "India must have the deepest sympathy for the Jews who have suffered so terribly during the recent persecutions in Europe." The appropriate solution to the Palestine question, as seen through Indian eyes, was one that must lie along the lines of the "formation of an Arab state with the inclusion of an autonomous Jewish area," and India would prefer to see this state independent at the earliest possible date.[5] India decided that it should support the Arab contention that Palestine "is essentially an Arab country and any decisions should have the consent of the Arabs . . . we cannot support any proposition which involves compulsion of the Arabs."[6]

The Indian stand regarding Palestine was based on political and strategic considerations: "We must not forget that India's relationship with Muslim countries of the Middle East is very close and must become much closer." India also took into consideration the importance of the Mediterranean to its communications, saying, "the security of those communications must depend upon the existence of an Arab world which is connected and can rely upon sufficient material support from friendly powers to enable it to retain its independence."[7]

All proposals for temporary arrangements or possible long-term solutions to the Palestine question, declared the Indian government, "must depend largely upon the Arab view and we do not wish at this stage to express any definite opinion." The end of the Indian provisional statement of principles regarding Palestine reflected India's short- and long-term strategies toward the Middle East, based on association with, and support for, the Arab positions.[8]

Although India failed to solve the Palestine problem in a way that would satisfy the Arabs, its position concerning the Palestine problem, concluded the Indian representative at the UN, V. Pandit, had proven to be correct. Arab states, she explained, "have throughout been appreciative of our attitude." As for the Jews, despite the fact that India took a pro-Arab stand, "Jewish spokesmen have privately expressed to us hope that there may be active cooperation between India and Jewish Palestine."[9]

India's positive image among the Arabs was enhanced as a result of the failure of the Arabs and India to prevent the partition of Palestine into two states, Jewish and Arab. On 30 November, the day after the approval of the partition plan, Shukri al-Quwatli dispatched a telegram to Nehru expressing the deepest gratitude of Syria and the Arabs for "the noble attitude of the Indian government" and its representatives to the UN for what he described as an "enthusiastic defense of the Arab cause in Palestine." The Syrian people and the Arabs, concluded the Syrian President, "shall never forget it."[10] On 3 December, Nehru received another letter, this time from the government of Saudi Arabia, which also expressed its deepest gratitude "for the honorable attitude" of India's delegates to the UN who took the side of the Arabs "against that unjust and oppressive resolution against Palestine." The letter concluded by promising that "the Arab nations will keep in memory your country and government, this good deed and genuine help in supporting right and justice, and will never forget this noble and honorable attitude."[11]

India's consistent pro-Arab stance was to have far-reaching repercussions on the reorganization of the post-colonial world. Successive Arab failures to pass resolutions in the UN in their favor (the Egyptian appeal to the Security Council of August 1947 and, soon after, the Israeli victories in Palestine), and the fact that most of the countries opposing the partition were from Asia (although China abstained), enhanced the sense of solidarity among Asian states. The Palestine experience laid the foundations for the formation of an Asio-Arab bloc in the UN, which was to gradually become—with the subsequent membership in the UN of many new independent states from Asia and Africa—the biggest bloc internationally. India, which had realized the enormous potential that could materialize should the Asian states unite under its leadership, took the initiative, and, from the late 1940s, attempted to translate this potential into a concrete and practical force.

Minor manifestations of Asio-Arab solidarity on inter-Asian and international affairs were seen in the first and second inter-Asian conferences of 1947 and 1949 in New Delhi. The first conference, which dealt with the furthering of the anti-colonial struggle in Asia and relations between the newly emerging independent states, was unsuccessful because of the lack of unity among its participants, because of criticism from the Arab delegates of the agreement of conference organizers to the presence of Jewish delegates from Palestine, and because some Asian countries expressed their fear that India was seeking the leadership of free Asia. The second conference in January 1949 expressed support for the cause of Indonesian independence, while the inclusion of two African states (Egypt and Ethiopia) in the conference was intended to illustrate the Afro-Asian character of the summit.[12] In his speech at the conference, Nazim al-Qudsi, the Syrian representative, declared that his country "welcomes the strengthening of political and economic ties with the countries of Asia here present, for our mutual safety and prosperity. Syria believes that a regional and permanent

understanding within the framework of the United Nations will be benefi-
cial to all the nations taking part in it."[13] As a result of the second
conference, cooperation in the UN between representatives of those countries that participated in the conference increased considerably. By the end
of 1950, the Asio-Arab bloc was consolidated and now constituted an
important and influential separate grouping. 'Abd al-Rahman 'Azzam, the
then Secretary-General of the Arab League, revealed that the Asio-Arab
bloc was established in 1949 over the question of Indonesia's independence:
"We rallied round India to support Indonesia, and that was the birth of the
Arab-Asiatic group. There was then India, the Philippines and China—
Nationalist China—and the Arab states."[14]

The outbreak of the Korean War in June 1950 led to an escalation of the
Cold War on all fronts and put non-alignment to a severe test. The "policy
pursued by the non-aligned countries," explained N. P. Nair, "that of India
and to some extent of Yugoslavia,"—both members of the SCUN at that
time—contributed in some measure "to a lessening of the tension and to
creating the necessary atmosphere for peaceful negotiations between the
two blocs."[15] The Korean War and the determination for peace also helped
to bring about a greater sense of unity among the Arab and Asian countries in the UN. Nair concluded that the two blocs (the Soviet and the West)
recognized the value of the peace efforts initiated by the non-aligned
nations.[16]

From the beginning it was India that assumed the leadership of this
group in its initial meetings in the UN in 1950, and provided guidance in
the process of the political awakening of Asia after centuries of colonial
rule. To quote Michael Brecher:

> The Indian National Congress served as a model for the intelligentsia of South-
> east Asia and to a lesser extent of the Middle East. India's freedom in 1947 was
> the major break in European control of the Asian rimland and hastened the
> coming of independence throughout the area . . . The withdrawal of the British
> power from the sub-continent also influenced the course of events in the Middle
> East, for, with the loss of its imperial bastion, England could no longer retain its
> paramount influence in the Arab world.[17]

The Arab-Asian group was composed of twelve countries, most of them
Arab: Egypt, Iraq, Lebanon, Saudi Arabia, Syria, and Yemen. Four more
were Muslim—Afghanistan, Indonesia, Pakistan, and Iran—and only two
were non-Muslim—India and Burma. The year 1953 saw the expansion of
the original group when more independent Asian and African (Ethiopia
and Liberia) countries joined, transforming it from an Arab-Asian into an
Afro-Asian group. That same year also saw close cooperation and warm
relations between Muslim Indonesia and Arab countries.[18] On 12 October
1953, Nehru had a meeting with Sunarjo, the Indonesian Foreign Minister.

In the course of their conversation, the latter suggested that their countries take steps to consolidate the Asian-African group of states. Sunarjo suggested that representatives of these states organize a conference somewhere beyond the UN headquarters. Nehru replied that he had welcomed the formation in the UN of the Afro-Asian group, and that he would like to make it "a firmer group than it was."[19] In principle, he accepted the idea of a conference, but expressed concern that "the larger the number of countries in the group, the vaguer would be their common ground." Such a conference, he reasoned, "should be preceded by a good deal of preparation." In Nehru's view, the real test would be a country's reactions to the Cold War: "was it aligned with any particular group or did it wish to pursue an independent policy [of] trying to avoid war and even to keep out of war if it was declared?"[20] Nehru preferred to see a smaller group of neutralist states so that a high level of cooperation could be achieved between them.

Internationally, India supported Arab countries that were struggling to gain their full independence from foreign domination. The Egyptian Ambassador in India admitted that his country was taking inspiration from India's struggle for independence. When Egypt unilaterally abrogated its 1936 treaty with Britain on 8 October 1951, Nehru expressed his view at a press conference that India's sympathies were with national aspirations, and Egypt, like other Asian and African countries, was struggling for national independence. He spoke of global shifts in the balance of power, noting that no equilibrium had yet been found, even as the old colonialism was disappearing from Asia: "Insofar as Egyptian nationalism is concerned, and Egypt's claims, etc. are concerned, we obviously always sympathize with them."[21] The Indian leader drew a distinction between Egypt's claims for full sovereignty over the Suez Canal and its claims to Sudan: "We do not think that Sudan or any territory should be controlled by foreign powers ultimately. What exactly Sudan should do is primarily the concern of the Sudanese, and also, of course of others, more especially of Egypt because of the waters of the Nile, etc." Nehru also criticized the military actions conducted by British troops in the Suez Canal area, maintaining that the introduction of new British troops in the Suez Canal zone was a fresh war effort.[22] Although Nehru repeatedly stressed that the Sudanese people should have the opportunity to decide upon sovereignty, he also formally recognized King Farouk's new title—King of Egypt and Sudan.[23]

Soon after the July 1952 coup, the new Egyptian interim leader, General Najib, appealed to the Egyptian armed forces and people "to emulate Gandhi in selfless devotion to the fatherland." India, its ambassador to Egypt declared, appreciated Najib's statement, which indicated a friendly approach to India.[24] As far as the Anglo-Egyptian dispute over the abrogation of the 1936 treaty and the future of Sudan were concerned, the ambassador said, the new Egyptian government could not suddenly reverse the policy of the previous Wafdist government regarding Sudan "without becoming very unpopular and even risking their existence as a government. In the delicate situation of today, they have to move warily." He recommended to his government that India should not do anything to embarrass the new Egyptian regime "when there is some likelihood of their proceeding on [the] right lines if left to themselves. I feel that any British attempt to utilize the present difficulty of Egypt to get some kind of a decision in their favor in regard to the Sudan, will not meet with success and might well aggravate the difficulty. We should therefore not be parties to it."[25] By September 1952, Nehru, like many other foreign politicians and observers, regarded Najib as Egypt's new leader. His main concern was to improve India's poor image as perceived by *al-Ikhwan al-Muslimun*, "the most important" organization in Egypt at that time. Nehru desired to do so because "General Najib is supposed to be a member of it."[26] Nehru asked his embassy in Cairo to send him an updated appraisal of the situation in Egypt and suggested that India should launch a propaganda campaign toward the Islamic countries aimed at presenting the positive dimensions of Hinduism. On 20 September, in a message to *Saut al-Sharq*, a magazine published by the Indian Embassy in Cairo, Nehru sent his greetings and good wishes to the people of Egypt and the other Arab-speaking countries. India, he stated, desired closer bonds with Egypt and the Arab world: "We have to understand each other and if we do so, we [will] see often that there is much in common between us."[27]

In mid-1953, Nehru called upon both Egypt and the UK to settle the dispute between them in a way that would avoid national humiliation for both countries. Nehru warned that, if allowed to fester, the dispute could give "rein to nationalist feelings which might spread over other parts of Africa with no good results." Some speeches made by Egyptian leaders were "offensive and irritating and scarcely conducive to a settlement," he noted. However, even if these leaders might be difficult to deal with, they were in power and their regime appeared to be popular. He therefore believed that Britain must find the appropriate avenues through which to open a constructive dialogue with them, because it seemed to him that "the points of dispute were few" and so small that it would be "extraordinary if they proved insoluble." He went further, expressing his own view about Najib's personality: "[I] had seldom come across a more pleasant and friendly sort of person than General Najib, who seemed to be the last person to make difficulties in negotiation."[28] Nehru would not like to see an agreement imposed upon Egypt by superior Western powers, "regardless of the consequences." If no positive steps were taken, he warned, "the situation might well grow worse."[29] The objective, he concluded, must be to further the prospect of a satisfactory settlement with Egypt. Such a settlement was particularly important "now that the international atmosphere had been much improved by the success of negotiations in Korea."[30]

Between 23 and 25 June 1953, Nehru made an official visit to Egypt as a guest of Egypt's military rulers. His image of Egypt's new regime was ambivalent. In a private letter to Lord Mountbatten (the last British Viceroy to India) from Cairo, he wrote that Egypt was ruled by the Revolutionary Command Council (RCC)—a ruling body composed of young army officers—which decided all social and political changes taking place in Egypt. On principle, Nehru declared, "I do not like this much. And yet, on the whole, I have been rather impressed by this Council. It consists mostly of young and earnest officers. Najib is a frank and likable person. Some of the other men, notably Colonel Nasser and Salah Salim, are probably the most important members of it. They create a favorable impression, but of course they are all very inexperienced." Nehru observed that decisions made by the RCC were popular and that the new government had the backing of a large number of Egyptians. He would not, however, predict "what the future will bring."[31]

Nehru's visit to Cairo had been useful, and he expressed satisfaction with its results.[32] His talks with Egypt's leaders covered, among other topics, the broad trends of international affairs and the great changes that had taken place as a result of the renaissance of Asia and the agitation in Africa. Nehru noted that "the old balances had been upset. Europe and America, however, though in a sense conscious of this fact, [are] unwilling to accept its consequences. Hence many of their difficulties."[33] One major theme had captured the attention of Egypt's new leaders in their conversations with him: what had happened in London during the Commonwealth Prime Ministers' Conference of early June 1953 concerning Egypt. Nehru told them that the British government was anxious to come to an agreement with Egypt, but Prime Minister Sir Winston Churchill argued that his country had already offered fair terms to Egypt, although the British were willing to resume negotiations.[34] Although reluctant to commit himself to interfering in this matter, Nehru stated that Egyptian sovereignty must be fully recognized, but "that strong language did not help and . . . [only raised barriers] to any calm consideration of the problem. They could remain quite firm in regard to the issues, but it would be helpful to put their case forward in moderate language."[35] Nehru modestly admitted that his talks in Cairo had created some impression on Egypt's new leaders. This, he said, became noticeable in their language in public, which tended to be somewhat more moderate than before. To support his claim, he referred to other diplomats in Egypt and foreign leaders who had come to the conclusion "that this must have been due to my presence there." Nehru also referred to a speech made by Salah Salim in early July that dealt with foreign affairs, and, according to Nehru, part of his analysis "appeared to me to be an echo of what I had said."[36] There was a good rapport between Nehru and Najib, and the two paid earnest compliments to each other. When Najib presented Nehru with album of photographs taken during Nehru's stay in Cairo, the inscription read: "To the great leader of the East, Mr. Jawaharlal Nehru, with true affection and great esteem of Egypt and Egyptians." On 11 July 1953, Nehru sent Najib some of his books in exchange and wrote to him: "I should very much like to have the criticism of a competent Egyptian authority on what I have written about Egypt [in my book *Glimpses of World History*].[37] Nehru also praised Ismail Kamal, the Egyptian Ambassador to India, for an address on India he gave in the Egyptian Foreign Office. "I am very grateful to you," Nehru wrote, "for your able advocacy of India before your own people."[38] Moreover, he asked K. M. Panikkar, India's Ambassador to Cairo, to convey his deep gratitude to Najib for his hospitality and for "the very friendly way in which he and his colleagues received me in Cairo. I have come back with the pleasantest of memories of my brief stay there."[39]

At a press conference in Cairo on 25 June 1953, Nehru reiterated his commitment to non-alliance with any power grouping, and ruled out the possibility of consolidating a third bloc. India's interest, he stressed, was to maintain friendly relations with all powers:

> That naturally flowed from our previous policies and from the fact that we think that we serve our own cause and the cause of the world best in that way. Now, some people have thought in the past of what they call a third bloc. I venture to say that that approach is not a right approach. I do not like the first bloc or the second bloc. Why should I like a third bloc? But I have suggested that a right approach to it is a third area which does not align itself for war . . . I think that it would be a good thing for the countries concerned, and for the world at large, for this third area, which I call [a] no-war area, to grow in extent. It will exercise a powerful force, a powerful influence, in favor of peace . . . Now, how to do it? I do not think this kind of thing should be done by what I call formal alliances and treaties. Because as soon as you talk of formality in this, you get back to that bloc idea. So it is really a question of informal friendly cooperation and understanding each other's viewpoints.[40]

Nehru dismissed the possibility of an armed Soviet invasion of the Middle East in peacetime. He did not share a common view with Britain, which maintained that it was of the utmost importance for it to continue keeping its troops in the Suez Canal Zone for the purpose of containing Soviet expansionist plans in the Middle East.[41]

Following the renewal on 30 July 1953 of Anglo-Egyptian discussions in Cairo—and after several weeks of talks about the Canal Zone—the two countries made significant progress, and it looked as though a solution to the dispute was only a matter of time. Nehru was pleased with this development and asked his representative in London to convey to Lord

Salisbury, the British acting Foreign Secretary, "in a friendly way our sense of satisfaction" at the progress so far made during the Cairo talks. He expressed his wish that a final accord would soon be achieved. Nehru's wish was not realized, however. By October 1953, the talks had become dead-locked. The British demand to allow their forces to return to the Canal Zone in the event of an attack on Turkey, Iran, or Pakistan, or any of the Arab states, was responsible for the stall in talks. The Egyptians also objected to the presence of 4,000 British technicians in the Canal Zone.[42] Nehru's reaction to this development demonstrated an increasing tendency toward Arab support. The proposal that the UK should reoccupy the Suez Canal Zone in the event of any future war, or whenever they chose to do so, "is something which I would never accept if I were an Egyptian. That means that Egypt must inevitably join a war, whatever its nature . . . in the long run Britain will suffer a good deal. The UK is loosing all the sympathy and goodwill which they got on the Indian settlement."[43]

By the end of 1953, India regarded Egypt as the foremost country in West Asia. Middle Eastern politics, Nehru stressed, were largely governed by what happened in Egypt: "Cairo is one of our most important centers . . . Egyptian newspapers go all over the Arab world."[44] India was developing an interest in Africa, but essentially looked toward western Asia. India's main approach to the Middle East was therefore through Egypt. Nehru appointed Panikkar Ambassador to Egypt because he was "one of our most senior and most experienced diplomats whose judgment we value". The other Indian heads of missions in the Middle East "should always keep in touch with him and even consult him when necessity arises."[45] Panikkar was India's foremost diplomat in West Asia. Besides his ambassadorial post in Cairo, he was also Minister to Syria, Lebanon, Jordan, and Libya. When Nehru informed Najib in late December 1953 that Panikkar would leave Cairo in the near future because he was appointing him to be "a member of a very important commission," he added that India attached "the greatest importance to this post and we shall, therefore, try to choose one of our ablest men in the Foreign Service for it."[46]

Another Middle Eastern issue that attracted Nehru's attention was the idea of Arab unity, which involved various schemes and was entertained by several Arab politicians, and was supported by Britain and other Western powers. Nehru held the view that India should not interfere or take any stand on the issue of Arab unity which he believed was solely and entirely an internal Arab affair. When, in late 1953, J. A. Thivy, Commissioner for the Government of India in Mauritius, recommended that Syria might include Lebanon as well as Jordan in the future, Nehru resolutely rejected the idea, considering it to be "a dangerous assumption." India was not working for a Greater Syria, rebuked Nehru, and it would be "completely improper for any representative of ours [India] to play the game, which the Great Powers have been playing for a long time past."[47] As far as India was concerned, "Syria, Lebanon and Jordan remain as they are, separate countries and we recognize the independence and individuality of each."[48]

When Britain and Egypt eventually settled their dispute, with the Anglo-Egyptian agreement for the withdrawal of British troops of July 1954, Nehru formally welcomed it. It was obvious, however, that he was not pleased with Nasser's consent to allow the re-entry of British troops into Egypt in the event of a future war. Nehru sent a laconic message to Nasser on 29 July 1954 expressing his wishes on the arrival at an agreement "satisfactory to both the parties concerned . . . it is welcome as giving satisfaction to the national aspirations of Egypt . . ."[49] Nehru was disappointed with the removal from power of Najib, whom he held in high esteem, and with whom he had developed close rapport. News of Nasser's ascendance was cautiously received, since, at the time, Nehru's opinion of Nasser and his military peers was not high: "We attach importance to Egypt from many points of view, but Egypt has to be seen in proper perspective. I read a pamphlet the other day by Nasser [*The Philosophy of the Revolution*] . . . I was rather surprised to read it, because it showed a great deal of earnestness, but also a great deal of immaturity."[50] Several months later, Nehru regarded "Egyptians or indeed Arab politics" to be "extraordinarily immature and wrapped up in their petty problems with little understanding of what is going on in the world." As for Nasser, Nehru explained, "[he] is a likable person"; however, again referring to *The Philosophy of the Revolution*, Nehru doubted Nasser's intellectual horizons: "When I read this book of his I felt disappointed, that is, in regard to his intellectual caliber."[51]

Moreover Nehru was not happy with Nasser's contradictory statements with regard to his foreign policy. On the one hand, Nasser declared that it was his intention to nurture close relations with the US and to persecute domestic communism, while on the other, he reiterated his commitment to the policy of positive neutralism and severely attacked the Western powers for their anti-Arab policies. At this historical juncture, Nehru suspected Nasser of opportunistic tendencies. In reference to Ali Yavar Jung's report of his talk with Nasser in which the latter was warned of the dangers involved in receiving military and economic aid from the US Nehru declared: "there can be no military aid without military alignment, whatever one may say about it. Even economic aid, unless very carefully handled, brings some risks." Egypt should consider an example from India, which had taken

a fairly independent attitude toward the US in matters of policy. We have even gone so far as to supply so-called prohibited articles to China, much to the indignation of the US. How have we managed to do so without leading the US to stop their economic aid? For the simple reason that we were perfectly prepared not to have that aid . . . The American position was weak because, in spite of their irritation with us, they attach too much importance to India and did not wish to worsen our relations . . . they often say that, if India is lost, Asia is lost.[52]

Continuing to criticize Egypt's policy toward the US, Nehru reasoned that Egypt's weak position was obvious when "Nasser says that he is afraid to recognize China because of American reactions. That is how policy is influenced by other countries . . ."[53] Moreover, since the conclusion of the Turco-Pakistani military pact in April 1954, Nehru had found Egypt's attitude toward defense plans of the Western powers for the Middle East to be "by no means clear." The Egyptians judged these matters from "some very limited point of view without taking into consideration the larger aspects"—there was no doubt that, "if Egypt joins this MEDO arrangement, it will be unfortunate."[54]

Nehru's distrust of the inter-bloc orientations of Nasser and the Arabs found its expression in his refusal to participate in the Jerusalem Conference—an Islamic Congress. Nasser suggested that India should be represented "in a semi-official way," because he felt that the participation of Indian Muslims would "help [in] keeping the Islamic congress above possible exploitation by Pakistan and also beyond politics as such."[55] Nehru politely declined this offer, saying: "I confess, I do not see how this can be done and what good it will do."[56] Nehru responded in similar way to the Lebanese Foreign Minister's suggestion that India should participate in the Jerusalem Conference; the Minister went even further in his attempt to persuade India: "if India were willing, [I] would insist on changing the name from Islamic to Arab-Asian conference."[57] Although Ali Yavar Jung, India's Ambassador to Cairo, recommended that India should reply positively to the Arab invitation and, by doing so, "cut out the possibilities of Pakistan seeking leadership in the region and using the conference for anti-Indian purposes,"[58] Nehru rejected his advice. "Normally, this would be difficult for us, as I do not quite see where we come into the picture," Nehru responded. "If Egypt or the Arab League join MEDO, this would become even more difficult. Major developments are taking place in the world and we have to judge these smaller matters in their light."[59]

The Road to the Bandung Conference, 1954–1955

The Colombo Conference, which took place in Ceylon from 28 April to 2 May 1954, was another link in a chain of conferences of Asian countries that paved the way to the Bandung Conference about a year later. The Colombo Conference, which was attended by the leaders of Ceylon, India, Indonesia, Burma, and Pakistan, was preceded by intensive international pressure from India and many Asian and Arab states demanding political negotiation to bring about the termination of the military struggle in Korea.[60] In line with India's pressure, the Colombo Conference devoted most of its discussions to Indochina, the admission of Communist China to the UN, the Palestine problem (to demonstrate goodwill toward the Arabs), and the need to hold a conference of Afro-Asian nations. At the same time, a hastened process of rapprochement between India and China occured, which culminated on 29 April 1954 (a day after the opening of the Colombo Conference) with the signing of an Indian–Chinese trade treaty on Tibet. The agreement was based on five principles that became the foundation of India's foreign policy and were later used as the basis for the convening of the Bandung Conference. These principles, which were called *Panchsheel*, were:[61]

1. mutual respect for each other's territorial integrity and sovereignty;
2. mutual non-aggression;
3. mutual non-interference in each other's affairs;
4. equality and mutual benefit;
5. peaceful coexistence.

Kimche argued that India's new orientation toward China was derived from its own opposition to the efforts made by the Western powers "to set up a military alliance [SEATO], which, in Indian eyes, was directed overtly against China."[62] In Nehru's view, China and India "would have to play important roles in Asia and the world, and it was necessary that they should understand and cooperate with each other. Their contacts should be friendly because of the five principles to which both had agreed."[63] He therefore took pains to persuade the other four participant Asian states in Colombo to open the Asian gates to China. At a later occasion, in a speech in Lok Sabha on 17 September, Nehru elucidated that the conception of *Panchsheel* meant that there might be different ways of progress, possibly different outlooks.[64]

On 28 December 1954, the five Asian states that had participated in the Colombo Conference held a preparatory meeting to the forthcoming Afro-Asian Conference in Bogor, Indonesia. In his opening address, Nehru expressed satisfaction in the growing influence of Asia "in the direction of peace." The forthcoming conference, he stated, "should help to place Asia and Africa in proper perspective in the world because the old perspectives no longer apply."[65]

An *Aide Memoire* prepared by the Political Committee and the Council of the Arab League and dated 20 December 1954 outlined the preliminary Arab approach to the forthcoming Afro-Asian conference. The document was sent to Nehru on 27 December, the eve of the Bogor Conference.[66] The *Aide Memoire* declared that the representatives of the Arab states, as members of the Arab League, had agreed on the necessity of participating in the forthcoming conference "in order to search for solutions to the problems facing them." The coming conference would offer "an excellent opportunity to strengthen the ties which bind the states of the Afro-Asian bloc under the emblem of their solidarity in the pursuit of common interests and of their attachment to the principles of right and justice in the conduct of mutual relations and their relations with the outside world." Participation of member states of the Arab League would contribute to the discovery of "happy solutions" to the problems to be discussed. The Arab League expressed its belief that the participant states in the conference would avail themselves of the "opportunity to affirm their attitude toward certain questions on which they have set their heart, such as Palestine, North Africa, the struggle against colonialism, and racial discrimination, not to mention other important international questions such as armament, the atomic bomb, and so on."[67]

The Arab League, however, conditioned its participation in the coming conference upon the non-participation of Israel:

> As it is understood that the congress will be of a regional character and the [Arab] League has so far followed the line of not participating in any regional conference with Israel, the Arab States are confident that such an eventuality will not arise and that under no circumstances will Israel be called to take part in the work of the congress.[68]

The question of Israel's participation in the conference was discussed in Bogor and was a subject of disagreement between the participants. It was U Nu, the Prime Minister of Burma, who insisted at the beginning of the conference on the inclusion of Israel among the invitees. Despite his eagerness to have Israel attend, however, he ultimately agreed not to press the point, because it was clear that "Israel's inclusion might result in non-cooperation by the Arab countries." Other participants—mainly the Pakistani Prime Minister—argued that the result of such a development, would be that "the Asian-African Conference would cease to have a representative character in a real sense."[69]

Nehru's analysis of this complex issue demonstrates the awkward dilemma that the five Asian leaders were facing. He held the view that "legally Israel should be invited, but if inviting Israel would mean non-participation by a large number of countries, it would be advisable to leave her out."[70] In a letter to Moshe Sharett, Israel's Prime Minister, Nehru explained the situation: "At the Colombo Conference, the subject of Israel was brought up by the Prime Minister of Pakistan with a view to condemning Israel lock stock and barrel. Some of us were not agreeable and since then much has been said in Pakistan about India not supporting Pakistan in this matter at Colombo."[71] Nehru continued with an analysis of the current state of affairs in India–Israel relations:

I had a talk with U Nu . . . I told him that India recognized Israel about two years ago but that we had not exchanged diplomatic representation. There was no basic objection to this; indeed, normally this follows recognition. But we had felt that we might not to be able to serve the cause we have at heart if at this juncture we exchanged diplomatic representation. I am convinced that the problems of Israel and the Arab countries can only be solved by some settlement between them. It is possible that at an appropriate moment, we might be of some service in this matter. But, unfortunately, this whole question is wrapped up in passion and prejudice and it is no easy matter to find a way out. If we established diplomatic relations with Israel at the present juncture, this would not facilitate our task.[72]

Although Nehru wanted the inclusion of Israel in the Colombo Conference—with a view to establishing diplomatic relations—geopolitical considerations prevented him from doing so: Muslim Pakistan was his northern neighbor, and then there were the Arab countries from West Asia. Eventually, the leaders who objected to Israel's participation imposed their view. In order to win Arab support at the expense of India, the Pakistani newspapers reported unfounded "information" that India insisted on the inclusion of Israel among the invitees. The existing tension between India and Pakistan found its expression in disagreement on major issues. India suggested that, in the final communiqué, reference be made in some form or other to the five principles (*Panchsheel*) earlier agreed upon with China and Yugoslavia. Pakistan resisted the suggestion on the grounds that "these principles were part of the UN Charter, and if they are to be included, reference to the collective security measures and other provisions of the UN Charter should also come in."[73] The Indian Ministry of External Affairs concluded that Pakistan did so because it was not "very happy at India's lead in creating [an area of peace] in the world on the basis of the *Panchsheel*." Furthermore, Pakistan felt that "her agreement with America and her participation in the SEATO is somehow inconsistent with these principles."[74]

Many of the articles published in the Indian press were critical of Nehru's pro-Arab stand and the decision at the Bogor Conference to exclude Israel. On 17 April 1955, a day before the opening of the Bandung Conference, the *Bharat Jyoti* declared that Israel was the only Asian country that had genuine cause "to fear aggression and needs a co-existing world to achieve peaceful progress."[75] Israel was the "only oasis of progress in the forbidding desert of reaction in the Middle East." As for the Arabs, the paper harshly censured the nature of the existing Arab regimes:

Feudal regimes in Saudi Arabia, Jordan and Iraq and military dictatorships in Egypt and Syria will be represented in Bandung and can be expected to add their voice to the plea for co-existence. But the Arab countries refuse to co-exist with Israel and sit at the conference table with it. Indeed, they made it a condition of attending the conference that Israel is kept out. So, in the name of co-existence, the sponsoring Colombo powers black-balled a country which has already achieved, despite the most adverse and trying conditions, a society which Prime Minister Nehru only hopes he will be able to establish in India ten years hence . . . [Nehru] prefers the friendship of Colonel Nasser to that of Mr. Moshe Sharett, the Prime Minister of one of the most progressive democracies in Africa, Asia or indeed any other part of the globe.[76]

The press in Burma expressed similar views. On 15 April 1955, the Burmese newspaper *The Nation* suggested that the question of Israeli participation should not be raised in Bandung. Israel should be a member of any group that claimed to represent all independent countries of Asia and Africa. "The studied insult of the Arab countries in prevailing upon the Colombo Powers to omit Israel is a blot on the escutcheon of the new organization,"[77] *The Nation* concluded.

The joint communiqué issued on 29 December showed that India and Pakistan had to make a compromise over the inclusion of the *Panchsheel* principles. The purposes of the next Asian-African conference would be:[78]

1. to promote goodwill and cooperation among the nations of Asia and Africa, to explore and advance their mutual as well as common interests, and to establish and further friendliness and neighborly relations;

2. to consider social, economic, and cultural problems and relations of the countries represented;

3. to consider problems of special interest to Asian and African peoples, e.g., problems affecting national sovereignty, and of racism and colonialism;

4. to review the position of Asia and Africa and their peoples in the world of today and the contribution they can make to the promotion of world peace and cooperation.

It was agreed by the five Prime Ministers that the conference would be held under their joint sponsorship in the last week of April 1955 in Indonesia. They decided to invite the following countries: From Asia— Afghanistan, Cambodia, Communist China, Iran, Japan, Laos, Nepal, Philippines, Thailand, Turkey, North Vietnam, South Vietnam, and the Asian-Arab countries of Iraq, Jordan, Lebanon, Saudi Arabia, Syria, and Yemen; and from Africa—the Central African Federation (the only one to decline the invitation), Ethiopia, the Gold Coast, Liberia, and the North African Arab countries of Egypt, Sudan, and Libya.

The communiqué gave prominence to the fact that the five leaders "did not desire . . . that the participating countries should build themselves into a regional bloc." They expressed delight at the results of the Geneva Conference on Indo-China and the cessation of hostilities. They also expressed their concern "in respect of the destructive potential of nuclear and thermo-nuclear explosions for experimental purposes which threaten . . . the world," and called for a halt to nuclear experiments.[79]

Soon after the conclusion of the Bogor Conference, the US launched an aggressive campaign aimed at persuading as many countries as possible to decline their invitations to the Bandung conference. Because the Arab countries were to be widely represented, pressure was put on Egypt, the biggest and most influential Arab state, not to participate. The US hoped that, if Egypt could be persuaded to stay away, most of the other Arab states might be expected to do likewise. The Americans were upset that the People's Republic of China was among the invitees at the expense of the Nationalist Chinese Government of Formosa.[80] The US argued that, "to sit down at the conference table with the People's Republic of China to the exclusion of Nationalist China will amount to recognition of the former."[81] Ali Yavar Jung, the Indian Ambassador to Cairo, ruled out any connection between participation in the conference and automatic recognition of Communist China. Although Arab countries did not recognize Communist China, he maintained, "we have always felt that they are not obsessed with the same hostility to that government as the United States." The Arab countries, he believed, "would have no objection to participation at the conference on the ground[s] of the presence of the People's Government of China."[82] As for Egypt, Ali Jung said that, despite American pressure, it had made no objection to the presence of Communist China in the conference. Nasser had told Jung that "he would be interested to meet Chou En-Lai, and I know for certain that he is very anxious to begin by opening trade relations with China."[83]

The Lebanese newspaper *al-Anba'* wrote that the invitations extended to Arab states by the Colombo Powers to participate in the coming Afro-Asian conference,

> fell as a bomb in the White House, which imagined Arab and Asian states listening to the arguments and viewpoints of Red China. After this, the White House decided to launch a campaign preventing Arab states from attending the conference. This is being undertaken by US ambassadors in Arab capitals and signs of interference has appeared in Syrian circles.[84]

The popular daily paper *al-Jarida* wrote that the US feared that coming into contact with Communist China at the conference would lead the Arab states to recognize the communist state and support its aspirations for a seat in the United Nations.[85] The pro-communist paper *al-Hadaf* went even further, stating that the "American Embassy [has received] instructions to stop Lebanon from participating in the Asiatic conference."[86] The neutralist Kamal Jumblatt, the leader of the Lebanese Progressive Socialist Party, declared in an interview that, for Lebanon to join either one of the international camps would be ruinous. Only by adopting a policy of neutralism could Lebanon and the Arabs gain respect from both camps. The establishment of a neutralist Afro-Asiatic bloc was one of the major elements in preventing a third world war, because neither the East nor the West could begin a war when one-third of the world's population stood against it. In Jumblatt's view, Communist China should be represented in the Asio-African conference, and should be admitted to the UN, since it was impossible to ignore such a large and populous country.[87]

The Egyptian government and press had solidly supported the Bogor joint communiqué.[88] According to Jung, the coming conference had attracted a great deal of attention in Egypt. On 8 January he met with 'Abd al-Khaliq Hassunah, the Secretary-General of the Arab League. Hassunah drew his attention to two matters arising out of the Bogor joint communiqué: First, the absence of any mention of the Secretary-General of the Arab League from the list of invitees; and second, the absence of representation of the movements for freedom in North Africa. In Hassunah's view, if these movements had even been asked to send observers, that would have been a source of further encouragement to them in their struggles for independence. The Indian Ambassador explained that the list of invitees was composed of states, not persons or institutions. He could not see any reason, however, that would prevent Hassunah's participation.[89] The answer to the second matter, explained Jung, was based on similar reasons: movements for freedom in North Africa were not invited because they did not represent independent states or states that were on the way to full independence. "That did not mean lack of sympathy for the movements, which had been specifically mentioned in one of the resolutions passed at Bogor," he explained, but "it looked as though there would be no place for observers as such in the structure contemplated for the conference."[90]

At the same time, the Egyptian Minister of Foreign Affairs Mahmud Fawzi suggested to Jung the idea that "it might perhaps be better to hold informal consultations beforehand about the subjects so as to avoid getting into bickerings at the preliminary stages of the conference itself." Jung replied that five Colombo powers had already created the machinery to launch an agenda for the conference, and that each country would also be permitted to suggest subjects of its own. He informed his superiors in New Delhi of Fawzi's suggestion, however, and asked to be alerted to any developments so that he could keep the Egyptians informed.[91] In reply to Jung's letter, the Indian Ministry of External Affairs endorsed Jung's view, but added that the intention of the five sponsoring countries was to avoid contentious issues or disputes between two or more countries participating at the conference. The emphasis was to be on the "larger issues that unite the participating countries, rather than [on] particular and contentious problems dividing two or more countries." The Indian Ministry of External Affairs suggested that, if the Egyptian government had any ideas in the fields of economic, cultural, and political cooperation among the countries participating at the conference and wanted to exchange such ideas, India would welcome such dialogue. Jung was asked by his superiors to "keep us informed of the way in which the Egyptian government's mind is working in regard to the Afro-Asian conference."[92] The Indian Ministry of External Affairs expressed its regret that the US and the Western powers had adopted a "mocking attitude" toward the Bandung conference. The Colombo powers, it emphasized, "have no desire at all to set up any rival organization to the United Nations or to the SEATO, or to set up a third bloc, or in any way to work against any of the existing power blocs."[93]

Early to mid-February saw the initial stages of the consolidation of the new international axis—Belgrade–Cairo–New Delhi—which later evolved into an international camp of the non-aligned countries, while Tito, Nasser, and Nehru were to become its leaders. Muhammad Hasanain Haikal, Nasser's confidant and chief speaker, said that the three leaders complemented each other: "Nasser was the man of convictions and actions, Tito the man of calculations and balances, and Nehru the man of intellectual articulation and hesitation . . . they behaved like the Musketeers: 'all for one and one for all'." Haikal maintained that they were the prophets and statesmen of the concept of non-alignment—a doctrine which was highly important to the peace and development of the world:

> Sandwiched between the super powers of the Soviet Union and the United States and their certain—even if accidental—victims in a nuclear war, Nasser, Tito and Nehru did not try to form a third bloc but strove to remain independent, hoping to settle international problems on their merits without regard to the policies of the cold war powers. In this way they felt that they could bring pressure to bear on both Russia and America without bias, using the United Nations and the international rule of law as their weapons.[94]

On 5 February, Tito held a seven-hour meeting with Nasser and some of his colleagues on the Yugoslav cruiser *Galeb* during its passage through the Suez Canal. Tito had just visited Nehru in India and was on his way back to Yugoslavia. Upon Nehru's advice, he stopped in the Suez Canal to meet with Nasser. In the course of their conversation, Tito advised Nasser not to involve himself in military alliances with the West. He presented Nasser with Yugoslavia's policy toward the inter-bloc conflict. At the conclusion of their meeting, they issued a joint communiqué stating that the talks were marked "by an atmosphere of cordiality and mutual understanding" that reflected the friendly relations between the two countries.

The meeting had been an opportunity to exchange views on international problems and to discuss "questions of a more direct interest" to both parties. Although relations between them were developing in a promising manner, the two leaders felt that "increasing efforts should be made to take advantage of all existing possibilities for a further and more favorable development of these relations."[95] Soon after, Jung, the Indian Ambassador to Cairo, called on Tito on board the *Galeb* at Port Said. Tito informed Jung that he had had honest talks with Nasser, and he expressed his conviction that "Egypt did not intend to get involved in power entanglements." Tito also praised India for the progress it had made since gaining independence. Jung noted in his report to Delhi that Wing Commander 'Ali Sabri, the Egyptian Director of Political Affairs who had been present at the Nasser-Tito meeting, told him that Tito had spoken "in terms of the highest praise of India's foreign policy."[96]

By mid-February Jung had reported to his superiors that Egypt admired India's independent stand in international affairs, and would like to play the role in the Middle East that India had played in Southeast Asia. Moreover, there was "a particular desire at the present stage, to break Egypt's isolation by drawing closer to India and to gain India's moral support in Egypt's fight against military pacts involving power entanglements."[97]

On 15 February, in the shadows of the conclusion of the Turco-Iraqi military pact and the preparations for the Bandung Conference, Nehru began a three-day visit to Egypt, during which a variety of issues related to world affairs were discussed. At the conclusion of the visit, Jung noted that Nehru commanded "the respect, admiration and affection of the Egyptian Prime Minister and his colleagues," and that, "in many spheres of activity," the visit foreshadowed far closer cooperation than ever before between India and Egypt.[98] Haikal wrote of the meeting: "I believe that before they met, Nehru had a limited interest in Nasser—a strategic interest—because this was the time to talk about a pact encompassing the whole of the Islamic world, and such a pact would have given Nehru's enemy, Pakistan, a great depth of power throughout West Asia, and it would have put India in a very difficult position."[99]

Nasser fought against such a pact, instead arguing for an Arab pact which, under no circumstances, should be linked to one of the great powers. Nasser's approach suited Nehru perfectly in light of his dispute with Pakistan. Haikal's recollection of the Nehru-Nasser three-day dialogue was that it had been one of harmony and mutual understanding. The visit opened an era of close friendship and alliance between the two leaders: "Nasser was big and strong, a man of action. Nehru was slight and fragile, a man of thought." According to Haikal, Nehru told Nasser, "the more we talk the more I discover we have the same thoughts."[100]

The effect of Nehru's visit electrified the Middle Eastern scene, "with the exception of Baghdad, where press statements were laconic." The joint communiqué and the press statements, added Jung, were given the widest publicity and were "the subject of talks in different circles for a number of days." Sabri al-'Asali, the Syrian Prime Minister, commented on Nehru's visit, emphasizing existing common features between non-aligned African-Asian countries, and that the "future of free Arab countries must be viewed increasingly in terms of their economic and social development."[101]

A US report based on a reliable Egyptian source adds an important dimension to Nehru's visit. In contrast to the prevailing opinion that the two leaders had reached a higher level of understanding on various international issues and that Nasser embraced Nehru's concept of neutralism, the US report revealed that Nehru did not encourage Nasser to follow his policy of neutralism. Instead, he expressed his opinion that Egypt's most pressing problem was domestic and that Nasser would be wise to devote his attention and energy to internal issues. Referring to information given them by officials from the Indian Embassy, US diplomats in Cairo explained Nehru's move:

> The Indians have not considered as a point in India's favor the pronounced proclivities for neutralism that Egyptians [have] expressed during periods when their national feelings run high. The Indians doubt the sincerity of Egypt's periodic neutralistic announcements. They believe that so long as there is a possibility of Egypt ultimately entering Western alliances, India cannot accept at their face value the recent statements of Egyptians favorable to neutralism, because if the Egyptians were not sincere, their "temporary neutralism" would only serve to discredit the neutralist concept. The attitude of the Indians is that they don't want the "coinage" debased.[102]

The US diplomats assumed that Egypt's declarations in favor of neutralism were an emotional reaction to the Turco-Iraqi Pact, rather than a long-term policy shift. India, certainly, could not regard it as a permanent policy as long as there was still an existing possibility that Egypt might join the Western military alliances.[103]

The following months, however, showed that Egypt's opposition to such military alliances was firm. Along with Syria, Egypt became the spearhead of neutralism in the Middle East. In line with the US report, there were significant differences in the essence of neutralism as perceived by Nehru and Nasser. The former adhered to ideological/doctrinaire neutralism emphasizing his total opposition to the Cold War—its methods, stratagems, and general climate; it viewed the rivalry between the two power blocs as a constant threat to world peace, and therefore maintained that the Cold War must be neutralized and an "area of peace" must separate the two rival blocs. Nehru believed that the Afro-Asian leaders had to play a major role in international affairs in order to bring about a *détente* in the Cold War. Nasser became the standard-bearer of positive neutralism—a utilitarian doctrine based on the principle of manipulating the Cold War in order to advance the interests of the neutralist state by gaining aid and benefits from the two blocs. Nasser believed that positive neutralism would be more advantageous than being allies of one bloc alone.

On 6 April 1955, India and Egypt signed a treaty of friendship at the Ministry of Foreign Affairs in Cairo. According to the terms of the treaty, the governments of the two countries announced a shared identity of views and objectives on certain fundamental national and international issues. They agreed to work for the preservation of peace, promote bilateral cultural relations, and cooperate in agricultural and industrial development. The Egyptian press gave wide publicity to the event, suggesting that it was appropriate that the treaty should be signed on the eve of Nasser's departure for India en route to attend the Bandung Conference. The *New York Times* also noted the significance of both the treaty and the timing of the signing ceremony.[104]

In January 1955, the Indian Ministry of External Affairs asked Jung to prepare a report on the political situation in the Middle East, with special reference to relations between the surveyed countries and the great powers. The completed report, which was submitted by early 1955, described the Middle East as an "area [that] bears many signs of instability," with the exception of Turkey and Afghanistan.[105] There was little doubt, the report stressed, that "today the area is under predominantly American influence and, whether willingly or acquiescently, the British play only second fiddle." Eventually the British reluctantly accepted the thesis first articulated by John Foster Dulles in mid-1953 that the Middle East Defense Organization (MEDO), as proposed in 1951, was not an immediate possibility. Dulles proposed instead the implementation of a "linear" defense, along the southern border of the USSR by joining the "northern tier" of nations. This change, the report suggested, was possibly a result of the recent insistence of Egypt on a purely Arab defense organization—a matter, which hastened "the conversion for fear that it might dish the prospects of an eventual MEDO." Initial British opposition to the Turco-Pakistani Pact of April 1954, the report maintained, was derived from dual considerations: the innovation of a bilateral American tie with a Commonwealth nation (Pakistan) and the shifting of the defense focus from the Suez Base to the "northern tier." Once the new thesis began to be effected by the US, "it reduced the importance of the [Suez] base and its evacuation became [only] a question of time." The US strategic thinking "placed more value on Ankara and Peshawar than on Suez: thousand-mile radii drawn from those two bases reach Budapest, Stalingrad, Baku, Tashkent . . . while a similar radius from Suez hardly touches even the fringes of Soviet territory. It is into this pattern of thinking that the British seem now to have fitted themselves . . . "[106]

The report argued that US influence was predominate in Iran, Iraq, Turkey, Lebanon, and Saudi Arabia, while in Libya the US shared influence with the British, "the prize which the weak can give to the strong." Only two Arab countries—Egypt and Syria—remained comparatively independent, "but Syria is divided by factions and there is a considerable body of opinion in favor of merger or federation with Iraq. In Egypt, Colonel Nasser is sitting in an opposition and he has not had Peron's time to establish himself." The report noted that in recent years (1953–5), Soviet pronouncements in the UN Security Council on frontier incidents between Israel and Jordan "evoked a resolution of thanks from the Jordanian Parliament and frightened and annoyed both the Americans and the British." There was also a marked improvement in the trade relations between countries in the area as a whole and with communist countries. Egypt was even trying to establish relations with Communist China.[107]

The report concluded by stating that India should not be discouraged or confused by "the picture of disunity, of political differences, instability and dependence, and of economic and social under-development of the countries dealt with in this survey." Rather, India should consolidate a positive approach toward countries constituting this part of the world because:

> They, like many others, are subject to certain pressures, which they are less able to withstand either due to their geographical location or lack of national leadership or their present state of development. The importance of the area and of its policies cannot be under-estimated from the Indian point of view, and it would be a mistake to think of it only in the context of the votes that it commands in the United Nations. It may be that the taking [up] of arms by Pakistan is of more direct consequence to us in India than the chain of "linear" defense with Turkey, but the one goes with the other as long as the inspiration and the weapons are the same. SEATO, despite its dangers and its extra-territorial ramifications, can be treated with less discomfiture because it is likely to remain still-born on account of the absence in it of Burma, India and Indonesia: our interests of peace go beyond our frontiers and, in the Middle East, that region's version of SEATO, now about to be consummated, requires the counter-parts of Burma, India and Indonesia to counteract the present efforts to draw the region into the area of cold or hot combat. Indian diplomacy has nothing to offer to this area except the sincerity of Indian conviction, India's truly impartial attitude and her support, whatever the stakes, for causes which, however lost they may appear, will not be compromised on the alter of international expediency . . . It is of consequence that this area should be an area of peace . . . [108]

A month before the opening of the conference, it became apparent that there would be no common Arab front on issues involving the Western position in Asia. The signing of the Turco-Iraqi Defense Pact in February 1955 and counter-measures taken by Egypt, Syria, and Saudi Arabia had deepened the traditional rivalry between Iraq and Egypt—two countries vying for hegemony in the Arab world. Arab states, suggested a US intelligence report, were likely "to move increasingly in the direction dictated by their own national interest." Egypt would aim at "stealing the limelight from Iraq and thereby regaining some of the prestige it lost both at home and abroad" following its failure to prevent the conclusion of the Turco-Iraqi Pact.[109] According to the report, the Israeli attack on Gaza on 28 February 1955 was one of the main reasons Nasser attended the Bandung conference. His failure to take strong counteraction had caused a certain amount of unrest within the Egyptian army, "with the result that the regime seems inclined to assume a position more independent of the West."[110] The Israeli raid also enhanced Nasser's determination "to air the Arab case on Palestine at Bandung and make a strong bid for support from the members of the conference."[111] A few days before the conference convened, there were enough indications to support the assumption that Nasser, like Nehru, intended to pursue an independent line on international affairs at the proceedings.[112] In a speech he delivered to Egyptian army officers on 28 March, Nasser made it clear that Egypt would adopt policies that would serve Egypt's interests first. He presented the guiding principles of Egypt's foreign policy: Egypt was for self-determination, against imperialism and foreign domination, and for the freedom of all peoples.[113]

In Syria and Lebanon there was marked activity by members of the SCP and the SPP, indicating that the communists and their fronts in the Arab areas would seek to launch an appeal—which was to be forwarded to the Arab parliaments and the Afro-Asian conference—to outlaw atomic and hydrogen bombs. The American intelligence report assumed that the communist leader Khalid Bakdash, who was then a member of the Syrian Parliamentary Foreign Affairs Committee, could be expected to lead this appeal.[114]

The Afro-Asian Conference: The Arab Perspective

The leaders of the five sponsoring countries and those of 24 of the 25 invited countries (the Central African Federation had declined the invitation) met in Bandung, Indonesia, for seven days (18–24 April) to discuss problems of common interest to the countries of Asia and Africa. The Afro-Asian conference, called the Bandung Conference, dealt with ways and means by which the peoples of Asia and Africa could achieve fuller economic, cultural, and political cooperation.[115] There was no balance between the representation of countries from both continents: there were more Asian states (24 of 29 states[116]), which also played a far stronger role than the few African states. After the first two days of discussions, the conference dissolved itself into three committees: economic, cultural, and political. The political committee consisted of the heads of all delegations, and was the main forum. The conference succeeded in demonstrating that there was a broad Asian-African consensus on general issues; all participant countries had a shared memory of colonial and semi-colonial domination. Although discussions in the committees disclosed fundamental differences of views on some international issues, the conference itself achieved a notable success, as concluded by the Indian delegation, "by voicing unanimous opinion of Asia and Africa on a wide range of subjects."[117] A US intelligence report maintained that the consensus reached by the participating countries was: "strong enough to discourage communists, neutralists and anti-communists from splitting it apart . . . Everyone at Bandung avoided a discussion of the mainsprings and direction of Asia['s] and Africa's fundamental social transformation now in process. In any event, they felt they shared enough: similar past experiences with Western imperialism; similar problems of cultural change and social dislocation; similar aspiration for status and prosperity."[118]

The conference succeeded in resolving the contentious issue of whether to accept Nehru–Chou's five principles (*Panchsheel*), which were related to peaceful co-existence and cooperation. The *Panchsheel* were enlarged and transformed into ten, and the term "peaceful co-existence" was changed upon Chou En-Lai's suggestion to "living together in peace" and was based on the following principles:[119]

1. Respect for the fundamental human rights and for the purposes and principles of the Charter of the UN;
2. Respect for the sovereignty and territorial integrity of all nations;
3. Recognition of the equality of all races and of the equality of all nations, large and small;
4. Abstention from intervention or interference in the internal affairs of any other country;
5. Respect for the rights of each nation to defend itself singly or collectively in conformity with the charter of the UN;
6. Abstention from the use of arrangements of collective defense to serve the particular interests of any of the big powers; and abstention by any country from exerting pressure on other countries;
7. Refraining from acts or threats of aggression of the use of force against the territorial integrity or political independence of any country;
8. Settlement of all international disputes by peaceful means such as

negotiation, conciliation, arbitration, or judicial settlement, as well
as other peaceful means of the parties' own choice in conformity
with the Charter of the UN;
9. Promotion of mutual interest and cooperation;
10. Respect for justice and international obligations.

Many of the ten principles could easily be fitted in with Nehru's doctri-
naire/ideological neutralism. Clause 6 was a victory for neutralist countries
that were against regional military alliances under Western auspices
(SEATO, the Baghdad Pact, etc.). Egypt, which was ideologically closer to
India and led the struggle against military alliances in the Middle East,
would be the one to initiate the insertion of clause 6 into the final communiqué.[120] Nasser also welcomed the approval of the ten principles by the
participant states.[121]

Despite the fact that the neutralists—India, Burma, Indonesia, Egypt,
Syria, etc.—appeared to emerge victorious at the conclusion of the conference, a close reading of the conference deliberations shows that they did
not, at any stage of the conference, put forward plans to form a new international bloc. As an American report put it, they did not intend "to secure
an endorsement of neutralism," though they wanted to ensure that no big
power gained major influence in Asia, which, in their view, could threaten
Asian independence. "Their aim was broader—to show that negotiations
and agreement are possible regardless of ideological differences and that
Asian and African states can set the world a moral and practical example
along this road. Their point was not so much to settle Cold War issues as
[it was] to create an atmosphere in which peaceful settlement would become
easier."[122]

Although not a neutralist, Chou En-Lai, the Indian delegation reported,
made an excellent impression on all delegations by "his sincerity and
moderation." He did not put forward controversial issues, and made it
clear that China's objective was "to enlarge areas of agreement among
participating countries rather than use the conference for bringing up issues
which would divide Asian-African countries." It was mainly due to his
patience, tact, and earnestness, the delegation said, that "unanimity could
be achieved on the resolution on colonialism and dependent peoples."
Chou En-Lai was described as being friendly with all participating delegations, "particularly those from the Middle East."[123]

As for the pro-Western nations—Iraq, Pakistan, Turkey, Iran, and
others—who composed about one-third of the participating states, they did
not let their inferiority in numbers to stop them from defending their alignment with the Western powers in defensive military pacts; they also
attacked and condemned communist colonialism. They attempted to link
disarmament with the prohibition of nuclear and thermonuclear weapons

in their interpretation of colonialism in order to include the East European countries within the concept of what they called new colonialism.[124] The inclusion in the final communiqué of the clause declaring that "colonialism in all its manifestations is an evil and should speedily be brought to and end," implied that, not only Western, but also Soviet colonialism, was part of the equation too.

Middle Eastern countries (12 of 29 states) constituted the largest single group at the conference.[125] If we add Pakistan to that list—which took the Arab line on Palestine, and did not consider Turkey to be anti-Israeli— there were actually 13 countries championing Arab causes including the issue of Palestine and the problem of the Arab North African countries. A senior member of the Indian delegation reported that:

> Because of the sheer numerical strength of their representation, the Middle East and Arab countries could not be ignored; they played a prominent part at the conference and influenced its deliberations . . . [however], they also appeared to show, at any rate at the beginning of the conference, much greater preoccupation with their own problems than the larger problems of war and peace and co-existence. Thus the Arab countries displayed a much too regional and Arab outlook and their contribution to the success of the conference was not in proportion to the strength of their representation.[126]

Among the Middle Eastern countries, Syria took a neutralist stand and generally accepted the Indian and Burmese approach. The Syrian attitude, stated B. F. H. B. Tyabji, a member of the Indian delegation, was in refreshing contrast to that of Iraq and Iran, who acted, along with Turkey and Pakistan, as the spokespersons of the Western powers at the conference. The Syrians, he noted, "[were] of considerable use to us." However, the political situation in Syria was "so unstable that one never knows when it may change. Even during the conference, a change seemed to come over the Syrian attitude after the news of the assassination of her chief of the General Staff, who apparently was a strong supporter of an independent policy, was received."[127] Jordan and Saudi Arabia also took moderate positions at Bandung. Jordan occupied an intermediate position. "Within the limitations imposed on her by her treaty with the UK," Tyabji noted, "Jordan gave a pleasant and rather unexpected exhibition of alertness and independence from the leading strains of Western power politics." As for Saudi Arabia, Sudan, and Yemen, they were "content to doze in the background." Tyabji concluded that, in Syria, Saudi Arabia, Sudan, and Jordan, there were strong political elements that were "striving to pursue an independent line, distinct from those prevalent in the ruling circles in Iraq, Lebanon, and of course Turkey and Pakistan. Every effort should be made to strengthen these elements and feelings."[128]

As for Egypt, the Indian delegate argued that the conference enhanced its reputation. Those who had expected Nasser to behave in the "flamboyant fashion of a military dictator, were disappointed. The more discerning . . . were impressed by his moderation, charm, and real ability to handle tricky diplomatic situations such as those which frequently arose in the Sub-Committee set up to draft the resolution on human rights. He presided over this Sub-Committee with marked distinction, discretion and ability."[129] Nasser played the role of mediator in discussions on world peace and cooperation and on the problems of colonialism and dependent peoples. His efforts saw to it that agreement was reached on the decision to abstain from use of collective defense arrangements serving big power interests.[130] It was also due to pressure exerted by Nasser and the Arab delegations—mainly Syria—that the conference declared "its support of the rights of the Arab people of Palestine and called for the implementation of the UN resolutions on Palestine and the achievement of the peaceful settlement of the Palestine question."[131] According to an Indian report, China sought to please the Middle Eastern countries by fully supporting them on this issue. In contrast to China, India expressed "sympathetic but reasonable and logical views," placing emphasis "not so much on the rightness of the Arab case but on the desirability of settling the question by peaceful negotiations." This Indian approach "was made to appear almost anti-Arab and evoked unfavorable comments in Arab circles."[132] Nehru's approach did not please his closest ally, U Nu, the Burmese leader; according to senior Burmese delegates, there was an agreement between U Nu and Nehru in which the latter would guarantee that there would be no resolution of the Arab–Israeli conflict. Nehru failed to fulfill his commitment, and yielded to intense pressure exerted by Nasser and the Arab delegates. Consequently, U Nu, who did not want the regional conflict included in the conference resolutions, found himself isolated and with no influence on this matter. Throughout the conference, U Nu and the Burmese delegation were "attacked and slandered" by Arab delegates for being friendly with Israel. The Burmese delegation reported that, to their "bad fortune," they were neglected by their "distinguished big brother [Nehru] and after a short period of time were even raped by him," so that, by the end of the conference, they were forced to accept the dictation of the majority.[133] Following Arab pressure, the conference also passed a resolution expressing support for "the rights of the people of Algeria, Morocco and Tunisia to self-determination and independence," and calling on the French "to bring about a peaceful settlement of the issue without delay."[134]

Nasser's performance in Bandung was appreciated in Egypt. Upon his return on 2 May 1955, a general holiday was proclaimed. He received a warm welcome by a huge crowd gathered along the streets of Cairo. Nasser told the crowds: "I declared in the name of the Egyptian people at Bandung that our internal policy was to establish social justice and get rid of feudalism and imperialism and its supporters, and that your foreign policy was [a] fully independent policy."[135] He then pledged that Egypt would work for the creation of independent countries everywhere so that they would no longer be tools in the hands of the major world powers. Nasser's prestige, reported the *Manchester Guardian* from Cairo, "has never been higher than today, and for the Junta it was a recovery sorely needed . . . [Nasser] now has a tentative proposition to offer his own personal political philosophy of neutralism, which won him sidelong glances of admiration at Bandung."[136] Indian diplomats declared that the part Nasser played at Bandung had added considerably to his stature. The Egyptian press crowned him one of the Big Three at Bandung along with Nehru and Chou En-Lai. Indian diplomats in Cairo reported that Nasser's contribution to the conference had undoubtedly been effective: "his part as the Chairman of the important sub-committee which succeeded in evolving a formula on colonialism acceptable to everybody won him laurels; to his championship of the Arabs of Palestine was attributed the unanimous declaration of support for them as against Israel; and he has been credited with a reasoned espousal of the nationalist cause in North Africa and the inclusion in it of the case of Algeria."[137] Nasser told the Indian Ambassador that Bandung was his greatest experience, and that he valued the personal contacts he made with the leaders of the different countries represented there. The role of some delegations, Nasser stated, convinced him even more of the value of steering his country clear of affiliations with the West and the East. Moreover, he had come back with greater self-confidence. [138] The implications of the Bandung Conference on Egypt's foreign policy were analyzed by 'Ali Sabri of Egypt's ruling elite during a conversation he held with W. Pankowski, the Polish *Chargé d'Affaires* to Cairo. Sabri noted that, at the Bandung Conference, Nasser realized that he could rely on the strength of the Afro-Asian peoples and that, after the last British detachment left Egyptian soil in July 1956, he would be able to conduct Egypt's foreign policy even more freely. Following the Bandung Conference, the international situation changed:

> The USA became aware that they could no longer count on Egypt's being a pliant tool in their hands. The United States began to use various ways of exerting pressure on Egypt, economic and political pressure, as well as trying to create disturbances within the country . . . The relations with the USSR and people's democracies have been improved, and economic relations with the Chinese [People's] Republic have been established. These facts reduce to zero the threat of American economic pressure. It is difficult for the [United] States, or Great Britain, to threaten to boycott Egyptian cotton when Egypt has customers in the countries of the Eastern camp.[139]

Although Nehru took pains to demonstrate a united Chinese–Indian front at the conference and in Asia, according to a variety of reports, both Western and Asian, Chou stole the show from Nehru to play the role of the chief actor at the conference. Rawle Knox of the *Observer* argued that Chou En-Lai "did everything that was asked of him and did it supremely well . . . His support of the Arab case against Israel, for instance, won him a solid group of friends who would like to see Communist China inside the United Nations."[140] Chou En-Lai, maintained Knox, did better than Nehru because, when the former pronounced his simple plan "to live and let live," he knew that China was the only country that most of the participating countries were afraid to live with. The choice, he stressed, was not between being anti-communist and neutralist, but between being anti-communist and trusting Chou En-Lai: "Many of the delegations were quite sure that India had the right idea about world peace; but when this idea was expressed in Indian metaphysics it began to float right above the lesser heads. Their attention wandered—to return to the single issue of whether Mr. Chou En-Lai was or was not a man to be believed."[141]

Overall, the Bandung Conference was a remarkable success. A feeling of common purposes among the Asian and African countries became more and more evident. The conference had opened a new chapter not only in Asia and Africa, but on the global stage.[142]

Two meetings between Nasser and Nehru which took place in New Delhi before, and after, the Bandung Conference, and Nasser's impressive performance in Bandung paved the way for closer cooperation between the two leaders in international affairs. Several steps taken by Nasser in the first months of 1955 had proven to Nehru that Nasser was not going to ally with either the Western or the Soviet bloc. His uncompromising struggle against the Baghdad Pact and all military alliances under Western auspices, and the consolidation of closer ties with the USSR and its satellites, had gradually enhanced Nehru's confidence in Nasser.

On his way to Bandung, Nasser stopped in New Delhi on 14 April, to meet Nehru—their second meeting within two months. Nasser took the opportunity to address his host with a long account of the existing tension along the Arab borders with Israel and the tremendous pressure exerted by the Western powers on Egypt to accept their initiatives in the Middle East. In order to demonstrate his desire to pursue an independent inter-bloc policy, Nasser enquired how far India could help him in obtaining "military supplies, aeroplanes, 25-pounder ammunition and the like." He even asked India to sell Egypt certain military equipment that was manufactured by India. Nehru's reply was: "anything that we produced we might be prepared to sell but we could not possibly get aeroplanes for them or anything else from outside. In fact, we were short of these ourselves."[143] The whole issue of arms raises questions. We now know that, several months before Nasser's departure to Bandung, he had already concluded an arms deal with the Soviet bloc.[144] The Soviets were willing to provide Egypt with, relatively speaking, advanced arms, and part of these had already begun to arrive in Egypt. Nasser's enquiry was intended, first, to demonstrate to his host that he felt strong and independent enough to purchase arms from sources which were neither associated with the Western powers nor with the Soviet bloc. Second, his arms deals with the Soviet bloc were kept top secret; very few people in Egypt knew about them. At that stage, his relations with the Western powers were very tense, and the unveiling of his arms deals with the Eastern bloc could have led to further deterioration, a development that he wanted to avoid.

On 1 May 1955, on his way back from Bandung, Nasser stopped in New Delhi for another meeting with Nehru. At Nasser's initiative, the discussions concentrated on democracy in the Arab world generally, and in Egypt in particular. Nasser told Nehru that the democratic parliamentary system had failed in Egypt because, every time a new regime was elected, there was widespread corruption. He was not happy with the current state of affairs in Egypt in which the country was ruled by a revolutionary group. Nasser ruled out the old parliamentary system, stressing that "as soon as parties came in, they would be bought up by foreign powers and financed by them as they used to be financed previously." Egyptian newspapers, he went on, were similarly financed by foreign powers and individuals.[145] Hence these institutions were at odds with his new foreign policy of neutralism. He sought for an alternative system and asked for Nehru's advice. The latter replied that "a long term of military rule or dictatorship was not likely to succeed, [but] . . . If it [the government] brought in radical reforms and gradually changed the political and economic structure of Egypt, people would be interested in these changes and not think of democracy as such for the time being." Nehru stated that although he firmly believed in democracy, he understood the complicated situation that existed in Egypt. Democracy is a great thing, he said, but "there must be the basis for a democracy to be there [in Egypt] before democracy could function properly. It could not function with widespread corruption."[146]

The conversation then shifted to the political situation in Syria and defense arrangements between Arab countries. Political stability in Syria was volatile; nobody knew what might happen there. Egypt, said Nasser, had suggested a pact between Syria, Saudi Arabia, and Egypt for self-defense. One of the terms of this pact was that "no one member country should have a military pact with another country unless two-thirds agreed to it." Syria, added Nasser, "had laid down some extraordinary conditions for joining this pact of self-defense. They wanted joint forces and a joint command and the basis of contribution suggested put the heaviest burden on Egypt." Nehru ridiculed the idea of such a pact. Why, he asked, [was it] necessary to copy the NATO parallel and have a joint command and all that. Each country could build up its defense forces to the best of its ability and there could be constant consultation between them for defense and like purposes. After all, what was the defense pact aimed against? It could be either against Israel or against some major invasion by a great power. Personally I did not think that there was any danger of such an invasion. If there was a world war, then of course all kinds of things would happen. Therefore, in effect they were thinking in terms of Israel. It was clear that in the unfortunate event of a war with Israel, the burden would fall on Egypt. Saudi Arabia did not even have a common frontier with Israel. Syria would do little.[147]

Nasser's meetings with Nehru enhanced the rapport between the two leaders. On 2 May, in a letter Nehru sent to Homi Bhabha, who was leaving for Europe on 6 May, Nehru suggested that Bhabha stop in Cairo to meet with Nasser. Egypt was governed by "a small military group with the support of the army," said Nehru, and was passing through a difficult period. The military group "is a good group, honest and seeking the welfare of Egypt. The whole record of the Middle-Eastern countries is one of corruption and being bought up by foreign powers . . . This is, perhaps, relatively less in Egypt than in some of the West Asian countries. Colonel Nasser . . . is a good man and trying his best to face and overcome these evils."[148]

As far as the Indo-Pakistani dispute was concerned, Nehru could feel comfortable and confident that Nasser's sympathy lay on India's side. On 9 April 1955, when Nasser went to Karachi for a short visit on his way to Bandung, Egyptian decision-makers—including Nasser himself—did every thing possible to convince Indian officials that they regarded the visit to Pakistan as "a necessary, but comparatively unimportant, interlude in contrast to the visit to Delhi to which they attached overwhelming importance."[149] Nasser, who objected to the Turco-Pakistani military pact, and later the Baghdad Pact (of which Pakistan was a member state), was able to agree with his Indian hosts on two issues: the Arab–Israeli conflict; and the friendly relations between Muslim peoples and countries. Nasser and Anwar al-Sadat, the then Secretary-General of the Islamic Congress, informed the Indian diplomats in Cairo that Egypt's interest in the Islamic Congress was based "primarily, on her desire to prevent Pakistan from making it an instrument of her leadership."[150]

Another indication of the acceleration of the process of rapprochement between India and Egypt can be seen in a conversation between Nehru and Sayed Ismail al-Azhari, the Sudanese Prime Minister, which took place on 30 April 1955 in New Delhi.[151] In the course of their conversation, Nehru subtly sided with Egypt in its controversy with the Sudanese government over future relations between the two states. The Egyptian government wanted a union, whereas the Sudanese government wanted full independence, although they were willing to cooperate with Egypt in many other matters. Nehru pointed out to his guest that "inevitably there could be many common interests . . . between Egypt and Sudan and it was obviously desirable for friendly relations between the two countries." Nehru was in Egypt's favor, stating: "There appeared to be no reason why even an independent Sudan could not have the closest relations with Egypt." He welcomed an idea of "joint Egyptians–Sudanese commissions for the Nile Waters as well as for defense and foreign affairs."[152]

Nehru's desire to develop closer relations with Arab countries, which were against military alliances with foreign powers, was manifested in his four formal meetings with Emir Faysal bin 'Abd al-'Aziz, Crown Prince and Prime Minister of Saudi Arabia, during his three-day visit to India (2 –5 May 1955).[153] Their talks focused on international affairs, including the question of Saudi Arabia and other Arab countries recognizing Communist China. Faysal asked whether such recognition would lead to communist infiltration; the Arab countries, he explained, were religious and did not approve of communist atheism. Nehru ruled out such a possibility and stressed that China was not under the thumb of the Soviet Union; although the two countries had friendly relations there existed a certain potential rivalry between them. Faysal then referred to words uttered by representatives of foreign powers that India was inclined toward communism and, by its policy, was encouraging the spread of communism—that it was "alleged that India was after the leadership of Asia and that India was opposed to the Arabs and their interests."[154] Faysal made it clear that he did not believe any of this.

Nehru ridiculed the pro-communist allegations, giving his host a long description of India's struggle for independence, which was achieved without the help of outside countries. India was not and could not be anti-Muslim because there were many religions within India, the chief ones being Hinduism, Islam, and Christianity, and India "could only be a strong united nation if there was unity among these various groups and religions and each had freedom to function and an equal place in the country." As far as India's attitudes toward the Arab countries were concerned, Nehru pointed out that India's record in the UN and elsewhere in the past seven or eight years showed its consistent friendliness with the Arabs and their cause. India had no conflicts of interest with the Arab countries. Past associations, history, culture, and geography, Nehru declared, had all "brought us near each other and we wished to develop closer association with them to our mutual advantage." As regards Israel, India's sympathies "had been and were now with the Arabs, who had suffered so greatly." India was anxious, however, to settle the Arab–Israeli problem by means other than employing "vigorous speeches," which could only antagonize the conflict. Nehru warned that, in the future, Israel was likely to become stronger militarily. Israel would never have been formed without the support of the US and Britain, and could not continue to exist without their sponsorship. These two Western powers were also the motivating power behind the Turco-Iraqi Pact, which had split up the Arab countries and made them weaker. If there should be another war in Palestine, "the burden of this would fall on Egypt." Saudi Arabia had no common frontier with Israel, and thus would remain out of it, and the contribution of other Arab countries would be minimal.[155]

Nehru explained his overall objection to all kinds of military pacts:

In the present context of atom and hydrogen bombs, war had become still more objectionable and the old armies were not much good. We objected [to] the military pacts in East and West Asia because those pacts were a projection of some old conception, which had no relevance today. They did not even add to the military potential of the area or assure security. In fact they did the reverse and made a country hostile to some other country and thereby increased its insecurity. Also this dependence on pacts and on other countries lessened the feeling of self-reliance and actually, therefore, reduced the strength of the country.[156]

As for the allegations that India was seeking to play a leading role in Asia, it would appear that Nehru found it difficult to refute. "Of course one could do no more than contradict," such allegations, Nehru said: but ultimately, "deeds and what we did would prove or disprove this allegation."[157]

Emir Faysal agreed with India's general foreign policy of independent non-alignment. Saudi Arabia, however, had to deal with the US, which was anxious to help it in various ways. The Saudis, he said, had no objection to accepting US help—just as India had accepted it—but he made it clear that such help must be without strings.[158]

Syria and the Neutralist Camp—India and Yugoslavia

Ba'thist Neutralism: Between Nehruism, Titoism, and Nasserism

By the mid-1950s, the Ba'th had already been influenced to a great extent by Nasser's inter-bloc policy, particularly following the formation of the Baghdad Pact and the Bandung Conference (both 1955). The principles of Nasser's policy of positive neutralism can be found in a statement made by 'Ali Sabri, Director of Egyptian Air Force Intelligence and Nasser's confidant in January 1954, that "Egypt's new [foreign] policy was intended to maintain a position of independence from the Soviet and Western blocs and to obtain what it could from both sides without becoming committed to either."[159] Since the mid-1950s, Syrian–Soviet relations, like Soviet–Egyptian relations, were in a process of rapprochement. Following

Shepilov's visit to Syria in June 1956, relations between the USSR and Syria were upgraded and the groundwork was prepared for the conclusion of military, economic, and commercial agreements. In an article published by his party organ *al-Ba'th*, 'Aflaq explained the logic behind the Soviet–Syrian rapprochement. In his view, both countries found themselves facing the same enemy:

> It has become clear today that the interests of the Arab Nation and the Soviet Union meet, and have met for a long time on more then one vital point. The Arab nation struggles for political and economic liberation from Western imperialism, while the Soviet Union sees the continuation of the Western military and economic occupation of the Arab land as a direct danger to its existence. Therefore when it supports the Arabs and provides them with arms and economic aid, it does not aspire to more than closing the Arab countries to Western imperialism and preventing it from using them as a theatre for its war operations and an economic source for augmenting its influence and hegemony. If it is the duty of the Arabs to be realistic and know what interests have changed the Soviet Union's policy toward them and brought it closer to their path and their friendship; it is also realistic to recognize the fundamental difference, which separates the socialist countries and capitalist countries. It is in the interests of the socialist countries to be loyal to the principles of their societies based on liberty, justice and peace and opposed to imperialism and exploitation.[160]

In 1957, 'Aflaq described and analyzed the tenets of his party's doctrine of "positive neutralism" [*al-Hiyad al-Ijabi*]. The Arab Nation [*al-umah al-'Arabiyya*], stated 'Aflaq, "has no interest in the collapse of one of the two world camps. The collapse of the socialist [Eastern] camp means the victory of imperialism and capitalism, whereas victory of communism means the victory of an ideology which negates both nationalism and freedom."[161] The fact that neutralism had become a worldwide movement, said 'Aflaq, may serve as clear-cut proof that the two international blocs were ideologically mistaken: there was room for other doctrines. The recruitment of various forces for the purpose of terminating imperialism was the most important goal of all freedom-loving nations. The price for the realization of that goal, however, must not be subservience to the Eastern bloc. If Syria joined in with the Eastern camp, 'Aflaq declared, they might quickly eradicate the imperialists, but Syria must not take this route because they could lose their independence as a result.[162] The purpose of neutralism, the Ba'th declared, was to reach simultaneously world and domestic peace. Positive neutralism also had a cultural face—it refused to embrace either Eastern or Western values. Positive neutralism did not accept blind adherence to one international school or blind hostility to a certain regime or philosophy. The task of positive neutralism was to prevent the outbreak of a conflict between democracy in its Western sense and social justice in its accomplished socialist form. Each of the two international camps were competing to shape the future the way it wanted.[163]

Although the Ba'th advocated a doctrine of balanced positive neutralism and negatively viewed both world camps, the development of political events in Syria and the Middle East in the 1950s gradually led to a change in Syria's policy toward the inter-bloc conflict. The ideological scale began to slowly, and pragmatically, move toward the Eastern bloc. The Western image in the Arab world in the 1950s became increasingly negative because its policies in the region went against Arab interests. Examples included efforts to establish military pacts (which divided the Arab world after the formation of the Baghdad Pact),[164] the extended Anglo-Egyptian conflict (which reached its peak with the Suez crisis of 1956), the Eisenhower doctrine of 1957, Western support for Israel, and, finally, the alleged attempt by the US to overthrow the Syrian government in August 1957. Syria did not feel that it had much choice but to seek help from the enemies of the Western powers. In contrast, the record of the Soviet bloc in the Middle East was steadily pro-Arab with no apparent strings attached. In its insistence on pursuing its military alliances, Western imperialism, the Ba'thists accused, "is not only aimed at fighting the Eastern camp but also aspires to terminate the zone of positive neutralism . . . Whoever claims that there was a danger of Russian attack proves his complete ignorance in international affairs."[165] According to al-Bitar, the real threat to the Arabs came from the Western powers, Britain and France, when, with Israel, they attacked Egypt in 1956. Only the USSR, India, and China, he declared in early 1957, "supported the Arab Nation when Egypt was attacked. In contrast, we cannot forget the British and French aggression; how can we disregard it and today attack the USSR? We are not friends of the USSR because she is communist, but because she stood on the Arab side when it [the USSR] defended its [Syria's] sovereignty . . . All that the Arabs ask is that the West understand, like the East did, the real danger that threatens them."[166]

The reason behind Syria's economic agreements of 1957 with the USSR were explained: "when the US assaults the region in order to enable her and Israel to profit at the expense of Arab liberty, and by imposing an economic blockade on Syria, it is just natural that we would aim at developing friendly relations with all countries in the world only on the basis of mutual benefit, and in order to achieve cooperation without political strings so that our sovereignty and independence would not be jeopardized."[167] The economic talks with the Soviets, which were based on, and supportive of, the Bandung principles and the policy of non-alignment ['Adam al-Inhiyaz], were described as "a new victory for Syria's positive neutralism." Western imperialism would not strangle Syria's economy, the Ba'thists declared, and, by cooperating freely with other countries, they would develop and defend their country.[168]

Ba'th leaders and theoreticians repeated that their close relations with the Soviets were a direct result of their troubled relations with the West. They emphasized the ideological differences between their socialism and Soviet communism, and stressed their non-alignment with either of the two blocs, and explained that political cooperation with local communists was restricted and temporary—both were anti-Western and opposed military pacts inspired by the West. The Ba'thists monitored this cooperation closely and were aware of the risks involved. They considered the communists to be serving foreign interests, which temporarily paralleled those of the Ba'th, as 'Aflaq explained: "No positive aims brought us together. We were not, for instance, cooperating in a campaign for the betterment of the working class. The communists had never really acquired rights of citizenship to enable such collaboration to take place." The Syrian Communist Party was in fact "an organization for manipulating the working class, the bourgeoisie, and the students to promote the objectives of Soviet foreign policy against pacts, alliances, and ties with the West."[169] The Ba'th praised the Soviets for their extended help to Syria, but also mentioned the support of other countries such as India, China, and Yugoslavia (Ba'th theoreticians, including 'Aflaq, regarded Tito highly). The Ba'thists were ideologically closer to Nehru, Nasser, and Tito than to the Soviet Union. 'Aflaq praised, in particular, Tito's courage because he refused to yield to Soviet pressure.[170]

The Implications of the Bandung Conference on the Syrian Political Scene

Relations between India and Syria began rapidly developing following the Bandung Conference. This was a natural development, because Syria accepted Nasser's leadership and his inter-Arab, as well as his inter-bloc, policies, and Nasser became Nehru's close ally in the non-aligned and Afro-Asian movements.

On 6 April 1956, Syed Mahmud, Minister of State in the government of India, arrived in Damascus for a six-day visit as a guest of the Syrian government. In a statement he made at a press conference, Mahmud stressed the support given by India to the Arab world. India, he said, supported the Arabs in the United Nations. In order to satisfy his Syrian hosts, he made it clear that, despite the fact that India recognized Israel, he did not expect that diplomatic relations between India and Israel would be established. India, he continued, had always been against imperialism, but it did not believe in violence. He hoped that a solution would be found to the Kashmir problem. The underlying theme behind Mahmud's visit, as noted by a British report from Damascus, was to recruit support for India's view of the Kashmir issue among the anti-Western members of the Arab world.[171]

Mahmud's visit was also a prelude to Nehru's arrival in Syria on 21 June, when he landed at Damascus airport and was warmly received by Syria's heads of state. Among the invitees at a cocktail party at the Indian Legation later that day were the communist leader Khalid Bakdash and a number of leaders of the Ba'th Party, which, according to a British report, appeared to be closely linked with the Indian Legation in Damascus. Several hours later a dinner party was given in Nehru's honor by President al-Quwatli, who, in his welcoming remarks, praised Nehru's past and present efforts to free India and other countries from imperialism and alluded to the fact that Nehru was persistent in his refusal to allow India to join military alliances "which could only have the effect of breeding wars."[172] In his reply, and in his other talks with his Syrian hosts, Nehru showed much sympathy for the Algerian people's struggle for liberation and expressed his support. However, he mentioned neither the Palestine nor the Kashmir issues. In his attempts to establish himself as the moral leader of the Afro-Asian movement, he stated that the newly independent states had a further, heavier task awaiting them—"the raising of the standards of living and dignity of their own population—a task which would absorb their energies for many generations to come."[173] The visit was conducted in a friendly atmosphere, and was designed to nurture and further develop relations between the two countries, which shared similar views on inter-bloc issues.

Syria and the Arabs could be satisfied with India's stand throughout the Suez crisis. Nehru pursued all possible channels to avoid war and seek a diplomatic solution to the situation. On 8 August, before the outbreak of hostilities, he announced his government's position, stressing that India would participate in the August 16 conference in London on the understanding that "attendance would not injure the interests or sovereign rights of Egypt which could not and would not attend a conference about which it had not been consulted."[174] India's first consideration, Nehru declared, was to work for "a calmer atmosphere and a rational outlook," and made it clear that India supported Egypt's right to nationalize the Canal. In his view, the coming conference could reach no final decision without Egypt's acquiescence. He agreed that the Canal was important internationally and that it was therefore necessary to keep it open for international navigation, but he criticized the US for "precipitating the whole affair not only by withdrawing its aid offer to Egypt, but also by the provocative manner of the action." He concluded his statement by criticizing both France and Britain for their preparations for war and noted that the attitude of the Western powers had caused much resentment in Asia.

Since his election (1955), the President of Syria al-Quwatli was busy furthering his country's foreign relations with Eastern bloc countries and

Egypt, India, and Yugoslavia—the leaders of the non-aligned movement. Several days after Eisenhower's doctrine was announced, al-Quwatli paid a state visit to India from 17 to 27 January 1957. He was accompanied by a gallery of notable political and military figures—among them, Salah al-Din al-Bitar and the Syrian Army Commander-in-Chief General Tawfiq Nizam al-Din. On his arrival, al-Quwatli was welcomed at the airport by Rajendra Prasad, the Indian President, and Nehru, the Prime Minister. Al-Quwatli chose to focus his first speech on the "aggression that had been committed against Egypt." This was only "one [piece of] evidence to show that, through the Arab world's policy of non-alignment and positive neutralism, they [the Arabs] were able not only to save their countries from the devastation and destruction of war, but to prevent this incident from developing into a global war." Later on, aiming to please his hosts, al-Quwatli stated that Syria's brand of neutralism was based on non-alignment—"Syria would not be submissive to either of the blocs"—and denied rumors that Syria allowed the USSR to build military bases in its country. Al-Quwatli also attacked the Baghdad Pact, describing it as the "outcome of the engineering of imperialists."[175]

Aware of the sensitivity his hosts displayed whenever Pakistan (which was a full member of the Baghdad Pact and in conflict with India over Kashmir) was mentioned, Salah al-Din al-Bitar criticized the Pakistani government at a press conference, declaring that Pakistan "was working hand in hand with the West." Syria had been accused of becoming a communist military base because it bought arms from the Eastern bloc; but Syria had no other choice but to buy arms from the Soviet bloc, because "we were not allowed to have these arms from the West." Syria paid for the arms they got from the Eastern bloc nations and was convinced that the Soviets "had no ambitions in our countries." The USSR was not seeking "any privileges either in Syria or the Arab world." When al-Bitar was asked about his government's reaction to the Soviet invasion of Hungary of late 1956, he preferred to remain mute, saying that he did not know enough about the subject. (In contrast, Nehru was highly critical of the Soviet invasion of Hungary.) Al-Bitar attempted to belittle the consequences of the events. He rationalized his stand by saying: "while you read so much about atrocities in Hungary you rarely hear of what is going on in Algeria, where massacres [are] being carried out with NATO arms."[176]

The attitude of the Indian press toward the visit was mixed; however, the general coverage of the visit was positive from the guests' point of view. The organ of the Congress Party, the *Hindustan Times*, approved warmly the "close identity of views shown to exist between Syria and India." The *Times of India* expressed a more complex approach to India's policy toward the Israeli–Arab conflict. On the one hand, the paper expressed satisfaction with India's policy of maintaining and consolidating friendly relations with the Arab world; on the other, the newspaper questioned whether India should consider an Israeli withdrawal from Sinai as "vital and necessary." When the two countries issued a communiqué at the conclusion of the visit, the newspaper protested against the absence of any reference to the events in Hungary. This may have been, the paper claimed, "because the Syrians found Nehru's revised and more sober judgment of events there unpalatable." The weekly *Eastern Economist* maintained that "it was unreal to talk in terms of the absence of a vacuum in the Middle East; it existed and the question really was by whom it was to be filled." The weekly affirmed that if "the Middle Eastern countries were left to themselves the vacuum would be filled by the Soviet Union; this was just what President Eisenhower's plan was designed to prevent."[177] The underlying theme the *Eastern Economist* expressed was that India should not let one of the two superpowers fill the vacuum in the Middle East, but should take the initiative to improve its own position in that area.

Indian officials were pleased with what they described as al-Bitar's moderate approach in international affairs and emphasized that, "the value of the visit lay in the reassurance which the Syrian visitors gave them that they were not in the hands of the Russians." The Indian hosts were also satisfied because of the "strong desire" displayed by their guests "for closer relations—leading to a federation—with Egypt, Jordan, and Saudi-Arabia."

The communiqué issued on 22 January at the conclusion of the visit revealed a "close similarity of views over a wide range of international problems" between the two states, and reiterated their commitment to regulate their international relations on the basis of the Bandung principles: peaceful coexistence, non-aggression, and non-intervention, which they commended to all nations. "The policy of non-alignment pursued by the two countries," the communiqué declared, "can best contribute to peace and harmony and to the realization of the Bandung principles." Although not mentioned by name, special emphasis was placed on the positive role played by India and Yugoslavia during the Suez crisis: "progressive forces working for freedom and stability and for the realization of the national aspirations of the people in this area [the Middle East] should be encouraged so that they may help in healing divisions and conflicts." Both countries expressed satisfaction with the "increased authority" of the UN exercised throughout the Suez crisis. The UN, however, could not succeed in resolving that crisis without the support of the two major superpowers—the US and the USSR. The US and the Western camp, though, were also criticized: "intervention by the Big Powers in the form of military pacts and alliances is detrimental to peace and stability in the Middle East. The Baghdad Pact has caused bitter conflicts and divisions in the Arab world and has greatly increased international tension." The communiqué concluded by stating categorically that "colonialism in all its manifestations is an evil which should be brought to an end," and both Syria and India expressed their desire to further strengthen their relations.[178]

The next few months saw a marked increase in relations between the two countries. On 14 June, Nehru arrived in Damascus for a short visit and was accorded a tumultuous reception at the airport by all the Syrian cabinet ministers. The following description, similar to that given by most of the Syrian press, shows how popular and admired Nehru was in Syria:

> Damascus has never before seen so many officials at the airport to greet a visitor. Damascus beauties released white pigeons and a crowd estimated at about 10,000 chanted "welcome to the hero of world peace" and "long live the leader of Asia". The procession from the airport passed along crowded streets and under banners bearing slogans of the "long live the Bandung Conference and its resolutions" type.[179]

At a dinner given by al-Quwatli in honor of Nehru, differences emerged regarding the way both leaders comprehended and referred to the term "positive neutralism." Al-Quwatli repeated his well-known view; Nehru, for his part, preferred to define the policy of positive neutralism as the policy of "non-adherence." The foreign policies of the two countries, he said, were much the same. India's adherence to the policy of non-alignment preceded the Bandung Conference "for she had long been conditioned by her past struggle to pursue this particular policy." He described how India had fought Britain, "the greatest empire the world has known in order to attain her independence," placing special emphasis on the peaceful means this struggle employed. Both Syria and India were faced with many problems, Nehru declared, which must be solved peacefully—the approach to world affairs had to be made "with patience and in good spirit." He criticized those countries that had participated in the Bandung Conference, namely Iraq and Turkey, which had quickly forgotten the principle of non-interference in the affairs of other countries put forth by the conference.[180]

The Indian press gave large coverage to Nehru's visit, referring to Nehru's warm welcome and to banners decorating the streets of Damascus that proclaimed "long live the Indian–Syrian twin policy of neutralism," and called Nehru the "great defender of the peoples' rights and freedoms," and "the hero of world peace."[181]

Commenting on Nehru's short visit, Salah al-Din al-Bitar was reported to have said that the visit enabled the Syrian people "to express their love and respect for the Indian leader in recognition of his attitude toward Arab issues, especially his bold stand against the tripartite aggression against Egypt last November." Al-Bitar went on to say that Syria and India were in full accord in their views on international affairs.[182]

The growing tension between Syria and its neighboring pro-Western countries, coupled with the deterioration of relations with the US and the West, demonstrated to Syria that the two other international blocs—the Eastern bloc and the movement of the non-aligned countries—stood firmly behind it. Since mid-1957, there had been a marked rapprochement between Yugoslavia and Syria. On 8 July, Salah al-Din al-Bitar arrived in Belgrade for a five-day visit as an official guest of the Yugoslav government. Al-Bitar held talks with the Yugoslav heads of state, and the visit was given prominent emphasis in *Borba* and *Politika*, the two leading Yugoslav papers. In the formal speeches, the community of interests between the two countries was emphasized,[183] while, in his interviews with the press, al-Bitar chose to focus on the socio-economic cooperation between the two countries. A British source reported that he spoke of "the renaissance of the Arab peoples and the development of the lands of the Middle East on socialist lines. In Syria they were demanding agrarian reform, a planned economy and increased industrialization ... The socialist movement, which was most advanced in Syria, was gaining strength in other Arab states."[184] Yugoslavia provided Syria unconditional aid, al-Bitar stated, so that his government could meet these reform demands successfully. Economic cooperation with Yugoslavia was of great importance to Syria. Al-Bitar gave as an example Yugoslavia's aid in the completion of the Latakia port. Yugoslavia had strong economic interests in Syria: the conclusion of contracts for the development of further civil engineering projects. (Yugoslavia found, however, that in order to realize its economic interests in Syria it had to compete with a number of Eastern bloc countries that showed similar interests, and which were, like Yugoslavia, favorably treated by Syria.) In reference to the exacerbating crisis with Syria's neighbors and the West, al-Bitar declared that Syria and the progressive Arab states wished to live in independence, but "they were being constantly harassed by foreign intervention aimed at destroying their unity. It was for this reason that the Baghdad Pact, Israel, and the Eisenhower doctrine were all equally unwelcome." Syria would preserve its independence and sovereignty, and "in common with Egypt, would continue to support other Arab states in their struggle for unity, solidarity, and full liberation."[185]

Following al-Bitar's visit, some "diplomatic circles" in Belgrade argued that Syria might be trying to interest the Yugoslavs in a share in the supply or delivery of arms; but it was more likely, according these sources, that the strongest interest of the two countries in each other was the development of further civil engineering projects in Syria, such as the port of Latakia. One of Yugoslavia's main competitors in this regard was Bulgaria, which was part of the Soviet bloc.[186]

On 1 September, the Yugoslav scholarly organ, *Review of International Affairs*, interviewed al-Bitar. In the course of the interview, al-Bitar referred to the recent tension on Syria's borders and stated that the outcome of the Suez crisis showed that "strength lies no longer in guns and bombers but in . . . world public opinion." He attacked military blocs and the Eisenhower doctrine and quoted Ba'th Party doctrine that the unity of all Arabs could only be brought about within the framework of "humanistic socialism." He declared that "Yugoslav–Syrian friendship is firmly based on [a mutual] identity of views on international problems and on economic cooperation."[187]

The Yugoslav government and press continued to show great interest in Syria. On 2 September, *Borba* published an interview with Khalid al-'Azm, who complained that Syria was misunderstood by the West: Syria sought peace, freedom, and independence, but the West and in particular the US, accused it of being "somebody's satellite." Al-'Azm argued that Syria–Yugoslav relations dated back to before the Bandung Conference, and were symbolized in the construction of Latakia Port. The two countries had much in common—"a history of imperialist domination and the need to develop their great mutual resources." Al-'Azm, known for his pro-Soviet stance, made it clear that Yugoslavia belonged to a wider camp of countries who offered assistance "without any ulterior motive." He gave marked emphasis to the recent agreements concluded with the Soviet Union and Czechoslovakia for economic assistance—also "without strings."[188]

The Yugoslav press gave wide coverage to the development of political events in Syria in August and September, when tensions with the West reached their peak. *Borba* and *Politika* dedicated their editorial articles on 10, 11, and 12 September to Syria. The main points made by these papers were: First, the internal political changes in Syria, including changes within the army, were entirely Syria's own affair; second, the current crisis in Syria's relations with the West was the result of its refusal to join the Baghdad Pact, and its objection to the Eisenhower doctrine; and, third, as a small country, Syria did not pose a threat or challenge to its neighbors, and the appropriate place to deal with the current tension was the UN. Moreover, arms deliveries to the Middle East by both international blocs only served to increase tension and instability in "a sensitive part of the world" and could subsequently lead to war, while economic aid to the countries of the region could prove to be more conducive to peace.[189]

The thesis that there were diverse approaches within the Syrian government vying to shape and implement Syria's inter-bloc policy in accordance with their own principles gains credence when one examines an interview Michel 'Aflaq, the Secretary-General of the Ba'th Party, gave on 11 October 1957 to *Nova Makedonija*, an organ of the Macedonian Socialist Alliance of Working People (SAWP). 'Aflaq stated that Syria's foreign policy since the conclusion of the Baghdad Pact was based upon three principles, which, he argued, were imposed by his party upon the other parties:

national independence, Arab federation, and neutralism between the two superpower blocs. 'Aflaq maintained that, of these three principles, neutralism was the most criticized by the Western powers, who repeatedly said that the countries of the Middle East were being threatened by Soviet invasion or infiltration. In order to strengthen the Baghdad Pact, which had proved to be powerless, the West was putting great pressure on more Arab countries to join it. As far as the Syrian political scene was concerned, 'Aflaq said, there were political forces who wanted to join the pact, but there were also those forces—including the communists and the Ba'thists—who were against the idea. Although there were no ideological points of contact between the Ba'thist-socialists and the communists, in certain cases they had cooperated. The communists were opposed to imperialism and the Baghdad Pact, but they were not neutralists like the Ba'thists and allied themselves with the Soviet bloc. Syria, 'Aflaq declared, could not cooperate with the Western bloc, because it represented an imperialist grouping. There were three reasons for the conflict with the West: First, Syria was pursuing a purely Arab policy and favored the emancipation of the occupied Arab countries; second, the military ambitions of the Baghdad Pact and the Eisenhower doctrine were introducing another form of political–military pacts; and third, there was the issue of arms delivered to Israel and the West's determination to strengthen it to the disadvantage of its Arab neighbors. The Arabs, 'Aflaq argued, must continue their struggle to eradicate these three problems. While struggling for those objectives, the Arabs were permitted to maintain economic and trade relations with the West. 'Aflaq elucidated Syria's policy of positive neutralism:

> If the West is willing to give us help as the USSR does, demanding no conditions, then we are going to accept it. In point of fact, Western powers use money to overthrow the progressive government in Syria and some other countries, in an endeavor to return reactionary governments to power . . . As regards the relations with the Eastern bloc countries, economic, trade and technical, they are based on neither political nor military conditions. They do not, even indirectly, request that we should change our political neutrality. In a way we prefer the Eastern bloc because we have many more points of contact.[190]

As far as socio-economic issues were concerned, 'Aflaq noted that the Ba'th Party chose its own way to progress and develop—for the last 15 years, it had been combining Arab nationalism with revolutionary socialism. Before the formation of the Ba'th, he stressed, the social problem in Syria had not at all been expounded. The Ba'th Party placed the revolutionary struggle at the heart of the national struggle and maintained that national liberation was unfeasible without the participation of the masses. He accused Arab governments of a permanent tendency toward separatism—a reflection of which, he declared, could be found in the Arab League.[191]

A visit of a high-level Ba'thist delegation of theoreticians—among them 'Aflaq, Jamal al-Atasi, and 'Abd al-Karim Zuhur from Syria, Jubran Majdalani from Lebanon, and the Egyptian Ahmad Baha al-Din—arrived in Belgrade on 10 November for a two-week visit. The delegation came to engage in theoretical discussions with representatives of SAWPY represented by the theoreticians Svetozar Vukmanovic, Petar Stambolic, Avdo Humo, Ales Bedler, and Punisa Perovic. The main themes to be discussed were Yugoslavia's social system, the internal development of Arab countries, economic and development projects, and Middle Eastern affairs.[192]

In his speeches and interviews, 'Aflaq argued that although his Ba'th Party had not yet managed to effect considerable change in the social structure in Syria, in accordance with its doctrine it had played a large role in the process of Arab liberation by imposing its foreign policy "even on the reactionary parties." The Ba'th, he declared, held the view that the Arabs were one nation and therefore the party opposed any adherence by Arab countries to military alliances. The struggle in Syria was twofold: a struggle for national independence, and a struggle for economic development. As for the first, "pressure and plots from outside had prevented success . . . but the Ba'thists were seeking to remedy this through broad and active cooperation with all friendly countries." The struggle for economic progress had only begun, and social reform would soon be introduced. The Ba'th Party and the progressive forces, he believed, would strengthen their power in the Syrian elections scheduled for September 1958. Some minor reforms had already been introduced: the peasants had been given security of tenure, and state lands had been distributed to small farmers. The Ba'th Party, which was part of the "national front" that had a majority in the Syrian parliament, included in its program Ba'thist ideological tenets such as "non-adherence to blocs, industrialization, willingness to accept foreign aid and cooperation provided that it [was] without strings, the raising of the standard of living, higher taxation of big land-owners and capitalists, and the purchase of arms from abroad provided that this was in harmony with the interests of the country's independence." 'Aflaq declared that his party was active in all Arab countries and maintained contacts with foreign socialist parties, while its relations with the SAWPY had furnished proof that "each country was following its own road to socialism."[193]

On 24 November, a day after the conclusion of the visit, *Borba* published the joint communiqué, which revealed more information on the content of the discussions. As far as the inter-bloc conflict was concerned, the two parties were in agreement that a "race in armaments and political–military blocs . . . [might] only further strain the international situation." It was therefore necessary to continue efforts to achieve initial and partial agreements "with a view to opening the road to a total solution of the disarmament problem . . . One of the important tasks of [the] socialists and progressive forces is [the] strengthening of [the] authority of the UN . . . [which might] and must play an important role in preserving and consolidating peace, as well as in the solution of the big world problems that require the joint efforts of the whole international community, such as the problem of development of the underdeveloped countries."[194] Both parties believed that the non-aligned countries should be actively involved in easing tensions between the East and the West within the framework of the UN, and that, by doing so, they might reduce the risk of a global war. The two parties also condemned the policy of pressure and interference as practised by the Western powers in Syria and certain Arab countries.

The SAWPY and the Ba'th Party regarded cooperation between their organizations as highly important. They pointed to the fact that painstaking efforts would also take place in the future to develop mutual relations "by exchanging experiences and views on important questions" by means of frequent meetings. Such cooperation, they concluded, would strengthen relations between Yugoslavia and the Arab peoples, and would benefit the forces of peace and socialism.[195]

Cooperation between the two parties continued in the following years, but was to undergo changes after the formation of the United Arab Republic (UAR). Nasser, who now ruled both Syria and Egypt, was the sole determinant in issues concerning state and society; however, his decision to embark on the path of socialism with his announcement of the "shift towards socialism" in July 1961 was made after a systematic and thorough dialogue with his Ba'thist colleagues. His brand of socialism, detailed in *Egypt's Incomplete Revolution*, owed much to the reigning ideologies in Yugoslavia and India, and the socio-economic legislation that followed the "shift towards socialism" in 1961 had much in common with the Ba'th Party platform of 1947. Nasser took pains to demonstrate that his decision to embrace socialism was motivated by his country's own interests. He declared that the UAR's brand of socialism and its pursuit of economic development lay in non-alignment, and noted that Egypt's socialism placed special emphasis on the abolition of artificial class barriers and the establishment of full liberty and democracy, including the rights of freedom of conscience and property ownership. This ideological non-alignment of domestic policy was, in practice, no more neutral than Nasser's non-alignment in foreign affairs; ideologically, it was closer to Eastern European doctrine than to Western concepts. Nasser's Arab socialism was a fusion of nationalist and Islamic ideas with socialism; it was a nationalist socialism in the sense that it accommodated itself to particular Arab and Egyptian circumstances. Arab socialism thus rejected proletarian internationalism and emphasized the distinctiveness of the Arab Nation.[196]

4

Communism, Syria, and Neutralist Trends

The period 1954–8 may be regarded as one of the least stable in Syria's modern history. It began in February 1954 with the overthrow of Adib al-Shishakli, the military dictator, and the subsequent free elections of September–October 1954, which reinstated a civilian government, and concluded in February 1958, with Syria becoming part of Nasser's ambition in the Middle East following the formation of the United Arab Republic.

Under Shishakli (1949–54) Syria had embraced a rigid policy of neutralism that was ideologically based on anti-Western sentiments—both the US and Britain were blamed for being the foster parents of Zionism and Israel. The hostility toward the West and the rise of neutralism were not, however, translated into a perceptible change in Syria's relations with the USSR, relations that had been in a state of slow but constant improvement since the mid-1940s. The right-wing politicians who had ruled Syria both before and after Shishakli's overthrow held a more positive attitude toward the West, but they lacked the courage of their convictions and were prone to left-wing pressure and street-level protests. Several months after the downfall of Shishakli, Ibrahim al-Astawni, the Secretary-General of the Ministry of Foreign Affairs, and other highly-placed Syrian officials—all belonging to the old traditionalist elite—privately expressed their pro-Western sentiments. In a conversation in early May 1954 between al-Astawni and Ahmad Shuqairi, the Assistant Secretary of the Arab League, the former was reported to have said that "the foreign policy of the Arab states was nonsense," since it, first, alienated "the friendship of all those [Western] countries, who, despite minor offences against the Arabs, were the only ones capable of helping Syria without infringing her sovereignty," and, second, brought the Arab countries "nearer to the Soviets—the real enemy of all the world." Al-Astawni's third point was that Israel "was now a fact, unpleasant though that might be to the Arabs, and so the sooner the Arabs dealt with it on that basis the better." He concluded by expressing his view that the Soviet Union, and not the West, was the real enemy of the Arabs.[1]

As a result of the elections of 1954, the anti-Western forces in Syria increased their power base, and the face of the Syrian political scene changed significantly. The country now entered into an era of political instability. Left-wing parties and independent politicians, who were politically alert, scored election successes disproportionate to their strength within the population. In spite of this, the newly-elected Parliament reflected a broad range of political allegiances in Syria. One of the most prominent outcomes of the elections was the appearance of the leftist Ba'th Party as the third-largest party in the Syrian Parliament (it gained 16 out of 142 seats). Syria was also the first Arab country to legally allow the participation of the Communist Party in democratic elections. Khalid Bakdash, the leader of the Communist Party, was elected as deputy for Damascus, coming third in the national poll—an impressive achievement. Although the party had only marginal representation in the Parliament, it was to become an influential political factor in Syrian politics in the following years. Amongst the many elected independents was the distinguished pro-Soviet politician, Khalid al-'Azm, known as the "Red Millionaire." Al-'Azm headed a group of independents that consisted of about 30 deputies. The Syrian left, now represented by several parties and individuals, could act as a counterweight to the conservative and traditionalist politicians.[2] There was close cooperation between the socialist Ba'th Party, al-'Azm's group, and the Communists, who together acted as a vocal opposition to the cabinet of Faris al-Khuri, a nationalist leader of the old guard who was a right-wing independent.[3] The balance of power in Syria's Parliament, therefore, rested with a heterogeneous group of independents, some with right-wing, and others with left-wing, sympathies.

Members of the old traditionalist elite, which was divided into two main rival parties, lost much of their power since they failed to nurse their constituencies. Although they still dominated Syria's two largest parties, neither of the parties commanded an absolute majority. A coalition government became inevitable. On 29 October 1954, al-Khuri managed to form a new government composed of the two traditionalist nationalist parties—the People's Party and the National Party. It was necessary, however, to make a gesture toward the strong left-wing opposition. The new coalition announced its adoption of a foreign policy of neutralism and its opposition to making any alliances with non-Arab powers.[4]

The Rise of Neutralist and Communist Influence following the Formation of the Baghdad Pact

Bakdash's electoral achievement boosted communist activity in Syria. Communist propaganda activity intensified and communist literature was

now sold openly in bookshops, and communist papers were freely distributed to trade unions where communists exercised influence. The reasons
for the relatively good performance of the Communist Party in the elections were explained by a British report:

> [The Communists] drew their support mainly from the large towns. Social condi-
> tions no doubt played their part in winning votes for the party, but other factors,
> such as the appeal of communism to the frustrated younger generation of intel-
> lectuals and the search for some form of protest against the Western attitude
> towards the Palestine question, also played their part. The increase in commu-
> nism in Syria during 1954, taken in conjunction with the general trend to the left
> and the government's reluctance to take any really effective measures against it,
> is an unfortunate development.[5]

The political void created by the downfall of al-Shishakli was exploited
by the Communists, who seized the opportunity of political freedom to
intensify their overt activity. The communist-oriented "League of Syrian
Writers," held its third annual meeting in Damascus in early July. The
meeting was attended by members from all parts of Syria, the majority of
whom were communists or fellow-travelers. The participants expressed
"their responsibility as writers to point out the dangers of plans and
alliances threatening the country with occupation and destruction."[6] The
organization succeeded in penetrating the Syrian press: at one point,
according to a British estimation, at least 40 percent of all Damascus newspapers had one or more known communists or fellow-travelers on their
staff who were also members of the League. Most of these journalists were
under thirty-five years old and were, according to the British,

> an unusually hard working group with an *esprit de corps* which leads them to help
> one another financially . . . they received financial support from some outside
> source. This tends to be confirmed by their willingness to accept lower salaries
> than equivalent non-Communist journalists. Though many of them were
> educated in schools belonging to various French organizations, they are now
> notable for their anti-Western attitude.[7]

After the removal of al-Shishakli, the sale of communist literature translated into Arabic increased considerably and was sold out within a few days
of its arrival in Syria.[8]

On 16 July, the Syrian Peace Partisans, another influential communist-
oriented organization, held a conference in Damascus attended by 113
delegates and guests from all over Syria. The conference, which was
presided over by the well-known communist fellow-traveler, Sa'id Tahsin,
declared that it was an independent movement and would welcome anyone
who wished to defend peace. The conference's Political Committee urged
all "honest Syrians to unify their efforts in order to foil the plans of the

colonizers, to support the Arabs and their peoples in their struggle against the colonizers and to denounce the use and even the testing of Atomic and Hydrogen bombs."[9] Although the conference decided not to officially support any candidates at the forthcoming elections, it enabled individual Peace Partisans to freely undertake political activities.[10]

From the strategic point of view of the Soviets, of all the Arab countries, Syria was the one to receive most attention because of its proximity to Soviet borders. Throughout 1954, stated a British report,

> [Syria] was in fact a special target for Soviet propaganda and communist activity. The banning of the Communist Party in some neighboring Arab countries seems to have made Syria the pivot point of the Cold War in this area. The staff of the Soviet Legation in Damascus increased considerably during the year and some satellite missions were opened. The Soviet Union also participated on a large scale at the Damascus International Fair in September and, in the absence of British and American official pavilions, created a considerable effect.[11]

Soviet–Syrian relations had been improving throughout al-Shishakli's period in power. As part of their growing interest in the Arab world, the Soviets had, since the early 1950s, supported Arab causes brought before the Security Council related to the Israeli–Arab conflict. When, on 19 October 1953, the dispute between Israel and Syria over the Jordan Waters diversion scheme (the Benot Yaacov Project) was discussed in the UN Security Council, the Soviet Union took Syria's side. On 22 January 1954, the Soviet Union voted against a draft resolution that was submitted by the three Western powers (the UK, the US, and France), despite the fact that these powers had taken pains during the deliberations to formulate their draft in such a way that it would appease the Soviets. This draft, while criticizing Syria for interfering with regional development projects, also censured Israel for ignoring instructions issued by General Bennike, Chief of Staff of the UN Truce Supervision Organization.[12]

On 12 January 1955, when Turkey and Iraq officially announced their intention to conclude a military treaty—a move supported by the Western powers—Soviet anxiety increased. They feared that Syria might be the next Arab country to join the Western military pact. No one, declared *Pravda*, doubted the hostile attitude of these Western blocs to the Soviet Union. The Soviet public could not be indifferent to the "machinations of the aggressive circle of the US, Britain and their accomplices, which are taking place on the borders of the USSR."[13] Nasser, who interpreted the Baghdad Pact as a Western attempt to isolate Egypt in the Middle East and bring the Arab world under Iraqi leadership, took pains to establish a united Arab front against the Iraqi plans. He hosted a conference of Arab Prime Ministers in Cairo from 22 January to 6 February 1955, but his efforts, which achieved only scant success, split the Arab world into rival camps.

Syria was represented at the conference by its Prime Minister, Faris al-Khuri, who had committed himself since taking office not to associate Syria with any military alliance with foreign countries. Al-Khuri adopted a hesitant approach when Egypt raised the question of condemning Iraq and its leader Nuri al-Said for their decision to take part in a military alliance with the West. The overall failure of the Cairo Conference had immediate repercussions for the Syrian political scene.[14] Considerable pressure was exercised by the US and Britain on Syria to join them in a military alliance, but such a step was met with disapproval by an anti-Western Syrian public. Pressure by both the public and the opposition led to the downfall of al-Khuri's government, and the left-wing bloc in the Syrian Parliament managed to gain a majority to form a new government.[15]

According to Nehru and the Syrian Minister to India, a declaration in Cairo made by Nehru on 16 February against military pacts had had a great effect in Syria and led to immediate demonstrations against the government, which was suspected of secretly joining the Baghdad Pact. In his statement, Nehru said that:

> [I am] completely opposed to military alliances as an approach to international problems. Such arrangements in the atomic age, whether in West Asia or Southeast Asia, caused irritation and suspicion and added to general insecurity instead of ensuring security . . . We must think not in terms of war but prepare for peace. If the world is foolish enough to have war, I wonder what good alliances can be.[16]

The government, said Nehru, "fell as a consequence and a new government was established . . . this government is very much opposed to the pact between Turkey and Iraq."[17] The Syrian Minister informed Nehru that Syria, in common with Egypt and Saudi Arabia, was definitely against the pact and they "were thinking of having an [Arab] mutual security pact, a clause of which would be that they should not join military pacts with other countries."[18]

The Soviet approach regarding Faris al-Khuri's stand on the Turco-Iraqi agreement seemed ambivalent. A few months after its formation, the Soviets expressed their satisfaction with Faris al-Khuri's statement that Syria was against participating in aggressive blocs. Al-Khuri was quoted by *Pravda* as saying that "we reject any alliance and any agreement contradicting the interests of the country or able to deprive it of sovereignty, independence and freedom."[19] During the Cairo Conference the Soviets again praised him for his firm refusal to join the Baghdad Pact.[20] However, the Soviets were pleased with the downfall of his government on 7 February, only a day after the conclusion of the Cairo Conference. The al-Khuri government, stressed *Izvestiia*, collapsed as a result of its tendency to approve the policy of military blocs in the Arab East.

There may be several explanations for this Soviet ambiguity. First, the Soviets were disappointed that, owing to "pressure from the Western powers," the Cairo Conference of Arab Prime Ministers refused to "satisfy the demands of the public which insisted upon resolute and open condemnation of the Turco-Iraqi treaty."[21] Reports emerged in the Egyptian press that were critical of al-Khuri's sympathy toward Iraq and his refusal to condemn the Turco-Iraqi treaty.[22] The second reason was because of developments on the Syrian political scene: the coming to power on 13 February of the leftist bloc. The al-'Asali government was dominated by Khalid al-'Azm, who held two key positions: Minister of Defense and Minister for Foreign Affairs. Within a short period of time, Al-'Azm—supported by a wide group of independents and the two leftist parties (the Ba'th and the Communist Party)—became the chief architect of the rapidly growing Soviet–Syrian rapprochement.[23]

Khalid al-'Azm's positive attitude toward the Soviet bloc derived from "their mutual" understanding of international affairs. He stressed that his cooperation with the Communist Party was confined to that mutuality and did not include domestic or socio-political affairs.[24] His rapprochement with the Soviets and Communists, he explained, was motivated only by utilitarian and practical reasons—their mutual struggle against imperialism, and Syria's need for Soviet aid in various fields. Communism as a practicable ideology for Syria was out of the question: "the more I was fascinated by the Soviet achievements," he said, "the more I was convinced that communism was not the right way for us."[25] Although Syria had declared its adherence to the policy of neutralism in the inter-bloc conflict, he believed that the Soviets, unlike the Western powers, were willing to extend aid to Syria with no political or financial strings or conditions. The Soviet Union was a friendly state that "understood our [Syria's] real situation, and we established with her relations [such as those] existing between two brothers who are not interested in each others assets . . . We did not give the Soviets anything in exchange and we did not tie ourselves with them in military or political agreements."[26]

In a conversation with the British Ambassador to Damascus that took place soon after his ministerial appointments, al-'Azm stated that the new government was opposed to communism. In his view the best way to fight the spread of communism in Syria was not "by open opposition and repression," but by "raising the standard of living and improving the conditions of labor so that the seeds of communism may not take root."[27] Al-'Azm stressed that Syria found it difficult to develop close ties with the West because the latter, in particular Britain and the US, were responsible for the creation of Israel, and they continued to maintain friendly relations with the Jewish state, supplying it with heavy weapons, and refusing, in contrast, to provide the Arabs with similar arms. By doing so, they exposed the Arab countries to possible Israeli aggression. Al-'Azm declared that the offer of friendship would be made to those countries who had shown sympathy and help toward settling the Palestine problem and demonstrated a willingness to support Syria in other matters.[28] While al-'Azm's stated policy *vis-à-vis* the inter-bloc rivalry was one of non-alliance, his attitude toward cooperation with the Western camp was negative. Nevertheless, he was fully aware that Syria had an urgent need of foreign aid—politically, economically, and militarily—and such aid could only be obtained from one of the two rival blocs. He therefore embraced the principles of positive neutralism, yet with closer affinity for the Soviet bloc.

The primary item in the political program of Sabri al-'Asali's government was the reconfirmation of the principle of Syria's non-participation in foreign military blocs. This caused a great deal of satisfaction in Moscow and Cairo, and indignation in Iraq, Turkey, and the West. The Soviet press often reported that the Western-aligned states were exerting pressure on the Syrian government to join the Baghdad Pact and warned that the Soviet Union would not remain indifferent to such pressures.[29]

The threat from Turkey and Iraq to Syria reached a climax soon after Syria joined Egypt and Saudi Arabia on 6 March in publicly condemning Iraq and the Baghdad Pact. The three Arab countries also urged other countries not to join the Turco-Iraqi Pact, or any other military pacts, but to set up a joint pact for Arab defense and economic cooperation.[30] The Syrian government received warnings from Turkey and Iraq, and, on 20 March, it was reported that these countries had concentrated their forces near the Syrian borders.[31] The Soviet Union responded quickly to the Turkish threat. On 23 March, Molotov met with Farid al-Khani, the Syrian Minister to Moscow, and informed him that the USSR supported Syria's attitude *vis-à-vis* Turkey and was prepared to intervene if necessary to assist Syria in maintaining its independence and freedom.[32] On the same day, Khalid al-'Azm received the Soviet Minister to Damascus to discuss the Soviet attitude toward the dispute.[33] Al-'Azm informed the Soviet Minister of a copy of the *aide memoiré* presented to him by the Turkish *Chargé d'Affaires*. This paper made it clear that the proposed Syrian–Egyptian pact was considered a hostile act by Turkey, and that Turkey would revise its policy toward Syria should the latter go ahead with the pact. The Syrian Foreign Minister also brought a warning letter given to him by the Turkish Prime Minister, who was quoted as saying: "We are at the end of our patience. If you speak of Alexandretta, we will speak of Aleppo. If you wish to break off relations, we are ready to do so." He also blamed Egypt and Syria for launching a war of propaganda against Turkey and Iraq by attempting to poison Turkish–Iraqi relations.[34]

In March 1955, during the deliberations in the UN Security Council following the Israeli attack of 28 February in the Gaza Strip in which 39

Egyptians and eight Israelis were killed and many were injured, the Soviet government attacked the Turco-Iraqi Pact and held that the policies of Western powers of "forming military blocs" were responsible for the growing tensions in the Middle East.[35] Several occurrences took place in the first half of April that created a situation requiring an immediate Soviet response. First, on 5 April 1955, Britain joined the Baghdad Pact as a full member. This development was coupled with continual pressure on Syria to join the Pact. On 18 April, the Afro-Asian conference convened in Bandung. The main message that the participants of this conference were to deliver was their objection to all military alliances and to demonstrate that there was an Afro-Asian consensus on international affairs. The Soviets wanted to endorse all those countries that took a hostile stand with regard to the Western military plans, and to assure them that it would stand behind them in case of future conflict with the West. Two days before the conference opening, Vasily V. Kuznetsov, the Soviet Deputy Foreign Minister, addressed the conference with a statement praising "the struggle of the Asian and African countries against any form of colonial domination, and for their political and economic independence."[36]

On 16 April the Soviet Ministry of Foreign Affairs issued an official statement on security in the Near and Middle East. The situation in this region, it was stressed, had deteriorated considerably owing to Western pressure for participation in military pacts. The Soviets made it clear that they could no longer remain indifferent to the establishment of foreign military bases on Middle Eastern territory. Such actions had a direct bearing on the security of the Soviet Union because of the proximity of those countries to Soviet borders:

> Ultimatums have begun to be made that Syria should join the Turco-Iraqi alliance, and these demands are accompanied by threats calculated to intimidate the government and people of Syria and to force Syria to change its position of non-participation in aggressive military blocs ... Great pressure is also being brought to bear on Egypt, on whom demands are being made that she change her negative attitude to the Turco-Iraqi bloc and that she should not support Syria ... If the policy of pressure and threats against countries of the Near and Middle East continues, this matter will have to be considered in the United Nations ... [the Soviet government] will defend freedom, independence and non-interference in the internal affairs of the states of the Near and Middle East.[37]

The Syrian and Egyptian governments expressed their satisfaction with the Soviet statement, and Farid al-Khani called on Molotov on 23 April to express his government's gratitude for the interest and attention displayed by the Soviet government. In return, the Soviet Foreign Minister assured Syria that the USSR would firmly maintain its position as set out in the published statement.[38]

Left-wing Syrian papers welcomed the Soviet statement as strengthening

Signing the formation of the United Arab Republic: Presidents Shukri al-Quwatli (Syria) and Gamal Abdel Nasser (Egypt), *al-Musawwar*, 7 February 1958.

Discussing the future of the union: Sabri al-'Asali, the Syrian Prime Minister (left), Akram al-Hawrani, a Ba'thist leader (second left), Egyptian President Nasser (second right) and the Syrian President al-Quwatli (right), *al-Musawwar*, 28 February 1958.

Greeting an old friend: Tito, the Yugoslav leader, and Nasser, the President of the UAR at the opening ceremony of the Belgrade Conference of non-aligned countries, *al-Musawwar*, 15 September 1961.

A post-Bandung meeting: Nehru, the Indian leader and his new ally Nasser, the Egyptian leader, Cairo, *al-Musawwar*, 15 July 1955.

Changing shifts: Shukri al-Quwatli, the newly elected Syrian President, at a meeting with his predecessor, Hashim al-Atasi (right), Damascus, *al-Musawwar*, 27 August 1955.

Spreading smiles in Cairo: Sa'id al-Ghazzi, the Syrian Prime Minister (white suit, left), Nasser
(center), and the Saudi Crown Prince, Emir Faysal bin 'Abd al-'Aziz (right), satisfied with their
consent to conclude a mutual military pact, *al-Musawwar*, 14 October 1955.

Following the formation of the UAR: Nasser and Nehru among the world's great leaders, a caricature in *al-Musawwar*, 7 March 1958.

Whither is Syria heading? One of many demonstrations in Damascus calling to object Western military defense arrangements and to adhere to a policy of neutralism, *al-Musawwar*, 17 December 1954.

A demonstration of Syrian women in the streets of Damascus remonstrating against the Four Powers' proposal to the Arabs to participate in the formation of a MEC, *al-Musawwar*, 15 November 1951.

The Cairo Conference of Arab leaders in response to the imminent Turco-Iraqi mutual defense pact. Faris al-Khuri, the Syrian Prime Minister, is in the middle between Nasser (left) and the Saudi Crown Prince, Emir Faysal bin 'Abd al-'Aziz (right), *Akhir Sa'ah*, 26 January 1955.

The opening speech of the Bandung Conference by Ahmad Sukarno, the Indonesian leader, *Akhir Sa'ah*, 27 April 1955.

the hand of those governments that were trying to carry out the wishes of the people by adopting a neutralist attitude.[39] In an interview in *al-Jumhur* (a Syrian anti-Western independent paper) about two months later, Khalid al-'Azm, the influential Syrian Minister, expressed his belief that the Soviet attitude toward Syria had had a definite effect on the easing of foreign pressure on his government. The Soviet Union, he said, had informed Western powers that it would retaliate in the event of pressure on Syria by any other country. The Soviet Union was undoubtedly a friendly country and Syria respected it. He repeated his argument that there was a difference between the Soviet Union as a country and its communist doctrine. Syria did not approve of communism as a social system because "it was not consistent with her position, customs, and traditions." The Syrian government opposed communism "not by imprisonment and intimidation, as was the case in certain Arab countries —notably Iraq—but by introducing a system of improved social services, which undermined support for communism."[40]

Al-'Azm represented Syria at the Bandung Conference, where he delivered a speech that reinforced his government policy of neutralism and opposition to all military alliances and blocs. He attacked the Western powers, stating that, "there can be no peace with imperialism, aggression, and lack of freedom." The cause of Palestine, he said, was one of the causes that threatened world peace. Israel was established "as an outcome of imperialism and anti-Semitism . . . the legitimate people were up-rooted from their homeland . . . Israel is a pocket left behind the line of imperialism in its desperate retreat." In the battle for world peace, the peoples of Asia and Africa, al-'Azm declared, must have faith in their capacity and potential, since all the Afro-Asian nations had plenty of both:

> It is true we are under-developed in the military and economic fields. It is equally true that we do not possess nuclear and other weapons of mass destruction. But still our contribution can be great and decisive. With our combined will, if we earnestly will [it], we can veto a catastrophic war or bring it down to a minimum. Without us a world war cannot be waged. We command the greatest of manpower, of raw material, of war fuel, of military bases, and of strategic positions. We are a great asset to arrest war and establish peace.[41]

Unlike the US—which had tried to prevent the Bandung Conference from taking place—the USSR regarded the conference as a positive development. On 8 February 1955, Molotov had referred to the anticipated conference in a speech he delivered before the Supreme Soviet, stating that the conference would symbolize the positive changes "which have taken place lately in Asia away from colonialism."[42] The Soviets praised the conference and its resolutions; they were particularly pleased with those calling for the abolition of collective defense arrangements that served the interests of the great powers and the abstention by any country from exerting pressure on other countries.[43] The conference was a great success for Soviet foreign policy and represented, as David Dallin put it, "a landmark in post-Stalin foreign policy, a symbol of communist–neutralist cooperation, and a step forward into the Asian and African World."[44]

On 12 June, al-'Azm made a statement to the press before his departure to San Francisco to attend the meeting of the United Nations Assembly. He said that his attitude toward international affairs remained unchanged since the Bandung Conference and expressed his hope that the new spirit of unity which had pervaded the conference would continue to spread— that "peace would be realized by the nations renouncing alliances and disputes and following the path of collaboration." He reiterated the same points of his Bandung speech and called for the implementation of the decisions made there.[45] Standing before the UN Assembly, he declared that Syria was determined to realize the tripartite pact (with Egypt and Saudi Arabia) despite efforts of the Western powers to dissuade the three countries from signing it. He advised the Western powers not to try to obstruct the proposed pact, because it "was a step toward the unity desired by the Arabs."[46]

Jordan's Experiment in Neutralism

The question of whether Jordan would join the Baghdad Pact was a subject of intensive maneuvers within the Arab world, between those elements who wanted Jordan to join the pact and those who opposed the idea. The vast majority of the Jordanian public—in particular the large Palestinian population, whose antipathy toward the British and the pro-British Hashemite dynasty in Iraq had always been strong—expressed strong vocal opposition to the idea. Favoring Nasser's independent inter-bloc policy, they supported him in Egypt's rejection, along with Syria and Saudi Arabia, of the Baghdad Pact. These three countries conducted a propaganda campaign that stressed the necessity of purging the Arab Legion of British officers while, at the same time, maintaining its loyalty to the Jordanian throne. Opposition to the Baghdad Pact also came from within the Arab Legion itself. In early December 1955, one hundred and fifty legion officers were said to have sent a "strongly worded" letter to King Hussein opposing Jordan's entry into "foreign pacts." Hussein reportedly showed the letter to General Glubb Pasha, the commander of the Arab Legion, but was said to have refused to allow the immediate dismissal of the signatories, as Glubb Pasha recommended.[47]

The Syrian government, and in particular al-'Azm, was involved in an endeavor to prevent Jordan from joining the Baghdad Pact and the pro-Western camp. A joint visit to Amman by al-'Azm and Salah Salim on 3 March 1955 was intended to achieve that goal. After meeting Taufiq Abu al-Huda, the Jordanian Prime Minister, al-'Azm reported that the Jordanian government would be happy to join the Saudi–Egyptian–Syrian front if it received a subsidy of around £5 million a year, as well as economic assistance. In exchange, Jordan was prepared to dispense immediately with the services of Glubb Pasha and other British officers in the Arab Legion. King Sa'ud of Saudi Arabia consented to provide a substantial part of the subsidy, as did Egypt.[48] Their efforts, and continuous Egyptian–Syrian endeavors in the latter part of 1955 and early 1956, were eventually crowned with success. Jordan did not join the Baghdad Pact, and, for a short period of time (October 1956–April 1957) joined the camp of the Arab neutralists—the Cairo–Riyadh–Damascus axis. Public opinion in Jordan was opposed to the Baghdad Pact and King Hussein took this into account, although at the onset of 1956, he was still reluctant to accept offers made by Egypt and Saudi Arabia to provide Jordan with aid in order to free it from British help. W. Pankowski, a Polish diplomat in Cairo, noted that Hussein was wary of Egyptian revolutionary ideas possibly spreading in Jordan—and that the King was well aware "that the struggle against colonialism may oust him from his throne. On the other hand, he cannot openly take a stand in favor of the continuing British presence, since, in doing so, he would arouse almost all people against him, with the exception of some tribal chiefs who do not constitute a decisive force. From this follows Hussein's policy of avoiding taking a clear stand."[49] A few weeks later, a Polish political report from Cairo noted that the struggle for Jordan between Britain and the Egyptian–Saudi–Syrian axis had intensified. Britain had not yet given up the idea of making Jordan join the Baghdad Pact. Their main targets in this effort were King Hussein and the chiefs of the Bedouin tribes. The Polish report, which based its facts on information received from 'Ali Sabri, stressed that the British warned King Hussein not to ally himself with Nasser since the latter would eventually act against him by taking all possible measures to overthrow his monarchy. The British strove to persuade King Hussein that Britain was his only true ally. The British, noted the report, were not successful in this endeavor. However, as a result of these British efforts, Jordan had so far not spoken out regarding the proposal from Egypt, Syria, and Saudi Arabia to jointly offset the Jordanian budget deficit. The main obstacle preventing Jordan from joining the Baghdad Pact was the opposition of the great majority of its people, or, as 'Ali Sabri put it, "Egypt was counting first and foremost on public opinion in Jordan and took pains to strengthen the resistance of Jordanian society to the countries joining the Baghdad Pact."[50] By March 1956 King Hussein had yielded to public pressure, dismissing Glubb Pasha as the Commander of the Jordanian Legion and joining the anti-Baghdad camp led by Egypt. This move was followed by the exchange of messages (8–17 March 1956) between King Sa'ud, al-Quwatli, Nasser, and King

Hussein regarding Arab aid for Jordan.[51] The Polish Legation in Cairo regarded the dismissal of Glubb Pasha and the appointment of Jordanian General Radi 'Innab as a victory of the national forces in Jordan. The move was a hard blow to British prestige not only in Jordan, but also in the entire Arab world; it enhanced the prestige of Egypt and of Nasser personally, since it was he who had set the dismissal of British officers from the Arab Legion as a condition for giving financial aid to Jordan. This development, the Polish Legation concluded, was an indirect victory for Nasser, while also increasing King Hussein's standing in the Arab world and inspiring confidence in him.[52]

On 19 January 1957, a treaty of solidarity was concluded in Cairo between Jordan, Saudi Arabia, Syria, and Egypt. According to their earlier proposal, Syria, Egypt, and Saudi Arabia took it upon themselves to "share in the expenditure emanating from the obligations falling on the government of the Hashemite Kingdom of Jordan, as a result of [its] policy of cooperation and solidarity for bolstering Arab existence and independence, [for] the total amount of 12,500,000 Egyptian Pounds annually . . . Jordan shall devote the Arab [financial] aid to the Jordanian Hashemite armed forces including the National Guard Forces."[53] This generosity was designed to fill the financial void that would be created by the severance of the Jordanian–British military alliance two months later. On 13 March 1957, Sulaiman Nabulsi, the Jordanian Prime Minister, sent a note to the British Ambassador in Amman informing the latter of his government's decision to terminate the Anglo-Jordanian treaty of 15 March 1948. The note called on the British to withdraw their forces "stationed in Jordan for the purposes of the 1948 Treaty" as soon as possible.[54] Another step forward in Jordan's shift toward neutralism occurred when, on 27 February, at the conclusion of a meeting in Cairo of King Hussein, Nasser, al-Quwatli, and Sa'ud, it was declared that "they are determined to protect the Arab Nation against the evils of the Cold War, to keep it away from the conflicts of [that war], and to adhere to the policy of positive neutrality, in order to preserve their national interests." They also emphasized that "the defense of the Arab world should emanate from within the Arab Nation, in the light of its real security and outside foreign pacts."[55] Prior to this statement, King Hussein was alarmed by the rise of pro-communist propaganda in Jordan in anti-Western circles. On 7 January 1957 he approved the Eisenhower Doctrine, and, on 31 January, in a letter sent to Prime Minister Nabulsi, he expressed his concern regarding the danger of communist infiltration "in our homeland." He warned that he would never permit Jordan to become "a battlefield for a cold war that will be followed by a devastating and annihilating war; [for this will happen] if the Arabs allow others to infiltrate their ranks." Jordan, stated King Hussein, should be "immune to communist propaganda and Bolshevist ideas. And we have to resist everything repugnant to our leanings and convictions."[56] The power struggle in Jordan between the king and his left-wing government had been rapidly coming to a head. King Hussein, noted a US intelligence report,

> is now publicly committed to a pro-Western position from which he could no longer draw back. The most vocal of the nationalist extremists, especially the Prime Minister and the Minister of State of Foreign Affairs [and], 'Abdulla Rimawi [the leader of the Ba'th Party] have repeatedly declared themselves for "positive neutrality" as defined by Nasser, and they, too, would now find it difficult if not impossible to backtrack. This has raised the stake in Jordan . . . the life of the monarchy itself is at issue. The crisis becomes sharper and more immediate as both sides "dig in" and strive to tighten alignments.[57]

In April 1957, when the Jordanian government decided to establish diplomatic relations with the Soviet Union and receive Soviet aid, King Hussein reacted swiftly and dramatically. His tilt toward anti-Western neutralism was short-lived. When he felt that the future of his monarchy was in danger following the rise of pro-Nasserite neutralists and left-wing and pro-Soviet forces, he shifted the pendulum of orientation back to the side of the Western camp. In the second half of April he dismissed Nabulsi's government, which had been elected some six months earlier, for its decision to establish relations with the USSR. He took advantage of the Eisenhower Doctrine to rescue his reign.[58]

Al-Ghazzi's Right-Wing Cabinet and the Continuity of al-'Azm's Neutralist Policy

Although there were still active and influential pro-Hashemite and pro-Western forces in Syria,[59] several factors were to determine Syria's continuous shift toward neutralism: First, Syrian public opinion was strongly opposed to foreign power entanglements; second, the Syrian Parliament ratified the anti-Iraqi line and the opposition to military pacts as manifested by the Cairo Conference—any successive government wishing to make fundamental changes of policy would have to have the consent of a parliament controlled by anti-Western representatives; and third, there were strong elements in the Syrian army who were opposed to foreign domination and adhered to neutralism. One of these was Colonel 'Adnan al-Maliki, a staunch supporter of the planned Syrian–Saudi–Egyptian defense organization. Colonel Maliki was due to have taken over from Colonel Shawkat Shuqair as Chief of Staff of the Syrian army, but he was assassinated on 22 April 1955.[60]

On 20 September, Sa'id al-Ghazzi, the new Syrian Prime Minister, re-endorsed before the Parliament the main principles of his government's foreign policy—similar to those outlined by al-'Azm on several previous occasions—despite the fact that this government had strong ministerial representation of the right-wing People's Party.[61] Soon after its establishment, al-Ghazzi's weak government yielded to Egyptian pressure to finalize a defense pact. Signed on 20 October, the pact set up a joint Syrian–Egyptian military command. This was followed by an identical mutual defense pact between Egypt and Saudi Arabia, in which it was stated that the contracting parties would "consider any attack on the territory or forces of one of them as an attack on them both. Consequently, and in exercise of the right of individual and collective self-defense, they undertake to extend speedy assistance to the attacked country and to take immediately all measures and use all means at their disposal, including armed forces, to repel the attack and restore security and peace."[62] As a consequence of these alliances, Egypt's influence in Syria grew. The Syrian–Egyptian pact was a prototype for the Saudi–Egyptian pact, with two major differences: First, the Syrian–Egyptian pact was within the framework of the Arab League, whereas the Saudi–Egyptian was not; second, while the Syrian–Egyptian pact provided for "consultations when serious tensions affecting the security of the Arab states in the Middle East develop," the Saudi–Egyptian pact provided for consultations only when such tensions developed that would affect the security of the specific contracting parties. These differences, the Indian Minister to Syria noted, underlined the Syrian desire not to completely alienate Iraq. The Saudi Arabian motives were just the reverse, because of dynastic rivalries between the Saudis and the Hashemites. According to the Indian diplomat, "the machinery provided in either case for fulfilling the purposes of the [defense] pacts consists of a Supreme Council, a War Council, and a Joint Command; provision is also made for embarking units, installations, and bases to be placed under the joint command."[63] The stand taken by the Saudi Arabian government with regard to its inter-Arab politics and inter-bloc issues is analyzed by a US intelligence report:

While Saudi Arabia's dynasty remains genuinely anti-communist, it has aligned itself in Syria with forces which are anti-Iraqi, neutralist, and deeply resentful of American support of Israel, and it has exerted a great influence on Syrian politicians through the use of funds derived from oil revenues and advances on such revenues. The group of advisers around the Saudi king is to a considerable degree either anti-foreign or at least anti-Western and the attitude of the Saudi government has become increasingly intransigent toward the US and the UK. The renewal of the Dhahran air base lease will under these circumstances cause considerable difficulties and it is conceivable that the price demanded for base rights may be raised to exorbitant heights. The Arabian American Oil Company has been plagued increasingly by various demands from the government, which so far the company has tried to fulfill. Saudi Arabia has so far not made any definite answer to a Soviet request for the establishment of diplomatic relations and to Communist China's invitation to Crown Prince and Foreign Minister Faysal to come for a visit. Also, a reported arms offer by the Soviet bloc has not yet been acted upon. From the attitude of the Saudi government, it appears obvious that it is holding out on these various offers in order to bring maximum pressure to bear upon the US, probably with regard not only to US base rights but also to Saudi's boundary disputes with Great Britain.[64]

Since the conclusion of the Baghdad Pact, Saudi Arabia had found increasing appeal in the multifaceted concept of neutralism as it evolved out of the Bandung Conference. Saudi participation in the Afro-Asian conference in Bandung indicated a search for additional forums from which to plead for support in its most immediate controversies with its neighbors. At that stage, Saudi neutralism was not based on ideological principles, but rather represented a search for additional tactics to put pressure on the West to change its policies toward Saudi Arabia and the Middle East.[65] The Saudi approach was based on the pattern of "negative neutralism." Saudi Arabia, in line with that concept, took an independent line in international affairs. It consolidated its approach on international affairs on merits and in line with its national interests and principles, and not on the basis of commitments or alignment with either the Eastern or Western blocs. Saudi Arabia rejected self-embroilment in the Cold War and remained outside the framework of the Cold War, refusing to participate in its power arrangements or to take part in its antagonisms.

From its formation in September 1955 until its downfall in June 1956, al-Ghazzi's government strengthened its relations with the USSR and the flow of Soviet arms to Syria increased considerably.[66] The West had hoped that the right-wing government and the election of the conservative Nationalist Party leader, Shukri al-Quwatli, as President of Syria (August 1955) might check the increasing instability and growing trend toward a neutralist and anti-Western attitude. These hopes were, however, not realized. Al-Quwatli, who had been subsidized by Egypt and Saudi Arabia during his six-year exile (1949–55), was totally dependent on those two countries, both of which had consistently backed the Syrian left because of its opposition to the Baghdad Pact. Al-Quwatli also had to be careful not to antagonize the influential left-wing in the Syrian army. Saudi–Egyptian influence in Syria was endorsed by the "little RCC," the strongest military faction which was led by Major 'Abd al-Hamid Sarraj.[67]

On 15 February 1956, al-Quwatli, alarmed at the drift to the left called on political parties to unite and to form a national government with a national program. Despite the fact that the Ba'th Party tried to sabotage al-Quwatli's initiative, a so-called "national covenant" was drawn up that included the following principles for Syria's foreign policy: opposition to imperialism and Zionism; neutralism in the inter-bloc conflict; the purchase of arms from any foreign country willing to sell without conditions; the strengthening of relations with Egypt; the subsequent unification of all Arab states; and freeing the Jordanian Arab Legion from British control. These principles were identical to Nasser's formula of positive neutralism.

The national covenant was based on two factors: hostility to the Western powers and their Middle Eastern allies; and the nurturing of friendly relations with the Soviets. Although these principles were designed to be in agreement with the Ba'th political platform, the Ba'thists continued to oppose al-Quwatli's national covenant, embarrassing the government on issues related to the conflict with Israel and the union with Egypt. The French actions in Algeria against the FLN (the Algerian Movement for National Liberation) were also fully exploited by the Ba'th Party and the Muslim Brothers, who organized anti-Western demonstrations throughout Syria and called for the economic, political, and cultural boycott of France. The Syrian Parliament followed suit, condemning French policy toward Algeria. Intense pressure from the left to ban exports of wheat and cotton to Algeria and France, despite the fact that these exports were crucial to the health of the Syrian economy, eventually led to the resignation of Sa'id al-Ghazzi's government on 2 June 1956.[68] The tactic al-Quwatli employed to check leftist influence had achieved exactly the opposite results, and by the end of the month, the leftist bloc was back in power again.

Al-'Asali's New Cabinet: The Growing Influence of Ba'thism and the Rise of Communism

Al-'Asali formed a new government which was composed of the Ba'th (which now held the Ministries of Foreign Affairs and Economy) and al-'Azm's Democratic Bloc of Independents. (Al-'Azm himself only joined the government on 31 December as Minister of Defense.) The right also had minor representation in this government, including the pro-Western Majd al-Din al-Jabiri, who became Minister of Public Works.[69]

The Syrian left had gained strength as a result of the increased prestige enjoyed by the USSR, which had the advantage of having no "imperialist" history in the Arab world. Soviet strategy in Syria since the mid-1940s had espoused no unpopular causes in Syria and devoted itself mainly to exploiting Syrian hostility toward the Western powers and their efforts to assume leadership and initiative in the Middle East. The Soviet Union had also taken the Arab side in the Arab–Israeli conflict, including supplying large quantities of arms to Egypt and Syria and a policy of backing these two countries politically on the international scene.

After the downfall of Shishakli, the USSR pursued a policy of keeping the communists and itself in the background, leaving the limelight to Syrian political forces that favored its aims. Eager to exploit the Syrian–Arab anti-Western trend, and speaking on behalf of the Soviets, Khalid Bakdash had already announced in 1953 that "the communists of Syria and Lebanon are ready to support any government issuing from a National Front without requiring for themselves any position of power . . . Syria is not communist; it is national and Arab and it will remain so."[70] Several regional developments in the Middle East contributed to the influential rise of the Syrian communists. The first was the Baghdad Pact of 1955, which deepened existing cleavages in the Syrian political scene. This state of affairs offered "a golden opportunity to the well-organized and ably led Communist Party." In line with Moscow's policies, the party adopted a posture of respectability and vigorously supported the nationalist goals. The second development related to the increasing Soviet popularity following the conclusions of arms deals with Egypt in 1955 and Syria in March 1956. Many Syrians, suggested an American intelligence report, were not so much pro-communist as they were anti-West, hence pro-Soviet. For them, "Moscow is not the home of international communism, but the seat of the only great power which supports the Arab cause."[71]

The communists were also influential within the Syrian army, which remained the most likely unifying force in the country. The fine pro-leftist groups in the army were in the ascendancy, one of which was communist. The communists also carried some influence within the strong military faction of the Ba'th Party. The two groups allied themselves with the strongest faction, the "little RCC" led by Major 'Abd al-Hamid Sarraj. Despite its anti-communist approach, the "little RCC," which opposed the Baghdad Pact and was anti-Iraqi and pro-Saudi–Egyptian, was willing to cooperate with the two leftist groups.[72]

In a British report that reviewed the political events of 1955, it was noted that communism had become "respectable" and "Syrians—who in the past shunned the Russian embassy and Khalid Bakdash, the communist deputy—now visited the embassy and do not mind being seen talking to Bakdash in public."[73] In March 1956, communists and fellow-travelers made a big event out of the presentation of a "Stalin Peace Prize" to Shaykh Muhammad al-Ashmar, a long-standing Syrian communist who was the honorary President of the Partisans of Peace movement in Syria, as well as a member of the World Peace Council. The Soviet Union sent a delegation of three respectable figures to present the prize, among them Shaykh Diya al-Din Burkan, a Muslim theologian. The presentation ceremony was organized by the Syrian Partisans of Peace. In their speeches at the ceremony, the three Soviet delegates praised the prize winner and the whole Syrian people "for their struggle in the cause of peace against foreign military pacts."[74] The Soviet delegates, who were warmly received by official and non-official Syrians, were invited to visit the Prime

Minister in his office and also had several meetings with religious and left-wing figures.[75]

Communism in Syria was on the increase and enjoyed considerable public support; this can be seen by the large demonstration held at the airport to welcome the return to Syria of Khalid Bakdash on 1 April after a long visit to the USSR, where he had attended the Twentieth Congress of the Communist Party. The demonstration attracted wide attention in Syria; the crowds "were amongst the largest and most enthusiastic ever seen there and that they provided an impressive demonstration of the support which the nationalistic anti-Western Left can command."[76] The large number of participants and the enthusiasm shown caused concern among political circles in Syria opposed to the increasing influence of the extreme left. In a speech delivered at Damascus airport, Bakdash said that the confidence and support he enjoyed were due to his hostility to the imperialist policy of military alliances. Communism, he declared, had worked, and would continue to work, for national unity in order to safeguard Syrian independence. To that end, he declared, the SCP welcomed cooperation with the parties of the right—the Muslim Brotherhood and the Ba'th Party. The goal was to destroy the Baghdad Pact and to repel imperialist aggression committed either directly or through Israel, the "agent of imperialism."[77]

Soviet Steps into the Syrian Political Arena

Sir John Gardener, the British Ambassador to Damascus, reported to the Foreign Office that Syria's self-confidence had grown significantly in early 1956. Syria was no longer frightened of Israel's military might for several reasons. First, Syria had concluded a military pact with Egypt in October 1955. The image of Egypt in Syria as a mighty military power had increased following the arrival of powerful arms from the Soviet bloc countries (arms were also arriving in Syria from the same sources). Syria also believed that the USSR would help it in any future troubles it might have with its pro-Western neighbors. Syria saw signs that the West had recognized "the Arabs' strong bargaining position over oil and over the Soviet intervention in Middle Eastern affairs," and therefore they would be anxious to support Israel through the supply of arms. These developments had "given the Syrians an unwonted sense of power and with it anti-West feelings have grown."[78]

From 22 to 25 June, Dmitrii T. Shepilov, the Soviet Minister of Foreign Affairs, made an official visit to Damascus. He was accompanied by Grigorii Zaytsev, Chief of the Near and Middle East Division in the Soviet Ministry for Foreign Affairs. Shepilov's visit was another important step in the process of rapprochement between Syria and the USSR.

Upon his arrival he was greeted at the airport by Salah al-Din al-Bitar, the new Syrian Minister of Foreign Affairs, who expressed Syria's desire for a closer union with Egypt as an essential step toward Arab unity. Al-Bitar also referred to the struggle against imperialism and Israel. Lasting friendship, he stated, was only possible with those countries in favor of peace and liberty in accordance with the resolutions made by the Bandung Conference. Shepilov expressed his hope that his visit would lead to closer cooperation between Syria and the USSR. He praised Syria for its pursuit of a policy based on equality and non-intervention in other people's affairs.[79] The following day, the Soviet guest met the Syrian Parliamentary Foreign Affairs Committee presided over by Ihsan Jabri. In a statement to the press he made at the end of their meeting, Jabri said that the attention of Shepilov had been drawn to the problems of Algeria and Israel. Israel, he told Shepilov, represented an artificial state which in the long term could not survive and therefore constituted an element of instability in the Middle East. Jabri thanked the Soviet Minister for the attitude taken by the Soviet Union toward Arab interests within the UN. Shepilov, declared Jabri, had offered unconditional aid to Syria and all Arab countries to help them assert their rights. The communiqué published later on the same day, following the conclusion of Shepilov's meeting with the Syrian Prime Minister, al-'Asali, displayed the same spirit.[80]

At a state dinner at the Presidency that night, Shepilov attacked imperialism, which he declared had failed "and was now trying to restore its position by such devices as the Baghdad Pact, which had subjected Syria to much pressure. But countries which had known liberty would never let themselves be tricked again into the servitude of colonialism." The object of his visit to Syria was to bring about a lessening of tension in the Middle East. The Soviet Union, he stressed, "possessed no military bases in this area and did not wish to promote misunderstandings between Arab countries . . . The Soviet people . . . had admired the heroism of the Syrian people in refusing to be forced into aggressive alliances and they therefore wished to establish relations with Syria in accordance with the principles of the Bandung Conference."[81]

Shepilov devoted his third and fourth days in Syria to detailed discussions at the Ministry of Foreign Affairs; here the focus was on bilateral relations between the two countries, including the promotion of economic relations between Syria and the Soviet bloc. The Secretary-General of the Ministry of Foreign Affairs said that the two parties conducted discussions on economic schemes, the industrialization of Syria, and the question of Syrian products finding a market in the Soviet Union and satellite countries.

A close scrutiny of Shepilov's talks in Syria reveal certain disagreements, the most prominent of which was their approach to Israel and the Palestinian issue. The Syrians tried to persuade Shepilov to alter the Soviet government's current official position that the Soviet Union would work for "a mutually acceptable settlement of the Palestine problem." Reliable Syrian sources, however, revealed that Shepilov "got no nearer to the Syrian view than to say on one occasion that the USSR would be on the Arab side in bringing about a settlement . . . Syria must have patience in this matter." Alleviating the disappointment of his hosts, Shepilov promised "to supply the Syrians with all the arms they require."[82]

If the Soviet stand on the conflict with Israel caused dissatisfaction, the talks on economic relations were much more fruitful. The continued deterioration of political relations with the Western powers was affecting Syria's economy, and there was an urgent need to look for alternatives to its traditional markets in the West. Since exports of wheat, barley, and cotton constituted a major source of Syria's foreign exchange, the Syrian economy was very sensitive to changing conditions and dislocations in the international market. It was to a large extent, dependent on the export of a few agricultural commodities, and on the willingness of a few countries to import its produce. Until 1956 France, Lebanon, Britain, and the US had been Syria's leading trading partners. These four countries accounted for nearly 50 percent of Syria's trade in 1955; for the same year, Syria's trade with Soviet bloc countries accounted for less than 2 percent of the total. As a result of Syria's decision to impose a boycott on the shipment of wheat to France in reprisal for French North African policies, France had threatened to curtail its purchases of cotton from Syria—a tangible threat to the Syrian economy, since France imported around 60 percent of Syria's cotton. Iraq, which had been one of the main importers of Syrian textiles, had also virtually halted its imports from Syria in 1955 because of disputes over the Baghdad Pact and Arab relations with the West.[83] Economic considerations had swung in favor of closer ties with the Soviet bloc in order to seek new markets for its agricultural and industrial production. Since early 1955, Syria was engaged in concluding bilateral treaties with Soviet bloc countries which had expressed a willingness to buy Syrian products (cereals and cotton) in exchange for a lucrative role in Syria's program of economic development—roads, railways, and ports.

Throughout 1956, Syria signed bilateral trade and payment agreements with most Soviet bloc countries. These agreements provided for Syrian exports of agricultural goods and textiles in exchange for manufactured products, especially capital goods. The most significant trade development was the Czech–Syrian arms deal which was announced in May 1956. According to this deal, Syria was to receive between US $23 million and

US $30 million in arms from Czechoslovakia; payments were to be made in cash, wheat, cotton, and other commodities. In mid-1956, the Syrian Eastern Development Corporation was established for the purpose of handling "trade with Soviet Bloc countries as well as to undertake the construction of industrial plants, develop shipping transportation agencies, and provide for other commercial services."[84] Already in March 1956 a Soviet technical delegation had visited Syria to talk with Syrian governmental officials and private interests regarding the industrial development of Syria. Another mission, headed by Heinrich Rau, East German Minister of Trade and Deputy Prime Minister, visited Syria in early May.[85]

Syria wanted to exploit the substantial opportunities arising from growing Soviet interest in the Middle East and the fact that the Soviets were keen to establish their influence in the region. The Soviet bloc could provide both military (arms) and economic (money and technical services) aid, as well as international support for Arab causes, including taking the Arab side in the conflict with Israel. Soviet willingness to assist Syria in many fields was unconditional as long as Syria continued to reject Western military arrangements in the Arab world and adhered to the principles laid down by the Bandung Conference.

During Shepilov's meetings, the Syrians had politely declined his idea of a political and defense agreement with the Soviet Union. At the conclusion of his visit, Shepilov offered his Syrian hosts aid in the construction of the Latakiya–Jazirah railway, grain storage facilities, airports, and other projects of infrastructure construction that had been recommended by the International Bank of Reconstruction and Development in its survey of Syria. Shepilov also offered financial aid necessary to undertake the building of the Yusuf Pasha Dam on the Euphrates. His offers were formulated in a general way, leaving room for more detailed talks in the future. More Soviet offers to construct industrial establishments were put forward during a second visit of a Soviet technical mission which arrived in Syria in July.

Soviet bloc efforts to get involved in the construction of industrial and infrastructure projects were crowned with success with the unofficial announcement in September that East Germany had been awarded a contract to build a cement plant at Aleppo.[86] Soviet bloc offers of economic aid were also intended to gain a foothold in Middle East oil operations. Czech efforts in late 1956 to win the contract for the construction of the Homs oil refinery near the Iraq Petroleum Company's pipeline demonstrated how this policy of favoritism worked. From the spring of 1956, there were intense negotiations over who would get the contract. The final duel was fought between a privately owned Anglo-American firm, Procon, and a Czech firm backed by its government. Although Procon's offer was highly competitive and more favorable, the Syrian government found it impossible to award the contract to a Western firm because of the inter-ference of left-wing elements within its hierarchy that favored the Czech offer, despite the fact that "the technical capabilities and material quality of the Czech firm were recognized to be inferior." Al-Ghazzi's government favored Procon, but with its downfall the next government, dominated by the left, awarded the contract to the Czechs in the spring of 1957. A contract worth Syr £54 million was signed with the Czechs for the construction of the oil refinery, with the payments to be staggered over a period of several years.[87]

Syrians and the Soviets gave prominence to their success, promoting a cultural agreement designed to create the conditions for the spread of Soviet cultural activity in Syria. An account of Shepilov's visit and its possible repercussions is given by Sir John Gardener, who stated that, although no specific agreements were concluded during Shepilov's visit, it had had

> a very great effect on the general political situation. By tradition and by economic interests, Syria has, despite the creation of Israel, continued to look to the West. This visit with its prospect of economic help from the USSR has diverted Syrian eyes to that quarter. The USSR and its policies have, through greedy hopes, perfervid nationalism and reactions against Israel, become popular. This will probably complete the process already begun of making left-wing parties and their doctrines respectable, and is likely to find concrete expression by the formal removal of the present ban on the Communist Party whose membership and importance is thereby likely to increase. Conversely, the right-wing political parties which stand for friendship with Iraq and the West generally will undoubt-edly find their task more and more difficult, for the Syrians are expert climbers on the bandwagon.[88]

Strong anti-Western sentiments in Syria gave the Soviet bloc an oppor-tunity to strengthen its political and economic ties with Syria. The Soviets had an advantage over the Western powers—they did not have a "colo-nialist" or "imperialist" record in the Middle East. Soviet bloc efforts in Syria, an American intelligence report correctly suggested, "are also abetted by pro-[Soviet] bloc political elements, which are more influential than in any other Arab state."[89]

Commercial and cultural relations were also developing between Syria and China, and agreements in these fields were concluded in mid-1956. In August 1956, a Chinese Commercial Representation was established in Syria. During a visit of a Chinese cultural mission in August, its members called upon the Syrian Prime Minister to deliver a message from Chou En-Lai, the Chinese Prime Minister, in which he alluded to the fact that "friendly communications" between the two countries were first estab-lished during the Bandung Conference. Since then, Chou stated, "cultural and commercial relations between the two countries are increasing daily and the friendship between the two nations has been cemented more and more."[90] In his reply, the Syrian Prime Minister expressed his "gratification at the consolidation of friendly relations which had followed Syrian recognition of the People's Republic," and that he hoped that cultural and commercial relations between the two countries, which were based on the recent agreements, would be further developed.[91]

Syria and the Suez Crisis: The Rise of "Pro-Soviet Positive Neutralism"

Nasser's decision of 26 July 1956 to nationalize the Suez Canal led to a growing tension between Syria and the Western powers—particularly Britain and France, the two main shareholders of the Suez Canal Company and who stood to be worst affected by Nasser's move. Syria, tied to Egypt by their military pact of October 1955, took Egypt's side, justifying Nasser's move and offering support to Egypt by all means possible. Prior to Nasser's announcement of nationalization, when news of the US Department of State's decision to refuse to finance the building of the Aswan Dam had reached Syria, anti-Western feeling flared up and the Syrian Ministry of Foreign Affairs protested to the US Ambassador. Anti-Western feelings increased following Nasser's July decision. Both the press and politicians launched virulent attacks on Britain, France, and, to a lesser degree, the US, for their reaction to the nationalization of the Canal. Akram al-Hawrani, one of the Ba'thist leaders, gave speeches and urged the government to close the pipeline from Iraq if the Western powers took action against Egypt.[92]

On 3 September, in a speech at the graduation ceremony for new officers at the military school at Homs, President al-Quwatli affirmed the solidarity of Syria and the Arab world with Egypt. He attacked the "imperialist powers for their aims of expansion and exploitation to which the Arabs refuse to submit." The imperialists had allied themselves with the Zionists. The establishment of a military alliance with Israel was designed in such a way that the latter would be used as "a springboard for an attack on the Arab world." The Western powers had also "waved the threat of a third world war at Egypt, merely because she [Egypt] had recognized her resources: this clearly shows that they covet our fortune, our resources, and our land, and that they intend to appropriate them indefinitely." Al-Quwatli concluded his speech by declaring that Syria had been by Egypt's side from the beginning and "shall spare nothing in defense of right and honor."[93]

An eleven-day visit (4–14 September) to Syria by fifteen deputies of the Soviet Parliament headed by M. Sinin continued the chain of visits of

Soviet bloc delegations to Syria. At a dinner party held at Bludan in honor of the Soviet delegation, Nazim al-Qudsi, the Speaker of the Syrian Parliament, warmly welcomed the Soviet guests. In a speech he addressed to the Soviet deputies, he declared that unity was the keynote of Arab aims. As long as the Arabs were divided, he stressed,

> The Great Powers would be impelled by motives of greed to loot Arab wealth and compete for strategic positions in the Arab countries. The Arab world was therefore full of gratitude to any nation, which would support them unconditionally, irrespective of strategic positions and social principles, in the task of liberation and in the elimination of Israel, which had been established in the Arab homeland as a tool of intervention by the Great Powers.[94]

In his reply, Sinin deliberately disregarded al-Qudsi's remarks about Israel. Rather, he emphasized the interest of the Soviet people in the Arabs and noted that the teaching of Arab history was now a compulsory item in the curricula of Soviet secondary schools. Sinin also praised Syria's modern industrial development and its success in agriculture in contrast to the lack of progress made by the imperialists.[95] During their visit, the Soviet delegation had met all of Syria's heads of state and toured textile factories in Damascus, a sugar factory in Homs, and a number of major and provincial towns. The Soviet guests had expressed their support of the Egyptian nationalization of the Suez Canal and agreed with the need to work for a peaceful solution.[96]

Official Syria continued to show decisive support for .Egypt and its struggle throughout the Suez crisis. The Syrian government expressed its gratitude to all those countries that supported Egypt, among them the Soviet Union. In a speech delivered by Salah al-Din al-Bitar, the Minister of Foreign Affairs, in Aleppo on 28 September, al-Bitar stated that Egypt's nationalization of the Suez Canal Company had been taken by Britain and France (and behind them, the US), "as a pretext to restore their imperialist prestige in the Middle East, and so they concentrated their forces and held conferences and prepared everything to attack the Arabs." At this critical moment for Egypt and the Arabs, friendly states were siding with them; the Foreign Minister stressed that it was "his national duty to strengthen the attitude of these friends." Although al-Bitar and his Ba'th Party were consistent in their opposition to communism as an ideology, the Foreign Minister called upon Arab journalists to stop attacking Communist Russia, which was firmly supporting the Arab struggle for liberation.[97] Such criticism was displayed by right-wing newspapers during the visit of the Soviet Parliamentary delegation in early September. *Al-Ittihad*, for example, voiced suspicions of Soviet expressions of friendship and asked whether the Soviet deputies really represented the people or whether they were merely "the nominees of [Nikolaii] Bulganin and [Sergeyevich]

Khrushchev."[98] Stopping aggression by the imperialist powers, explained al-Bitar, "depends on the support of Powers friendly to the Arabs,"[99] and the Soviet Union was indeed "Syria's best friend."[100]

In early October, the Syrian press reported that al-Quwatli accepted Shepilov's invitation to visit the USSR on 30 October.[101] The intimate atmosphere in Soviet–Syrian relations provided a good basis for deepening and strengthening these relations. Between June and October, the number of diplomatic missions of communist countries had grown considerably. Both Soviet and Czechoslovak missions had extended their staffs by receiving new diplomats with high qualifications. Military technicians from Soviet bloc countries had arrived to instruct the Syrian army in the use of Soviet weapons. The British Embassy in Damascus reported that, "the vigorous leftist elements in the present government, represented by two Ba'th ministers, seems to have paralyzed the conservative, pro-Iraqi faction." This development had been reinforced by the effect of the Suez crisis on Syrian public opinion, "which has been to discredit the Western powers and increase Russia's popularity."[102] According to this report, the Soviets were active in increasing their popularity, pursuing a vigorous propaganda campaign. In order to impress the Syrians, Soviet bloc countries spent a great deal of money on their pavilions at the Damascus International Fair (1–31 September 1956). A large number of Soviet bloc technicians took part in building and running these pavilions. Although the West also had quite an impressive representation in the Fair, and "the quality and competitiveness of their goods showed up well in comparison with Soviet bloc goods," the very weight of the Soviet bloc participation "impressed the public and again provided a front-window for the public display of communist activities."[103] There were also continuous close contacts and a mass of complementary activities between Syria and Eastern European countries.[104]

A few days before al-Quwatli's departure to Moscow, al-Bitar, who was due to accompany the President, had a meeting with the British Ambassador to Syria. The meeting took place on 24 October on the latter's initiative in order to discuss British–Syrian relations following the Suez crisis. During their talks, Gardener complained that, with the exception of Iraq, Syria and the Arab world, "were preoccupied in pursuing their own nationalistic aims to the exclusion of legitimate and established rights of commerce and of navigation of the West, and that they preferred the friendship of Russia to that of the West, which had been more helpful to them than Russia was ever likely to be."[105] Al-Bitar considered Gardener's analysis "too severe," but agreed that animosity toward the West "had gone too far"; however, he concluded that the differences between the Western powers and the Arabs were "too wide to be bridged except very slowly."

Gardener suggested in reply that "a start could and should be made with the Canal, which is now the key to Arab–Western relations." Egypt, stressed Gardener, had initiated the crisis, and it should therefore "now come more than half-way in accepting a solution which would give the governments of the West the guarantees which [are] essential to maintain the standard of living of their people." Al-Bitar expressed his view that "Egypt would not dare for some years at least to do anything to interfere with shipping through the Canal." He believed that a solution to this crisis could therefore be deferred "until Arab–Western relations had improved." Al-Bitar also regarded Britain's association with France over the Canal as an unwise move. Gardener managed eventually to persuade al-Bitar to urge Nasser "to make a liberal approach" to Britain over Suez, though al-Bitar expressed his fear that "this gesture would not be met in the same spirit" by Britain. Responding promptly to al-Bitar's words, Gardener reported that "while I could make no promise, [I believed] the gesture was well worth making."[106] Gardener did not know about the Anglo-French-Israeli clandestine talks on a jointly planned attack on Egypt due to begin a few days later.

Official Syria remained mute following the entry of Soviet tanks into Budapest on 24 October to suppress the uprising in Hungary, which was a rebellious Soviet satellite state.[107] The left-wing press made no mention of these events, preferring to concentrate on the arrest of anti-colonial Algerian leaders by France. In contrast, the right-wing press made the most of the suppression in an attempt to discredit the USSR as a trustworthy ally, and attempted to raise questions regarding the quality of the friendly Soviet attitude toward Syria. Right-wing papers criticized "those elements in Syria" who favored closer relations with the USSR, referring them to the outcome of the Hungarian uprising and the fate of other satellite countries. *Al-Insha'* criticized left-wing papers and Radio Damascus for not reporting the uprising, writing that, "at the very moment when Eastern European countries are beginning to throw off the Soviet yoke the Syrian supporters of Soviet domination are increasing their propaganda in favor of a regime that would bring about the enslavement of Syria."[108] The right-wing paper *al-Qabas* was even sharper in its criticism of Radio Damascus, noting that "in suppressing this news [Radio Damascus] has become more communist than the satellites."[109]

Martial law was proclaimed throughout Syria at midnight on 29–30 October, soon after the Anglo-French-Israeli military actions began against Egypt. Ba'thist politicians and officers in the army wanted to take military action against Israel, but were prevented from doing so by Nasser. There was some fear that Iraq, or possibly France, would intervene to protect the oil pipeline from Iraq. On 2 November, the Syrian government announced its intention "of breaking off diplomatic, consular, and cultural relations with Britain and France." It gave the two ambassadors twenty-four hours to leave. The government also announced that it would protect the pipeline and the foreigners employed on it.[110] Syrian politicians, press, and public opinion had reacted violently to the Anglo-French military attack on Egypt—the country with which many Syrians favored federal unity.

In the shadow of two international crises in which great powers from the two rival international blocs were involved—one in Eastern Europe, where the Soviet Union appeared to be the aggressor; and the other in the Middle East, where Britain and France were the attackers—Shukri al-Quwatli's four-day visit to the Soviet Union commenced as planned. Al-Quwatli arrived in Moscow on 31 October accompanied by a distinguished entourage, which included his ministers of Foreign Affairs, Defense, and Agriculture, and by the heads of the Central Bank and the Information and Propaganda Department. Although the date of al-Quwatli's visit had been arranged before the crisis began, events in the Suez Canal Zone occupied a central place in the talks. Upon his arrival, al-Quwatli stated at the airport that he was "happy to be in a country which had broken the bonds of colonialism and was showing the way for other countries to follow."[111] The following day, al-Quwatli held talks with Voroshilov, during which he talked about the Arab struggle for liberation and of "the attempts of the imperialists, in alliance with Zionism, to halt Arab progress." The attack on Egypt, he declared, was an attack on the whole Arab world. He praised the Soviet Union for standing on the side of the Arabs: "We are grateful to the Soviet Union for adopting this position and therefore state here that we are ready to develop and maintain the most friendly relations with your great country." At the Kremlin reception on the last day of the visit, Voroshilov attacked Israel, Britain, and France. The joint communiqué issued at the conclusion of the visit condemned the three countries for their "open and unprovoked aggression against Egypt and for their failure to heed the UN General Assembly's resolution calling for the cessation of hostilities and the withdrawal of foreign troops from Egypt."[112] In the course of his visit, al-Quwatli had met the Soviet heads of state. Reports from Moscow also revealed that al-Quwatli had spent a great deal of time meeting with Soviet military figures to discuss possible Soviet military help in support of Egypt, including the possibility of dispatching Soviet "volunteers" via Syria. The issue of expanding trade and commercial transactions including arms supplies was also discussed.[113]

Al-Quwatli's efforts to persuade the Soviets to take military measures to help Egypt did not meet with success. Al-Quwatli heard many words of sympathy and support for Egypt and the Arabs for their struggle against imperialism, but no actual plans ever materialized. His visit had no great practical significance. With or without the visit, argued the author of a British account of al-Quwatli's visit, "Soviet influence in Syria, already strong, is bound to increase as long as the present tense situation in the Middle East continues." Al-Quwatli's visit gave the Soviet hosts, "the best possible opportunity of impressing on the president and his companions that the Soviet Union is the only true friend of the Arabs in their struggle against Western domination."[114]

At the conclusion of the Suez crisis, two countries emerged victorious. Although Egypt was defeated militarily, internationally it gained an impressive political victory over the Anglo-French-Israeli coalition. Not only was the coalition forced by the United Nations to withdraw their forces from Egypt unconditionally, but they failed to achieve most of the political goals they had set themselves prior to going to war. The other victorious country was the Soviet Union, which, except for paying lip service to the support of Egypt in the international arena, did not perform any substantial actions. The threats it made of sending "volunteers" and of the possible use of the atomic bomb went largely unheeded; however, the threats of action were in themselves sufficient to secure the USSR as the Arabs' main ally and friend. Many in Syria held the opinion that it was not the action of the United Nations or the US that led to the prompt ceasefire, but the Soviet threat to bomb London and to send "volunteers" to support Egypt on the ground. The British Foreign Office considered the Soviet moves as tactical bluffs and intended to achieve several goals:[115] to encourage the Arab and Afro-Asian states to make extreme demands both inside and outside the UN, and to ensure that Soviet intervention would be credited with any developments satisfactory to the Arabs; but not to outstrip Afro-Asian opinion by independent action, for which there had been no call in the UN. The British concluded that Bulganin's proposal for joint Soviet–American action against Anglo-French military actions showed that the Soviet leaders realized the danger of unilateral intervention. Soviet threats of military supplies or volunteers, they maintained,

> contain at the present time a large element of bluff, although in the long-term the [Soviet] bloc will no doubt remain a source of arms supplies and other assistance. Nevertheless, the Soviet Union's interests are best served by keeping the Middle East in a state of turmoil and they will try to perpetuate the present confusion. Soviet prestige is already heavily committed and the Soviet Government have carried bluff dangerously far. If the situation in the Middle East deteriorates further still and if the Arab states ask the Soviet government to implement their recent vague promises and threats, they would probably feel impelled to send "volunteers" and urgent material help of at any rate token significance to the Arabs. In that case the most obvious and least dangerous point of entry for the Soviet Union would be Syria, where Soviet aid would be used against Israel rather

than against British and French forces. Rapid assistance for Syria would have to be sent by air, but there are few airfields in Syria suitable for jet aircraft.[116]

The probability that the Soviets would implement their threats throughout the Suez crisis and send volunteers[117] was seriously discussed by the Western powers at diplomatic and military levels. The British Military and Air Attachés in Moscow, who were asked to evaluate the capabilities of the Soviets to realize such threats, held the view that, for objective and subjective reasons, the prospects were very low. The Military Attaché argued that a Soviet division needed 11,000–15,000 fighting men "plus a share of supporting services amounting to some 5,000 or more, and that moreover would consume some 500 tons of supplies a day during operations. It would clearly be a long job to build up a base in Syria for Russian military operations." The Air Attaché pointed out that "a major operation of preparing runways and pre-stocking jet fuel would be needed before the Soviet Air Force could operate from Syria: at least 6–9 months preparation would be needed before the bomber operations could be mounted."[118]

The way the Suez crisis ended was to have positive consequences for the Syrian left which had supported Nasser and even wanted to take an active part in the war. Nasser's image in Syria was of someone who had scored a military and diplomatic victory over the Arabs' traditional imperialist enemies. Soon after the war was over, left-wing elements took advantage of the Anglo-French humiliation to seek and eliminate their right-wing opponents. Left-wing military officers were involved in rooting out right-wing elements both inside and outside the army. There were many arrests, and the final step in the transfer of power from the right to the left took place on 11 December with the formation of a Parliamentary National Front composed of more than half of the deputies, with the object of opposing "plots against the state, imperialism and the Baghdad Pact."[119]

The development of events after the outbreak of the Suez War caused great concern in Turkey and Iraq, Syria's pro-Western neighboring countries. On 11 November, Nuri al-Sa'id asked for a meeting with Sir M. Wright, the British Ambassador to Iraq, to express Iraq's concern about the growing Soviet involvement in Middle Eastern affairs, in particular in Syria. Al-Sa'id informed Wright of his recent talks with the Turkish Prime Minister, who had made it clear to him that Turkey could not stand by and allow Syria to become virtually communist or controlled by Communist Russia. If the Soviets were in earnest in attempting to control Syria, the Turkish Prime Minister had stated, "the West would react strongly and . . . it would be made plain that Russian action could lead to a third world war." Unless the Soviets intended to provoke war, a possibility which he ruled out, it was necessary "that their bluff should be called by firmness on the part of someone. If this were done, the tension in the Middle East would be considerably diminished and Nasser would no longer be able to pose to the Arab world as being able to count upon Soviet support in Syria, ostensibly on behalf of aid for the Arabs against injustice."[120] The Turkish Prime Minister assumed that NATO was giving urgent consideration "to the danger of their flank being turned and that Turkey's attitude would depend to a large extent on NATO's views."[121]

The British Foreign Office responded immediately to this information by instructing its embassy in Ankara to inform the Turkish government that Britain deemed it an advantage in keeping the North Atlantic Council informed of developments in Syria. The Foreign Office suggested that the Turkish government might instruct the Turkish delegation at NATO "to call the attention of the council to the situation and pass [on] all suitable information which [the] Turkish government receive about Syria and the Soviet threat."[122] Although, compared to the Turkish and Iraqi Prime Ministers, the Foreign Office was less alarmed by the Soviet moves in Syria, it wanted to assure Britain's two allies that "the military and intelligence staffs of NATO are very much aware of the dangers of Soviet intervention in the Middle East including Syria and are watching the situation closely."[123]

Turkey was closely monitoring the activities of the Soviets in Syria. On 15 November, the British Embassy in Moscow sent the Foreign Office information received by the Turkish Air Attaché in Moscow, who had in turn received it from "a very important source." According to this information, Marshal Zhukov and the Syrian Minister of Defense (who accompanied al-Quwatli during his visit) met in Moscow twice on 9 November and signed a military treaty that included the following clauses:[124]

1. The USSR would provide Syria with aircraft, tanks, and guns;
2. The Soviets would establish operational jet units in Syria as soon as possible, either by flying them in or by shipment, and would train in the Soviet Union some Syrian pilots and technicians;
3. The Soviet Union would provide technical and logistical teams to develop four existing Syrian airfields to modern standards and to build three new ones.

According to the Turkish Air Attaché, there were political and economic footnotes attached to this agreement that were based on benefit and utilitarian considerations. The extent of Soviet military and economic aid to Syria would be directly related to the "military facilities" that Syria would offer in return. In return, Syria expected the Soviets to support its claims for a Greater Syria through geographic alterations to its borders with its neighbors—Israel, Lebanon, Turkey, and Iraq.[125] There is no clear-cut evidence to establish whether this deal was signed, and, if so, whether it was under the terms stated above. The subject of Soviet arms making their way to Syria was an established fact. One arms deal between Syria and the USSR was known to have been concluded in early 1956. By the end of October 1956—and with no connection to the Suez War—Syria, under the terms of the deal, had received from the Soviet bloc some 100 medium tanks, 100 armored personnel carriers, 50–100 self-propelled guns, and about 100 other guns of various calibers, together with large quantities of minor armaments, ammunition, vehicles, wireless, radar and other equipment. About 20 MiG-15 aircraft ordered by Syria were delivered to Egypt for assembly and then dispatched to Syria; and bombs and rockets for these MiGs were (possibly) delivered to Syria directly. The total value of this arms deal was estimated to be about Syr £20 million. Reliable reports indicated that negotiation for purchasing MiG-17s and other advanced military equipment had been ongoing since al-Quwatli's visit to Moscow.[126]

Reports from Damascus confirmed the arrival of Soviet bloc arms to Syria. These reports could not be specific with regard to the types or quality of the arms, but substantial quantities of various weapons were arriving from the Soviet bloc—taxation in Syria was being increased to pay for them. Reports also confirmed that Soviet technicians were resident in Damascus. The Soviet bloc military build-up within Syria was not a short-term project. So far, it had been limited to the supply of aircraft, arms, and other forms of military equipment, and although Syria had to pay for these purchases, the terms of payment were thought to be generous. There appeared to be no restrictions on what the Syrians could order.

At the same time, there was no reliable evidence of an imminent build-up in Syria of military and air concentrations. The possibilities of sending airborne and seaborne troops to Syria on short notice were limited for several reasons. First, the Syrian airfields were not up to handling large numbers of transport aircraft, serving as bases for Soviet jet aircraft, or providing them with the necessary support facilities, such as storage for special fuel. Second, sea-routes from the Soviet Union to Syria would have to embark at Black Sea ports, which meant that, on their way to Syria, they would have to pass through the Turkish straits. There the Turks could easily monitor and control the passage of heavy vessels making their way to Syria for military purposes. If this happened, "the Turks would be entitled to hold up such vessels under the Montreux Convention." Any Soviet threats of launching a military effort from Syria was, according to the reports,

a medium-term [danger] rather than an immediate one. Syria will probably be reinforced with Soviet equipment, advisers and technicians in the next few months and these could be supplemented by small groups of "volunteers" at short notice. The Russians might then be able to manipulate the situation to bring about renewed fighting between Israel and the Arab states or a renewed Arab attempt to deny the Suez Canal or other oil supply routes to the West. From the Soviet standpoint, Syria probably provides a better opportunity than Egypt under present circumstances. The Russians probably hope that, as there are no UN or British forces there, a gradual build-up would not attract so much attention and would not bring into operation President's Eisenhower's threat of American action to prevent the arrival of forces in the Middle East.[127]

By the end of 1956, the British Embassy in Moscow concluded that the Soviet operation in Syria was a double one. First, arms, equipment, and a certain number of Soviet instructors were being supplied to Syria to strengthen the local armed forces and provide a pool from which potentially dissident elements in neighboring Arab countries could draw. Second, a Soviet stockpile was being built up in Syria so that, if the Soviets decided to play a direct military role in Syria, they would already have many of the supplies they would need waiting for them.[128]

Recently declassified Polish documents have confirmed that, in late 1956, an arms deal was concluded between the Syrian and Polish governments for a total amount of US$7,785,160 worth of goods. The deal included 1,000 aviation bombs (FAB-500s), four radar stations of the Nysa type, and other weapons. The arms deal was to be fully implemented by the end of 1957.[129] On 6 December 1956, in a speech delivered at a Syrian university, President al-Quwatli confirmed that Syria had obtained Soviet arms. Syria, he declared, was exercising a sovereign right. These arms deals reflected Syria's policy of positive neutralism—manipulation of the inter-bloc conflict in order to advance Syria's national interests. If the Western powers declined its requests for arms, Syria would then buy them from the rival Eastern bloc: "Arms were not available and we could not get them from those who had been plotting, delaying and deceiving, and, simultaneously, preparing the aggressive Zionists for new conquests in Egypt, Lebanon, Jordan, and Syria." Al-Quwatli made it clear that relations with the Soviets were friendly, but denied rumors spread by Western sources of an alleged communist danger. These powers feared that Syria was about to become "one of the iron-curtain states; they even directed accusations—involving our loyalty to our religion and nation—as if either were any of their business; in actual fact, however, they were afraid lest we should break through the imperialist curtain which, for many years, they have imposed on us in order to make us eat the crumbs at their tables, while resources of our country remain common booty for them, but strictly denied to us."[130]

Turkey felt most threatened by the recent Soviet moves in Syria and had taken great pains to convince its NATO allies of the seriousness of these developments. The Turkish Air Attaché in Moscow had revealed alarming information on aggressive Soviet plans for Syria. In Moscow, however, US and British diplomats were in agreement that "[the Attaché] is not a reliable source, since he is a poor observer, is inclined to be alarmist, and has an obvious ax to grind in trying to persuade the Americans and ourselves [the British] of the dangers of the Syrian situation."[131] On 28 November, at the NATO Council Meeting, the Turks circulated a statement expressing "the grave view they took of developments in Syria, which presented a threat to Lebanon as well as to the Baghdad Pact Powers."[132] The British representative at this meeting, Sir Christopher Steel, belittled the importance attached to the Soviet threat in Syria by his Turkish counterparts. "There was no firm evidence to support the more alarmist of the reports about the presence of large Soviet reinforcements, particularly aircraft, in Syria," he noted. Syria was, however, "the obvious point of entry into the Middle East for the Soviet Union and the situation there presented a potentially dangerous threat to NATO's Eastern flank which must be countered by all practicable means. The problem was to know what means we could adopt."[133] The answer to this was not possible, the British concluded, "as long as the Americans maintain their detached attitude towards the Soviet threat. NATO pressure on the United States would be all to the good."[134]

An accurate and enlightening analysis of the internal Syrian political situation and its relation to Soviet involvement in Syria's affairs was provided by Kamil Chamoun, the Lebanese President, during his conversation with the British Ambassador to Lebanon on 7 December. The role of al-Quwatli in this game, he explained, was not crucial, because he was largely a prisoner of the left-wing and nationalist elements in the government "and could quickly be reduced to a powerless figurehead." Chamoun held the view that the Syrians were becoming deeply involved with the Soviets, both militarily and economically. In order to check this development there was an urgent need to change Syria's government. Such a move was impossible under the current circumstances, "owing to the firm grip which the army had on the country and the large number of opposition leaders either in jail or exile." The West, suggested Chamoun, could do no more than monitor the situation closely.[135] A similar picture of the situation in Syria was provided by the Turkish ambassador to Damascus during his conversation with the British ambassador to Beirut, which took place the following day in Beirut.[136] The British Foreign Office came to the same conclusion with regard to the impotent nature of the Syrian government, stating that "the real power is wielded by a clique in the army and a group of politicians who are communists, fellow-travelers, or pro-Russian. The atmosphere in Damascus and the provincial cities is becoming increasingly worse and conditions there resemble what one would expect to find in a communist state. Pro-Western elements are under constant police surveillance and liable to arbitrary arrest."[137]

John Foster Dulles, the US Secretary of State, declared that in his view, neither the US nor any other state could use external force to prevent Syria from becoming a Soviet satellite if the Syrian government wished to do so. Dulles, however, doubted "whether any country could long remain a satellite unless that country had a border next to the Soviet Union. While, therefore, Syria might become a satellite for a time, he did not think that it was beyond the power of the free world to win her back in due course."[138]

Pressure exerted by the army and the left on al-Quwatli and on the nationalist Prime Minister Sabri al-'Asali finally resulted in a government reshuffle on 31 December. The reorganized government was composed of entirely new ministers, apart from Prime Minister al-'Asali and the two former Ba'thist Ministers who continued to hold the same portfolios. Left-wing politicians were heavily represented in the new government; right-wing parties and independents were excluded. One of the most important changes was the return of Khalid al-'Azm, who now held the positions of Minister of State and *Chargé* of Defense.[139]

Syria's pro-Soviet orientation was the result of a combination of intense Arab nationalism and political radicalism. The Israeli, Turco-Iraqi, and Western menaces, taken seriously by many Syrians, were to play a major role in stimulating pan-Arab feelings—a development that translated into a desire to develop close relations with "victorious" Egypt. The rise of radicalism in Syria and Egypt, which had begun as a reaction to the Western powers and Israel, soon adopted a socialist character and was directed against the old traditionalist elite—the land and property owners, the entrepreneurs and industrialists, and the existing social order. The combination of radicalism and nationalism was a strong phenomenon among officers in the Syrian army—to all intents and purposes, the most influential element in Syrian politics. Socio-economically, these officers, like their Egyptian counterparts, were mostly of lower middle-class origins. They felt a natural affinity with their Egyptian partners, and saw in the possibility of Soviet military and economic aid a powerful weapon to use against Israel and the West, with its Middle Eastern allies. At that stage, although Soviet influence in Syria had grown steadily over the past few years, the country had still not completely fallen into the Soviet embrace. The then existing state of affairs in Soviet–Syrian relations was analyzed by a British report:[140]

The USSR had undoubtedly secured a certain foothold in Syria, largely because of the latter's support for Egyptian policy and because of the instability of Syrian internal politics. Whether the USSR will be able in the future to increase her hold on Syria largely depends on the success of the Soviet policy towards Egypt and on the influence which the pro-Soviet military faction is able to wield in Syria. At the moment the Syrian leaders, like their Egyptian allies, apparently feel confident that they can use Russian support for their own ends without becoming mere instruments of Soviet policy.

Attempts by the Soviets and their local communist followers to expand their control over Syria would grow a great deal in the following year. By late 1957, the struggle for hegemony over Syria would be between two of Syria's strongest allies, Egypt and the USSR; a regional power versus a global superpower. In the course of this struggle, the Ba'th and other anti-communist elements in Syria would ally themselves with Nasser's Egypt.

5

Syria's Rival Schools of Neutralism and the Road to Union

The process of gradually removing right-wing politicians from power was successful only as long as the army officers supported the tactic. However, this method of government reorganization led to social discontent in Syria's towns, which had been the strongholds of the traditional right-wing elite for many years. Reports indicated that anti-government activity was going on in the periphery. On 5 February 1957, right-wing elements distributed pamphlets in Aleppo attacking the government for its left-wing tendencies. It was reported that bombs were even being thrown, though these were intended to intimidate and terrify rather than to kill. Parents were subsequently urged to keep their children away from school because the local authorities could not guarantee their safety.[1]

In a message to the US Congress on 5 January 1957, President Eisenhower requested authorization for an economic program and for a resolution on communist aggression in the Middle East. This message was better known as the Eisenhower Doctrine. The doctrine stipulated that the US would reply positively to requests made by any country in the Middle East asking for military assistance to protect its territorial integrity and political independence against overt armed aggression "from any nation controlled by international communism." Eisenhower accused the USSR of creating instability in the Middle East and noted that its interests in the region were solely "that of power politics. Considering her announced purpose of communizing the world, it is easy to understand her hope of dominating the Middle East."[2] The Eisenhower Doctrine was directed toward two countries in particular: the USSR, whose expansionist ambitions in the Middle East the US wanted to discourage; and Egypt, with the aim of making it plain to Nasser that, if his aggressive and subversive policies against pro-Western regimes did not stop, the US would not hesitate to act against him.

Official Syria's immediate reaction to the Eisenhower Doctrine created a degree of confusion, and Syria's policymakers employed a "wait and see" tactic. On 7 February, Salah al-Din al-Bitar, the Foreign Minister, told Soviet visitors to Damascus that, if the Eisenhower Doctrine would be imposed by the US, it would be rejected. If, however the doctrine was simply an American analysis of the Middle East, then the Arabs had their own analysis to put forward. When the Americans understood this analysis, al-Bitar said, there could be cooperation.[3] On the same day, Prime Minister al-'Asali issued a statement in response to the Eisenhower Doctrine that concurred with al-Bitar's comments. Al-'Asali refuted Western allegations that Syria had become communist; the fact that Syria had purchased arms from the communist bloc did not mean that Syria was becoming communist, he stated. The influential pro-Soviet Defense Minister, al-'Azm—who, on 7 February, also issued a moderate statement emphasizing Syria's adherence to its policy of neutralism in the inter-bloc conflict—would adopt an adverse approach to the American President's doctrine. Al-'Azm was encouraged by the Soviet warning issued on Radio Moscow on 7 February to the Arab world that any nation permitting a foreign power to set up military bases would expose itself to the threat of the Soviet atom bomb. On 10 February he told the Soviet paper *Pravda* that Syria categorically rejected the Eisenhower Doctrine. A day earlier, Akram al-Hawrani, a prominent Ba'thist leader, had reaffirmed Syria's commitment to neutralism and denied on Radio Damascus that Syria wished to join any bloc.[4] By June, al-Bitar was persistent in his opposition to the Eisenhower Doctrine. Fully committed to his party's adherence to neutralism, he stressed that "Syria did not wish to belong to any bloc so as not to be hampered in its foreign policy and was prepared to receive economic aid from any source, excepting only [aid offered under] the Eisenhower Doctrine."[5]

The US Embassy in Damascus reported in late January that Syria was steadily becoming "an inefficient police state in evolution toward subservience to either Egypt or Russia." Syria, the report noted,

[had all the] classical machinery of a police state: effective one-party government (the national pact, with the opposition ceasing to oppose); a perpetual state of emergency (and with it censorship, so exercised as to cut out all news and comments favorable to the West); purging of the administration of pro-western elements; dependence of the government on army (purged), secret police, and an inner cabinet; selective taxation designed to weaken the wealthiest classes; plans under consideration for state trading organizations as a basis for bilateral agreements with the East.[6]

Syria was characterized by the report as xenophobic, anti-Zionist, anti-Western-Christian, and pan-Arabist. The Syrians, it was concluded, had an "immodest conviction" of their ability to "outsmart the Egyptians, the Russians or anyone else."[7] Future events would demonstrate that the report's conclusion was incorrect; Syrians were, in fact, insecure and had low self-esteem with regard to their ability to defend their independence. Because of this, they became an object of manipulation for both Egypt and the USSR.

In order to consolidate their hold on Syria, the Soviets appointed diplomats to Damascus with a wide knowledge of Arabic and the Arab world. These Soviet "Arabists," who were extremely active, produced a daily information bulletin. Jamil Hasan, the Third Secretary at the Pakistani Legation in Damascus, reported that there were also six or seven Soviet army officers in Syria who served as technical advisers, and that Soviet subjects had been brought into Syria on satellite passports. The "Russians," Hasan noted, were popular in Syria, "where it is universally believed that it was Bulganin's ultimatum which brought about the cease-fire at Port Said."[8]

In early June 1957, Soviet–Syrian relations, which had been developing rapidly since late 1955, reached one of their peaks with the conclusion of a political agreement which committed both countries to undertake: (a) not to allow US forces to use Syrian bases; (b) not to take action to defend any Arab state against communist subversion; and (c) not to allow Syrian bases to be used by other Arab forces. In return Syria was to receive increased shipments of Soviet arms.[9] Clause (b) referred mainly to Jordan and Lebanon, two adjacent Arab countries experiencing subversive activity by pro-Soviet Arab elements. As far as clause (c) was concerned, it is not clear which Arab state was interested in using Syrian bases other than Egypt. Relations with Hashemite Iraq at the time were at a low ebb, which meant that Iraq was not likely to be permitted to use military facilities in Syria. If this clause referred to Egypt, it was meaningless, since Syria and Egypt were bound by a military pact (October 1955) with a joint command.

The development of events in the Syrian political scene since late 1956 indicated that pro-Soviet elements within Syria had the advantage over their right-wing rivals. It looked as though it was just a matter of time for Syria to become a Soviet zone of influence. Under these circumstances, the Soviets did not need Nasser's anti-communist Egypt to distract from this development. Both Egypt and the USSR were vying for domination over Syria. The two countries sensed that Syria would soon have to voluntarily relinquish its independence, opening it up to external rule. The underlying motive behind the Soviet demand from Syria to agree to clause (c) was to smooth the way for their future takeover of the country. What the Soviets did not take into account was that the Syrian left was divided between two groups—the influential Ba'th Party, whose members were Arab nationalists and wanted Syria to be fully united with Egypt; and those who were pro-Soviet, communists and their fellow-travelers, who wanted to see Syria become a Soviet ally. The Soviets underestimated the political strength of the Ba'th and the decisive role played by its army officers, the true leaders of Syria.

A remarkable change had taken place in inter-Arab relations in late 1956 with the conversion of King Sa'ud of Saudi Arabia—who had been anti-Hashemite and pro-Nasserite—to the Eisenhower Doctrine, and reconciliation with Iraq and Jordan, coupled with the increasing isolation of Syria and Egypt. The Soviets made an effort to "seal off" the effects of this realignment and prevent Syria and Egypt from reconsidering their own positions *vis-à-vis* the Eastern bloc. To achieve this goal, the Soviets sought to aggravate inter-Arab differences and tensions between Egypt, Syria, and the West. The "Red Millionaire" Khalid al-'Azm contributed to this effort by attacking King Sa'ud for siding with the West and leaving the pro-Egyptian Arab camp.[10]

By the end of June, it was widely reported by Western and local Syrian sources that preparations were underway in Syria for a new political purge and the establishment of a communist-dominated government and administration. British diplomats in Beirut reported the landing of new Soviet arms and the arrival of a Soviet submarine at the port of Latakia.[11]

On 24 July, Khalid al-'Azm began a two-week visit to the USSR at the head of a high-level Syrian delegation. Talks were held with the highest level of Soviet policymakers, including Khrushchev, Bulganin, and Marshal G. Zhukov, Minister of Defense. The joint communiqué published on 6 August at the end of the visit revealed the purpose of the visit and its results. The discussions, which took place in "an atmosphere of friendship and cordiality," dealt with political, military, and economic issues. The visit was conducted in the shadow of the Eisenhower Doctrine, which had caused some concern in Syria about possible US plans to protect its interests in the Middle East. The Syrians needed Soviet reassurance, as they had in early 1955 in connection with the Turco-Iraqi threat. The Soviets manifested "a sincere sympathy for the efforts of the Syrian government [which were] aimed at consolidating the political and economic independence of the country and at liquidating as quickly as possible the remains of colonialism."[12] The extension and development of economic cooperation was discussed, culminating in an agreement in which Soviet–Syrian cooperation would be carried out

> through the organization of projects of geological prospecting, [and] research and the drawing up of plans for, as well as the construction of, industrial and other plants. The Soviet authorities will delegate their specialists in Syria for this purpose and will supply the equipment and materials that are lacking in the country . . . an economic delegation composed of experts of the appropriate different branches will go to Syria soon for the purpose of implementing the agreement reached on economic cooperation . . . the Soviet side declare that economic and technical cooperation will be carried out without any conditions

of a political or analogous nature, on a basis of equality and reciprocal economic advantage, of non-interference in internal affairs and complete respect for the national dignity and sovereignty of the Syrian Republic.[13]

Although the word "arms" did not appear in the communiqué, both parties regarded the arms deal of late 1955 as a positive step that had "contributed to the development of reciprocally advantageous commercial ties" between Syria and the USSR. The communiqué alluded to the fact that the talks also touched on questions of payment for deliveries made previously; that is, arms deliveries.

On 7 August, al-'Azm arrived in Prague for a three-day visit to conduct talks on economic and technical aid. He returned to Damascus on 10 August, and several days later rendered an account of his visit to the USSR and Czechoslovakia. Al-'Azm thanked the people and government of the USSR for their political, diplomatic, and economic support of Syria in the international field. He also emphasized that, while other countries had refused to provide Syria with arms, the Soviets did so, enabling Syria "to purchase arms to increase the strength of our beloved army."[14] He listed the main public works projects (rail, road, air, and harbor), irrigation and hydroelectric schemes, and industrial plans which Syria was interested in executing. The World Bank, al-'Azm declared, had insisted on attaching various unacceptable conditions to the necessary loans; the Soviets, however, had agreed in principle to help Syria carry out these projects, with payments spread out over a long period of time. Unlike the West, the Soviet Union had declared that it would not interfere in Syria's internal affairs "nor does it want to interfere with our political or social systems." The Soviets were purely motivated by a desire to strengthen Syria's economy, to consolidate its regime, and to secure its independence. Al-'Azm refuted allegations of Soviet and communist plans to take over Syria: "The Russians have no ambitions in our country. Their country is enormous . . . [therefore] there is no necessity for territorial expansion into any other country. Thus neither Syria nor any other country is the object of territorial ambitions."[15] The economic blockade imposed on Syria by the West, concluded al-'Azm, would come to an end with the agreement of both the Czechs and the Soviets to on take surplus Syrian agricultural and industrial production.[16]

An aid agreement was signed in October 1957 in which the Soviets agreed to finance the construction of the Euphrates Dam and other projects worth an estimated $90 million. They also promised to add about $40 million more in October 1964, a pledge, which was not entirely fulfilled.[17]

August 1957 witnessed a severe deterioration in US–Syrian relations. The Eisenhower Doctrine rejected by the Syrian government, and the special relations that were developing between Syria and the Soviet bloc, both contributed to this development. On 12 August, Syria announced that it had uncovered an American plot to overthrow the Syrian government, and the following day the Syrian authorities expelled three US diplomats whom they accused of plotting the coup. These charges were regarded by the Department of State as "fabricated" and "unfounded."[18] Several days later, Nizam al-Din, the moderate Syrian Chief of Staff, was replaced by 'Afif al-Bizri, an officer who was thought to be pro-Soviet and affiliated with local communists.[19] On 24 August, Loy Henderson of the US State Department arrived in Turkey to discuss with its leaders the situation in Syria, where he also met with the leaders of Iraq and Jordan. In a report to his superiors at the end of his visit on 5 September, he expressed his deep concern that Syria might be falling prey to international communism—a development, which, in his view, could jeopardize the security and independence of the whole area.[20]

Salah al-Din al-Bitar ridiculed Western allegations of a communist takeover, stating in a press conference: "It is only in Syria's atmosphere that one can understand the truth of the Syrian situation."[21] The Syrian government considered Henderson's mission a failed attempt to drag Iraq and Turkey into a military action against Syria. The government paper *al-Ra'i al-'Amm* suggested that the members of the Baghdad Pact had put heavy pressure on Henderson to persuade the US government to join the Pact. Henderson's only conclusion, noted *al-Ra'i al-'Amm*, seems to have been "that Syria should be isolated with a cordon sanitaire."[22]

Although the heterogeneous left-wing camp had already completed consolidating its hegemony over the Syrian political scene, there were still calls in its various papers for an administrative purge, "because Syria must be able to make proper use of the economic aid which the Soviet Union had promised," which Khalil Kallas, the Minister of National Economy, said amounted to almost Syr£1 billion. He also declared that Syria had found "the markets she needs for her agricultural products and that Syria has been able to obtain unconditionally from the Soviet Union all the assistance she needed."[23] Prime Minister al-'Asali embraced the Ba'th doctrine of positive neutralism, which was already practised by Nasser's Egypt—a policy aiming at exploiting the Cold War and the inter-bloc rivalries by playing the Western bloc off against the Soviet bloc and vice versa in order to advance Syria's national interests. Al-'Asali did not rule out the development of economic ties with the West. He explained, however, that Soviet offers of economic aid were preferred to US or International Bank offers because they were unconditional and were attractive economically.[24] Evidence that economic and commercial relations between Syria and the Western powers were at low ebb could be found in the absence of British and American representatives at the annual Trade Fair in Damascus, where there was enthusiastic participation of Eastern bloc countries. The outstanding foreign pavilion that year was that of the USSR.[25]

On 3 September, the Syrian *Chargé d'Affaires* in Ankara told the Turkish newspaper *Ulus* that his government's policy with regard to inter-bloc conflict was, and remained, neutralist. He described allegations that Syria was sliding toward communism as unfounded; Syria would accept no aid to which any conditions were attached. He ruled out the possibility that Soviet aid would place Syria under Soviet influence and lead to the spread of communism in the country. The purchased Soviet arms should not be seen by "a strong nation like Turkey" as competition or an act of provocation on Syria's behalf, but as a Syrian move intended to "strengthen herself against Israel."[26]

The Syria of late 1957 was characterized by its Janus-faced foreign policy—on the one hand, al-Bitar, the Ba'thist Foreign Minister, was active in advancing his party's ideology of Arab unity by bringing Syria closer toward a union with Egypt. In early September, the two countries signed an agreement for future economic union that provided for the appointment of a joint subcommittee to discuss detailed plans. On the other hand, al-'Azm, the Defense Minister, in alliance with the communists, was doing everything possible to bring Syria closer to the Soviet Union. His visit to the Soviet bloc was fruitful as far as Syria's economy and military needs were concerned.

By early October 1957, Nemchina, the Soviet Ambassador to Damascus, could express his satisfaction with the process of the rapid radicalization that was going on in Syria. The anti-Western political parties that nurtured closer cooperation and relations with the Soviets were supported by the vast majority of the Syrian public, noted the Ambassador. In Syria, unlike other Arab states, public opinion exercised great influence over the government. The army in Syria played a major role in state affairs, and the fate and duration of its governments depended on the willingness and interests of key army officers. Currently, the army was anti-imperialist and anti-American. US efforts to manipulate Syrian army officers in order to overthrow incumbent governments only served to increase hatred in the army for America.[27]

The process of radicalization was taking place amid an intense power struggle within Syria between progressive and reactionary forces. This situation was influenced to a great extent by a tense international situation, in general, and by US efforts to rehabilitate the Western position and influence in the Levant, in particular. The explanation for the Western failure in Syria, said the Soviet Ambassador, was that Syria, unlike other Arab countries, had two large and influential anti-Western parties: the SOP, which enjoyed the support of students, intelligentsia, and workers, but lacked the support of the peasants and the army; and the Socialist Ba'th Party, which conducted an intensive anti-imperialist struggle and enjoyed much influence among army officers, soldiers, intelligentsia, and the petit-bourgeoisie. The two parties had a growing influence on the internal political situation in Syria. According to the Soviet Ambassador, there was a high level of cooperation between the two parties despite the fact that there were certain disagreements between them on internal affairs.[28] This Soviet analysis of the current existing state of affairs in Communist–Ba'thist relations was soon to become irrelevant. The last weeks of 1957 witnessed a growing power struggle between the two parties arising out of disagreements about Syria's foreign orientation. The CPS wanted to fully commit to the Soviet Union, believing that it would serve their overall interests; the Ba'thists wanted to maintain Syria's positive neutralism and continued to cling to the view that full union with Egypt was inevitable and necessary.

An accurate picture of Syria's internal situation and its attitude toward the inter-bloc conflict was portrayed by Nehru, who maintained close relations with both Syria and Nasser's Egypt. In an attempt to refute Western allegations of a communist conspiracy and Soviet takeover of Syria, Nehru wrote a personal letter to the British Prime Minister Harold Macmillan in which he explained Syria's awkward situation:

> I have been watching developments in Syria for many months and I paid a brief visit to Damascus in June last. I found then a prevailing fear of being surrounded by hostile forces backed by some of the Great Powers. Economic pressures were being exercised against them. There was an intense national feeling and a desire to do everything for self-preservation. Owing to certain military alliances, notably the Baghdad Pact, the countries surrounding Syria were becoming progressively more hostile to it, and the Syrians believed that these countries had the powerful support of the United States. They further believed that a deliberate attempt was being made to isolate their country and thus bring pressure to bear upon them so as to change the regime there.[29]

Nehru admitted that the involvement of army officers in politics had recently become more noticeable, stressing that some of them were pro-communist. Nehru declared that he was assured that communism had little strength or organization in Syria.

Nehru ruled out the possibility of a Soviet takeover in Syria similar to the one that had occurred in Czechoslovakia in the late 1940s. Syria had no common border with the USSR and did not have a strong Communist Party, as was the case in Czechoslovakia. Since the death of Stalin, who was responsible for the aggressive action in Czechoslovakia, the position of the Soviet Union had changed. The vast majority of the Syrian officers were "young [and] intensely inexperienced," and Nehru believed they had the urge and desire to preserve Syria's independence. He was also certain that these officers had no intention of attacking any neighboring state. If, however, "they are driven to extreme courses by fear of any military or like action against them, then they may well rely even more [up]on the Soviets." An attempt to moderate Syria's position was being made by friendly neutralist states such as Egypt and India—both of whom were exercising their strong influence on Syria to show restraint *vis-à-vis* its neighboring countries—in particular with regard to Turkey, which had concentrated troops along its border with Syria. In order to achieve stability in that region, there was an urgent need to remove the "fear of armed intervention from either side or of attempts to change regimes by external pressure." Nehru was referring to the US plot to overthrow Syria's regime. He concluded his letter by establishing that, in any future conflict between communism and nationalism, the latter would prevail:

> Arab nationalism is a basic fact in all these countries and communism is not even a distant prospect. But if nationalism is driven to take help from communism then the combination of the two might certainly be strong. The right course would appear to be to prevent such a combination from taking place and to allow nationalism to grow independently and to work out its destiny.[30]

Nehru considered the so-called communist danger a non-existent threat—an imaginary scenario designed by external forces hostile to Syria.

In the second half of September, a close scrutiny of statements and interviews made by Syrian politicians and high-ranking military officers covering the main spectrum of political views in Syria supported Nehru's analysis. Salah al-Din al-Bitar accused the Western powers of violating the United Nations Charter by trying to overthrow the incumbent democratic regime. The Syrian government, al-Bitar stated, was contemplating the possibility of complaining to the UN about US naval movements "off the Syrian Coast and Turkish troop concentrations near the Syrian border." The current political and security instability in the Middle East was inextricably bound to the Eisenhower Doctrine, which was:

> An extension of military pacts created by the US which had weakened the ability of the United Nations to solve international problems and secure a stable peace for the whole world. The US was using economic and military aid to turn Arab States against one another.[31]

Al-Bitar expressed his objection to the Cold War tactics being employed by the West, in particular the US. Israel, in his view an imperialist bridgehead, had been serving the joint interests of imperialism and Zionism in the Middle East "promoted by the Eisenhower Doctrine." The US plans for Syria, concluded al-Bitar, had failed for two reasons: First, the US ignored the national awakening of the Arab peoples; and second, Syria continued to adhere to a policy of positive neutralism.[32] Like al-Bitar, General 'Afif al-Bizri, the new Syrian Chief of Staff, attacked US activities in Syria, describing alleged movements of the US Sixth Fleet within Turkish territorial waters as "a show of muscle." Al-Bizri reckoned that the US might drive other nations to attack Syria because, in his opinion, the US was seeking to occupy Syria, "not directly by means of military occupation, but by placing Syria in a state of subservience politically, economically and militarily to the US." Syria, al-Bizri stated, would continue its policy of positive neutralism.[33]

President al-Quwatli defended Syria's foreign policy and persisted in not giving in to Western pressure. At a graduation ceremony at Homs Military College, accompanied by al-Bizri, he declared that Syria "would never sell herself to any of the two rival world camps for military purposes." Syrian cooperation with the Soviet Union, he explained, was based on principles of mutual interest, and communism had no influence on Syrian policies. Al-Quwatli claimed there was a connection between Zionism and Western imperialism, warning that "Imperialist–Zionist plans [were] aimed at expanding Jewish immigration into Israel and supporting Israel with arms." Such a policy, he maintained, could cause another "large-scale conflict in the Middle East."[34]

In September 1957, the Secretary-General of the right-wing opposition People's Party, Ma'aruf al-Dawalibi (one of the first Arab leaders to publicly advocate neutralism and closer relations with the Soviets), reiterated his adherence to neutralism in a statement to the press. The People's Party, he declared, fully supported the present government's foreign policy of positive neutralism. It was his view that the policy of positive neutralism "formed part of the National Charter subscribed to by the People's Party, and this had been Syria's policy since 1950." The reason his party did not join al-'Asali's government derived from disagreements on "the distribution of ministerial posts." On 28 September al-Dawalibi referred to the reasons behind the recent Soviet–Syrian rapprochement. The Soviets, he declared, "do not need our oil and have no interest in us. It is sufficient for them that we should ban oil to the USA and that the area should be free, independent and neutral in order that their overall political plan may be successful. On these points our interests coincide and the Soviet people's desire that the people of this area should be free is apparent. Syrian–Soviet rapprochement does not mean communist control; this contention is pure imperialist intrigue."[35]

Khalid Bakdash, the leader of the Communist Party, also refuted allegations that Syria was about to be taken over by international communism. In an interview with the Lebanese communist paper *al-Nur*, he claimed that world opinion "would not be deceived by American propaganda to the effect that Syria had aggressive intentions against her neighbors and had been converted into a communist or Soviet base." Syria, he stressed, did not stand alone in "resisting imperialist plots." Arab nationalism "would be victorious in Syria, because of the unity of the Syrian people and their preparedness to defend freedom in every inch of Syrian territory, the support of Egypt reinforced by the solidarity of the Arab people, and the position adopted by the Soviet Union in warning the Western powers and Turkey that she would not stand idle in the face of any aggressive moves."[36]

As a demonstration of power, two units of the Soviet Fleet, the cruiser *Zhdanov* and the destroyer *Svobodny*, arrived in Syria in late September for what was described as "a goodwill visit of indefinite duration to Latakia." The Soviet Vice-Admiral commanding the fleet said that his country was "always ready to support Syria against any imperialist aggression." The visit was followed on 18 September by the arrival in Damascus of a Soviet delegation of experts to discuss the development of the Syrian economy with the Syrian Economic Development Board. The visit was in response to al-'Azm's August visit to Moscow.[37] Al-'Azm and al-Bizri paid a formal visit to the units of the Soviet Fleet at Latakia, and al-Bizri, in an attempt to ease tension, declared that "there was no connection between the Soviet Fleet's visit and Turkish troop concentrations on Syria's border." The Soviet Vice-Admiral followed al-Bizri's moderate declaration with the statement that "this was a goodwill visit to sincere friends."[38]

In an attempt to appease Syria's anger and fears about its pro-Western neighbors' intentions, King Sa'ud arrived on 25 September in Damascus. Sa'ud affirmed that his country would resist any aggression against Syria or any other Arab state from whatever source it might come. He asserted his belief that Syria was not a threat to any other Arab state. The following day, Sa'ud was joined in Damascus by the Iraqi Prime Minister, 'Ali Jawdat al-Ayyubi and the Lebanese Acting Foreign Minister, Jamil Makkawi, in a public show of Arab solidarity with Syria. In an interview with the Lebanese paper *L'Orient*, al-Ayyubi expressed satisfaction with his talks with Syria's leaders and declared his hope that relations between the two countries would soon be restored to their previous friendly terms.[39] It was also reported by the Syrian press that al-Quwatli assured al-Ayyubi that Syria was not and never would be communist, and would never "give up her policy of Arab liberation and the accumulated stocks of Soviet arms [which were] solely for the purpose of defending herself against Israel." The Syrian press welcomed the newly-established discussions with these countries and maintained that they signified a closing of the Arab ranks and the beginning of the resolution of inter-Arab quarrels. The common theme in most papers was Syrian–Saudi brotherhood and the recognition of Saudi Arabia's unwavering support of Syria's freedom and independence. The press also predicted that the Syrian–Saudi relationship would be strengthened by the visit and that it would help to consolidate inter-Arab relations.[40]

Endeavors made by the conservative Arab countries to appease Syria proved largely unsuccessful. A secret, lengthy, analytical report prepared by the Polish Legation in Damascus on the situation in Syria, noted that the arrival of King Sa'ud in Syria signified his return to the

Syrian–Egyptian camp. His recent pro-American orientation and the role he played in events in Jordan in April 1957 on behalf of American interests to protect King Hussein had achieved the opposite; his prestige at home and in the Arab and Muslim worlds, was significantly diminished. The aid he had extended to King Hussein contributed toward strengthening the Hashemites, Saudi Arabia's traditional enemies, and he was criticized by Saudi ruling circles and by senior officers in the Saudi army (who received their military training in Egypt and were therefore pro-Egyptian). The Polish report suggested that King Sa'ud's recent rapprochement with Syria and Egypt derived from his fears of Israel. He believed that only Egypt and Syria would be willing to help defend Saudi Arabia should Israel attack. On their part, Syria and Egypt did everything possible to convince him that the Israeli threat was real and dangerous. The process of restoring relations between Egypt and Saudi Arabia found its expression in recent deliveries of arms and jet aircraft from Egypt to Saudi Arabia.

The Polish Legation stressed that one should remember that King Sa'ud was still in close touch with the Americans, not only because of the oil factor, but also because of an "hysterical fear" of national liberation or progressive movements. Sa'ud's recent moves were in line with current US intentions to pursue a more moderate and flexible policy toward Syria. The previously aggressive approach of the US toward Syria had reached its peak in August 1957, when the Americans had attempted to overthrow the incumbent government and install a pro-US leadership. This move failed, but Syria had become alienated from the Arab mainstream. From Syria's viewpoint, therefore, Sa'ud's visit to Damascus helped to break down the walls of isolation imposed upon it following the announcement of the Eisenhower Doctrine and the April events in Jordan. Other Arab countries followed Saudi Arabia's lead and took a more sympathetic approach toward Syria. In his talks with his Syrian hosts, Sa'ud advised them to find a common language with the US by employing a policy of balanced positive neutralism. He also advised them to nurture economic relations with West Germany, from which economic aid could also be received with no conditions attached. His advice fell on attentive ears. Soon after Sa'ud left Damascus, a group of some 100 West German economic experts arrived in Damascus to examine the possibilities of extending aid to Syria.[41]

With the conclusion of Sa'ud's visit, several gestures of appeasement were made by the US toward Syria: Dulles expressed his willingness to meet al-Bitar, and he instructed US diplomats in the UN forums to stop attacking Syria. Sa'ud's visit made it possible for the US to pursue a different policy toward Syria.

The visit of the Iraqi Prime Minister was designed to achieve several goals, the Polish report declared. First, he hoped to calm domestic discontent, which had grown substantially as a result of the pro-Western stand taken by successive Iraqi governments, in particular that of the previous Prime Minister, Nuri al-Sa'id. Second, the exacerbation of the conflict with Syria could have led to the closure of the Iraqi oil pipeline which went through Syria, and that could have caused economic damage to both Iraq and Britain. The Syrian decision to invite al-Ayyubi was an expression of support for the current Iraqi government after a period of very poor relations between the two countries. The Polish Legation in Damascus maintained that one of the long-term repercussions of al-Ayyubi's visit in Damascus was the weakening of the Baghdad Pact, and the isolation of Turkey and the limitation of its ability to play a central role within the Arab world. Syria's relations with Lebanon, as well as with Jordan, remained tense. Syria encouraged opposition elements in both countries to continue their activities against their incumbent governments.[42]

Relations between Turkey and Syria had been cold for several years. Tension had grown tremendously since October 1957. Movements of Turkish forces along the border between the two countries, the report revealed, did not attract much attention in Syria, however, and the presence of Syrian military forces along the border was sparse. In unofficial talks, ruling and diplomatic circles in Damascus ruled out the possibility that Turkey would attack Syria. Syrian military sources revealed that most of the Syrian army forces were concentrated along the border with Israel, whom they considered to be Syria's main threat. Syria's self-confidence had also been significantly enhanced because of Soviet threats and warnings directed toward Turkey. The report pointed out that one of the Soviet bloc intelligence centers in the region, as well as the Syrian Foreign Ministry, provided information on the concentration of Turkish troops along the Syrian border. The Polish Legation in Damascus arrived at the following conclusions:[43]

1. Although activity related to the concentration of Turkish troops was exaggerated, Syria had reason to be concerned. According to official Syrian sources, there were ten Turkish divisions along the border. Soviet sources in Damascus estimated the total number of Turkish troops to be 50,000. Syrian fears were expressed in a Syrian complaint against Turkey made to the UN Security Council.

2. The US would have liked to attack Syria through Turkey and other neighboring states, but under the contemporary circumstances, it was unlikely. The report noted that the US had launched a "brutal" war of nerves against Syria during mid-August through to September 1957. This included pressure, threats, and blackmail: the US Sixth Fleet was engaged in maneuvers near the Syrian shores; there were conspiracy plots to overthrow the ruling Syrian governments; Henderson's mission, the concentration of Turkish troops

along the Syrian border, and the supply of arms to Jordan, also contributed to the US campaign. All these American actions were unsuccessful. The Syrian security services were adept at exposing the various plots, and the fact that the Americans used Middle Eastern countries such as Turkey, Jordan, Lebanon, and Iraq for their own perceived imperialist goals, had led to a further intensification of anti-imperialist feelings in Arab public opinion. Syria was isolated, but gradually it gained the sympathy of other Arab states, including Iraq. Consequently the Baghdad Pact was weakened, and Turkey threatened by the Soviets, had to back down. The US moves earned the opposite reaction—they led to the awakening of pan-Arab aspirations and calls for Arab unity.

3. The Turkish threat convinced Syria that it could expect real help only from the USSR and the socialist camp.

4. Nasser also understood that the Soviet Union alone was capable of helping Syria. He dispatched 2,500 Egyptian soldiers to Syria—a small force that, in practical terms, could not do much; however it had some moral significance. Nasser's move was intended to prevent further rapprochement between Syria and the USSR. The Polish report noted that Nasser's move received wide coverage in Syria.

5. While the Syrian government and the army exercised full control over the internal situation within the country, that task was not easy. Although the government gained a parliamentary majority, the opposition was quite strong. The National Party was also split between one group led by Prime Minister al-'Asali, which was in coalition with the left-wing bloc, and another group led by 'Abd al-Rahman Kayyali, which was supported by landlords and the bourgeoisie elements, and was in opposition to al-'Asali's government. The government therefore did not enjoy a wide majority; Akram al-Hawrani, a leader of the Ba'th Party, was elected Chairman of the Parliament by only a tiny majority. Attempts to stabilize the internal situation were made by al-Quwatli, who visited two centers of discontent—Jabal Druze and Aleppo. He promised the Druze, who were alleged to have been involved in the recent US conspiracy, that he would see to it that several economic projects would be developed in their area in order to improve the local welfare and standards of living. In Aleppo he tried to ease tension by promising the landlords and bourgeois elements of the traditional elite that the government's social policy would not be designed to weaken them, and he called on them to cooperate with the government.

The internal situation in Syria was tense, but there was also a high level of stability. The attitude of the Syrian government toward the external threats (Turkish, Iraqi, and American) appeared to be ambivalent. On the one hand, these threats were taken seriously and all possible measures to prevent an escalation to armed conflict with Turkey were pursued. On the other hand, the self-confidence of Syrian ruling circles in the government and the army was enhanced by the Soviet threats to take any action, including military, in support of Syria against any foreign intervention that would jeopardize Syria's territorial integrity and sovereignty.

On 15 October 1957, Salah al-Din al-Bitar sent a letter of complaint about "threats to the security of Syria and to international peace" to Dag Hammarskjöld, the Secretary-General of the UN. Al-Bitar pointed out that, "[f]or more than a year now, foreign actions affecting Syria and endangering its security and independence" had been in progress. Although the situation had calmed down by the beginning of October, al-Bitar wrote, "these actions have increased and intensified during the last two months, and more so during the last two weeks." Al-Bitar's complaint focused on Turkey and the US, though the latter was not mentioned by name. At present, he said, "there exists an actual military threat to Syria, resulting from the heavy, unprecedented, and unwarranted concentration of Turkish troops, up to several divisions, in close proximity to the Syrian–Turkish border. These troops are being constantly reinforced." There had been violations of Syrian air space by foreign military airplanes. Al-Bitar spoke of frequent Turkish acts of aggression toward Syria: armed raids, clashes, and shootings on the border. There had also been other actions taken by foreign elements (i.e., the US) of interference in "the affairs of Syria to sway its policy or overthrow its government . . . one of which was discovered. More recently, another attempt to overthrow the government of Syria by violent action was discovered." Turkey had given shelter to anti-Syrian foreign elements who were active "in their efforts to overthrow the government of Syria with foreign help, and to set up for Syria a government which would fall in line with the policies of certain foreign powers." Al-Bitar called on the General Assembly to deal urgently with his complaint by setting up a commission to investigate the situation on the Syrian–Turkish border and report to the Assembly. He threatened that "a war starting in the Middle East would . . . cause wide international complications" and could possibly endanger world peace.[44]

The following day, Andrei Gromyko, the head of the Soviet delegation to the UN, sent a letter to Hammarskjöld aimed at backing the Syrian request. Gromyko attacked both the US and Turkey, declaring that "there is reliable information that the Turkish General Staff, together with American military advisers, have worked out detailed plans for an attack by Turkey on Syria, which they intend to carry out immediately after the elections in Turkey on 27 October of this year." Present attempts to pretend that the tension along the Turco-Syrian border had decreased, he wrote, "are mere camouflage designed to mislead public opinion both in Turkey itself and in other countries, and to ensure the element of surprise in the attack on the peace-loving Syrian state." Gromyko praised Syria for pursuing "a consistent policy of defense of national independence and non-participation in aggressive blocs." He warned that if there were an armed attack on Syria by Turkey, "a member of the North Atlantic bloc (NATO), the conflict is bound to extend to other countries." The US, NATO's leading member, he pointed out, was planning to intervene directly "with its armed forces on the side of Turkey in the hostilities against Syria and it is prodding Turkey to commit aggression against Syria." It would be an act of awful ignorance Gromyko declared,

> not to realize that Syria would not remain alone in its struggle against aggression ... It is known also that a number of other Arab countries have spoken in support of an independent Syria and of the necessity to give assistance to Syria if aggression were committed against it. Also, on the side of Syria are the peace-loving peoples of other countries, in particular of the Soviet Union, which cannot regard impassively the military provocations that are being planned in the immediate proximity of the southern frontiers of the USSR.[45]

Gromyko concluded his letter by endorsing the Syrian demand that the UN intervene immediately to eliminate the possibility of the outbreak of war.

Henry Cabot Lodge, the US representative to the UN, reacted promptly to the Syrian and Soviet letters. In a statement to the General Assembly of the UN on 18 October, he refuted both nations' allegations, regarding them as "clumsy and flagrant fabrications." He hastened to welcome the Syrian demands for a UN inquiry, expressing his confidence that such an investigation would show "not only the absurdity of the charges against the United States and Turkey, but will also reveal the true source of tension in the entire area."[46] A week later, in another statement he delivered before the General Assembly of the UN, Lodge spoke in a firmer tone, noting that the US had been concerned over recent developments stemming from Soviet infiltration into the Middle East. He blamed the Soviets for stirring up the atmosphere in the Middle East against the US by spreading false information concerning US war plans in the area. "We have heard of American 'plots' from Soviet representatives on previous occasions," ridiculed Lodge, adding that "these American plots" were invented in Moscow. In a counterattack directed toward the Soviets and Syrians, Lodge blamed these two countries for planning and preparing for war in the area: "The Soviet government has been sending large quantities of arms to Syria, including jet aircraft, tanks, armored vehicles, etc. There is no question whatever of challenging any country's right to acquire arms . . . But we are entitled to inquire regarding the motives behind sending such large quantities of arms into a potentially explosive area at a particularly tense moment, because such shipments in such circumstances inevitably heighten tensions." He dismissed each of the Soviet–Syrian allegations, showing that they did not correspond with the historical facts and blamed the Soviets for conducting a war of nerves against Turkey accompanied by intimidation and threats of military attack. According to Lodge, the Soviets were responsible for the current tension because it served their goals in the area. By creating the appearance of threats to Syria's security, and then pretending to remove the threats, they wanted to pose before the world as the savior of the Arabs. The Soviets evidently believed that "their agents and sympathizers inside Syria will make political gains from the artificial threat of war which has been generated." Finally, by the creation of an artificial war scare, the Soviets hoped to "further its expansionist purposes and . . . reduce the Middle East to the status of the captive nations of Eastern Europe."[47]

Referring to recent Soviet activities concerning the Turco-Syrian crisis, Sir D. P. Reilly, the British Ambassador to Moscow, stated that he found it hard to locate the reasons why the Soviets "have continued to work up an air of crisis over Syria when it seems that they can no longer hope to benefit by so doing." In generating tension, the Soviets had succeeded in getting Egypt, along with other Arab states, to firmly commit to the support of Syria. Syria was less isolated now in the Arab world, and the Soviets could attribute that to themselves. In Reilly's view, the Soviets, who had made many gains in Syria, now needed a period of relative quiet to consolidate their position. Reilly concluded that their present tactic of creating a tense atmosphere in the international arena would have a bad effect on Soviet prestige abroad.[48]

Within a few months Syria would fall into Egyptian hands. Syrian policymakers would decide to unite with the Egyptian camp, leaving the solid and friendly Soviet–Syrian relationship, and joining Nasser's political climate and pan-Arab aspirations. If there were any Soviet plans to take over Syria or to turn it into one of their satellite states, they were now relegated to a low level of priority. The Soviets had to face a regional challenge by one of their problematic allies in the Arab world—Nasser's Egypt. One that had its own agenda, and which did not necessarily run parallel with Soviet Middle Eastern policies and interests.

In the latter half of November 1957, the Turco-Syrian crisis had calmed and the Syrian press switched its resources from its campaign against Turkey to Israel and King Hussein of Jordan. There were still a few reports of incidents on the Turkish border, but, by and large, there was a significant easing of tension between the two countries.[49] In a statement made in late November, al-Bitar stressed that nothing new had happened and that the Syrian government "hoped that the situation would improve and that the West would understand the justice of [our] cause . . . Syria sincerely desired to live in peace and to collaborate with those countries which wanted to maintain peace and build a world in which justice and equality alone would predominate."[50] In early December the Syrian government paper, *al-Ra'i al-'Amm*, declared that the "Turkish threat to Syria had ended"; consequently, both Syrian and Egyptian governments should hasten the steps toward effective union between the two countries.[51]

It was not easy to remove Syria from Soviet and Egyptian circles of influence. The policymakers and decision-makers in Syria were not al-Quwatli and his followers, but rather the left-wing camp—the Ba'th Party in particular. It was in the interest of both the Ba'th leaders and the Soviets to keep the crisis with the Western powers and the neighboring countries reasonably realistic. Neither the theory of the external threats toward Syria from its adjacent neighbors, nor the theory of internal threat—the danger of communist takeover—were based on solid evidence or logic.[52] In a conversation with the leader of a British parliamentary delegation that visited Lebanon, Shawkat Shuqayr, the former Chief of Staff of the Syrian army expressed his belief that "the Syrian army had by no means been won over, by the communists." He reckoned that there were only "a handful of communists in the army and relatively few outside it." He correctly predicted that, "other left-wing elements would sooner or later combine to oust the communists and fellow-travellers from their present positions of influence."[53]

Two main subjects had continued to engage Syrian politics: relations with the Soviets, and possible union with Egypt. Around these two subjects there was a power struggle between, on the one hand, the pro-Soviet elements within the government and their communist supporters, and on the other, the Ba'th Party and other forces within the government, which included President al-Quwatli, who wanted to pursue a policy of positive neutralism—that is, to maintain close and intimate relations with the Soviets, but from an independent position (based on Nasser's model of neutralism).

The mainstream in Syrian politics followed the Ba'th line, including the People's Party, which was the main opposition party. A debate in the Syrian Parliament on the prospects of Soviet–Syrian economic relations took place following the unanimous ratification by the Parliament of the Soviet–Syrian agreement for economic and technical aid. Despite the fact that there was hardly any opposition to the agreement, Ma'aruf al-Dawalibi, the People's Party leader, was accused by the pro-government press of creating doubts about the government's ability to repay the Soviet loan without monopolizing Syrian exports for that purpose. Expressing the government view, *al-Ra'i al-'Amm* regarded such fears as groundless, "because the agreement provided that Syria could repay Russia either in goods or in currency and there was no reason why Syria should make payment solely in goods."[54] A similar view was held by Hasan Jabbara, President of the Economic Development Council:

> Syria would repay Russia in Syrian produce only if Syria were unable to sell her goods on the international market . . . it was a good thing for exporters to know that no matter how the world market stood they could always ship their goods to the Soviet Union.[55]

Akram al-Hawrani expressed his satisfaction that the agreement was approved by the Parliament. Such an agreement fitted in with Syria's policy of positive neutralism, since it was "tangible proof of the Soviet Union's unconditional friendship for Syria." Continuing al-Hawrani's line, his Ba'thist colleague, Khalil Kallas, stated that "the West could not match the excellent conditions provided by the agreement with Russia." Prime Minister al-'Asali's statement on the agreement reinforced its line of positive neutralism, stating: "the agreement would not stop Syria from making similar agreements with Western countries on a basis of equality."[56]

In November, Michel 'Aflaq headed a Ba'th Party delegation on a visit to Yugoslavia at the invitation of the Yugoslav Socialist Party. 'Aflaq, who did not hide his dislike of Soviet communism both as an ideology and a political doctrine, was influenced to a great extent by the Yugoslav model of socialism. In a statement he made on his arrival in Belgrade, he declared that the Yugoslav brand of socialism "suited the temperament of the Arabs who have always been careful to reconcile their nationalism with their socialist aspirations."[57]

The Soviets viewed the concept of positive neutralism with a certain degree of cynicism. This concept, explained Nemchina, the Soviet Ambassador to Damascus, had two aspects—Arab and international. The first was related to the struggle of the Arabs against imperialism and colonialism. However, Nemchina stressed that Syrian neutralist policy was not actually neutral when Arab, African, and Asian peoples were struggling for independence against imperialism and colonialism. Syria firmly supported these peoples' struggles for liberation. The international aspect of neutralism meant the need to maintain peaceful coexistence between countries with different socio-political and economic systems. This did not mean that Syria accepted the moral and philosophical principles of the Western system, but that it followed the principles of peaceful coexistence in order to save mankind from the danger of annihilation as a result of war.[58]

As a member of the Afro-Asian movement that had emerged from the

Bandung Conference, Syria was active in organizing and hosting conferences related to the advancement of that movement's goals. In the first half of November the Afro-Asian Lawyers Conference took place in Damascus. The opening ceremony was attended by al-Quwatli, Akram al-Hawrani, Sabri al-'Asali, 'Afif al-Bizri, and other leaders. In his speech, al-Quwatli directed his attack on Western imperialism as the creator of Israel, which put pressure on Syria and the Arabs when Israel was in danger. In line with previous resolutions made by the Afro-Asian movement, the West was slandered and condemned, whereas the activities of the Soviet Union in Eastern Europe (Hungary, Poland) were not mentioned. The Lawyers Conference considered the treaties signed between the Western powers and Afro-Asian states as "unequal treaties," and they were declared "to be void." The conference recognized acts of nationalization as "a legitimate means of supporting a national economy." The Baghdad Pact, NATO, and SEATO were described as aggressive blocs.[59]

A further step on Syria's road to union with Egypt was made in mid-November, when a joint session of Syrian and Egyptian deputies took place in the Syrian Parliament. Statements made by Akram al-Hawrani, al-'Asali, and Anwar al-Sadat—who headed the Egyptian parliamentary delegation (35 members)—made it clear that the Ba'th view of neutralism was accepted by all the speakers. In reference to inter-bloc and foreign affairs, future unity would be based only on Arab nationalism and that "Syria and Egypt belong neither to East nor West." Nevertheless, a clear-cut distinction was drawn between the "good" and "bad guys." The Soviet bloc was praised for the help it had provided to both countries in difficult times in the past, and the help it continued to provide. In contrast, the Western camp—"imperialism and Zionism"—that had always fought "Arab aspirations towards unity and freedom have not ceased to put pressure on Syria to renounce her policy of liberation."[60] Arab unity, the Ba'th maintained, was a guarantee of positive neutralism. Arab protection of positive neutralism meant defending their liberty, unity, and national messages. The political independence of the Arabs from imperialism was connected with positive neutralism. Positive neutralism and Arab unity were inextricably bound.[61]

Two processes were operating in parallel at the end of 1957 and early 1958: discussions on unification between Egypt and Syria, led by the Ba'thists; and attempts to tighten relations with the Soviet bloc, led by al-'Azm and his supporters. Al-'Azm wanted to conclude more attractive agreements with the Soviets so that his image and prestige would be enhanced within the government and the domestic political arena. At that stage, his main rivals were the Ba'thists—his "yesterday" allies. Al-'Azm's influence within the government grew substantially following his appointment in late 1957 as Minister of Finance, in addition to his influential position as Minister of Defense. Al-'Azm had good reasons to be wary about any possible union with Egypt. He had not forgotten that it was Egypt and Saudi Arabia who firmly supported his rival Shukri al-Quwatli during the presidential elections of August 1955. Indian sources alluded to the fact that, although al-'Azm favored the idea of a Saudi–Egyptian–Syrian defense organization in April–May 1955, he was "playing cautious and was in no hurry about it pending the final result of his alternative efforts to woo Iraq into a position which would prevent the break-up of the Arab League."[62] Despite the fact that Syria and Egypt were in fundamental agreement on non-alignment and the avoidance of entanglements with the Great Powers, al-'Azm did not want "merely another old Collective Security Pact, with dictatorship in Egypt and Kingship in Saudi Arabia . . . [al-'Azm] does not think the moment is ripe for a federation with them, but [he] desires something near to it and more than the old arrangement."[63] Such a pact was concluded several months after the downfall of al-'Asali's government, in which al-'Azm was its key figure.

The architect of the process of rapprochement between Syria and the USSR, al-'Azm was highly regarded by Moscow. When he arrived in Moscow on 9 December 1957, the Soviets did everything possible to make his visit a great success. A Soviet aircraft flew al-'Azm and his entourage in from Damascus. The Syrian press reported Khalid al-'Azm's appointment as Deputy Prime Minister just before his departure to Moscow—a move which "was designed to strengthen his hand in his talks with the Soviet authorities."[64] The official purpose of his visit was to discuss the Syrian–Soviet Economic Aid Agreement. The press reported that, among other things, al-'Azm was trying to obtain a revision of the terms of payment stipulated in the agreement. The formal purpose of his visit was achieved with the ratification on 11 December of the economic aid agreement of 28 October 1957. Al-'Azm's delegation also visited Budapest en route to Moscow and held talks with the Hungarian Prime Minister. Al-'Azm offered a controversial comparison between the Hungarian uprising and Syria's internal strife when he spoke of similarities between the struggles of the Hungarian and Syrian peoples to maintain their freedom. He stated: "You have crushed a plot which was in fact a foreign plot. We did the same and we are determined to frustrate any further attempts at leading our people off the chosen road."[65] His rivals considered this comparison as proof that he was "heart and soul with the Soviets."[66] On 17 December, al-'Azm held a meeting with Khrushchev, and on 19 December an agreement aimed at broadening commercial relations between the two countries was signed. According to the agreement, the USSR would purchase Syrian cotton and grain, and Syria, in exchange, would import goods of Soviet make, "including machinery, equipment, and other materials." On 21 December, a day after the visit was concluded, a final communiqué was published. A close reading clearly indicates that the August–September crisis was over. Syria expressed its gratitude to the Soviet people and government for "the determined stand of friendly support of Syria . . . during the period when the threat of aggression hung over Syria in connection with the foreign plot against the independence and territorial integrity of the Syrian Republic."[67] The Syrian press reported that the Soviets would give Syria "two *Ilyushin* 402 airliners and another especially constructed aircraft as a present to President al-Quwatli."[68]

Support for al-'Azm's pro-Soviet orientation came from an unexpected source—Mgr. Alexandros Tahan, the Patriarch of the Greek Orthodox Church in Syria, who visited the USSR in November. Tahan said in Moscow that "he had been made aware of the affection which the Russian government and people have for the Arabs in general and for the Syrians in particular." The Russians, he declared, watched with understanding Syria's struggle to preserve its freedom. He urged the Arabs "to show a similar affection and sympathy towards the Russians."[69] Another distinguished Syrian visitor to visit Moscow was Munir al-Rayis, the editor of the Damascus daily *al-Barada.* In an article he wrote for *Pravda*, al-Rayis praised the "friendliness of the Soviet people, who are always ready to lend support to the people of Syria."[70]

In early December, two reliable sources representing two of the leading countries of the non-aligned movement—the Indian and Yugoslav Ministers to Lebanon—provided the British with information regarding the recent fissures in the leftist government then in power in Syria. Jansen, the Indian diplomat, told his British counterpart that "he had heard on good authority" that al-Hawrani had appealed to Lebanese journalists, mainly pro-Western, to be more positive about him. He told them that he was "at heart a convinced anti-communist." According to al-Hawrani, he had associated himself with "communists and fellow-travelers only in order to reach a position of strength from which he hoped eventually to be able to lead Syria into the anti-communist camp." Although Jansen could not see any possibility of the replacement of the present Syrian government, he believed that there were good prospects of "a serious split between the Ba'thists and the pro-communists and that something might come about on the lines of the plan which al-Hawrani was reported to be contemplating."[71]

A similar picture was drawn by Milos Lalovic, the Yugoslav Minister to Lebanon who was formerly accredited to Syria. Lalovic noted that most of the Ba'thists had recently concluded that aligning Syria with the Soviets was a dangerous move. The Ba'thists according to Lalovic, wished to renew normal relations with the West—a move derived from their adherence to the doctrine of positive neutralism. Lalovic had good evidence for that information, part of which was based on what Michel 'Aflaq, whom he used to meet frequently, told him. Lalovic also revealed that there were close links between the Ba'th Party and the SAWPY, and he outlined the positions of some of the main political figures in Syria with regard to Soviet–Syrian relations. Al-Quwatli, whose influence was currently not strong, was on the side of the moderates—those who favored positive neutralism. Akram al-Hawrani was anti-communist. "The real nigger in the woodpile," stated the (racist) Yugoslav Minister, was Khalid al-'Azm, who, "for reasons of personal ambition, had decided to throw in his lot with the communists; he seemed to think he was smart enough to use the Russians for his own ends, but he would soon be undeceived and would be the first to be sacrificed if ever the communists should take full control of Syria."[72] Khalid al-'Azm's alliance with the communists was based on opportunistic and utilitarian reasons.

Further information on the power struggle taking place within the Syrian government was provided to the US State Department by reliable Syrian and Egyptian sources. According to them, strong pressure was being applied by al-'Azm and 'Afif al-Bizri on the Syrian government to appoint Khalid Bakdash as a minister, allowing all anti-imperialist forces in Syria to be represented in the government. Both al-Hawrani and Prime Minister al-'Asali resisted this pressure, but agreed to "a compromise by which al-'Azm should be given greater responsibility as Deputy Prime Minister." Both al-Hawrani and al-'Asali were "much alarmed," as the latter put it, "at the expansion of communist influence." The two agreed that, in order to check the rise of the communists and prevent the possibility that they might win the forthcoming elections in 1958, both the Ba'th and Nationalist parties must join forces together. Al-'Asali and al-Hawrani expressed their disgust with al-'Azm, "who, in his ambition to be President, was prepared to go to any lengths in [his] collaboration with the communists and the Russians."[73] The two expressed the hope that Egypt would assist them in counteracting the communist threat. The US Embassy in Cairo was informed by Muhammad Hasanain Haikal, Nasser's propagandist and confidant, that Nasser had checked information provided to him by the US concerning 'Afif al-Bizri's communist record and found it to be accurate. According to Haikal, Nasser would exercise his influence in Syria to see to it that al-Bizri's powers were dismantled.[74]

Other foreign diplomats continued to report the growing rift within the Syrian left involving the Ba'th Party, in opposition to al-'Azm and his communist allies. In mid-December, Suter, of the Swiss Legation at Damascus, confirmed Lalovic's version of events in a conversation with the British Ambassador to Lebanon.[75] Suter offered his opinion that "more and more Syrian politicians seem genuinely anxious to disengage from a totally pro-Soviet policy [of al-'Azm's faction] and to get back to 'positive neutralism' in which they would try to maintain a neutral line between the

two big power blocs." Suter also said that 'Afif al-Bizri was losing popularity and that the Turco-Syrian tension had recently calmed down. The
postponement of the municipal elections, he explained, was derived from
a fear of a victory for the communists. Many in Syria were impressed by

> pro-communist propaganda which made the most of the assistance to Syria
> which had been offered by the Soviet Union. As the only organized party in Syria,
> the communists were in a position to get the maximum benefit from this during
> an election and the Ba'thists recognized that, though a communist victory would
> not signify that there were many convinced communists in Syria, the impression
> on world and particularly western opinion would be bad.[76]

By late 1957, the Syrian Communist Party faced a threat to its unity. A
group around Ilyas Murqis was in favor of adopting a Titoist policy,
focusing on the nationalist dimension by creating a separate "nationalist"
Communist Party in Syria as a counterweight to Bakdash's commitment
to international communism. Bakdash, whose image among many Syrians
and foreigners was that of a "Stalinist," managed to suppress the rebel-
lion.[77] Although the Soviets were pleased with the growing influence of the
communists and their fellow-travelers in Syria, they also recognized that
their Syrian comrades were motivated by their own political and strategic
interests. The Soviets learned to draw a clear-cut distinction between
ideology and politics. In 1956, Khrushchev had expressed the cynical
realpolitik relations between the USSR and Syria and Egypt: the USSR
supported Nasser, he said, although Nasser "even put communists in
jail."[78] In late 1957, he went further, stating that "the Soviet Union does
not intend to intervene in the internal relationships of the Arab states. If
Egypt hangs communists and Syria does not persecute them, these are
matters which are exclusively the concern of those states." Khrushchev
expected other countries, namely the Western powers, to follow suit,
because the USSR would not tolerate attempts by any country "to intervene in the internal developments of the Arab and other states, either with
force or with methods of corruption commonly used by capitalist governments, in order to keep satellite governments loyal to them in power against
the will of the people, or to bring them to power. There ought not to be any
doubt that we communists will stand wholeheartedly on the side of the
progressive movements which must in any case win the historical
process."[79]

Khrushchev's moderate approach with regard to non-intervention in the
internal affairs of other countries did not take into account Nasser's view
on this matter. When he realized that Syria's political instability might play
into the hands of the Soviets and their Syrian communist allies, Nasser
directly intervened in Syria's internal affairs. Through his Ba'thist allies, he
orchestrated a brilliant move that led to full unification with Syria under

his sole leadership, leaving the Soviets and their Syrian allies trapped and stunned. Al-'Azm, the Soviets' main ally, was one of the only senior ministers to express vocal opposition to the Syrian–Egyptian Protocol drafted in Cairo in mid-January 1958. This document listed the main principles for the gradual process of unification between the two countries. Despite his objection, however, the Syrian cabinet, which was influenced to a large extent by the Ba'th Party and the army (who both desired unity with Egypt), approved the Cairo draft with all of Nasser's conditions.[80]

6

Nasserite "Positive Neutralism" and the United Arab Republic

The process of the amalgamation of Syria and Egypt into one state was completed in February 1958 with the formation of the United Arab Republic (UAR). The union was a victory in the short-term for both Nasser and the Ba'th Party—the adherents and promoters of the policy of positive neutralism. There were several explanations for the motives behind the decision to go ahead with unification. In a recent authoritative study on the United Arab Republic, Elie Podeh pointed out four immediate reasons behind Syria's desire for unification:

> First, the existence of a Soviet-communist threat—whether real or imaginary—to the regime, magnified by Western propaganda, convinced many that Syria was on the verge of becoming a Soviet satellite; the union, therefore, was to save Syria from that fate. Second, a new counter-elite, comprised of many officers and Ba'th Party members, challenged the position of the old conservative elite, made up of the landed oligarchy and wealthy merchants. Unable to attain power through the political system, the Ba'th saw the union as an alternative means to do so. Third, the army initiated the venture once its competing factions realized that no single group was capable of dominating the political system. Fourth, the old elite, which was not consulted in advance by the army or the Ba'th, accepted the union as the lesser evil in light of the circumstances prevailing in Syria. Soviet involvement, Ba'th domination, or military takeover were all possible scenarios that threatened to undermine the old elite's power base. Moreover it could not openly oppose the union since it had long espoused the doctrine of pan-Arabism . . . Moreover, the union could offer some tangible advantage to the industrial and commercial segments of the old elite, which might benefit economically from a merger with the larger Egyptian market. Thus all segments of the Syrian elite supported the formation of some association with Egypt though for different, even contradictory, reasons—a development facilitated by the strong appeal of pan-Arabism.[1]

Podeh maintained that Nasser's charismatic leadership played an important factor in the formation of the union. According to Podeh, Nasser was one of the chief advocates and distributors of the idea of pan-Arabism. Nasser's image personified the "proud Arab who fearlessly stood up to Western imperialism," and his speeches inflamed the Arab masses—a development that could not be ignored by Arab leaders who sought association with Nasser in the hope that such moves would strengthen their own shaky legitimacy. Podeh concluded that the appearance of a "strong personality at that particular historical juncture facilitated the formation of the UAR." For Podeh, the US had also played a central role in its formation. In late 1957, the interests of Egypt and the US had temporarily coincided. Although each was motivated by different interests, both nations wanted to contain the alleged communist threat in Syria. Nasser's main concern was that an unstable Syrian regime under communist or Soviet control might pose a challenge to his quest for leadership of the Arab world.[2]

By late 1957, the so-called communist danger and the external threat were no more than a manipulative means used by those elements in Syria, Egypt, and the West who wanted to check the process of the rapid expansion of Soviet influence in Syria. The struggle for power over Syria was between two external factors: Nasser's Egypt and the Soviet Union. Both had their own domestic agents who were motivated by self-interest; Nasser used the offices of the Ba'th Party and its supporters within the Syrian army. A Polish memorandum from Cairo explained the motives behind the Ba'th Party to seek union: "the ruling Ba'th Party felt itself so weak and susceptible to constant outside pressure, and threatened from within to such a degree that its leaders saw no option other than to seek for Nasser's patronage. The Ba'th offered Nasser a merger of Syria and Egypt into a single state. This step was in agreement with the wish of the Arab masses, [particularly] in Syria, where it was received with much greater enthusiasm than in Egypt."[3] The USSR took a full advantage of the growing influence of its main Syrian ally, Khalid al-'Azm. There had been a constant and constructive mutual feedback between al-'Azm and the Soviets: they both needed each other in order to achieve their goals in Syria—al-'Azm to become President and the Soviets to establish their hegemony over Syria.

Following the formation of the United Arab Republic (UAR) in February 1958, Nasser's battle against communism intensified. Syrian communists opposed the idea of Arab unity other than proletarian solidarity among the Arabs and association with international communism.[4] After the Suez crisis, when Nasser's image in the Arab world was that of a great hero, however, the communists realized that to oppose unity with Nasser would be politically incompetent. Therefore they supported unity based on a loose federal formula "which they thought might have protected their position in Syria."[5] As a result of their growing tension with the Ba'thists, the communists tried to embarrass their opponents by demanding a full union with Egypt; the communists thought that neither the Ba'th Party nor Nasser really wanted union. On 15 January 1958, the Syrian communists issued a resolution that declared: "the unity between Syria and Egypt will enhance the prestige of the two liberated Arab republics, increase their importance in the international realm and will serve the interests of the Arabs and international peace."[6] In late January 1958, when total union was a matter of days away, the communists called for "the necessity of an understanding between communists and Ba'thists who form the cornerstone of the National Front."[7] Once again they embraced the idea of federal union. One of Nasser's pre-conditions for union with Syria was the dissolution of all Syrian political parties—a condition that met with the approval of the Syrian authorities, and that consequently led to the abolition of the influential Syrian Communist Party (SCP). This development created friction between Nasser and the Soviets. Moscow's initial cool response to the formation of the UAR left no doubts about their reservations over the union.

The Emergence of the First Fissures in Soviet–UAR Relations and the Nasser–Khrushchev Ideological Warfare

The leader of the SCP, Khalid Bakdash, left Syria on 5 February 1958, attacking the dissolution of all Syrian political parties. He expressed fierce criticism of the UAR's internal policies, with the full backing of the Soviets for his activities and views. Bakdash declared on several occasions that the SCP would continue its work as before. Attending party congresses in several bloc countries, he was identified as the "Secretary General of the Syrian Communist Party."[8] An American intelligence report noted that, for the Soviets, Bakdash was the "pre-eminent communist leader in the Middle East and was thus useful to Moscow not only for what he could achieve in Syria but also as a factor in the development of other communist parties in the area."[9] The Soviets even allowed Bakdash to publish an anti-UAR article in the first issue of *Problems of Peace and Socialism*.[10] The article criticized Nasser's 1958 agrarian reform in Syria, stating that the UAR government was "incapable of solving this problem." Bakdash also accused the UAR of using Soviet bloc aid "as a bargaining tool with the West." He concluded by declaring: "We shall never give up our communist party."[11] Several months after the formation of the UAR, Nasser remonstrated strongly to the Soviets against the activities of their embassy in Syria during the pre-plebiscite period, and attacked attempts by Syrian communists to prevent the union between Egypt and Syria. In response, Khrushchev promised that such activities would be halted.[12]

Although displeased with the formation of the UAR, Moscow quickly adjusted to it. The Soviets even showed a degree of tolerance toward Nasser's neutralization of the SCP. A few months after the establishment of the UAR, Nasser was invited by the Soviets to visit the USSR—a tour which was supposed to celebrate Soviet–Egyptian relations. Nasser arrived in Moscow on 29 April accompanied by both his vice-presidents, 'Abd al-Latif al-Baghdadi and Akram al-Hawrani, and other senior officials from Syria and Egypt. Despite efforts by hosts and guests to create an atmosphere of cordiality and understanding, however, certain signs of discord were evident during Nasser's visit (29 April–16 May 1958). The Soviets were disappointed by Egypt's declared policy of positive neutralism. They expected Nasser to take a more radical anti-Western stand and were concerned about prospects for improved UAR–US relations. Soviet officials were said to have made it clear that they desired the USSR to be the only source of outside assistance to the UAR. This would mean that Nasser would be expected to employ a "pro-Soviet neutralism." The Soviets expressed indignation over Nasser's friendly relations with Tito; specifically, Khrushchev was angry about Nasser's forthcoming visit to Yugoslavia and he attacked Tito's policies.[13]

Nevertheless, throughout the visit Nasser showed himself to be a self-confident and intelligent leader. Despite his gratitude for Soviet military, economic, and diplomatic support, he displayed no obsequiousness and was not afraid to stand up to his hosts; he was by turns cautious, astute, and self-assured. He behaved toward his Soviet hosts as their equal and made it clear that he was not only Egypt's leader, but also the leader of an Arab nationalist movement, as well as a practicing representative of Islam. At the conclusion of Nasser's visit, Khrushchev, at the Kremlin reception on 15 May, went so far as to say: "We want the solidarity of the Arab people under your leadership. This is a guarantee that the colonialists will never return to your sacred land. You will have the necessary help from us."[14] The visit taught the Soviets a lesson on the nature of Arab nationalism, and Nasser's pan-Arab ambitions. It made them realize that, while there was much in common between their own aims in the Middle East and Nasser's ambitions, the scope for cooperation between them was limited by self-interest and wide ideological differences.[15]

Nasser's visit to Yugoslavia in July 1958 shed more light on Soviet–Egyptian frictions. According to Yugoslav sources, Nasser told Tito that "The USSR was pressing hard for 'independent apparatuses'" in Syria in both the military and political fields, including special privileges for the Soviet military personnel there and special liaison arrangements between the Soviet Embassy and the SCP.[16]

By mid-1958 Nasser could be pleased with the many achievements he had gained from his foreign policy, in particular the formation of the UAR. Soviet bloc countries were fully aware of the growing role and influence of

Nasser's Egypt. The Polish Legation in Cairo noted that a number of factors had contributed to Cairo becoming the center of Arab unity and that it would continue to be the heart of the Arab liberation movement. The whole of colonial Africa, stressed the Polish diplomats, was now looking to Cairo. Egypt's image in the Third World had been enhanced since early 1958, while serious economic difficulties in India and political troubles in Indonesia had prevented both Nehru and Sukarno from playing a leading role among the states of Asia and Africa. Neither Nehru, nor Sukarno, stressed the Polish report, could now openly proclaim to be struggling against imperialism, for they both still counted on help from the imperialist West:

> Millions of the oppressed in Asia and Africa look with hope and love at Nasser. He is the only one who is resolutely and consistently conducting a vigorous struggle against imperialism for complete independence of his country and for the Arabs' position in the world, and is winning this struggle.[17]

The Polish diplomats reported that Nasser and the Arab world were gaining in strength and importance. The economic and political potential of the Arab countries was developing. There was no doubt that establishing the best relations possible with the Arab countries was in the interests of the socialist countries:

> Freeing themselves from the foreign yoke, the Arab countries are striving to build up their economic potential as fast as possible and are beginning to develop industries. Due to this, they are becoming a perfect market for our investment industry. Some of these countries produce raw materials, which are of interest to our industry. Among us, one can often hear an opinion that at present we are not yet able to take an important place at these markets. However, our industry is developing and in a few years we will frantically seek new markets and new sources of raw materials. It seems that one should think about it now and to prepare the groundwork for our penetration to these markets by establishing friendly relations with the Arab countries. This has become a possibility because imperialist states have been forced to withdraw from many Middle East countries and the unfriendly feelings towards them is still running high. One should make an effort in order to enter these markets, because it is difficult to say what will happen tomorrow. One should also not lose sight of political aspects—at least because of the fact that there exist 10 independent Arab countries, and one should not neglect 10 votes at the UN.[18]

Interest in the Soviet bloc countries, the Polish report concluded, was growing because the Arabs regarded the countries of the socialist camp to be friendly and with no expansionist intentions toward their territories; the Arabs did not feel threatened by socialist countries. The socialist camp it was argued, should therefore seize the opportunity and make the most of these favorable conditions by trying to acquaint Arab countries with "our culture, our science and our technology," making it clear to their Arab counterparts that, by establishing close relations with them, they should have no fear of communist infiltration because the socialist countries had no intention of engaging in communist propaganda. In view of Egypt's primacy in the Arab world, efforts should be made in this direction in order to build solid and harmonious relations.[19] The Soviet bloc countries needed to draw a clear-cut distinction between ideology and realpolitik.

There was further evidence of Soviet–UAR differences during the special session of the UN General Assembly in August 1958. A reliable Egyptian source close to Nasser stated that the USSR had expressed disappointment with the Arab resolution on the Middle East adopted by the Assembly—a resolution that was not in line with the Soviet position, which was to condemn US and UK policies in the Middle East. The residues of the recent Soviet–Egyptian struggle for hegemony over Syria of late 1957 were an additional source of conflict between Nasser and the Soviets (despite the fact that the Soviets accepted the formation of the UAR as a *fait accompli*), and Nasser disliked the Soviet attempt to expand its influence in Yemen through the Eastern bloc economic and military assistance program. Recent developments indicated that the UAR was attempting to renew its activity in Yemen.[20]

Qassem's coup of July 1958, which raised expectations that Iraq was on its way to join the UAR, soon led to bitter disappointment for Nasser.[21] Qassem's alliance with Iraqi communists and his rapprochement with the USSR changed Nasser's approach to communism. He now blamed international communism for interference in Arab domestic affairs. This new view of Soviet intentions created tension and, subsequently, the mutual growth of ideological warfare. As early as September 1958, the communists in Syria and Iraq began to increase their activities. Concerned with these developments, Nasser took countermeasures to check them. The first serious Iraqi–UAR friction appeared in connection with the demotion, ouster, and arrest (between 12 September and 4 November 1958) of 'Abd al-Salam 'Arif, one of the main leaders of the Iraqi coup and a leading advocate of union with the UAR.[22] Since mid-September, a power struggle had taken place in Iraq that revealed cleavages within the new Iraqi ruling elite, mainly over the subject of Iraq's relationship with the UAR. Prime Minister Qassem, who had opposed immediate union with the UAR, had the advantage over the pro-Nasserite group—a development that created much indignation in the UAR. Qassem also maintained that it was not appropriate to combat communism in Iraq since he needed communist support. The Communist Party was one of only two significant parties in Iraq, and it had enjoyed a resurgence after the July coup. The party was allowed to distribute propaganda freely, and party members held government office. Like Qassem, the Iraqi communists opposed Iraq's union with the UAR unless the party's legality was guaranteed. The Iraqi Communist Party had gradually assumed the predominant role on this issue, because it alone had the organized capability to provide Qassem with the force and will to resist the pressures of pro-union groups.[23] The communists also encouraged greater Kurdish autonomy within the Iraqi state.

Increasing discontent over union with Egypt occurred in the fall of 1958. The principal dissatisfied elements were the conservatives and members of the Ba'th Party. This trend did not pose a tangible threat to Nasser's leadership, but local communists exploited the feelings of discontent in order to advance their anti-UAR campaign. In line with Moscow, the SCP supported the UAR's foreign policy but opposed Nasser's internal policies, including the dissolution of political parties. The SCP aimed at infiltrating the government bureau and the National Union—the only legal political organization. In response, Nasser acted harshly to suppress communism.[24]

The Kurdish question was another source of contention in Soviet–UAR relations. Following Qassem's takeover, the Soviets altered their traditional approach regarding the Kurdish question from firmly backing the "long-standing Kurdish aspiration for an independent Kurdistan" to fully supporting Qassem's efforts to play down Kurdish separatism and to secure Iraqi independence outside the UAR. Nasser's position toward the Kurdish question also wavered. Several weeks before Qassem's coup, Egyptian propaganda broadcasts were calling for Kurdish independence— possibly in response to the Iraqi alliance with the West. In September 1958, in an attempt to win Iraqi support and especially to encourage those pro-UAR elements within the new Iraqi regime, Nasser accused the USSR of "continuing support of Kurdish separatism."[25]

Nasser was angry with the Soviets because two influential pro-Soviet political factions in Iraq—the communists and the Kurdish Democratic Party (KDP)—supported the anti-UAR group within the Iraqi ruling elite—the group led by Qassem. Both the communists and the KDP agreed on 6 September to support the Iraqi Republic if Iraq preserved its independent identity—if it refused to join the UAR, and if Iraqi Kurds were recognized as a nation linked to Arab Iraq, a condition that was provided for by the new Iraqi constitution.[26]

From the Soviet viewpoint the new regime in Iraq proved to be an effective counterbalance to the existing union with Egypt—another source of concern for Nasser. Under Qassem, the Iraqi communists stepped up their activities, directing their attacks on Nasser and the UAR. Because Qassem opposed union with the UAR, he found the communists to be— temporarily—reliable partners.[27] In an effort to ease tensions, the Soviet leadership sent a member of the Presidium of the USSR Communist Party, Nureddin Mukhitdinov, to Cairo for an extended visit (17–26 September 1958). In the course of Mukhitdinov's meetings with Nasser, the latter complained that: "Communists in the Arab world were receiving liberal financing from the Soviet Embassy in Baghdad. In Syria the local communists were cooperating with conservative elements to obstruct the implementation of Syrian–Egyptian unification." Mukhitdinov denied the "existence of any link between the USSR and national communist movements." He went further, stating that Soviet support of the Syrian communists was impossible, as such a move "would be contrary to Khrushchev's policy of helping Nasser wherever possible."[28]

In spite of Mukhitdinov's words, however, Bakdash continued his harsh criticism of the UAR while enjoying the hospitality of Eastern bloc countries, which gave him free reign to direct his anti-Nasser campaign. On 14 December 1958, he issued a statement in the Lebanese communist weekly *al-Akhbar* that announced the separation of the Syrian and Lebanese communist parties. Bakdash also declared his objection to Arab union on Nasser's terms, calling instead for the establishment of separate governments and parliaments in the two regions of the UAR.[29] On 17 March 1959, while delivering a speech to the Polish United Workers Party Congress, he accused the UAR of making imperialist attacks on Iraq. He charged that: "The attempts of the imperialists to break up the friendly relations between the Arab countries and Russia coincided with the position taken by certain Arab circles." Bakdash's reference to "Arab circles" was a thinly-veiled attack, clearly pointing to "certain determined circles in the UAR"— Nasser and his inner circle—as being responsible for the current tension in UAR–Soviet relations. Bakdash quoted Khrushchev's indirect advice to Nasser not "to trust false friends" and fall into the American trap of "hypocritical smiles," but to remember that the USSR was the Arabs' true friend. Bakdash concluded by attacking Nasser's slogan of Arab unity, describing him as a representative of the Egyptian bourgeoisie who "aspired to achieve unity in conformity with their own class interests." In contrast, the "Arab liberation movement," of which Bakdash saw himself a part, sought to unify the "Arab world in the struggle against imperialism."[30]

On Nasser's orders, the press of both UAR regions reacted by attacking Bakdash's statements, saying that the Arab left "might become more dangerous to the Arab cause than its traditional enemies." Muhammad Hasanain Haikal, the editor of *al-Ahram*, made it clear that the UAR campaign against communism was a campaign against communism within the UAR: "it is in no way a campaign against communism, because communism as a system in other countries has achieved results that cannot possibly be ignored. But this cannot prevent us from believing that circumstances in our countries are different, and that what has succeeded in other countries would not necessarily achieve the same results in our countries." Referring to the Yugoslav–Soviet dispute, Haikal stated that "even within the communist orbit, differences in each country require changing the methods of application of Marxism." He praised Khrushchev, Tito, and Mao Tse-Tung as communists who "are considered heroes in our countries . . . however, despite our deep respect for these persons and for their doctrines as communists, we differ from them."[31] In his speeches and public statements, Nasser denounced the SCP for its "opportunistic" resistance and hostility to the Arab nationalist and unity movement, identifying the communists with "reactionaries" and Zionists.[32] The Soviets concluded that the rise of communism in Iraq following Qassem's coup favored an escalation of the activities of communism in both Syria and Egypt. As early as 1959, a US report stated, the Iraqi Communist Party was winning, largely by default, a major victory. "Its apparently well-calculated plan would make Iraq, although not an actual satellite, a major base for anti-Western propaganda and for penetration and agitation . . . The speed and vigor of the communist thirst has been a revelation—especially to Nasser— of Soviet intentions and methods . . . within a few months the communist drive will be difficult if not impossible for non-communist Iraqi elements to check unaided."[33]

The Soviets played a twofold game: First, they continued their policy of close cooperation with Nasser; and second, they increased covert and low-level official support to the communists in Syria and Iraq. The Soviets cherished hopes that the continual success of the Iraqi Communist Party would eventually lead to the emergence of a Soviet-oriented regime. The Soviets did not want to repeat the mistakes they had made in Syria in late 1957–early 1958, when they left the SCP's fate to Nasser's mercy. They were now willing to stand behind the communists even if it meant placing new strains on relations with Nasser, "so long as such a policy appeared profitable on balance,"[34] to quote a Western report. On 1 January 1959, the Soviet government paper *Izvestiia* accused the Cairo weekly *Akhbar al-Yaum* of slandering the USSR and of falsely reporting that progressive democratic forces in Iraq opposed friendly relations with the UAR.[35]

On 27 January, in a speech before the first session of the Twenty-First Congress of the Communist Party of the USSR, Khrushchev voiced an official Soviet criticism of Nasser's anti-communist campaign for the first time. It was wrong, he asserted, to accuse "the communists of acting counter to the national interests of the Arab peoples." Khrushchev branded as "reactionary" and "naïve" Nasser's anti-communist moves and his equating of Zionism with communism. He drew a distinction between the firm Soviet support for Nasser in the Arab struggle against imperialism and the Soviet support for progressive forces in their struggle with "internal reactionary forces." Nevertheless, he promised that the USSR would continue to support the newly "emancipated countries." He stressed that "differences on ideological questions should not hinder the development of friendly relations" with these countries. Although praising Nasser as a "prominent Arab nationalist leader," Khrushchev accorded, in the same breath, equal praise to Nasser's Arab rival, the Iraqi Premier Qassem.[36] At a Kremlin reception on 16 March for an Iraqi economic delegation, Khrushchev delivered a speech indicating that the USSR favored Qassem's regime over Nasser's and regarded it as more "progressive" than those "in neighboring Arab countries." He added that the USSR sided with those governments that considered their people's interests. He concluded his speech by indirectly warning Nasser that the USSR was "not indifferent to developments in UAR–Iraqi relations."[37] This anti-UAR attack came several days after a failed pro-Nasser coup took place in Mosul on 8 March. The Soviets firmly supported the Qassem regime and described Colonel 'Abd al-Wahhab al-Shawwaf, the leader of the revolt,[38] as a traitor acting in the name of foreign interests, who wanted to return Iraq to the Baghdad Pact.

In his prompt response to Khrushchev's speech, Nasser, on 18 March on Radio Damascus, denounced the Soviet Union for being identified with the Arab communists. Khrushchev's speech, stressed Nasser, "unmasked Moscow's plans against the Arabs," and he charged that the "Arab communists are agents of the Communist Party in Moscow." The Soviets were "initiating a new stage in their plans to dominate the Arab Nation now that imperialism had been defeated in the Middle East and Arab nationalism strengthened." The USSR had "switched from supporting a policy of positive neutrality and non-alignment to one of supporting communist parties, and this policy had brought the Arab people face to face with communist imperialism."[39]

Both the Soviets and Nasser were playing a power game aimed at testing each other's limits while knowing that they were not willing to break the rules of the game at that stage—Nasser and the Soviets could not afford a rift in their relations since it would not serve their short- and long-term interests. Nasser predicted that the Soviets were not likely to exert pressure on or threaten him, nor would they halt or withdraw economic, military, or any other types of aid to the UAR. From the Soviet viewpoint, there was nothing to be gained by doing so, because they were well aware that an open rift with Nasser could only have a negative effect on their relations with other Afro-Asian states that followed Nasser's policy of non-alignment. As Patrick Reilly, the British Ambassador to Moscow, correctly suggested, the Soviet government "would probably prefer to bide their time until the situation in Iraq has become clearer and they have a better idea of future possibilities there and in Syria." Taking into consideration the leaders' personal characteristics, Reilly concluded that "Nasser's propensity for speech-making, and Khrushchev's unwillingness to leave attacks unanswered, may make this difficult, and the Soviet aim will probably be to 'keep Nasser in play' with continued aid spiced with vague threats."[40] Moscow continued economic and military cooperation with the UAR.

Soviet bloc countries were not happy with Nasser's inter-bloc policy, which he exercised in the late 1950s. This policy included the repression of Arab communists, but acceptance of economic and other aid from communist bloc countries, as well as from the US and other Western states. "When one has nothing to lose, but has a chance of gaining everything, one can easily stake one's all," commented a Polish report on Nasserite neutralism. Nasser's foreign policy after he established his power, noted the report, bore "many marks of adventurism," and had the Soviet Union not rendered decisive help, affairs might have taken a bad turn. As Nasser's ideals were being realized—the establishment of the UAR, his success in the Bandung Conference, and his growing stature and prestige in Asia and Africa as well as the international arena—his inter-bloc policy was becoming more moderate and restrained. These features had manifested themselves during the crisis in Lebanon, when he repeatedly curbed the excessive zeal of enthusiastic Syrian army officers such as 'Abd al-Hamid Sarraj. Nasser had shown similar political behavior after the Iraqi coup of July 1958, when his intervention prevented the immediate nationalization of British petroleum companies. Nasser, the Polish report concluded, would most definitely not like to mobilize all the interests of imperialist states against the Arab cause. The Arab public, however,

> is realizing with increasing clarity that, without the help of the Soviet Union and socialist countries, it has no chance of gaining independence in its struggle with the overwhelming forces of imperialism. Therefore the public begins to feel gratitude toward socialist countries, the feelings of friendship are growing, as well as the belief that socialism itself is a good thing. This phenomenon is not to the liking of the Arab national bourgeoisie. That is the reason why it promotes the slogan of positive neutrality. That is why it tries to put obstacles against the socialist cultural and ideological infiltration, which is being received with growing receptivity in Arab societies. [However], it is doubtful that the final victory in the Arabs' struggle for national liberation will come soon. Imperialist powers have deeply-rooted interests in many Arab countries [and] they are still powerful enough to defend their interests.[41]

The Polish report drew a clear distinction between the Arab public, which favored the Soviet Union and its socialist satellites and was also showing interest and sympathy with socialist ideas, and the ruling national bourgeoisie, which adhered to the policy of positive neutralism and retained the interests and activities of the Western powers. Nasser was indirectly criticized for his manipulative use of the inter-bloc rivalry in order to promote his foreign policy.

Nasser's anti-communist offensive had in fact taken the anti-Western edge off his policy of positive neutralism. The motives behind Nasser's anti-communist campaign in the UAR were both political and ideological. Politically, he wanted to warn the Soviets that friendly relations with the Arab world could only be based upon respect for Arab neutralism in the inter-bloc conflict and non-interference in Arab internal affairs. Ideologically, Nasser was expressing his dislike of communism, because "communism is in its essence atheistic; I have always been a sincere Muslim . . . [and] it is quite impossible to be a good Muslim and a good communist. Second, I realized that communism necessitated certain control from Moscow and the central communist parties, and this, too, I could never accept . . ."[42] Nasser also believed that communism as a system could not provide an adequate basis for shaping the social and economic future of the Arabs. Nasser's neutralist policy was very selective. In certain foreign affairs issues in which Nasser had no political interest, he was neutralist or indifferent to the East–West conflict. In areas where he had a political interest, such as Arab affairs, he had never been neutralist; rather, he had been vying for hegemony, as in the case of Syria. In Arab affairs, Nasser maneuvered in such a way that the direct attempts of both the Western powers and the Soviet Union to gain a predominant position canceled each other out. In his efforts to thwart the indirect attempts of the two big powers to engage his influence—whether these attempts were in the form of the Baghdad Pact, in the case of the West, or support for local Arab communist movements, in the case of the Soviets—Nasser relied on the power of impasse and the area rivalry between the two world power blocs to provide him *ad hoc* support and ensure his immunity from effective retaliation. For Nasser, the greatest danger stemmed from the possibility that he would be maneuvered into a position of opposing both power blocs at the same time.[43]

The rise of communism in Iraq, and the growing tension between the USSR and Nasser, posed a challenge for Nasser. He took pains to speed up the normalization of relations with Western bloc countries. Already prior to the Iraqi coup—on the eve of his visit to Moscow—a US report revealed that Nasser responded positively to US overtures to normalize relations in phased stages. A West German loan was announced while Nasser "was sitting face to face with Khrushchev in Moscow, a move which was designed by Nasser to demonstrate his independence in conducting Egypt's international affairs." On 15 July, a day after the Iraqi coup, US marines landed in Lebanon at the request of the Lebanese government to defend it until the UN might be able to "guarantee Lebanese independence and political integrity." The US maneuver was intended to prevent a takeover of Lebanon by the UAR, which was allegedly involved in promoting subversive activities inside Lebanon in order to overthrow the pro-Western regime there.[44] Nasser interpreted US action in Lebanon as directly targeting his interests. He was also angry with the flow of Western arms to Israel. After the Iraqi coup, however, Nasser realized that Qassem's new regime with his communist allies, which were fully supported by the Soviets, had their own political agenda, which did not coincide with his and were even counter to the UAR's interests. This development prompted Nasser's attempts to rebuild the UAR's bridges with the West. By late September and early October, the US State Department disclosed that the UAR was deliberately conveying information about the situation in Iraq to the United States. In clandestine reports and in private conversations with Americans and other Western statesmen, UAR officials also began to express their alarm over US indifference to Iraqi developments and a continued Western hostility to Arab nationalism and Nasser. They wished to make it clear that the UAR was unable to fight a war on two fronts; to move against the communists and risk alienating the USSR without prior assurances that its Western rear would be protected.[45]

By the end of 1958, there was a marked improvement in UAR relations with both Britain and France. On 22 August, a settlement was reached with France, and on 20 January 1959, an agreement was initialed with Britain. Both agreements were aimed at liquidating the aftermath of the Suez War. After much hesitation, diplomatic relations between Britain and the UAR were reestablished in December 1959. This was preceded by a financial agreement between the two countries which permitted the unblocking of Egyptian bank balances in London in return for compensation. On 22 December 1958, West Germany offered capital participation in the construction of the Aswan High Dam. In November, Nasser asked the US to provide him with wheat, although he had earlier promised "he would never again do so." The speedy conclusion of negotiations at Nasser's request, said the Department of State, ran concurrently with an agreement in principle to negotiate with the US for "a double taxation treaty and the lease of the dredge *Essayons* for work on the Suez Canal." It was also noted that "a new cordiality to the West was also visible in the Cairo press." By May 1959, the United States Information Agency had reported a shift toward a Western orientation in the field of education—a growing interest in Egypt to replace Soviet and Chinese educational material with Western publications.[46] By the end of 1959, the United States granted some $140 million worth of aid to the UAR. The International Bank also granted a loan for the development of the Suez Canal, a notable success for the UAR, marking its return to financial respectability.[47]

The conclusion arrived at by the Department of State was that the "magnitude and the speed of the rapprochement with the Western world very probably helped stiffen—though it clearly did not determine— Nasser['s] decision to move against his local communists."[48] A Polish report from Damascus suggested that Nasser's attacks on the USSR and communism were intended to attract the attention of the West. Although

Nasser maintained friendly relations with the socialist camp, noted the report, the UAR would never allow communism to dominate the Arab world. The report concluded that Nasser's anti-Soviet and anti-communist campaign was "a kind of gesture to the West, in particular the USA, aimed at getting American economic help." Nasser's policy was intended to win the rest of the Arab countries over to his side in his struggle for leadership in the Arab world.

Nasser was accused of being an opportunist with shortsighted horizons; someone who did not hesitate to abandon yesterday's allies in order to gain immediate beneficiaries. The pattern of Nasser's behavior in the case of his Soviet ally was similar to his treatment of his main Syrian political ally, the Ba'th Party. He deprived the Ba'th of its monopoly over political and economic life in the Syrian province to bring Syria under his control, manipulating conflicts between leaders of the Ba'th and the National and Populist parties (the latter two parties were traditionally bourgeois institutions and, although dissolved by Nasser, they were still very influential and refused to remain outside the scope of political life in Syria). The Nationalist and Populist leaders also wanted to be involved in shaping political and economic affairs, and were against the monopolization of political life by the Ba'th Party. There were indications that Nasser endeavored to win them over to his side in his attempts to improve the political situation in Syria.[49] By spring 1960, his efforts achieved some success when representatives of the two bourgeois parties readily accepted positions in the state administration, expressing their willingness to cooperate with Nasser's regime. The Nasser–Syrian bourgeoisie honeymoon, however, proved to be ephemeral. Nasser politely declined a request made by the bourgeoisie to restore the previous economic system in Syria; he also rejected their plea for the removal of 'Abd al-Hamid Sarraj, the Minister of the Interior and the most powerful Syrian official in the UAR. Sarraj had been Nasser's most loyal and devoted collaborator in Syria. Nasser's idea to attract the Syrian bourgeoisie to cooperate with his regime had failed.[50]

Despite the existence of an open rift in UAR–USSR relations, Nasser's policy of positive neutralism still prevailed. Even at the height of its attacks on the UAR, the USSR maintained its aid program and indicated that, despite political differences, it sought to strengthen its cooperation with Nasser. By Soviet invitation, Field Marshal 'Abd al-Hakim 'Amir, Vice President of the UAR, visited the Soviet Union from 30 November to 10 December 1960. 'Amir's talks with his Soviet hosts were concerned with political, military, and economic issues. Reports from Moscow revealed that the supply of Soviet aircraft (MiG-15s and MiG-17s) were the major subject of discussion. During the visit, technical committees were formed to discuss questions of industrialization, planning, and political and military affairs. The USSR was determined to complete the Aswan Dam project as expeditiously as possible. 'Amir thanked the Soviets for their consistent support for the UAR, with special reference to the delivery of arms in 1955, support during the Suez crisis, and the building of the Aswan Dam.[51]

By late 1960, soon after the conclusion of 'Amir's visit, the Soviets once again attempted to induce Nasser to reduce his anti-communist campaign. This time, the CIA suggested that the Soviet move was probably because of growing sensitivity to the Chinese challenge to Soviet leadership of the world communist movement. The Soviet campaign began with an article published by *World Marxist Review* in December 1960 condemning the "reign of terror" in the UAR that "surpassed the horrors of the inquisition."[52] The CIA's explanation for this development was as follows:

> Along with the need to take up the cause of local communists to blunt the Chinese challenge, a further motivation for Soviet attacks at this time may have been the growing divergence of Moscow's and Cairo's political interests. The continuing Soviet attacks at time on Nasser's formulation of "Arab Socialism" suggest a concern that the successful implementation of such a program would blunt the appeal of the reformist and economic program of the Middle Eastern communist parties. Moscow's Congo policy created another problem. Although the UAR supported the ill-fated leftist Premier Lumumba, it pursued its own policy in the Congo and failed to back Soviet attacks on the UN operation and on Secretary-General Hammarskjöld.[53]

Soviet–Egyptian ideological disagreements culminated during a two-week tour of the USSR in April–May 1961 by a UAR parliamentary delegation led by Anwar al-Sadat. When the delegation met Khrushchev on 3 May, he seized the opportunity to rail against the UAR's socialist ideology and domestic measures:

> You say you want Arab nationalism and also socialism. We have different views on many issues . . . we are communists and you are not connected with this word. But history will teach you . . . If our people live better than you under the communist banner, then how can you declare yourselves adverse to communism? The people will tell you to go out . . . Communism consists of ideas and ideas cannot be buried in prisons . . . You [Arabs] say that you seek socialism. But you do not know much about socialism, which leads to communism. As a scientific phenomenon, socialism is the first step to communism. You are still in the first stage of your thinking, if you want to build up socialism . . .[54]

Sadat responded to Khrushchev's attacks only after he returned to Egypt and consulted with Nasser. While emphasizing in his reply to Khrushchev the basic differences between Soviet communism and Arab socialism, Sadat said:

The socialism we believe in is based . . . on the liberation and freedom of the individual. We aim at the destruction of exploitation and work for the elimination of class differences . . . we believe that the bloody character of the inter-class struggle can be avoided and that the imperative elimination of social anomalies can be accomplished within the framework of national unity. We also believe that there are a number of spiritual factors, including religion, which have their effects in addition to the accepted basis of material development.[55]

Nasser explained the reasons for the anti-communist campaign in the UAR: "We have not permitted the establishment of a communist party in Egypt because we are sure that it cannot act in conformity with its own will or work for the interest of the country." Communism in the UAR, Nasser concluded, would mean that "the country would have no will of its own, and we would follow the line of international communism and receive directions from it."[56]

In a lengthy conversation between Nasser and R.A.D. Ford, the Canadian Ambassador to Cairo, held in Cairo on 11 June 1961, the former shed new light on, and provided further explanations for, the current conflict with the Soviets. The basis of Egypt's policy had always been and would continue to be the development of independence, and Egypt would never be "under the thumb of anyone," Nasser declared. The Soviet Union's major mistake was that they had thought that, because his regime criticized Western capitalism as not being adaptable to Egypt's conditions, and because Egypt had adopted some aspects of socialism, Egypt had necessarily to follow the road to communism. Yet communism too, Nasser stated, was not applicable to the UAR, the Middle East, or Africa. Nasser relied on the Yugoslav experience in order to provide an explanation for his decision to outlaw communism and communists. The UAR experience in dealing with communists clearly showed that they were "traitors" acting on behalf of the Soviets. The Yugoslav experience taught that, in order to defend their independence after the split from Moscow in 1948, they had to arrest 15,000 pro-Soviet communists "and ever since they have had to keep up a continuous battle for their freedom, as I knew," recalled Nasser.[57] The Soviets had to understand that the Arabs were not going to gain their freedom and defend it at great cost from Western imperialism, only to later lose it to the Soviet Union. To Ford's question of whether the Soviets were not worried that, if the UAR's new model of socialism were successful, it might prove an effective obstacle to Soviet ambitions to win over left-wing opinion not only in the UAR but in Africa, Nasser replied:

You put your finger right on what I considered the essence of the present dispute, which was basically ideological but had its ramifications also in the struggle for Africa and the Middle East. In the UAR [we] were developing a kind of socialism, and it was working. It was neither Marxist nor capitalist. But it worked. It would make nonsense of Marxist historical inevitability. It would show that it was possible to develop a middle road, a social system independent of communism and capitalism. This upset the Russians, and above all the Chinese, who did not like their concept of the march of communism to be questioned.[58]

The roots of the Soviet–UAR conflict were ideological. Both were vying for influence in Africa and the Middle East—both wanted to export and impart their socio-economic system to countries in these areas. Nasser admitted that the UAR's brand of socialism was not necessarily the best for other countries "but at any rate it was more applicable than Soviet communism." Once again, he took Yugoslavia, his chief ally in the non-aligned movement, as an example, stating that the Soviets were afraid of independent communist systems such as Yugoslavia's proving attractive to other potentially pro-communist nations. Nasser explained that the Soviets did not like the way the non-aligned movement was going, and this was tied up with the question of the competition for Africa. Communism was not the solution for Africa, and the non-aligned movement should work out its own solutions, which would have to be something in between capitalism and communism. This solution would have to be adapted to the special conditions in each country. "There is no facile solution," Nasser concluded.[59]

Ford was on close terms with both Soviet diplomats in Cairo and high-ranking Egyptian officials, and often provided his superiors in Ottawa with first-rate reports and analyses on social, ideological, and political developments and trends in Egypt. While analyzing the Soviet motives behind the current crisis, Ford determined that the Soviet–Chinese differences of opinion about the right way to deal with former colonial areas was a fundamental factor in the Soviet–UAR quarrel. The Chinese accepted the situation so long as the UAR followed Soviet policy in Africa, even though suppression of communism in the UAR must have irked them. Nasser's retreat from extreme Soviet positions on Africa, however—as well as his association with Tito in a scheme to organize a new neutralist grouping, which might not be easy for Moscow to control or influence—must have aroused strong suspicion among the Chinese, and among many Soviet communists as well. The suppression of communism in the UAR, maintained Ford, was not a new problem, and, "while irritating to Moscow, is undoubtedly something that could be left to mature, except in the context of an ideological conflict, which I conceive of as being on one hand between the Russians and Chinese, and on the other between the Russians and the UAR."[60]

Another explanation for the Soviet–UAR crisis is provided by the Turkish representative at the CENTO meeting of 15 June 1961 in Ankara, who argued that the Soviet–Egyptian rapprochement of 1953–4 became possible because the two countries shared similar enemies—in particular, the Western powers, the supporters of Egypt's hated enemy, Israel.

Nasser's interests temporarily coincided with the Soviet Union's, and the latter found a valuable outlet in Egypt for its aims in the region, so the Soviets provided Egypt with arms, loans, trade, and diplomatic support. The USSR, unlike the Western powers, did not make overt demands in return and did not even appear to mind Nasser's imprisoning of communists. The Soviets presented themselves in this way with the sole aim that Egypt would mature and eventually become a communist regime. Nasser's maturity, however, grew in a different direction, to the disappointment of Khrushchev. Both countries' interests had come into conflict on specific issues such as the communists' opposition to the Syrian–Egyptian union, and Nasser's opposition to a communist takeover in Iraq. By 1959, these grievances led to the outbreak of ill-feeling between Nasser and Khrushchev. When comparing the rift that occurred in 1959 with the later one of 1961, the conclusion was, according to the Turkish representative, that the two crises were identical in origin.[61]

The Strengthening of the Tito–Nasser Alliance: The Road to the Formation of the Non-Aligned Movement

At the very end of the 1950s and early 1960s, Yugoslavia had taken India's place as Nasser's closest ally in the non-aligned movement. The attitude of Indian officials from the Ministry of External Affairs and the tone of the Indian press with regard to Nasser were, in sharp contrast to the past, unfriendly. The decline of Nasser's image in India began with his quarrel with Qassem, the Iraqi leader. The violence of Nasser's campaign against the Iraqi regime, together with the militant tone of Nasser's official anti-Israeli declarations, had tarnished his reputation in India, where the leadership wanted to see a peaceful solution to the Arab–Israeli conflict. His actions went counter to the India's accepted doctrine of "live and let live," noted C. M. Anderson of the Office of the High Commissioner for the UK, stationed in New Delhi. India's relations with Iraq, Anderson noted, in a letter to London, seemed to be friendly and closer than with the UAR. The Iraqi Ambassador, Hasan Qassem, was "very much in the limelight." The Indian government "appear to regard the new regime in Iraq to a certain extent as protégés whose requests for personnel are flattering [India had supplied three air force instructors and a number of civil pilots, engineers, and other ground staff]," Anderson wrote, adding that "a 'goodwill' delegation of Iraqi ministers is at present visiting Delhi."[62]

President Sukarno of Indonesia, visiting Cairo from 22 to 25 April 1960, followed India's attitude toward Nasser. When Nasser made a warm speech of welcome on Sukarno's arrival—referring to him as a hero of Bandung and praising his achievements on behalf of Afro-Asian solidarity—Sukarno brushed aside Nasser's compliments in his reply and refused to admit to any heroic qualities. The Indonesian guest did not make any complimentary return references to Nasser, but concentrated his speech on a dissertation about the inevitability of historical processes.[63]

A visit made by Nasser to Yugoslavia at the invitation of Tito from 13 to 20 June 1960—the seventh meeting between the two leaders—was another step up in strengthening relations between the two countries. The visit emphasized the solidarity between the two leaders. Reports of the intensive talks between the two leaders revealed Tito's latent desire to take a leading role in world affairs. Tito urged that the non-aligned countries should not stand on the sidelines waiting passively for the superpowers to determine and dictate their fate. He did not suggest that the non-aligned countries should create a "third bloc," which he stressed would merely inflame the already delicate world situation; but there was a need for greater activity on their part. The non-aligned countries, said Tito, should be "carrying out an exchange of views" and ought to "constitute the conscience of mankind."[64] Throughout their talks, Nasser expressed devotion to non-alignment, and the two leaders discussed the possibility of convening a conference of the non-aligned states, though the Indian Embassy in Belgrade made it clear that such a project would not be welcomed by Nehru. In a conversation between the British and the Indian Ambassadors to Belgrade on 28 June 1960, the latter was quoted as saying, "Tito has the misfortune of being a great leader at the head of a small country." For personal reasons, Nehru would find it difficult to take part in a conference under Yugoslav leadership. India's opposition to the Yugoslav initiative was also derived from its concern that such a gathering would isolate the Great Powers, including the USSR—a matter that would complicate India's relations with the Soviet Union at a moment when it needed Soviet support against Chinese influence in Asia.[65]

At the conclusion of Nasser's visit to Yugoslavia, he and Tito issued a communiqué from Brioni on 20 June:

> The two Presidents agree that responsibility for the preservation of world peace and security rests with all nations of the world, and not only exclusively with the Great Powers. For that reason, they firmly believe that now it is more important than ever before that all nations should continue their efforts to put an end to the Cold War, to create a better atmosphere in international relations, and to resist any policy based on the threat or use of force. With their ability to view objectively the general interests of mankind, the uncommitted countries, as well as those which are not directly involved in the Cold War, can play an increasingly useful role in that direction . . . They take the view that the latest proposals of the Soviet government on disarmament, which contain constructive points and contribute to a reduction of the existing differences of opinion, should facilitate the efforts to reach an agreement.[66]

214

Although this statement was formulated to reinforce adherence and the commitment of both leaders to the policy of non-alignment, the two leaders showed more sympathy toward the Soviet Union than the West. Nasser and Tito, however, represented two different brands of neutralism. Tito was a founder of, and firm believer in, the doctrine of negative neutralism; that is, he took an independent line in international affairs based on Yugoslavia's national interests and principles, and not on the basis of commitments or alignment with either the Eastern or Western blocs. Nasser was a founder of positive neutralism—a doctrine that was designed to manipulate the inter-bloc conflict to his own advantage. Tito and Nasser shared similar aspirations—they both wished to play a leading role among the non-aligned countries. However, during his visit to Yugoslavia, Nasser, as the above communiqué shows, made some ideological concessions to his host by sharing many of Tito's views on international affairs. Several reasons have been suggested for this. First, at the time of his visit, he was embroiled in an ideological quarrel with the Soviets. Second, his relations with the Western powers were cool—although some progress had been made—and he still harbored anti-Western feelings. Third, his relations with Nehru, his close ally, were strained. For these reasons Nasser needed to strengthen his alliance with Tito, who remained his main ally on the international scene.

A ten-day visit to the UAR by Edvard Kardelj, the Yugoslav vice-president—which started on 19 December 1960—continued the trend of mutual visits of statesmen from both countries. Although subjects concerning international affairs of interest to both countries were discussed, the focus of his visit was social and economic affairs. Nasser was determined to model the economy of the UAR on a Titoist pattern. Kardelj arrived in Cairo to prepare the forthcoming meeting of the Joint Yugoslav–UAR Ministerial Committee for Economic Cooperation, which was to take place in Cairo in March 1961.[67] Kardelj was the leading theoretician in the Yugoslav Union of Communists. Nasser's doctrine of Arab socialism relied heavily on the Yugoslav model, and Kardelj's visit was followed by intensive ideological cooperation between the two countries, culminating in July 1961 with Nasser's announcement of the "shift towards socialism"—which marked the outset of his socialist revolution.[68]

Tito's visit to the UAR from 18 to 23 April 1961 accelerated the process of convening the preparatory conference of non-aligned countries which was to take place in Cairo. During the visit, both leaders reached full understanding on all issues discussed. In the communiqué issued at the conclusion of the visit, they declared: "The two presidents resumed their review of the relations between Yugoslavia and the UAR and expressed their complete satisfaction concerning them, and their own, and their governments' determination to maintain their progress in every field."[69]

The idea of holding a conference of the heads of state of non-aligned countries, a CIA report declared, was developed and initiated by Nasser and Tito. The two leaders "share the view that as heads of small states with little influence by themselves, but with pretensions to broader leadership, the best means to advance their interests is to create a bloc of states which agree on general foreign policy and which might be brought to express their policy views collectively."[70] In May the two leaders formally invited governments of more than twenty non-aligned states to send representatives to a preparatory conference to be held in Cairo on 5 June 1961.

By early May 1961, the UAR's press had begun to report that Tito and Nasser's initiative was gathering momentum and that the two leaders had already received replies accepting the proposal for the conference from many invitees. Tito and Nasser, reported Nasser's mouthpiece, *al-Ahram*, had taken two factors into account while formulating the proposal for the conference: First, the conference should represent all adherents to the principle of non-alignment; and second, invitations should be addressed to all countries that were not members of multilateral or bi-lateral military pacts.[71] The Cairo press reported that the agenda of the proposed conference would be based on the following issues: the safeguarding of world peace; disarmament; the liquidation of colonialism; non-interference by major powers in the affairs of small countries; and general international problems.[72] *Al-Akhbar* expressed the belief that the non-aligned states would play an important role in the establishment of peace and the maintenance of a balance between East and West, and would block the return of colonialism to Asia and Africa.[73]

For Nasser and Tito, the attendance of India was of the utmost importance. Nehru—who was hesitant about whether to accept the invitation or not because of his fear that the meeting would only point up differences among the attending states rather than help to ease world tensions—finally replied positively. On 12 May, Krishna Menon, the Indian Minister of Defense, visited Cairo. He welcomed the convocation of the conference in the name of his government, and confirmed that the preparatory meeting would take place in Cairo at the ambassadorial level.[74]

Ambassadors or special representatives attended the Cairo preparatory conference, which went from 5 to 13 June. It was decided that the heads of state conference should open on 1 September in Yugoslavia. After an extended debate the participants agreed that a non-aligned state should have an independent policy based on non-alignment, be active in struggling for the independence of other countries, and would not belong to multilateral, bilateral, or regional defense pacts in the context of the Cold War, or have agreements to permit foreign military bases in that context.[75]

The Conference of Heads of State or Government of non-aligned states took place in Belgrade from 1 to 6 September 1961. The Belgrade

Conference, the first of non-aligned countries, may be regarded, according to D. N. Mallik as "a landmark in the evolution of the policy of non-alignment."[76] Tito stated that the conference was "the first concerted action of non-aligned countries," and Sukarno declared that it was initiated under "the conviction that non-alignment has become a growing force in the world . . . and that [the] time has now come to gather this force together, to turn it into a coordinated accumulated moral force."[77] The Belgrade Conference, like Bandung before it, recognized the fact that there were a variety of ideologies to which the participants adhered, but that they all accepted the principle that each country had the right to choose its own path of development. Sukarno, in his speech at the Belgrade Conference, provided a good description of how these countries arrived at the policy of non-alignment:

> There was no prior consultation and agreement between us before we adopted our respective policies of non-alignment. No. We each arrived at this policy inspired by common ideals, prompted by similar circumstances, spurred on by our experiences. There was no attempt to round off disagreements to make our policies identical. But not one of us, I think, will deny that we did inspire each other. The experience of one country in discovering that a policy of non-alignment is the best guarantee for safeguarding our national and international position has undoubtedly helped others to come to a similar conclusion.[78]

The Belgrade Conference marked the birth of the non-aligned movement and the emergence of Tito and Nasser, its architects and sponsors, along with Nehru, whose political reputation was in decline, as the chief leaders of the movement. The decrease in the stature of India, David Kimche stated, was dramatically shown at the Belgrade Conference. Nehru, Kimche declared,

> had not been among the original sponsors of the conference; he had in fact displayed little enthusiasm for it from the start. His reasons for eventually joining the sponsors were mundane and far from the idealistic motives which Nehru usually attributed to such events. India agreed to the conference mainly because the exclusion of China and Pakistan (neither of which was considered non-aligned) gave her a better chance to bring forward her own point of view to the detriment of her two adversaries. But at the conference itself Nehru failed to create a consensus behind his opinions: for him the question of peace and coexistence was of top priority, while for others, such as presidents Sukarno and Nkrumah, the continuation of the anti-colonial struggle was far more important."[79]

The Belgrade Conference took place against the background of mounting international tensions, aggravation of East–West intrigue, and the continuous struggle for national liberation in the Third World. Its greatest significance, declared Bimal Prasad, lay in its enunciation of certain fundamental principles, such as the declaration that the non-aligned countries "did not want to constitute themselves within a bloc and could not be a bloc." The participant countries also expressed the desire "to cooperate with any government which sought to contribute to the strengthening of confidence and peace in the world . . . the further extension of the non-committed area of the world constituted the only possible alternative to the intensification of Cold War policies."[80] The conference made it clear that "all peoples and nations have to solve the problems of their own political, economic, social, and cultural systems in accordance with their own conditions, needs, and potentialities."[81]

If the formation of the UAR was Nasser's major success in his inter-Arab politics, the formation of the non-aligned movement was his major success in promoting his leadership within Third World countries. At the height of his international success, however, only a few days after the conclusion of the Belgrade Conference, anti-unionist forces in the Syrian province of the UAR organized a military coup, which led to the disintegration of the UAR.

The Shift toward Socialism and the Demise of the UAR

The USSR–UAR ideological warfare came to an end soon after the introduction of Nasser's Socialist Laws of July 1961.[82] These laws marked the beginning of Nasser's Arab socialism, an idea that constituted one of his basic principles. One reason why Nasser decided to take such a step at this particular time, according to Western diplomats in Cairo, was that he was sensitive to Soviet criticism of his social policy following the drastic measures taken against communism. Nasser, the diplomats suggested, was dependent on Soviet arms supplies and financial support, and could not afford such a rift. He seemed to have believed that the introduction of socialist measures might appease Soviet anger over his anti-communist campaign.[83] However, his decision to embark on the socialist route was actually consolidated and determined earlier, in the late 1950s, and had almost nothing to do with either Soviet influence or pressure.[84] In any case, the shift to socialism was warmly received by the Soviets, albeit with certain reservations.[85]

To demonstrate that his decision to embrace socialism was purely motivated by Egypt's own interests and was an independent act, Nasser declared that Egypt's brand of socialism and its pursuit of economic development lay in non-alignment. The choice was not between capitalism or communism but between progress and stagnation. Nasser claimed that Egypt's socialism placed special emphasis on the abolition of artificial class barriers and the establishment of full liberty and democracy, including the rights of freedom of conscience and property ownership. This ideological non-alignment of domestic policy, was, in practice, no more neutral than Nasser's non-alignment in foreign affairs; ideologically it was closer to Eastern European doctrine than to Western concepts. Elements of Marxism, such as an emphasis on social rights at the expense of individual political rights, were evident. As in the Soviet model, Nasser's socialism placed great emphasis on detailed government planning and control, in contrast to Western ideas of freedom from government interference. Nasser's Arab socialism was a fusion of socialist, nationalist, and Islamic ideas. It was a nationalist socialism in the sense that it accommodated itself to particular Arab and Egyptian circumstances. Arab socialism rejected proletarian internationalism and emphasized the distinctiveness of the Arab Nation. It called for the unification of the Arab Nation under the leadership of Arab revolutionary forces.[86]

As for the Syrian province of the UAR, the Laws of Nationalization were a source of indignation among the old traditionalist elite that constituted the Syrian bourgeoisie. If fully implemented, these laws would have destroyed its economic and political bases of power. Podeh holds the view that these laws constituted "the most significant economic factor" leading to the demise of the UAR.[87] In the period 1958–61, despite all the efforts of Nasser and pro-Nasserite Syrian elements to weaken it, the Syrian bourgeoisie continued to be politically significant, and, moreover, had its supporters within the Syrian army. As Rabinovich declared, the group of officers who plotted the coup against Nasser, "was composed of at least two distinct elements. On the one hand were rightist officers . . . who seem to have been linked to the Syrian bourgeoisie and possibly also to conservative Arab regimes. The other headed by 'Abd al-Karim Nahlawi . . . seem to have had no strings attached but rather to have been moved by personal ambitions and by the grievances of the Syrian officer corps." Rabinovich asserted that some of the officers in the latter group did not want to see the demise of the union, but wished to impose upon Nasser the need to introduce some vital reforms. Nasser's refusal to negotiate with them, however, was decisive.[88]

The demise of the UAR in September 1961 also marked the temporary end of the phase of positive neutralism in Syria. Questions of national identity and Syria's inter-Arab politics became prominent in the period 1961–3. As far as Syria's inter-bloc policy was concerned, there was a sharp shift from positive to passive neutralism.

Conclusion

The Rise of the Neo-Ba'th and the
Gradual Demise of Neutralism

The rise of neutralism in Syria, which had begun in the mid-1940s, was not an exclusive phenomenon in the Arab world. This process also developed simultaneously in Egypt and other Arab countries. Neutralism was one of the immediate consequences of the conclusion of World War II, which marked the emergence of the post-colonial world. Many of the newly-emerged independent countries in Asia and Africa showed no desire to ally themselves with either of the two new international blocs—the East and West—following the outbreak of the Cold War. These countries rejected both capitalism and communism and were searching for a third alternative, for a socio-economic system that would suit them. Their search led to the emergence of nationalist socialism, which was formulated and practised by each country in accordance with its special needs, particular circumstances, and objective and subjective conditions. These countries were also seeking for an independent policy in international affairs—and many of them chose to embrace the doctrine of neutralism by expressing their intention to remain non-aligned in the East–West conflict. However, there were many different forms of neutralism. Many of the countries that opted for a policy of neutralism had formulated and implemented their own ideas of neutralism, and put emphasis on the special characters of their brand of neutralism.

Syria under al-Shishakli—in particular in the period 1949–51, when he acted as covert, unofficial leader of the country—and Egypt under the Wafd government (1950–2), embraced and practised the doctrine of neutralism. The essential difference between Syrian and Egyptian neutralism of the 1940s and early 1950s, was that Syrian neutralism was derived from resentment toward the West for what it perceived as the pro-Zionist-Israeli policies of the Western powers, the founders and defenders of Israel. This approach to neutralism, "anti-western neutralism," maintained that Syria should strengthen its links with the Soviet Union and, by doing so, Syria would position itself out of the Western camp should a third world war occur. There was moreover, a strong will to humiliate the West for the injustices it had caused the Arabs.

In addition to this pattern of neutralism, there was another school of Syrian neutralism—Ba'thist neutralism—which was highly ideological. While repelling both communism and capitalism, it offered an alternative formula—a united Arab world embracing the socialist socio-economic system—a form of nationalist socialism that had many similarities with the Indian and Yugoslav brands of socialism. As far as the inter-bloc conflict was concerned, the Ba'th, like Nehru's India, declared that Syria and the Arabs should not ally themselves with either of the two major blocs; rather, Syria must develop an independent policy. There was a slight difference between the Indian and Ba'thist patterns. Indian neutralism aimed at playing an active role in easing tensions between the East and West and removing the danger of the outbreak of a third world war. The Ba'th supported this principle, in theory, but in practice, there was no balance in its attitude toward both rival camps—the East and West. Although the Ba'th Party rejected communism, it looked, on the one hand, more favorably at the Soviet Union and, on the other hand, with resentment at the Western powers. Like many other Syrian political groups, it wanted to humiliate the West. In the early 1950s, the Ba'th pattern of neutralism remained strictly within the framework of theory.

Al-Shishakli emerged as Syria's sole leader in the years 1952–4, a period that was characterized by its lack of interest in the inter-bloc conflict. Syria's inter-bloc policy fell along with the pattern of passive neutralism. Politically, the Ba'th found itself situated on the margins of the Syrian political arena, with poor representation in the Parliament. It was only after the elections of 1954 that the Ba'th emerged as a rising force on the Syrian political scene. The party endeavored from 1954 to 1958 to further its doctrine, in particular in connection with its foreign policy, which had two major interrelated components—pan-Arabism and neutralism. The Ba'th became one of Syria's ruling circles following the formation of a united front of left-wing forces, which also included Khalid al-'Azm, the architect of Syria's relations with the Soviet bloc, and a group of independent politicians who gathered around al-'Azm. This front received the support of the communists, who, although they had only marginal representation in Parliament, did have a growing influence in the army and other state institutions. Foreign influences in Syria—Soviet and Egyptian—also marked this period. Within the ruling leftist front, there existed two neutralist trends. One was represented by the Ba'th—an ideological/doctrinaire neutralism, which at some point, as a result of the significantly growing Nasserite influence, shifted to positive neutralism. The second trend was that of al-'Azm's group, which adopted a clear anti-Western line, more extreme than that which al-'Azm practised in the early 1950s. Al-'Azm also adopted a pro-Soviet approach and acted, with reasonable success, to deepen the extent of Soviet involvement in Syrian affairs. Nevertheless, al-'Azm had no intentions of turning Syria into a Soviet satellite. This can be defined as positive neutralism with a pro-Soviet orientation. Besides these two neutralist trends, there existed a third way which resembled, in its essence, the neutralist trend of the early 1950s—an anti-Western approach that showed sympathy toward the Eastern bloc. This was the policy adopted by Prime Minister al-'Asali and President al-Quwatli. The group gradually allied itself with the Ba'th Party and embraced Nasser's doctrine of positive neutralism. By late 1957 and early 1958, most of the political forces determining Syrian politics supported the Ba'th Party's principles in foreign affairs; they favored positive neutralism and full political amalgamation with Nasser's Egypt. The road was paved for a union between Syria and Egypt.

Egyptian neutralism, which had been a ruling doctrine since the Wafd government took power in January 1950, can be delineated as calculative/pragmatic. In Egypt, as in Syria, there were diverse neutralist approaches. By the mid-1940s and early 1950s, anti-Western sentiments, which derived inspiration from the outbreak of the Cold War, had spread across Egypt. Egypt had failed to reach a satisfactory agreement with Britain to its extended dispute over the 1936 treaty, which had cast a heavy shadow on Egypt's sovereignty over its territory. Egypt's ruling elite accused the US of not exerting sufficient pressure on Britain to make concessions to Egypt, and therefore they came to regard the US as Britain's ally in the matter. This shattered the image of America as an anti-imperialist and anti-colonialist superpower. Syria and Egypt rejected categorically US efforts to settle the Arab–Israeli conflict peacefully. They also resolutely objected to the plans of Western powers to take part in establishing military alliances with the aim of preventing possible Soviet expansion into the Middle East. At the same time, a process of rapprochement between the two Arab countries and the USSR began to gather momentum. Both Syria and Egypt were nurturing relations with the Soviets in order to exert pressure on the Western powers. The continuous refusal of these powers to respond positively to Arab national demands led the Arabs to move even closer toward the Soviet bloc, which showed willingness to support the Arabs militarily, economically, and politically, with no strings attached.

This pattern of calculative/pragmatic neutralism became relevant again during Nasser's first years in power. In their first year-and-a-half in power, the Free Officers adopted a pro-American line and condemned domestic and international communism. They soon realized, however, that the hopes they cherished of the US providing them with military and economic aid and their belief that it would take their side in their dispute with Britain were to be dashed. By the end of 1953, Nasser embraced the doctrine of calculative neutralism implemented by the last Wafd government. This new direction started to bear fruit when Nasser concluded arms deals with the Soviet bloc and managed to secure economic aid from the Western camp, although his main success was his 1954 agreement with Britain, which led to the full evacuation of all British troops from Egypt. In the years 1956–8, Nasser put into effect the formula of positive neutralism, designed to manipulate the East–West conflict to his own advantage, and further Egypt's interests by trying to maintain correct and balanced relations with both blocs. Nasser wanted to secure maximum support and assistance in all fields from both international blocs. This form of neutralism, however, was rejected by the US, which refused to take part in Nasser's game. Nasser's inter-bloc policy consequently became less balanced: anti-Western and pro-Soviet. Nasser's hostile approach toward local communism indicated that he had no plans for Egypt to become a Soviet satellite; he made it clear that he was keen to preserve and protect Egypt's independence. Since the conclusion of the Bandung Conference, he had become one of the chief leaders of the Afro-Asian movement and the camp of non-aligned countries. Nasser's aspiration to secure Egypt's hegemony over the Arab world brought him closer to the Syrian Baʻth Party, as both Nasser and the Baʻth shared similar views with regard to the appropriate stand to be taken by the Arabs in the East–West conflict. The alliance between the two was strengthened in the course of the internal Syrian power struggle of late 1957–early 1958. Nasser took the Baʻth's side, and the decision to form a union between the two countries marked the defeat of those Baʻth rivals who had promoted their pro-Soviet neutralist approach. Following the formation of the UAR, the doctrine of positive neutralism reached its pinnacle. The years of the Syrian–Egyptian union were characterized by a more balanced positive neutralism.

With the collapse of the UAR, Syria returned for a short period of time to the pre-union parliamentary system, and the old politics and politicians continued to operate in an atmosphere of deceit and dishonesty, which led to political instability. The period September 1961–March 1963 has been commonly characterized as a period of "separatism" or "secessionism." Two of Syria's most important features of foreign policy—its inter-Arab and inter-bloc policies—signified a fundamental change to previous years. In Arab affairs, Syria found itself isolated. Nasser, who felt betrayed by the Syrians, refused to recognize the new Syrian regime, as did other Arab governments that procrastinated their act of recognition, employing the tactic of "wait and see." They waited until the new heterogeneous Syrian elite consolidated its grip in Syria and restored stability. The new elite included members of the old traditionalist right-wing elite, whose position was weakened significantly during the union period, in particular with the introduction of the socialist laws of 1960–1. There was also the multifaceted left-wing elite, which included elements from the Ba'th Party who, prior to the demise of the UAR, objected to Nasser's rule. Among this elite was Akram al-Hawrani, whose decision to participate in the "separatist regime" led to his expulsion from the Ba'th Party in May 1962. In the post-UAR period, the Ba'th was split and weak, and divided between those who had objected to union with Egypt and those who remained pro-Nasserite. The latter included the 'Aflaq–Bitar group—the forefathers of the party. Although they remained adherents of the idea of Arab unity, they concluded from their recent past experience that some amendments and modifications were necessary before making any further steps in that direction. The Ba'th, as well as other political groups, also had their supporters within the army.

As far as Syria's inter-bloc policy was concerned, the new government dropped Nasser's doctrine of positive neutralism and instead embraced the policy of passive neutralism. Syria's separatism aimed at turning the clock back to the first period of independence (1946–9)—to be independent of foreign influence, a period in which passive neutralism prevailed.[1] Although the Soviet Union had been the first major power to recognize Syria after the break-up of the union, relations between the two countries remained within the framework of "businesslike cooperation," as Khrushchev himself described it on 17 October 1961, before the Twenty-Second CPSU Congress.[2] Statements by Syrian politicians, such as those made by Ahmad Bashir al-'Azma—one of several Syrian Prime Ministers whose terms of power was short-lived—were intended to keep Syria out of the East–West conflict and to demonstrate its passive approach to it. On 22 April 1962, al-'Azma declared on Radio Damascus that Syria's foreign policy continued to be based on "the principles of positive neutrality and non-alignment with military blocs, non-participation in the Cold War, and respect for the principles of the UN Charter."[3]

Syria's policy of passive neutralism was to change again following the successful *coup d'état* of 8 March 1963. The Ba'th Party, the advocate of positive neutralism, became, for the first time in its history, the ruling body of Syria. The coup was carried out by a mixture of Ba'thist and pro-Nasserist (Unionist) elements led by an independent, General Ziyad al-Hariri. Salah al-Din al-Bitar, a co-founder of the Ba'th, formed a new government composed of Ba'thist and Unionist members. In its first weeks in power, al-Bitar's government acted together with the Iraqi Ba'th regime (which had taken over in Baghdad a month earlier) to implement the idea of unity with Egypt, a move, which, in the short-term, achieved the signing of the Tripartite Charter on 17 April. A few weeks later, however, anti-Unionist feelings among Ba'thist elements brought about a confrontation between the two groups that had fomented the March coup. The result was the ouster of the pro-Nasserist group following an attempted coup mounted on 18 July.[4]

The idea of union with Egypt was now irrelevant. Al-Bitar and the old guard, the advocates of Arab unity, went into decline. On 27 July, General Amin al-Hafiz, the oppressor of the failed Unionist coup nine days earlier, took over as President of the National Council of the Revolutionary Command, as well as Commander-in-Chief of the Army. On the inter-Arab front, al-Hafiz's first order was to set in motion a process within the Iraqi and Syrian Ba'thist regimes which would culminate in a union between the two countries. Al-Hafiz's policy was endorsed on 28 October by the National Congress of the Ba'th Party, which met in Damascus. The issue of broader Arab unity was therefore relegated. Prime Minister Salah al-Din al-Bitar resigned on 11 November after losing control of events; he was replaced by al-Hafiz, who formed his first Cabinet on the same day.[5] The principle of federal unity between Iraq and Syria, which was agreed to by the Sixth National Congress of the Ba'th Party, suffered a serious setback when the Iraqi Ba'th regime was overthrown in a successful anti-Ba'thist *coup d'état* in November. Amin al-Hafiz's efforts to resolve the crisis in Iraq were unsuccessful.[6]

In foreign policy, Syria's new leaders achieved some successes. In 1964, relations with many Arab countries had improved, so the new government was able to begin emerging from its isolation.[7] However, this development lost its momentum in the following year. Relations with Egypt were at a low ebb after Egypt ignored Syria's call for help following Israeli military action that destroyed Syrian canalization works forming part of the Jordan waters diversion scheme. Syria also took the side of the anti-Nasserite forces in Yemen and Southern Arabia that were trying to expel Nasser's invading army from Yemen.[8]

There was also a significant rapprochement with Soviet bloc countries throughout the period 1963–6. Although the Syrian leaders declared their adherence to a policy of non-alignment, they were ideologically and politically closer to the Eastern bloc than to the West:[9]

The Arab Socialist Ba'th Party had placed the question of the struggle against imperialism in its international and human framework and considered the socialist camp a positive, active force in the struggle against imperialism . . . The Party was the first to propose the slogan of positive neutralism as a broad line for Arab foreign policy and has always stressed the principle of "non-commitment" towards any of the international camps, but this formula meant fundamentally a determined revolutionary struggle of principle against imperialism. Therefore the party did not regard the two camps equally since the horizon of struggle of a colonized or semi-colonized people and of a homeland crushed and exploited by imperialism render the fundamental starting points of the socialist camp more harmonious with the interests of our Arab homeland and more in sympathy with our Arab people.[10]

The Ba'th regime departed from the passive neutralism pursued by their predecessors to re-embrace the doctrine of positive neutralism exercised by Nasser during the period of unification. This positive neutralism was not at all balanced but, rather, inclined toward the Soviet bloc. It was a pro-Soviet positive neutralism.

Syria's socio-economic policy also indicated a tilt toward the Eastern concepts of socialism. The Sixth Congress adopted a more radical concept of socialism than Michel 'Aflaq's previous moderate "Arab Socialism." The Ba'th had added to its terminology the Eastern Bloc idea of "popular democracy." That concept, it was said, "involves an extensive measure of democracy for the popular masses, but it also stresses at the same time the need to seclude the class and political forces hostile to the socialist revolution."[11] The road to scientific socialism was to be led by the revolutionary socialist vanguard—the "instrument of the masses in bringing about a transformation of the social and economic relations." However, "for this transformation to materialize in a comprehensive radical and human fashion, it should be brought about by the masses themselves; as for the socialist vanguard, it will play the role of mediator and leader (even if it is in power) that acts to direct the journey of the masses toward the socialist future in a scientific way and in a democratic style."[12] The years 1964 and 1965 had seen a remarkable shift toward socialism followed by a wave of nationalization in industry, external trade, and real estate, and these developments had produced social discontent and provoked an uprising in Damascus of merchants and religious leaders, suppressed by the authorities. Amin al-Hafiz's regime also made considerable progress in organizing large-scale economic projects, including the exploitation of Syria's oil resources.[13]

The officers' cabal, which was led by Jadid's military supporters, put an end to al-Hafiz's rule on 23 February 1966. This coup inaugurated a new era of intensified radicalization in both domestic and foreign policies. A provisional Syrian executive of the Ba'th Party was established that same day. The former leaders, Radio Damascus announced, among them General Amin al-Hafiz, Munif al-Razzaz, Salah al-Din al-Bitar, and Michel 'Aflaq, had been arrested and would be tried by a party court. The broadcast added that General Hafiz al-Asad (Jadid's main ally), the Commander-in-Chief of the Air Force, had also been appointed Minister of Defense. Colonel Ahmad Swaidani was appointed Chief of Staff. The provisional Syrian Executive explained its motives and declared its program. They blamed al-Hafiz for abandoning the principle of collective leadership and Prime Minister al-Bitar for betraying his socialist principles. It was also claimed that:

Appeals by the rank and file of the party in Syria for convening a Party Congress or an extraordinary meeting of the National Council had been ignored, they [the new leaders] took it upon themselves to summon meetings of both the Syrian and the pan-Arab Congresses, to maintain socialist measures of nationalization, and to study and deal with the country's economic difficulties on a "scientific" basis.[14]

The pro-Jadid civilian group, the anti-Nasserite *Qutriyyun* ["regionalists"] who were the ideological opponents of ʿAflaq, and the old guard, soon took their place throughout the state and party machinery. On 25 February, Nur al-Din al-Atasi was appointed Head of State, and Yusuf Zuʿayyin became Prime Minister. There was no doubt, however, that real power remained in the hands of the insurgent military officers. The Baʿth Party, notwithstanding its endeavor to broaden its base and gain popular support, had now clearly become a minority party ruled by an ʿAlawi military elite.[15] The external image projected by Syria's new leaders, at both the military and civilian levels, was negative: they were considered doctrinaire, extremist, and inexperienced.

The Jadid group's coup failed to improve Syria's troubled relations with Egypt and other Arab countries. The new regime was given a suspicious reception which only deepened Syria's isolation. As far as Soviet–Syrian relations were concerned, British diplomats appreciated that the coup of February 1966 would not change the existing state of affairs: Syria would remain dependent on the USSR for military, economic, and political support. These relations would not be impaired by Syria's growing cooperation with Communist China.[16] The diplomats reported that the Soviet Union and Syria "saw early this year [1966] such compelling reason to draw nearer the one to the other that it is quite possible that even without the coup of 23 February, the Syrian regime might have got to the point of requesting fulfillment of Russian promises for aid to the Euphrates Dam and found their request met."[17] This assumption was indeed correct; relations between the USSR and Syria reached their peak following the coup of February 1966.

Relations between the Soviets and the new Syrian ruling elite improved dramatically soon after the removal of the old Baʿth guard. A series of measures taken by the new Syrian rulers contributed to this development. First, the Baʿth regional command decided at a conference in March to "expand and deepen socialist transformations and to democratize the political life of both the party and the country as a whole."[18] Second, the coup was carried out by a group on the extreme left of the Baʿth Party. The new government included a new communist minister (Samih ʿAtiyya), albeit as an individual and not as a representative of the Communist Party. Moreover, on 13 April, the authorities permitted the return to Syria of Khalid Bakdash, the communist leader, after many years spent in exile.

Third, the government removed the premier, Salah al-Din al-Bitar, whom the Soviets considered a "gradualist, unworthy of the name of socialist." The regime, it should not be forgotten, was so lacking in other internal and international support that it had no choice but to continue Syria's pro-Soviet orientation.[19] Reports from Damascus revealed that the new Ba'th regime sought the support of the Syrian Communist Party (SCP) in order to broaden its political support base within Syria.[20]

The Ba'th–Communist alliance and the growing Soviet foothold in Syria stirred considerable anxiety in the West. The participation of communists in running Syria, even on an individual basis, was a sign that their influence, in comparison to the recent past, was increasing. Reports from Damascus by Western diplomats noted that "rumblings of discontent" about the new regime and its communist ally were widespread in Muslim circles.[21]

The process of rapprochement between Jadid–Asad's Ba'th and the USSR gathered momentum throughout the period 1966–70. The Jadid–Asad group wanted to improve their relations with the Soviets for several reasons, which can be classified into internal, and external threats to the regime's stability. First, the Ba'th Party had never enjoyed the support of the vast majority of the Syrian people, or commanded solid support in the country's traditional power centers. Following the coup of 23 February, Syria was ruled for the first time by military officers of 'Alawi origin, and, by removing 'Aflaq, al-Bitar, al-Hafiz, and the old guard, the new leaders lost the support of the town middle class and of many Sunnis who constituted the majority of the population. The 'Alawi elite relied on the army for its legitimacy to rule and to safeguard its interests *vis-à-vis* the townspeople. Second, in international affairs, the new ruling elite was characterized by anti-Western sentiments and opposition to imperialism. Domestically this was reflected in its implementation of social radicalism. The new rulers felt isolated in both domestic and external arenas. They were also desperate for legitimacy from other Arab countries. Their radicalism, however, made them an anathema to conservative Arab regimes, and their only hope was to be recognized by Nasser, who had already preceded them in pursuing a social revolution. Nasser had also incorporated into his establishment communists on an individual basis, and in 1965 the main Egyptian communist groups fell apart. Nasser's shift to socialism and the opening of the doors of his establishment for communists were welcomed and praised by the USSR.[22] It is probable that the Syrian leaders were influenced by the Egyptian model when they allowed communists to join the regime as individuals.

The Syrian leaders realized that the only way to be accepted by Nasser was through Moscow. By declaring an anti-Western policy and expressing a desire to implement radical socialism, they believed that they could improve their image in the USSR and thus abet the rapprochement between the two countries. Soviet economic, military, and international support could help them stabilize their rule. It would also help to consolidate a new Arab front of radical regimes with Egypt's participation as the key state.

The USSR had its own reasons for supporting the Jadid–Asad regime. First, the Soviets feared that the regime's domestic weakness and its lack of a foundation of legitimacy for its rule might strengthen the right and induce it to mount a coup. Second, the Soviets were aware that the Arab world was sharply divided into two camps—the conservative and the revolutionary. The former was led by Saudi Arabia, American-oriented and possessing great influence in the Arab world. The second camp was led by Nasser, whose status and influence in the Arab world decreased in the mid-1960s due to the war in Yemen among other reasons. It was important for the Soviets to strengthen Nasser and the revolutionary camp in the Arab world *vis-à-vis* the pro-Western camp. The inclusion of the radical and pro-Soviet Syrian regime into the anti-Western revolutionary camp could have achieved two results: the strengthening of the pro-Soviet and revolutionary Arab camp; and the serving of Soviet interests in the Middle East which derived from strategic Cold War goals. Third, the Soviets hoped that by supporting the Damascus regime at this crucial time they would pave the way for the penetration of communists into the establishment. Fourth, the USSR was afraid that if it did not act quickly, China might seize the opportunity to establish a stronghold in Syria. Both countries had vied for influence in Syria in the preceding decade.[23] The process of rapprochement between Syria and the USSR was therefore in the interest of both countries.

In late April 1966, at the conclusion of a visit of a Syrian delegation led by Prime Minister Zu'ayyin in the USSR, the Syrian adherence to non-alignment remained theoretical and meaningless since they made it clear that they followed the Soviet view on international affairs. The Syrian delegation condemned the "intervention of American imperialism" in South Vietnam and its aggression against the "Democratic Republic of Vietnam." American military involvement in Vietnam, both sides stressed, must cease immediately, since it created a serious threat to international peace. The two countries condemned all forms of colonialism and asserted their support for anti-colonialist movements struggling for national liberation and for social justice and economic prosperity. Special emphasis was placed on the anti-colonialist campaign led by the non-aligned countries. Those countries, the communiqué said, were in the vanguard of the effort to ease international tensions and consolidate peace and cooperation among nations. Syria and the USSR called for an international treaty on nuclear non-proliferation, urging the establishment of denuclearized zones in different parts of the world to help strengthen peace.[24]

The results of the Zu'ayyin delegation's visit were positive from Syria's point of view and effectively heralded a new era in Syrian–Soviet bloc relations. Other Eastern European countries followed the USSR's lead and strengthened their relations with Syria. Throughout 1966, a procession of delegations from East European countries and Syria paid mutual visits to one another, usually resulting in the signing of commercial agreements. Economically, Zu'ayyin's visit to Moscow was a major success. Damascus obtained the Soviets' unconditional recognition and support for the Ba'th regime. Soon after, the USSR successfully mediated between Syria and the UAR. Nasser adopted the Syrian Ba'th proposal, with Soviet backing, for a common front composed of Egypt, Syria, and Algeria—"the meeting point of the revolutions"—to rival the bloc of conservative Arab states. The ideological content of the "meeting point of the revolutions" bore a more radical revolutionary character than "unity of purpose" [wahdat al-hadaf].[25] Syria and the USSR could also congratulate themselves for consolidating the alliance of "progressive forces" in the Arab world. This new Arab alignment created concrete dividends for the Ba'th regime when Egypt and Syria concluded a defense agreement in November 1966. The pact bolstered the Ba'th regime's self-confidence, and this was soon reflected in developments along the Israeli–Syrian border. The aggravation of tensions and mounting violent clashes between the two countries, with Syria backed by anti-Israeli Soviet statements and by its defense pact with Egypt, helped pave the way for the June 1967 War.[26]

The humiliating Syrian and Arab defeat in that war led to the loss of the final vestiges of Syria's policy of positive neutralism. The following years were characterized by Syria's reliance and growing dependence on full Soviet support. The results of the June 1967 War were a hard blow for the Ba'th regime and the Soviets. The Syrians, as well as Nasser, needed to rebuild their military power in an effort to recapture the territories occupied by Israel, and only the Soviets were able and willing to provide the equipment. The Soviets did not want the Ba'th and Nasserite regimes to collapse and subsequently lose their influence and strategic strongholds in the Middle East after years of considerable investment in these countries. Hafiz al-Asad's takeover in November 1970 reinforced this development. As far as Syria's stance toward the Cold War was concerned during the period 1970–91 (the year of the disintegration of the Soviet Union), the policy of neutralism vanished. Although not a Soviet bloc country, Syria had gradually become almost fully aligned with the Soviet side in the Cold War—a virtual Soviet satellite in many international affairs. Evidence to support this argument could already be seen by Syria's decision to support the Soviet invasion of Czechoslovakia in 1968, contrary to the position of Tito and the vast majority member states of the non-aligned movement.[27] Another example was the support given by Syria to the Soviet invasion of Afghanistan in late 1979.[28]

Syria's foreign policy in the period 1946–61 was characterized by its constant search for foreign allies. Two major features of Syria's foreign policy developed along parallel lines in this period—its inter-Arab and inter-bloc politics. However, Syria's inter-bloc policy was inextricably bound to Egypt's. Syria's policy toward the inter-bloc conflict was not fully independent, but rather influenced to a great extent by the inter-Arab relationship. With the formation of the Baghdad Pact in the mid-1950s, the Arab world was divided into two camps—the "conservative," led by Hashemite Iraq (until 1958), and the "revolutionary," led by Egypt. Since early 1955, Syria had been allied with Nasser's Egypt, an alliance that reached its pinnacle when the two countries made the decision to unite in 1958. Since Syria had gained its independence, it found itself embroiled in a crisis of national identity. Rival political groups held different notions of Syrian identity and purpose. Some wished to promote unity with Hashemite Iraq, others desired to see political union with Egypt or at least to develop closer relations with it and with Saudi Arabia (until 1956–7). The Ba'th coups of 1963 and 1966 signified the victory of territorial nationalism over pan-Arabism. The Syrian forces who led the coups wished to establish Syria's independence in both domestic and Arab affairs. They wanted to see Syria improve its position within the Arab world, from being a weak and dependent state to becoming a strong, leading country, a development that was reinforced in al-Asad's period in power. And in Hafiz al-Asad's years in power, Syria did indeed become a regional Middle Eastern power, with its own agenda in Arab as well as international affairs. Since the late 1970s, as a result of Egyptian President Anwar al-Sadat's initiative to promote peace with Israel, Syria challenged his ambitions and managed to isolate Egypt in the Arab world. Until the mid-1980s, Syria led the Arab boycott against Egypt for its decision to make peace with Israel.

If, in the period 1946–61, Syria's inter-bloc policy was influenced to a great extent by its inter-Arab politics, things evolved in the opposite direction during the period 1970–91. Soviet–Syrian relations, in particular since the decline of Soviet influence over Egypt in the latter part of 1970s, influenced to a large degree Syria's politics in Arab affairs. Syria became the Soviets' chief ally in the Middle East, and because of its growing dependency on the USSR, it now followed the line dictated from Moscow. Relations between the two countries, however, eased following Mikhail Gorbachev's ascension to power in 1985. His policies of glasnost and perestroika, which marked the beginning of the end of the Cold War, did not suit Syria's Middle Eastern policy. Gorbachev's decision to improve relations with Israel and to seek for a peaceful solution to the Arab–Israeli conflict were coolly received in Damascus.[29]

When the Gulf War broke out in January 1991, Syria joined the anti-Iraqi coalition formed by the US. The war was concluded with victory for the US-led coalition. By late 1991 Syria found itself engaged in the Middle East peace conference held in Madrid; a conference initiated by the US government that aimed to reach a peaceful solution to the Arab–Israeli conflict. Both Syria and the USSR attended the conference and, by doing so, admitted American hegemony. A few weeks after the conclusion of the conference, the USSR disintegrated and the Cold War was officially over. This development marked the demise of the doctrines and policies of neutralism and non-alignment, which were born at the outbreak of the Cold War and were directly connected to the international treaties, agreements, and ideologies established under that conflict.

The end of the Cold War and the disintegration of the USSR placed Hafiz al-Asad in an awkward position. The emergence of the Russian Federation as the USSR's successor did not signify a positive development in terms of Syria's foreign relations. In the immediate post-Soviet era, Russia under Boris Yeltsin took a pro-Western line, a development, which was manifested in the Middle East when Russia considered Syria, Iraq, and Iran—old allies—to be more of an economic burden than a benefit. Syria was now viewed by Yeltsin's regime with much suspicion and kept at a distance. Moscow also nurtured relations with Syria's neighbors—Israel, Lebanon, Jordan, and Turkey. Its call for the withdrawal of all foreign troops from Lebanon displeased Damascus.

Russia's pro-Western line was, however, short-lived. The radical economic reforms did not have immediate positive results and the West did not provide the necessary funds to accomplish the economic revolution in Russia. Also, US plans to expand NATO's membership by admitting former Eastern bloc countries were condemned by Moscow. Russia realized that its relations with the US were no longer based on equality and therefore it was necessary to redefine and re-evaluate them. Consequently, a gradual shift in Moscow's relations with Syria and other Middle Eastern countries took place in the mid-1990s. Yeltsin had now placed greater emphasis on geo-strategic and economic aspects in his relations with Middle Eastern countries. Russian–Syrian relations continued to improve since Primakov, a Middle East expert himself, had replaced Kozyrev as Foreign Minister in 1996. By 1998, Russia did not hide its desire to play a larger role in the Middle East peace process. Primakov's policy towards Israel and its neighbors had, however, remained pragmatic, avoiding the old Soviet line of "enemies and friends." According to Primakov, "Russia had many options ahead of it, including the utilization of its traditional ties as well as the cultivation of new ones, to further its national aims in the Middle East."[30]

Syria was satisfied with Moscow's Middle Eastern policy, yet it realized that the key to the solution of the problems in the Middle East lied in the hands of the United States. The US war against Iraq in 2003 and the demise of the Iraqi Ba'th regime led by Saddam Hussein, who refused to comply with the new rules of the international arena—a single-polar world dominated by the US—left no room for maneuver for Bashar al-Asad's new regime in the international arena. The choices were stark and foreboding: either respond favorably to American requests and serve US interests in the Middle East or bear the unpleasant consequences.

Appendix

Modes of Practised Arab Neutralism

Listed by mode of neutralism. Chief features and definitions are given. *Countries that have practised the particular form of neutralism are listed in italic.*

1. Ideological/doctrinaire neutralism

Refers to a state that emphasized its total opposition to the Cold War—its methods, stratagems, and general climate. It viewed the rivalry between the two power blocs as a constant threat to world peace, and therefore maintained that the Cold War must be neutralized and an "area of peace" must separate the two rival blocs. The concept of non-violence was at the roots of this opposition.

This pattern was formulated and practised by Nehru's India. It was also practised by Burma under U Nu, and Israel between 1948–50. The Ba'th Party adhered to it in the period 1945–54.

2. Calculative/pragmatic nationalist neutralism

Embraced by countries that were under the hegemony or influence of one of the traditional great powers—Britain or France—and were embroiled in a struggle for national independence against these powers. One of the methods they employed to achieve that goal was the utilization of the emerging inter-bloc conflict in order to advance their national aspirations. The idea was that intentional improvement in relations with the Soviet bloc, in all fields, would definitely put pressure on the Western powers to alter their policies toward the Arabs. Also, in order to prevent the falling of these countries into Soviet zones of influence, the US, they believed, would exert enormous pressure on its allies Britain and France to evacuate their troops from the struggling countries. It was based on national interests and utilitarian purposes.

This pattern of neutralism was in fact exercised by Egypt (1943–4, 1950–2) and Syria (1944–6).

3. Anti-Western neutralism

The growing radicalization of the Arab intelligentsia from the mid-1930s and anti-Western sentiments, which were deeply rooted in Arab soil as a result of an extended struggle for liberation, were translated into action following the outbreak of the Cold War. Arab political circles, governments, and the general public had demonstrated their strong will to humiliate and punish the West for all the injustices and evils it had caused the Arabs. They totally rejected any possible alliance with the Western camp. Rather, they strengthened relations with the Soviet Union and by doing so positioned themselves out of the Western camp, arguing that should a third world war occur they would remain neutral.

Such a pattern was practised by Syria in the period 1949–51, and by Egypt in 1950.

4. Anti-Soviet neutralism

The rejection of both communism as an ideology and the Soviet Union as an imperialist power. This mode of neutralism ruled out participation in the Cold War on either side, but it did advocate closer relations with the Western powers.

Adhered to by the SSNP in Syria.

5. Passive neutralism

A manifestation of general indifference to the Cold War. A state that followed such a pattern showed no interest whatsoever in either the ideological or the political antagonism of outside powers and power groups.

Practised in Syria (1946–9, 1952–4, 1961–3) and Egypt (1944–7).

6. Negative neutralism

Refers to states that exercised an independent line in international affairs based on their national interests and principles, and not on the basis of a commitment or alignment with either the Eastern or Western blocs. The doctrine rejected self-embroilment in the Cold War, refusing to participate in its power arrangements or to take part in its antagonisms.

Practised by Yugoslavia under Tito and Saudi Arabia in the first part of the 1950s. Also adhered to by the main Iraqi opposition party, al-Hizb al-Watani al-Dimuqrati *[the National Democratic Party] at the onset of the 1950s.*

7. Positive neutralism

This pattern had sprung out of the policy of calculative/pragmatic nationalist neutralism. An independent state that wished to maintain close and balanced ties with both international blocs for the purpose of manipulating the inter-bloc rivalries in order to advance its foreign policy. It wanted to internationally demonstrate its independence and wished to play a major role in international affairs. Positive neutralism was nothing less than the revolt of non-aligned countries against the exercise of monopoly, by either party to the Cold War, in the supply of goods, services or capital to under-developed lands. It is their protest against unfair practices, discrimination, and the attachment of politico-military conditions to trade, economic aid, or technical assistance.

Practised by the UAR (1958–61).

8. Pro-Soviet positive neutralism

A failure to maintain the above balance led a given state to rely more on Soviet support and as a replacement it supported the Soviet bloc in inter-national affairs, but with a certain degree of independence. A state adhering to such a policy continues to maintain economic and political relations, including bilateral agreements, with Western powers, in order to exploit the rivalry between the two international blocs. However, the reliance on Soviet support was much noticeable and Soviet influence in that country rose significantly.

Practised by Syria (1955–8, 1963–7) and Egypt (1954–8, 1961–7).

9. Pro-Western positive neutralism

As above, but here the emphasis is on closer relations with the Western powers.

Such policy was practised by Sadat's Egypt (1974–7) and Israel (1950–67).

10. Pro-Soviet neutralism

Refers to a state which was supported by the USSR by all means, and in exchange fully supported the Soviet bloc in international affairs, but not yet formally allied with the Soviet bloc by becoming a Soviet satellite state.

Examples: Syria (1967–91), Egypt (1967–72) and Iraq (1958–63).

11. Pro-Western neutralism

Refers to a state which was supported by one or more Western powers, by all means, and in exchange fully supported the Western bloc in interna-tional affairs, but not yet formally allied with that bloc by becoming a Western satellite state.

Practised by Egypt's Free Officers in the period 1952–3. Jordan's foreign policies, except for a short period (1955–7), and the inter-bloc policies of Iraq over the period prior to the Baghdad Pact of 1955, are good examples of pro-Western neutralism.

Notes

Preface

1 See, for instance, Mohamad El-Sayed Selim, *Non-Alignment in a Changing World* (Cairo: The American University of Cairo, 1983); K. P. Karunakaran (ed.), *Outside the Contest: A Study of Nonalignment and the Foreign Policies of some Nonaligned Countries* (New Delhi: People's Publishing House, 1963); Richard L. Jackson, *The Non-Aligned, the UN and the Superpowers* (New York: Praeger, 1983); Laurence W. Martin (ed.), *Neutralism and Non-alignment: The New States in World Affairs* (New York: Praeger, 1962); Michael Brecher, *The New States of Asia: A Political Analysis* (London: Oxford University Press, 1964). A. W. Singham and Shirley Hune, *Non-Alignment in an Age of Alignments* (London: Zed Books, 1986); Mustafa Husayn Fahmi, *Siyasat 'Adam al-Inhiyaz* (Cairo: Dar al-Qawmiyya, 1962) [Arabic]; Sami Mansur, *Intiqasat al-Thawra fi al-'Alam al-Thalith* (Beirut: al-Mu'assasa al-'Arabiyya lil-Dirasat wa-al-Nashr, 1972) [Arabic]; Lutfi al-Khuli, *'Am al-Inkisar fi al-'Alam al-Thalith* (Cairo: al-Qahira lil-thaqafa al-'Arabiyya, 1975) [Arabic]; Kiyyali Ghalib, *Nazariyyat al-Thawra fi al-'Alam al-Thalith* (Beirut: Mu'asasat al-Ibhath al-'Alamiyya al-'Arabiyya al-'Ulya, 1973) [Arabic]; Clovis Maqsud, *Ma' na al-Hiyad al-Ijabi* (Beirut: Dar al- 'Ilm lil-Malayin, 1960) [Arabic].

2 David Kimche, *The Afro-Asian Movement* (Jerusalem: Israel University Press, 1973).

3 *Ibid.*, p. 83.

4 Bahgat Korany, *Social Change, Charisma and International Behaviour: Towards a Theory of Foreign Policy-Making in the Third World* (Leiden: Institut Universitaire de Hautes Etudes Internationales, 1976), 3–7.

5 Patrick Seale, *The Struggle for Syria* (London: Oxford University Press, 1965).

6 Fayez al-Sayegh, *The Dynamic of Neutralism in the Arab World* (San Francisco: Chandler Publishing House, 1964).

7 Gordon Wright, "Contemporary History in the Contemporary Age," in Charles F. Delzell, *The Future of History* (Nashville, TN: Vanderbilt University Press, 1977), p. 223.

8 This topic will be dealt with comprehensively in the Introduction.

Introduction: Neutralism in Retrospect: Definitions and Paradigms

1 Roderick Ogley, *The Theory and Practice of Neutrality in the Twentieth Century* (London: Routledge & Kegan Paul, 1970), pp. 2–5.

2 Julios Gould and William L. Kolb (eds.), *A Dictionary of the Social Sciences* (London: Tavistock, 1964), p. 467.

3 Edwin R. A. Seligman (ed.), *Encyclopedia of the Social Sciences*, Vol. 11 (New York: Macmillan, 1949), p. 360.

4 Gould and Kolb (eds.), *A Dictionary of the Social Sciences*, p. 468.

5 David Robertson, *A Dictionary of Modern Politics* (London: Europa Publications, 1985), p. 234. Robertson explains that, should a state desire to remain neutral in wartime, international law prevents it from taking the side of any of the belligerent parties, including giving permission for the use of its territory for war purposes. If it conforms to this policy, international law prohibits either party from attacking the neutral state. See also Michael Brecher, *The New States of Asia* (London: London University Press, 1964), p. 111. "Neutralism and Nonalignment," in David L. Sills (ed.), *International Encyclopedia of the Social Sciences*, Vol. 11 (New York: Macmillan Company, and the Free Press, 1968), p. 168.

6 Gould and Kolb (eds.), *A Dictionary of the Social Sciences*, p. 467.

7 *Ibid.*, p. 233. See also David Robertson, *The Penguin Dictionary of Politics* (London: Penguin Books, 1993), p. 344.

8 Robertson, *The Penguin Dictionary of Politics*, pp. 344–5.

9 Sills, *International Encyclopedia of the Social Sciences*, pp. 166–7.

10 Brecher, *The New States of Asia*, pp. 112–13.

11 Cyril E. Black, Richard A. Falk, Klaus Knorr and Oran R. Young, *Neutralization and World Politics* (Princeton, NJ: Princeton University Press, 1968), p. xi.

12 *Ibid.* On neutralization within the context of the post-World War II, see Clovis Maqsud, *Ma'na al-Hiyad al-Ijabi* (Beirut: Dar al-'Ilm lil-Malayin, 1960), pp. 31–5.

13 Black et al., *Neutralization and World Politics*, pp. xiv–xv. See also Ogley, *The Theory and Practice of Neutrality*, pp. 1–18.

14 Brecher, *The New States of Asia*, p. 113.

15 Ahmad 'Atiyyallah, *al-Qamus al-Siyasi* [The Dictionary of Politics] (Beirut: Dar al-Nahda al-'Arabiyya, 1980) [Arabic]. Unlike 'Atiyyallah, Mustafa Husain Fahmi uses Switzerland as an example for *al-hiyad taqlidi.* See his *Siyasat 'Adam al-Inhiyaz* (Cairo: Dar al-Qawmiyya, 1962), pp. 10–11 [Arabic].

16 'Atiyyallah, *al-Qamus al-Siyasi.* On the shift from neutralism to non-alignment in the course of the Belgrade Conference, see also Sills (ed.), *International Encyclopedia of the Social Sciences*, p. 166.

17 Fayez A. Sayegh, "Anatomy of Neutralism—A Typological Analysis," in *idem* (ed.), *The Dynamics of Neutralism in the Arab World* (San Francisco, CA: Chandler Publishing House, 1964), pp. 10–11.

18 *Ibid.*, pp. 28–9.

19 *Ibid.*, pp. 38–9.

20 *Ibid.*, p. 39.

21 *Ibid.*, pp. 64–5.

22 *Ibid.*, p. 70.
23 *Ibid.*, pp. 70–1.
24 David Kimche, *The Afro-Asian Movement* (Jerusalem: Israel University Press, 1973), pp. 22–3.
25 *Ibid.*, pp. 25–6.
26 *Ibid.*, p. 25.
27 Pandit Jawaharlal Nehru, *Toward Freedom: The Autobiography of Jawaharlal Nehru* (New York: John Day, 1941), pp. 228–31.
28 Rikhi Jaipal, *Non-Alignment* (Ahmedabad, Bombay: Allied Publishers Private Ltd., 1983), p. 8.
29 *Ibid.*, p. 9.
30 Julius K. Nyerere, "Non-Alignment and its Future Prospects," in Uma Vasudev (ed.), *Issues before Non-Alignment Past & Future* (New Delhi: Indian Council of World Affairs, 1983), p. 36.
31 Kimche, *The Afro-Asian Movement*, p. 24. See also Fahmi, *Siyasat 'Adam al-Inhiyaz*, p. 8.
32 N. Parameshwaran Nair, "Non-Alignment, History, Ideology, Prospects," in K. P. Karunakaran (ed.), *Outside the Contest* (New Delhi: People's Publishing House, 1963), p. 32. See also Malabika Banerjee, *The Nonaligned Movement* (Calcutta: Firma KLM Private Limited, 1982), pp. 43–4.
33 Banerjee, *The Nonaligned Movement*, p. 44.
34 Nyerere, "Non-alignment and its Future Prospects", p. 37.
35 Sills (ed.), *International Encyclopedia of the Social Sciences*, p. 167.
36 Banerjee, *The Nonaligned Movement*, p. 24.
37 *Ibid.*, p. 26.
38 Quotation from *The Programme of the League of Communists of Yugoslavia (1958)* (Merhavya: Mapam, 1959), pp. 56–7 [Hebrew]. See also Bnerjee, *The Nonaligned Movement,* p. 28.
39 See more on Israel's policy toward the inter-bloc conflict in Uri Bialer, *Between East and West, Israel's Foreign Policy Orientation 1948–1956* (Cambridge, UK: Cambridge University Press, 1990). See also Nadav Safran, *The United States and Israel* (Cambridge, MA: Harvard University Press, 1963), pp. 218–21.
40 Bialer, *Between East and West*, pp. 206–7.
41 Rami Ginat, "British Concoction or Bilateral Decision?: Revisiting the Genesis of Soviet–Egyptian Diplomatic Relations," *International Journal of Middle East Studies*, Vol. 31 (1999), p. 47.
42 The information on this period is based on my articles, "The Egyptian Left and the Roots of Neutralism in pre-Nasserite Era," *British Journal of Middle Eastern Studies*, Vol. 30, No. 1 (2003), pp. 5–24; and, "Nasser and the Soviets: A Reassessment," in Elie Podeh and Onn Winckler (eds.), *Rethinking Nasserism: Revolution and Historical Memory in Modern Egypt* (Gainesville: University Press of Florida, 2004), pp. 230–50.
43 The US resolution that recommended collective action to defend South Korea.
44 Rami Ginat, *The Soviet Union and Egypt, 1945–55* (London: Frank Cass, 1993), p. 113.
45 Rami Ginat, "The Egyptian Left and the Roots of Neutralism in pre-Nasserite Era," pp. 21–2.

46   *Ibid.*, p. 22.
47   *Ibid.* See also Ahmad Hamrush, *Qissat Thawrat 23 Yuliyu*, Vol. 1 (Cairo: Maktabat Madbuli, 1983), pp. 152–4 [Arabic].
48   "The Egyptian Left and the Roots of Neutralism in pre-Nasserite Era," pp. 22–3.
49   Ginat, *The Soviet Union and Egypt*, pp. 158–60.
50   Ginat, "Nasser and the Soviets: A Reassessment."
51   See: Ginat, *The Soviet Union and Egypt*, pp. 207–19. See also: Central Intelligence Report, "The Soviet Arms Offer to Egypt," in *CIA Research Reports: The Middle East, 1946–1976*, Reel 2, M5617, SOAS Library.
52   Ginat, *The Soviet Union and Egypt*, pp. 207–19.
53   "Soviet Bloc Economic Activities in the Near East and Asia as of November 25, 1955," Report, Office of Research, Statistics, and Reports, Clarence Francis Papers, Eisenhower Library. See also: CIA Intelligence Memorandum, "The Communist Economic Campaign in the Near East and South Asia," November 30, 1955, in *US Declassified Documents Reference System*, US, 1986, 002516, quoted from Ginat, "Nasser and the Soviets: A Reassessment."
54   Ginat, "Nasser and the Soviets: A Reassessment."
55   Quotation from Sills (ed.), *International Encyclopedia of the Social Sciences*, p. 167.
56   *Ibid.*, p. 169.
57   Kamil al-Jadirji, *Mudhakarat Kamil al-Jadirji wa-Ta'arikh al-Hizb al-Watani al-Dimuqrati* (Köln: Al-Kamel Verlag, 2002), p. 475 [Arabic].
58   *Ibid.*, pp. 476–7.
59   See a broader discussion on this subject in Chapter 5.

1   Syria's Road to Independence: The Emergence of "Pragmatic/Calculative Nationalist Neutralism"

This chapter is an outgrowth of my article "Syria's and Lebanon's Meandering Road to Independence: the Soviet Involvement and the Anglo-French Rivalry," *Diplomacy & Statecraft*, Vol. 13, No. 4 (December 2002).

1   Albert Hourani, *A History of the Arab Peoples* (Cambridge, MA: Harvard University Press, 1991), p. 320.
2   *Ibid.* Elie Kedourie, "The Transition from a British to an American Era in the Middle East, in Haim Shaked and Itamar Rabinovich (eds.), *The Middle East and the United States* (New Brunswick and London: Transaction Books, 1980), pp. 3–4.
3   Hourani, *A History of the Arab Peoples*, pp. 320–1. Meir Zamir, *The Formation of Modern Lebanon* (Ithaca and London: Cornell University Press, 1985), pp. 38–9.
4   William R. Polk, *The United States and the Arab World* (Cambridge, MA: Harvard University Press, 1965), pp. 261–3; Nadav Safran, *The United States and Israel*, pp. 36–8.
5   Kedourie, "The Transition from a British to an American Era in the Middle East," p. 6.
6   On the Constantinople agreement of 18 March 1915 between Russia and Great

Britain and France, see in details, George Lenczowski, *The Middle East in World Affairs* (Ithaca and London: Cornell University Press, 1980), 4th edition, pp. 75–6.

7   See a report on "Communism and Islam," prepared by the Research Department of the Israeli Foreign Ministry, 30 September 1951, Records of Israel Foreign Ministry (FM)2530/8/A, Ginzakh Hamedina, Jerusalem. See also "Soviet policy towards the Arab East," *Bulletin*, Institute for the Study of the USSR, Vol. 15, No. 3, March 1968, pp. 29–30. It is noteworthy that the first appeal of the Soviet leaders to "Muslim workers in Russia and the East" was already made on 3 December 1917. See full text of it in J. C. Hurewitz, *Diplomacy in the Near and Middle East A Documentary Record: 1914–1956*, Vol. II (London & New York: D. Van Nostrand Co., 1956), pp. 27–8.

8   See Ginat, "British Concoction or Bilateral Decision? Revisiting the Genesis of Soviet–Egyptian Diplomatic Relations," p. 40. See also *idem*, *The Soviet Union and Egypt 1945–1955*, pp. 3–7.

9   A well-detailed description of the capture of Damascus is given by Elie Kedourie in *England and the Middle East* (London and Boulder, CO: Mansell Publishing and Westview Press, 1987), pp. 119–22. See also *idem*, *The Chatham House Version and other Middle Eastern Studies* (Hanover and London: University Press of New England, 1984), pp. 33–51. David Fromkin, *A Peace to End all Peace, Creating the Modern Middle East 1914–1922* (Tel Aviv: Dvir, 1994), pp. 277–88 [Hebrew]. On the Arab revolt—the background, the campaign and the aftermath— see Richard Allen, *Imperialism and Nationalism in the Fertile Crescent* (London, New York: Oxford University Press, 1974), pp. 228–47. Peter Mansfield, *The Arabs* (London: Penguin Books, 1978), pp. 187–208.

10 Kedourie, *England and the Middle East*, pp. 128–9. On Faysal's Arab government see more in Philip S. Khoury, *Urban Notables and Arab Nationalism, The Politics of Damascus 1860–1920* (London, New York: Cambridge University Press, 1983), pp. 78–92.

11 Kamal S. Salibi, *The Modern History of Lebanon* (Delmar, New York: Caravan Books, 1990), p. 164.

12 Salibi, *ibid.*, p. 164. Kedourie, *England and the Middle East*, pp. 173–4. See also Lenczowski, *The Middle East in World Affairs*, pp. 88–95. Fromkin, *A Peace to end all Peace*, pp. 361–5.

13 On the creation of Greater Lebanon, see Zamir, *The Formation of Modern Lebanon*, pp. 38–98.

14 On 1 January 1925 the French unified the states of Aleppo and Damascus to what was now called the state of Syria, and in late 1936 incorporated Jebel Druze and Lattakia into the Syrian Republic. On 23 June 1939 France ceded to Turkey the sanjak of Alexandretta. On the territorial divisions see Lenczowski, *The Middle East in World Affairs*, pp. 315–19.

15 Lenczowski, *ibid.*, p. 315. On Khoury's analysis of the French rule in Syria, see Philip S. Khoury, "Syrian Political Culture: A Historical Perspective," in R. J. Antoun and Donald Quataert (eds.), *Syria: Society, Culture and Polity* (New York: State University of New York Press, 1991), pp. 20–2.

16 Kedourie, *The Chatham House Version*, p. 4. On the Anglo-French contrast in

making their Middle Eastern policies throughout World War I and immediately after, and the growing Anglo-French antagonism in the inter-wars period, see Christopher N. Andrew, "France, Britain, and the Settlement: A Reconsideration," in Uriel Dann (ed.), *The Great Powers in the Middle East 1919–1939* (London, New York: Holmes & Meier, 1988), pp. 157–71.

17 Lenczowski, *The Middle East in World Affairs*, pp. 321–2. Salibi, *The Modern History of Lebanon*, pp. 184–5.

18 Salibi, *The Modern History of Lebanon*, p. 185. Lenczowski, *The Middle East in World Affairs*, p. 322.

19 Salibi, *The Modern History of Lebanon*, p. 185. According to Lenczowski, Catroux' proclamation on Syria's independence was on 28 September. See Lenczowski, *The Middle East in World Affairs*, p. 323.

20 Quoted from Lenczowski, *ibid.*

21 *Ibid.*, pp. 323–4. On the growing tension between Britain and France and its repercussion upon these powers relations with local political groups, see Salibi, *The Modern History of Lebanon*, pp. 185–8.

22 It was only on 1 August 1945 that they were handed over to Lebanon.

23 Salibi, *The Modern History of Lebanon*, pp. 188–91. Lenczowski, *The Middle East in World Affairs*, pp. 324–5.

24 This resolution will be discussed later.

25 On the Soviet growing interests and activities in the Middle East in the first part of the 1940s, see Ginat, "British Concoction or Bilateral Decision? Revisiting the Genesis of Soviet–Egyptian Diplomatic Relations," pp. 39–60.

26 Ginat, *ibid.*

27 *Ibid.*

28 Telegram 34 from E. Spears, Beirut, 6 June 1944, Political Correspondence of the Foreign Office 371/40337, E3482/3482/89 (hereafter cited as FO371), Public Record Office (PRO), London.

29 Telegram 40 from Spears, Beirut, 25 June 1944, FO371/40337, E3907/3482/89.

30 Telegram 34, FO371/40337, *ibid.* On the Soviet–Iraqi dialogue, see telegram 386 from British Embassy Baghdad, 9 May 1944, FO371/40092, E2891.

31 Telegram 40, FO371/40337, *ibid.*

32 Telegram 398 from Spears, Beirut, 4 July 1944, FO371/40337, E3923/3482/89.

33 Telegram 398.

34 Telegram 359 from Foreign Office to Beirut, 11 July 1944, FO371/40337, E3929/449/G.

35 N. V. Novikov, *Vospominaniya Diplomata Zapiski 1938–47* (Moskva: IPL, 1989), p. 211.

36 Dispatch 26 from British Consulate, Damascus, 15 July 1944, FO371/40337, E4539/3482/89.

37 Ibid.

38 Novikov, *Vospaminaniya Diplomata Zapiski*, pp. 211–13.

39 *Ibid.*

40 Dispatch 26.

41 Dispatch 26.

42 Dispatch 26.

43 Telegram 439 from Spears, Beirut, 19 July 1944, FO371/40337, E4311/3482/89.

44 Novikov, p. 218.
45 Telegram 1944 from Sir A. Clark Kerr, British ambassador, Moscow, 26 July 1944, FO371/40337, E4467/3482/89. See full copies of the original telegrams in French in enclosure to telegram 72 from British Legation, Damascus, 2 August 1944, FO371/40337, E4870/3482/89. See also dispatch 31 from British Consulate, Damascus, 3 August 1944, FO371/40337, E5088/3482/89.
46 Telegram 472 from Mackereth, Beirut, 31 July 1944, FO371/40337, E4601/3482/89.
47 Telegram 472.
48 Telegram 426 from Foreign Office to Mackereth, Beirut, 7 August 1944, FO371/40337, E4001/3482/89.
49 Telegram 472.
50 Letter 30/63/44 from Mackereth, British Legation Beirut, 11 August 1944, FO371/40337, E5065/3482/89.
51 Letter 30/63/44.
52 Letter 30/63/44.
53 Dispatch 31 from British Consulate, Damascus, *ibid.*
54 Dispatch 31.
55 See copy of the original text, sent from British Embassy, Moscow, 5 August 1944, to Eastern Department, FO, in FO371/40337, E4807/3482/89.
56 See copy of the original telegram of Molotov in *ibid.* See also telegram 2045 from Sir A. Clark Kerr, British Embassy Moscow, FO371/40337, E4710/3482/89. Telegram 494 from Mackereth, Beirut, 7 August 1944, FO371/40337, E4763/3482/89.
57 Telegram 498 from Mackereth, Beirut, 9 August 1944, FO371/40337, E4795/3482/89.
58 This information was based on Lebanese reliable sources. See telegram 498.
59 Telegram 93 from Spears, Beirut, 19 September 1944, FO371/40337, E5981/3482/89.
60 Telegram 630 from Spears, Beirut, 3 October 1944, FO371/40337, E6045/3482/89.
61 Telegram 49 from Spears, Damascus, 27 October 1944, FO371/40337, E6623/3482/89.
62 See an enclosed memorandum to dispatch 37 from Terence Shone, British Legation, Beirut, 16 March 1945, FO371/45613, E1825/808/89.
63 *Ibid.*
64 *Ibid.*
65 *Ibid.*
66 *Ibid.*
67 On the connection between the Soviet Legation and the communist press, see dispatch 71 from British Legation, Beirut, 6 May 1945, FO371/45365, E3173.
68 *Jhoghovourti Tzain* (Beirut), 6 March 1945, enclosed to dispatch 71, *ibid.*
69 *Jhoghovourti Tzain* (Beirut), 10 March 1945, enclosed to dispatch 71, *ibid.*
70 See "Joint Manifesto of Syrian and Lebanese Communist Parties," enclosure to dispatch 807 from US Legation, Damascus, 22 October 1947, FO371/62129.
71 *Saut al-Sha'b* (Beirut), 11 and 12 February 1945.

72 *Saut al-Sha'b* (Beirut), 18 and 19 February 1945.

73 See Putski's speech in "Report on a Lecture on Syria and Lebanon," from British Embassy, Moscow, 20 June 1945, FO371/45613, E4586.

74 *Foreign Relations of the United States, Diplomatic Papers, 1944* (Washington: U.S. Government Printing Office, 1967), Vol. 5, p. 786. Quoted by Yaacov Ro'i, *From Encroachment to Involvement* (Jerusalem: IUP, 1974), p. 28.

75 Salibi, *The Modern History of Lebanon*, p. 190.

76 Ro'i, *From Encroachment to Involvement*, p. 28.

77 Ro'i, *ibid.* Salibi, *ibid.*, pp. 190–1. Lenzchowski, *The Middle East in World Affairs*, pp. 325–6.

78 Kedourie, *The Chatham House Version*, p. 7.

79 *Foreign Relations of the United States, Diplomatic Papers, The Berlin Conference*, Vol. 1 (Washington: US Government Printing Office, 1955), p. 960, and Vol. 2, p. 246. Quoted from Ro'i, *From Encroachment to Involvement*, p. 28.

80 Report No. 2500, "Spravki, informatsii otdela I drogoe o politicheskom polozhenii v Sirii, Palestine, Egipte, Livane, ob otnoshenii siriiskikh I livanskikh kommunistov k sionistkim organizatsiiam," prepared by the Department of International Information of the Central Committee of the Communist Party, 31 June 1945, Fond 5, Opis' 10, Ed.Kh.R. 821, Roll 7831, Rossiiskii goasudarstvennyi arkhiv Noveishei Istorii, Moscow (hereafter cited as RGANI-Ts.Kh.S.D.).

81 *Foreign Relations of the United States, ibid.*, Vol. 2, pp. 261, 318–19. Quotations from Ro'i, *From Encroachment to Involvement*, p. 28.

82 *Foreign Relations of the United States, ibid.*, p. 261. Quoted from Ro'i, *ibid.*

83 See the content of the Anglo-French agreement of 13 December 1945, in Hurewitz, *Diplomacy in the Near and Middle East, A Documentary Record: 1914–1956*, pp. 257–8. On the Ba'th Party criticism of the agreement, see Hizb al Ba'th al-'Arabi al-Ishtiraki, *Nidal al-Ba'th*, Vol. I (Beirut: Dar al-Tali'a, 1962), pp. 129–31.

84 Ginat, *The Soviet Union and Egypt*, pp. 69–70. Frank Roberts, the British Ambassador to Moscow, received some inaccurate details of the content of the secret treaties from the US ambassador there. He seemed to be skeptical about the likelihood that such treaties were signed. On the British version see letter 438/1/46 from British Embassy, Moscow, 9 April 1946, FO371/52860.

85 See the content of the Syro-Lebanese complaint of 4 February to the Security Council of the UN, in Hurewitz, *Diplomacy in the Near and Middle East*, pp. 258–9.

86 *United Nations Security Council, Official Records*, 1st Year, 1st series, No. 1, 21st Meeting, pp. 301–9.

87 Lenczowski, *The Middle East in World Affair*, p. 326.

88 See report by the US Central Intelligence Agency entitled: "Possible Developments from the Palestine Truce," 27 July 1948, in *US Declassified Documents Reference System* (US, 1975), 4F.

89 Pinhas Vazeh, *Hamesimah-Rekhesh* (The Mission—Arms Acquisition) (Tel Aviv: Ma'arkhot, 1966), pp. 153–7.

90 Ginat, *The Soviet Union and Egypt*, pp. 70–1.

91 "Syria: Annual Review for 1949," in dispatch 8 from P. M. Broadmead, British Legation, Damascus, 9 January 1950, FO371/82782, EY1011/1.
92 "Syria: Annual Review for 1949," *ibid.*
93 On Khalid al-'Azm's policy toward the three Western power, see Lenczowski, *The Middle East in World Affairs*, pp. 330–1. See also Patrick Seale, *The Struggle for Syria*, pp. 101–2.

2 The Rise of "Anti-Western Neutralism" in Post-Mandatory Syria

1 Roderick Ogley, *The Theory and Practice of Neutrality in the Twentieth Century* (London: Routledge & Kegan Paul, 1970), pp. 2–5.
2 On al-'Azm's political biography see in detail, FO371/82783, p. 6. See also Tel. 27 from Eyres to Attlee, E170/170/89, FO501/12/46.
3 On the formation of al-'Azm's cabinet in December 1949, see telegram 158 from Broadmead to McNeil, 31 December 1949, FO501/4, EY1015/4.
4 "The constitution of the Arab Resurrection," *Middle East Journal*, Vol. 13, No. 2, Spring 1959, p. 198.
5 On 'Aflaq's biography see FO371/82783. Memorandum on the Ba'th Party enclosed to letter 2/2/49 from British Legation, Damascus, 18 August 1949, FO1018/63, 405/3/49. See also Nabil M. Kaylani, "The Rise of the Syrian Ba'th, 1940–1958," *IJMES* (1972), Vol. 3, pp. 3–23. Norma Salem-Babikian, "Michel 'Aflaq, a Biographic Outline . . . ," *Arab Studies Quarterly* (Spring 1980), Vol. 2, No. 2, pp. 162–79. Gordon H. Torrey, "The Ba'th—Ideology and Practice," *Middle East Journal* (Autumn 1969), Vol. 23, pp. 445–57.
6 The two founded the Ba'th Party in 1940.
7 Salah al-Din al-Bitar and Michel 'Aflaq, *al-Ba'th wa-al-hizb al-Shuyu'i* (Damascus: 1944), quoted from Seale, *The Struggle for Syria,* p. 153.
8 Michel 'Aflaq, *Fi Sabil al-Ba'th* (Beirut: Dar al-Tali'a, 1963), p. 197.
9 *Ibid.*, p. 202.
10 Bitar and 'Aflaq, *al-Ba'th wa-al-hizb al-Shuyu'i*, in Seale, p. 153.
11 See more on Soviet–Syrian relations in the period 1944–46 in the previous chapter.
12 Michel 'Aflaq, "Arab nationalism and its attitude towards communism (1944)," quoted from Michel 'Aflaq, *Choice of Texts from the Ba'th Party Founder's Thought* (Firenze: Cooperation Lavoratori, 1977), p. 159.
13 Hizb al-Ba'th al-'Arabi, "Ra'y al-Hizb fi al-itifaq al-Britani—al-Faransi," in Hizb al-Ba'th al-'Arabi al-Ishtiraki, *Nidal al-Ba'th*, Vol. I (Beirut: Dar al-Tali'a, 1963), pp. 129–31.
14 Michel 'Aflaq, "The Reason for the Weakness of our Foreign Policy," 10 July 1946, in *Choice of Texts from the Ba'th Party*, p. 159.
15 *Al-Ba'th* (Damascus), 21 January 1948. Quoted from George J. Tomeh, "Syria and Neutralism," in Fayez A. Sayegh (ed.), *The Dynamics of Neutralism in the Arab World*, p. 124. On the Ba'thist anti-Zionist stand at the time, see also Moshe Ma'oz, *Syria and Israel From War to Peacemaking* (Oxford: Clarendon Press, 1995), pp. 79–80.
16 Michel 'Aflaq, "Siyasatuna al-Kharijiyya," in *idem, Fi Sabil al-Ba'th*, pp. 322–4.

17 Memorandum on the Ba'th Party, enclosed to letter 2/2/49 from British Legation, Damascus, 18 August 1949, FO1018/63, 405/3/49.
18 Itamar Rabinovich, *Syria under the Ba'th* (Jerusalem: IUP, 1972), p. 11.
19 Hizb al-Ba'th al-'Arabi al-Ishtiraki, *Nidal al-Ba'th* Vol. II (Beirut: Dar al-Tali'a, 1963), pp. 89–93, 185–9.
20 On the rise of Egyptian neutralism in the period 1950–52, see Ginat, *The Soviet Union and Egypt,* pp. 107–43.
21 Seale, *The Struggle for Syria,* pp. 101–2.
22 On Mustafa al-Siba'i's biography see in detail FO371/82783, pp. 22–3.
23 Siba'i made that statement on 12 March during a rally of his organization in Damascus. He is quoted from Seale, *The Struggle for Syria*, p. 102.
24 *Al-Qabas* (Damascus), 23 May 1950. See also dispatch 315 from James Hugh Keeley, US Minister to Syria, 5 June 1950, RG 59 783.00/6–550, Reel 1, M5680, SOAS Library.
25 See copy of the constitution in dispatch 53 from James Hugh Keeley, US Minister to Syria, 7 February 1950, RG 59, 783.00/2–750, Reel 1, M5680, SOAS Library.
26 See record of conversation between the two, in dispatch 167 from Owen T. Jones, US Chargé d'Affaires, Damascus, 27 September 1950, RG 59 783.00/9-2750, Reel 1, M5680, SOAS library.
27 *Ibid.*
28 Economically, the party advocated the nationalization of the main public utilities, state control of banks, distribution of state lands to landless peasants and small farmers, and the inauguration of a social security system and free medical treatment for the workers. See more on the party, its leaders, and constitution, in dispatch 220 and its enclosure from James Hugh Keeley, US Minister to Syria, 18 April 1950, RG 59, 783.00/4-1850, Reel 1, M5680, SOAS Library.
29 *Ibid.*
30 *Al-Balad* (Damascus), 1 February 1950; *al-Nasr* (Damascus), 3 February 1950. Dispatch 106 from US Legation, Damascus, 28 February 1950, RG 59, 783.5611/2-2850, Reel 5, M5680, SOAS Library.
31 On al-Dawalibi's political biography, see FO371/82783, p. 9.
32 SWB, Arab World, 12 April 1949, p. 49.
33 *Al-Misri* (Cairo), 9 April 1950.
34 SWB, Arab World, 22 April 1950, p. 57.
35 "Press summary for period April 1 to April 15," in dispatch 300 from US Legation, Damascus, 23 May 1950, RG 59, 983.61/5-2350, Reel 11, M5680, SOAS library.
36 The quotation from *al-Manar* is taken from dispatch 300, *ibid.*
37 The quotation from *al-Barada* is taken from dispatch 300, *ibid.*
38 Policy Statement, "Syria," Department of State, 26 June 1950, Reel 12, M5680, SOAS Library; "Quarterly Economic Report," pp. 9–10, enclosed to dispatch 147 from US Legation, Damascus, 12 September 1950, RG 59, 983.08/9-1250, *ibid.* See also Rami Ginat, *The Soviet Union and Egypt*, pp. 109–11.
39 See a record of conversation between Colonel 'Abbara and the Army Attaché, US Embassy, London, 20 April 1950, in dispatch 2180, 3 May 1950, RG 59, 783.5841/5-350, Reel 5, M5680, SOAS Library.

40 Policy Statement, "Syria" (see note 38 above). See also dispatch 552 from Jefferson Caffery, US Ambassador, Cairo, 24 May 1950, RG 59, 783.00/5-2450.
41 *Ibid.*
42 Khalid al-'Azm, *Mudhakkirat Khalid al-'Azm* (Beirut: al-Dar al-Mutaharir lil-nashr, 1973), Vol. II, pp. 234–40.
43 Al-'Azm, *Mudhakkirat*, Vol. II, pp. 235–7.
44 Dispatch 221 from James Hugh Keeley, US Minister to Damascus, 18 April 1950, RG 59, 683.84A/4-1850, Reel 11, M5680, SOAS Library.
45 *Ibid.*
46 *Ibid.*
47 *Ibid.*
48 Memorandum to the President by R. H. Hillenkoetter, Director of Central Intelligence, 27 April 1950, President's Secretary's Files, File Subject: CIA Memorandums 1950–1952, box 250, Truman Library, Independence, Missouri. See also telegram 821 from American Embassy, Cairo, 20 April 1950, Foreign Office Posts of the Department of State, Record Group (RG) 84, Cairo Embassy—General Documents, 1950–1952: 320, box 219, Washington National Records Center, Suitland, Maryland.
49 Telegram 206 from FO to British Embassy, Damascus, 13 May 1950, FO371/82794, EY10338/2. Telegram 128 from British Embassy, Damascus, 17 May 1950, FO371/82814, EY11338/2.
50 "Syria and Communism," a paper prepared by G. W. Finlaye, British Foreign Office, London, 14 June 1950, FO371/82792, Y1025/2.
51 "Syria and communism," *ibid.*
52 See record of conversation between Acheson and Bevin, 11 May 1950, *FRUS 1950*, Vol. V, pp. 158–60.
53 "Tripartite Declaration regarding Security in the Near East," *Department of State Bulletin*, XXII, 5 June 1950, p. 886.
53 Al-'Azm, *Mudhakkirat*, p. 242.
55 *Al-Nasr* (Damascus), 21 April 1950.
56 On Truman's speech of 19 April before the American Society of Newspaper Editors, see dispatch 281 from US Legation, Damascus, 15 May 1950, RG 59, 983.61/5-1550, Reel 11, M5680, SOAS Library.
57 *Al-Masa'* (Damascus), 24 April 1950. Dispatch 281, *ibid.*
58 "Press summary for the period 28 May to June 2," dispatch 355 from US Legation, Damascus, 21 June 1950, RG 59, 983.61/6-2150, Reel 11, M5680, SOAS Library.
59 *Al-Manar* is quoted in dispatch 355, *ibid.*
60 *Al-Nasr* is quoted in *ibid.*
61 *Al-Shabab*, is quoted in *ibid.*
62 *Al-Kifah*, is quoted in *ibid.*
63 *Al-Kifah* is quoted in dispatch 357 from US Legation, Damascus, 21 June 1950, RG 59, 983.61/6-2150, Reel 11, M5680, SOAS Library.
64 On Egypt's stand on Korea and the rise of neutralism, see Ginat, *The Soviet Union and Egypt*, pp. 112–18.
65 See Dispatch 227 from Cavandish W. Cannon, US Legation, Damascus, 8

November 1950, RG 59 783.00/11-850, Reel 1, M5680, SOAS Library. On the Syrian press reaction to the Crisis in Korea, see also, telegram 14 from W. H. Montagu-Pollock, British Minister to Damascus, 13 July 1950, FO371/82793, EY1026/1.

66 "Damascus Press Summary: July 1–7, 1950," in dispatch 26 from US Legation, Damascus, 20 July 1950, RG 59, 983.61/7-2050, Reel 11, M5680, SOAS Library.

67 The quotation from *al-Nasr* is taken from dispatch 26, *ibid.*

68 The quotation from *al-Nasr* is taken from "Press Summary for period July 8 to July 17," in dispatch 62 from US Legation, Damascus, 6 August 1950, RG 59, 983.61/8-650, Reel 11, M5680, SOAS Library.

69 *Al-Nasr* (Damascus), 5 December 1950.

70 *Ibid.*

71 *Al-'Alam* (Damascus), 8 August 1950. Dispatch 73 from US Legation, Damascus, 14 August 1950, RG 59, 983.61/8-1450, Reel 11, M5680, SOAS Library.

72 *Al-Qabas* (Damascus), 8 April 1951.

73 Telegram 177 from Montagu-Pollock, British Minister to Damascus, 8 July 1950, FO501/4, E10211/15.

74 See record of conversation between Nazim al-Qudsi, Prime Minister of Syria, and Paul C. Parker, US Treasury Representative in the Middle East, which took place in Cairo on 6 December 1950, enclosed to dispatch 1352 from Jefferson Caffery, US Ambassador, Cairo, 8 December 1950, RG 59, 883.00/12-850, Reel 5, M5680, SOAS Library.

75 *Ibid.*

76 Dispatch 270 from Harrison M. Symmes, Third Secretary of US Legation, Damascus, 18 December 1950, RG 59, 783.00/12-1850, Reel 1, M5680, SOAS Library.

77 Dispatch 227, *ibid.* See also *al-Kifah* (Damascus), 3 November 1950.

78 Dispatch 227, *ibid.*

79 See report entitled "Review of Syrian Political Parties and Some of their Recent Policies," prepared by US Legation, Damascus, in dispatch 406, 19 March 1951, RG 59, 783.00/3-1951, Reel 1, M5680.

80 *Al-Misri* (Cairo), 22 June 1950.

81 Telegram 19 from Montagu-Pollock, British Minister to Damascus, FO371/91846, EY1022/3.

82 *Ibid.*

83 "Review of Syrian Political Parties and some of their Recent Policies," *ibid.*

84 Hizb al-Ba'th al-'Arabi, "al-Sha'b al-'Arabi Yuridu Hiyadan Haqiqiyyan min al-Sira' baina al-Mu'askarin wa-yahdhiru al-Jami'a al-'Arabiyya min al-Indimam ila al-Kutla al-Gharbiyya al-'Isti'amariyya," 25 January 1951; enclosed to dispatch 350, US Legation, Damascus, 12 February 1951, RG 59 783.001/2-1251, Reel 3 M5680, SOAS Library.

85 Telegram 15 from Montagu-Pollock, British Minister to Damascus, 27 January 1951, FO371/91848, EY1025/3.

86 Seale, *The Struggle for Syria*, p. 103.

87 See more on the Four-Power proposals and the Arab and Soviet response in Ginat, *The Soviet Union and Egypt*, pp. 122–9.

88 See dispatch 578 from William L. Eagleton, Third Secretary of US Legation, Damascus, 2 April 1952, RG 59, 783.00/4-252, Reel 1, M5680, SOAS Library.

89 *Al-Ishtirakiyya* (Damascus), 27 March 1952.

90 *Ibid.*

91 Report on "Neutralism in Syria," prepared by Harrison M. Symmes, US Legation, Damascus, in dispatch 319, US Legation, Damascus, 23 January 1951, RG 59 783.00/1-2351, Reel 1, M5680, SOAS Library.

92 *Ibid.*

93 *Ibid.*

94 Dispatch 546 from US Legation, Damascus, 1 June 1951, RG 59, 783.001/6-151, Reel 3, M5680, SOAS library. The subject of the SPP is broadly discussed in the next sub-chapter.

95 Dispatch 10 from US Legation, Damascus, 9 July 1951, RG 59, 783.2/7-951, Reel 4, M5680, SOAS Library.

96 *Ibid.*

97 Dispatch 128 from James F. Leonard, Second Secretary of US Legation, Damascus, 28 August 1951, RG 59, 783.13/8-2851, Reel 4, M5680, SOAS Library.

98 *Ibid.*

99 *Ibid.* See also "Syria: Annual Review for 1951," in dispatch 30 from Montagu-Pollock, British Legation, Damascus, 8 March 1952, FO371/98913, EY1011/1.

100 King Abdullah was assassinated on 20 July 1951.

101 See full text of his statement in *al-Ahram* in enclosure No. 1 to dispatch 86 from US Legation, Damascus, 20 August 1951, RG 59, 783.551/8-2051, Reel 5, M5680, SOAS Library.

102 Dispatch 86 (see note 101 above).

103 *Ibid.*

104 *Ibid.*

105 On al-Hakim's personal views on foreign affairs, see dispatch 92 from US Legation, Damascus, 22 August 1951, RG 59, 783.13/8-2251, Reel 4, M5680, SOAS Library. See also dispatch 128 (see note 97 above).

106 Dispatch 92 (see note 105 above).

107 See more about the six weeks of UN debates on this complaint in Ginat, *The Soviet Union and Egypt*, pp. 119–22.

108 Dispatch 158 from US Legation, Damascus, 21 September 1951, RG 59, 783.13/9-2151, Reel 4, M5680, SOAS Library.

109 *Ibid.*

110 Dispatch 220 from US Legation, Damascus, 26 October 1951, RG 59, 783.13/10-2651, Reel 4, M5680, SOAS Library.

111 *Ibid.*

112 *Ibid.*

113 *Ibid.*

114 Faysal ruled part of pre-mandatory Syria from October 1918 to July 1920. He was expelled from Syria by the French mandatory authorities.

115 Alexandrettat became part of Turkey in the late 1930s and Palestine was lost by the Arabs to the Jews in the late 1940s.

116 On al-Hakim's interview to *al-Hayat*, see telegram 332 from Montagu-Pollock, Damascus, FO371/91850, EY1027/2.

117 See a copy of al-Hakim's letter to President al-Atasi in enclosure No. 2, dispatch 262, from US Legation, Damascus, 16 November 1951, RG 59, 783.13/11-1651, Reel 4, M5680, SOAS Library. See also "Syria: Annual Review for 1952," *ibid.*

118 See a copy of al-Hakim's letter to the Parliament in enclosure No. 3, dispatch 262 (see note 117 above).

119 *Ibid.*

120 On the political situation in Syria, the rifts within al-Hakim's government in October–November 1951 and the subsequent downfall of his government, see telegram 340 from Montagu-Pollock, Damascus, 11 November 1951, FO501/5, EY1016/23. See also a record of a conversation between Anthony Eden, the British Secretary of State, and Faris al-Khuri, the Syrian chief delegate to the UN, which took place on 12 November 1951 in Paris. Faris al-Khuri expressed views similar to al-Hakim's, describing al-Hakim as "a very courageous man." He could not succeed because "the rest of the cabinet led by the Foreign Minister, were against him on the question of [the] Middle East Command Proposals." See telegram 151 from Eden, London, to Montagu-Pollock, Damascus, 20 November 1951, FO501/5, EY1051/15.

121 See quotation from *Al-Fayha*'s article in enclosure No. 1 to Dispatch 203, from US Legation, Damascus, 17 October 1951, RG 59 983.61/10-1751, Reel 11, M5680, SOAS Library.

122 See Quotation from *al-Barada* in enclosure No. 1, dispatch 203 (see note 121 above).

123 See quotation from *al-Manar* in enclosure No. 1, in dispatch 203 (see note 121 above).

124 *Al-Sha'b* is quoted in enclosure No. 1, dispatch 203 (see note 121 above).

125 Telegram 224 from US Legation, Damascus, 18 October 1951, RG 59, 783.56/10-1851, Reel 5, M5680, SOAS Library.

126 On the contradictory approaches among American policymakers with regard to arms sales to Israel and its Arab neighbors, see R. J. Watson, *History of the Joint Chiefs of Staffs*, Vol. V (Washington: 1986), pp. 326–29. See also P. L. Hann, *Strategy and Diplomacy in the Early Cold War: United States Policy toward Egypt, 1945–1956* (unpublished Ph.D. dissertation, Vanderbilt University, 1987), pp. 371–91.

127 See telegram 364 from Montagu-Pollock, Damascus, 29 November 1951, FO501/5, EY1015/28. On the events that led up to al-Shishakli's second coup d'état, see in detail, Telegram 181 from Montagu-Pollock, Damascus, 11 December 1951, FO501/5, EY1015/78.

128 "Syria: Annual Review for 1951," *ibid.* See also "New Syrian Government Statement of Policy," in dispatch 103 from A.C.I. Samuel, British Legation, Damascus, 19 June 1952, FO371/98915.

129 "Syria: Annual Review for 1951" (see note 128 above).

130 See more on its founders and formation in Tareq Y. Ismael and Jacqueline S. Ismael, *The Communist Movement in Syria and Lebanon* (Gainesville: University Press of Florida, 1998), pp. 7–20. See also Suliman Bashear, *Communism in the Arab East, 1918–1928* (London: Ithaca Press, 1980). Ilyas Murqis, *Ta'arikh al-Ahzab al-Shuyu'iyah fi al-Watan al-'Arabi* (Beirut: Dar al-Tali'a, 1964).

131 Ismael, *The Communist Movement*, pp. 20–38.
132 *Ibid.*, p. 41.
133 *Ibid.*, pp. 42–3. See full text of his report in Khalid Bakdash, "For the Successful Struggle for Peace, National Independence, and Democracy We Must Resolutely Turn toward the Workers and the Peasants," *Middle East Journal*, Vol. 7, No. 2 (Spring 1953).
134 *People's Struggle* (Beirut), No. 20, 1 January 1951, enclosed to dispatch 364 from US legation, Beirut, 15 February 1951, RG 59 783.001/2-1551.
135 The figures are taken from report entitled "General Survey of Communist Activities in Syria," enclosed to dispatch 294 from US Legation, Damascus, 31 December 1950, RG 59, 783.001/12-3150. See also *al-Ayyam* (Damascus), 16 August 1951.
136 See "General Survey of Communist Activities in Syria," enclosed to dispatch 294 (see note 135 above).
137 *Ibid.*
138 *Ibid.*
139 See a secret report entitled "The Partisans of Peace—Most Prominent Communist Front Organization in Syria," prepared by the US Legation in Damascus and enclosed in dispatch 283 from Damascus, 30 December 1950, RG 59, 783.001/12-3050, Reel 3, M5680, SOAS Library.
140 Dispatch 1926 from Caffery, Cairo, 12 February 1951, RG 59, 774.001/2-1251.
141 Dispatch 546 (see note 94 above).
142 Dispatch 283 (see note 139 above).
143 *Ibid.*
144 *Ibid.*
145 *Ibid.*
146 Thirteen delegates who were of many varieties with little common background except their attachment to peace and communism. Among this group were two shaykhs (Muhammad al-Ashmar and Salah al-Za'im), several lawyers (Nasuh al-Ghaffari, Mustafa Amin, and Falak Tarazi—all communists), a judge (Ibrahim al-Hamzawi who was employed in 1944 by the Soviet intelligence bureaus established in the Soviet Legation in Damascus to collect political and economic information and in 1947 visited the USSR), a parliamentary deputy ('Abd al-Salam Haydar), and a law student ('Abd al-Majid Jamal al-Din); Sa'id Tahsin, Joseph Musali and Ahmad Abaza were communists. See more details in enclosure 1, dispatch 283 (see note 139 above).
147 See dispatch 283 (see note 139 above). See also dispatch 1926 from Caffery, Cairo, 12 February 1951, RG 59, 774.001/2-1251.
148 Dispatch 283 (see note 139 above). See also *People's Struggle* (Beirut), No. 21, 15 January 1951, enclosure to dispatch 364 (see note 134 above).
149 See Monthly Report of Communist Activity in Syria, enclosed to dispatch 398 from US Legation, Damascus, 12 March 1951, RG 59, 783.001/3-1251.
150 Several reports maintained that *al-Nasr* (circulation circa 3,000) received subsidies in some form from the Soviets. See dispatch 294, *ibid.*
151 *Al-Nasr*, 30 November 1950.
152 The tract was issued jointly by the Central Committees of the Syrian and Lebanese communist parties at the "last days of November 1950." The full text

of the tract is enclosed to dispatch 351 from US Legation, Damascus, 13 February 1951, RG 59, 783.001/2-1351.

153 See enclosure to dispatch 351 (see note 152 above).

154 Enclosure to dispatch 351 (see note 152 above).

155 *People's Struggle* (Beirut), No. 20, 1 January 1951, enclosed to dispatch 364, *ibid.* See also *People's Struggle* (Beirut), No. 21, 15 January 1951, enclosed to dispatch 364 (see note 134 above).

156 Enclosure to dispatch 351 (see note 152 above).

157 See monthly report of communist activity in Syria attached to dispatch 342 from US Legation, Damascus, 12 February 1951, RG 59, 783.001/2-1251, Reel 3, SOAS Library.

158 Monthly report of communist activity in Syria, dispatch 342 (see note 157 above).

159 See Monthly Report on Communist Activities, enclosed to dispatch 77 from US Legation, Damascus, 13 August 1951, RG 59, 783.001/8-1351.

160 Monthly Report on Communist Activities, enclosed to dispatch 77, *ibid.*

161 On the demonstrations and their results, see dispatch 87 from US Legation, Damascus, 20 August 1951, RG 59, 783.00/8-2051.

162 See dispatch 87 (see note 161 above). See also "Monthly Report on Communist Activities (August 1951)," in dispatch 151 from US Legation, Damascus, 17 September 1951, RG 59, 783.001/9-1751.

163 Dispatch 77 (see note 159).

164 *Al-Salam* (Damascus), No. 7, 18 August 1951. Enclosure 2, in dispatch 104 from US Legation, Damascus, 27 August 1951, RG 59, 983.61/8-2751.

165 *Al-Salam* (Damascus), No. 8, 25 August 1951. See also dispatch 151 (see note 162 above).

166 *Al-Salam* (Damascus), No. 9, 1 September 1951. See also *al-Salam,* No. 10 and 11, 8 and 15 September 1951.

167 *Al-Salam*, No. 9.

168 See copies of these articles in dispatch 155 from US Legation, Damascus, 19 September 1951, RG 59, 783.001/9-1951.

169 *Al-Jil al-Jadid* (Damascus), 24 August 1951.

170 *Ibid.*

171 Dispatch 346 from US Legation, Damascus, 12 February 1951, RG 59, 983.61/2-1251.

172 See dispatch 491 from US Legation, Damascus, 11 May 1951, RG 59, 983.61/5-1151.

173 *Al-Jil al-Jadid* (Damascus), Part I, 23 April 1951, enclosure 1 to dispatch 491.

174 *Ibid.*

175 Lenin of course was not a Jew.

176 *Al-Jil al-Jadid*, Part II, enclosure 2 to dispatch 491.

177 *Ibid.*, Part III, enclosure 3 to dispatch 491.

178 *Ibid.*, Part IV, enclosure 4 to dispatch 491. See also dispatch 346, *ibid.*

179 *Ibid.*, Part V, enclosure 5 to dispatch 491.

180 See the article in enclosure 1, dispatch 402 from US Legation, Damascus, 14 March 1951, RG 59, 783.5/3-1451

3 Neutralism in Practice: Syria and the Consolidation of the Arab-Asian Group

1 "The United Nations," Note, 5 September 1946, Ministry of External Affairs, File No.6 (58)-cc/46, in NMM&L, *Selected Works*, Second Series, Vol. 1, p. 440.

2 Nehru's speech was broadcasted by Radio New Delhi on 7 September 1947. See its content in Jawaharlal Nehru, *India's Foreign Policy, Selected Speeches, September 1946–April 1961* (Delhi: The Publication Division, Government of India, 1961), pp. 1–3.

3 *Ibid.*, p. 3.

4 A. K. Damodaran, *Jawaharlal Nehru: A Communicator and Democratic Leader* (New Delhi: Sangam Books, 1997), pp. 119–20. On the development of cultural and political relations between India and Egypt in 1944, see for instance, Political and Services Department, S.32/39-A, S.131/19223-B, S.131/18698-B and S.131/8307-B, Department of Archives, Government of Maharashtra, Mumbai, India. On the development of agricultural relations between the two countries see, for instance, letter 48/Agri/5 from A. H. Layard, Counsellor, Office of the High Commissioner for the UK, New Delhi, 19 February 1948, File No. F.31-68/48-O.S.V., National Archives of India, Janpath, New Delhi (hereafter cited as NAI with appropriate filing). See also Letters D.896/48—O.S.V. and S.No(3) from Indian Ministry of External Affairs, and Commonwealth Relations, New Delhi, 28 February and 3 May 1948, File No. F.31-68/48-O.S.V., NAI.

5 Telegram 3172 from Ministry of External Affairs, New Delhi, to Asaf Ali, Washington, 23 April 1947, File No. 46(1) AWT/47, NAI.

6 Remarks at a Cabinet meeting, 23 April 1947, Cabinet Secretariat Papers, NMM&L, *Selected Works of Jawaharlal Nehru*, Second Series, Vol. 2 (New Delhi: Jawaharlal Nehru Memorial Fund, 1984), pp. 492–3.

7 Telegram 3172.

8 Telegram 3172.

9 Telegram GA-268.

10 Telegram 51 From Shukri al-Quwatli, President of Syria, Damascus, to Nehru, New Delhi, 30 November 1947, File No. 7 (8)—UNO-I.

11 Telegram 126 from Foreign Ministry, Jeddah, to Ministry of External Affairs, New Delhi, 3 December 1947, File No. 7 (8)—UNO-I.

12 Kimche, *The Afro Asian Movement*, p. 34. Renate Wunsche, Marion Linder and Roswitha Voigtlander, *The Struggle of the Movement of Non-Aligned Nations for Peace, Disarmament and Development—An Important Factor of Modern International Relations* (Berlin: Akademie-Verlag, 1985), pp. 12–14. N. Parameshwaran Nair, "History, Ideology, Prospects," in K. P. Karunakaran (ed.), *Outside the Contest*, pp. 32–3.

13 Kimche, *The Afro-Asian Movement*, p. 34. On the conferences see more in *idem*, pp. 31–6.

14 Kimche, *ibid.*, p. 55. See also *idem*, p. 36. On the rising importance of the Arab–Asian bloc in the UN, and the Soviet efforts to win its support, see Ginat, *The Soviet Union and Egypt*, pp. 108–9.

15 N. Parameshwaran Nair, "History, Ideology, Prospects," pp. 34–5.

16 Nair, *ibid.*, p. 35.

17   Michael Brecher, *Nehru A Political Biography* (London: Oxford University Press, 1969), pp. 226–7.
18   Kimche, *The Afro-Asian Movement*, pp. 36–43.
19   See note from Nehru to Secretary-General, Foreign Secretary and Commonwealth Secretary, 12 October 1953, in *Selected Works of Jawaharlal Nehru*, 2nd Series, Vol. 24, pp. 553–4, NMM&L, New Delhi.
20   Note from Nehru to Secretary-General, 12 October 1953, p. 554.
21   See Nehru's remarks at a press conference took place in New Delhi on 3 November 1951, in *Selected Works of Jawaharlal Nehru*, 2nd Series, Vol. 17, pp. 541–6, NMM&L, New Delhi.
22   *Ibid.*
23   See Nehru's remarks at a press conference, New Delhi, 24 July 1952; and note from Nehru to Foreign Secretary, New Delhi, 3 August 1952, in *Selected Works of Jawaharlal Nehru*, 2nd Series, Vol. 19, pp. 637–41, NMM&L, New Delhi.
24   Note from Nehru to Foreign Secretary, p. 640.
25   Note from Nehru to the Foreign Secretary, *ibid.*, pp. 640–1.
26   See letter from Nehru to S. Radhakrishnan, 3 September 1952, in *Selected Works of Jawaharlal N Nehru* 2nd Series, Vol. 19, pp. 642–3, NMM&L, New Delhi.
27   See message to *Sawt al-Sharq*, 20 September 1952, New Delhi, in *ibid.*, p. 643.
28   Minutes of the third meeting of the Commonwealth Prime Ministers' Conference, London, 5 June 1953, in *Selected Works of Jawaharlal Nehru*, 2nd Series, Vol. 22, p. 404–5, NMM&L, New Delhi.
29   *Ibid.* See also Nehru's press conferences in London, 8 and 10 June 1953, *ibid.*, pp. 407–11.
30   Minutes of the fourth meeting of the Commonwealth Prime Ministers' Conference, London, 8 June 1953, *ibid.*, p. 406.
31   See personal letter from Nehru to Lord Mountbatten, Cairo, 24 June 1953, *ibid.*, pp. 411–16.
32* Letter from Nehru to Syed Mahmud (he led the Indian delegation to King Faysal's coronation), 29 June 1953, *ibid.*, p. 419. On his visit to Egypt, see also Political and Services Department, File No. 2727/46, Department of Archives, Government of Maharashtra, Mumbai, India.
33   Note from Nehru to the Secretary-General, MEA, and Foreign Secretary, 8 July 1953, p. 534, in *Selected Works of Jawaharlal Nehru*, 2nd Series, Vol. 23, NMM&L, New Delhi.
34   Anglo-Egyptian talks on the Suez Canal question were opened on 27 April 1953 and were suspended indefinitely on 6 May 1953. See cable from Nehru to B. G. Kher, New Delhi, 5 July 1953, *ibid.*, Vol. 23, pp. 531–2.
35   Note from Nehru to the Secretary-General, MEA, *ibid.*, p. 533.
36   Note from Nehru to the Secretary-General, MEA, *ibid.*, p. 534.
37   Letter from Nehru to K. M. Panikkar, India's ambassador to Egypt, 11 July 1953, *ibid.*, Vol. 23, pp. 535–6. See particularly fns 3 and 4.
38   Letter from Nehru to Isma'il Kamal, Egypt's ambassador, New Delhi, 2 July 1953, *ibid.*, Vol. 23, p. 531.
39   Letter from Nehru to Isma'il Kamal, *ibid.*, Vol. 23, p. 531.

40 See Nehru's press conference in Cairo, 25 June 1953, *ibid.*, pp. 416–17.
41 *Ibid.*, p. 418.
42 Cable from Nehru, New Delhi, to B. G. Kher, London, 9 September 1953, *ibid.*, Vol. 23, pp. 536–7, and fn 3.
43 Letter from Nehru to K. M. Panikkar, Embassy of India, Cairo, 13 October 1953, in *Selected Works of Jawaharlal Nehru,* 2nd Series, Vol. 24, p. 618, NMM&L, New Delhi.
44 Note from Nehru to the Foreign Secretary, New Delhi, 15 November 1953, *ibid.*, Vol. 24, p. 556.
45 Note from Nehru to the Foreign Secretary, *ibid.*, Vol. 24, p. 556.
46 Letter from Nehru to Muhammad Najib, Cairo, 28 December 1953, File No. T/53/1445/37—MEA, Vol. 24, p. 619. Panikkar was replaced by Ali Yavar Jung.
47 Note from Nehru to the Foreign Secretary, New Delhi, 15 November 1953, *ibid.*, Vol. 24, p. 556.
48 Note from Nehru to the Foreign Secretary, *ibid.*, p. 556.
49 See Message from Nehru to Nasser, New Delhi, 29 July 1954, in *Selected Works of Jawaharlal Nehru,* 2nd Series, Vol. 26, p. 523, NMM&L, New Delhi.
50 Letter from Nehru to Ali Yavar Jung, India's ambassador to Cairo, 17 July 1954, in *ibid.*, Vol. 26, p. 522.
51 Letter from Nehru to Ali Jung, 8 September 1954, *ibid.*, Vol. 26, p. 524.
52 Letter from Nehru to Ali Yavar Jung, 8 September 1954, *ibid.*, p. 525.
53 Letter from Nehru to Ali Yavar Jung, 8 September 1954, *ibid.*, p. 525.
54 Letter from Nehru to Ali Yavar Jung, 9 September 1954, *ibid.*, pp. 526–7. The Turkish–Pakistani pact was the first layer of the West's Northern Tier defense plan. This plan was born in mid-1953 following Dulles' extended visit to the Middle East in May 1953. Dulles concluded that a Middle East Defense Organization (MEDO) was no longer a possibility. He therefore formulated an alternative plan, which maintained that new efforts were to be concentrated on building a defensive alliance in the northern tier (refers to Middle and Near East countries bordering on the USSR), which would include Pakistan, Iran, Syria and Turkey. See Ginat, *The Soviet Union and Egypt*, p. 167.
55 Letter from Nehru to Ali Yavar Jung, 8 September 1954, *ibid.*, pp. 525–6, and fn 4, p. 526.
56 Letter from Nehru to Ali Jung Yavar, 8 September 1954, *ibid.*, pp. 525–6.
57 Letter from Nehru to Ali Yavar Jung, 9 September 1954, *ibid.*, p. 527.
58 Letter from Nehru to Ali Yavar Jung, 9 Sseptember 1954, *ibid.*, p. 527 and fn 3, p. 527.
59 Letter from Nehru to Ali Yavar Jung, 9 September 1954, *ibid.*, p. 527.
60 Wunsche, Marion and Voigtlander, *The Struggle of the Movement*, pp. 14–15.
61 Kimche, *The Afro-Asian Movement*, pp. 47–8.
62 *Ibid.*, pp. 49–50.
63 *Ibid.*, p. 49.
64 Jawaharlal Nehru, *India's Foreign Policy, Selected Speeches, September 1946–April 1961*, pp. 99–100.
65 Nehru's speech was delivered on 28 December 1954. See the full text of his speech in Ministry of Information, Republic of Indonesia, *The Bogor*

NOTES TO PP. 97–101

Conference, Cl. No. V4: IPN54, J52, Library of the Indian Council of World Affairs, New Delhi, pp. 18–21. See also *idem, Bogor (Road to Asian-African Solidarity)*, Cl. No. V4: IPN54 J51, pp. 15–16.

66 See telegram D.O. No.0001/185/54 from Ali Yavar Jung, Embassy of India, Cairo, 27 December 1954, File No. 1(8)—AAC/55, NAI.

67 A full text of the Aide Memoire is attached to telegram D.O.No.0001/185/54, *ibid.*

68 *Ibid.*

69 See "Note on the Meetings of the Prime Ministers of the Five Colombo Powers at Bogor in Indonesia on December 28 and 29, 1954," by S. Dutt, Indian Ministry of External Affairs, 9 January 1955, File No. 1(8)—AAC/55, NAI, New Delhi.

70 "Note on the Meetings of the Prime Ministers of the Five Colombo Powers at Bogor," *ibid.*

71. Letter from Nehru to Moshe Sharett, Israeli Prime Minister, 5 June 1954, *Selected Works of Jawaharlal Nehru*, 2nd series, Vol. 26, pp. 527–8.

72 Letter from Nehru to Moshe Sharett, *ibid.*, p. 528.

73 "Note on the Meetings of the Prime Ministers of the Five Colombo Powers at Bogor," *ibid.*

74 "Note on the Meetings of the Prime Ministers of the Five Colombo Powers at Bogor," *ibid.*

75 *The Bharat Jyoti* (Bombay), 17 April 1955.

76 *Ibid.* See also *The Pilot* (New Delhi), 29 April 1955. See more on the Indian press reaction to the exclusion of Israel from Bandung, in News to Israel Legations Abroad, No. 1030, from Israel Ministry of Foreign Affairs, Department of Information, 7 June 1955, FM2564/8, Israel State Archive (hereafter cited as ISA).

77 *The Nation* (Rangoon), 15 April 1955. See also *The Burman* (Rangoon), 25 April 1955. See more on this subject in FM2564/8, ibid.

78 "Joint Communiqué by the Prime Ministers of Burma, Ceylon, India, Indonesia and Pakistan," 29 December 1954, Bogor, File No. 1(8)—AAC/55, NAI.

79 *Ibid.*

80 See letter No. 9/PR/55 from Arthur S. Lall, the Permanent Mission of India, UNO, 10 January 1955, File No. 1(9)—AAC/55, NAI.

81 Letter No. 9/PR/55, *ibid.*

82 Letter D.O.No.1—AA/55 from Shri Ali Yavar Jung, Ambassador of India, Cairo, 24 January 1955, NAI, File No. 1(9)—AAC/55, NAI.

83 Letter D.O. No. 0001/25/55, from Ali Yavar Jung, Cairo, 31 January 1955, File No. 1(9)—AAC/55, NAI.

84 *Al-Anba'* (Beirut), 14 January 1955.

85 *Al-Jarida* (Beirut), 11 January 1955.

86 *al-Hadaf* (Beirut), 11 January 1955.

87 See Kamal Jumblatt's interview in *al-Hadaf* (Beirut), 6 January 1955.

88 See Monthly Report (16 December–15 January 1955) No. 20(3)/54, prepared by the Embassy of India, Cairo, 20 January 1955, File No. 23—R&I/55, NAI.

89 Hassunah eventually participated in the conference as a member of the

Egyptian delegation, which included also, Prime Minister Nasser; Salah Salim, Minister of National Guidance; Mahmud Fawzi, Foreign Minister; 'Ali Sabri *Chef du Cabinet* to Prime Minister Nasser. See letter No. CA-6175 from US Embassy, Cairo, 18 March 1955, Cairo-Embassy—General Records, 1955:050-3213, File Subject 310 Afro-Asian Conference—Djakarta, Record Group (RG) 84, Box 262, US National Archives, Suitland.

90 See record of conversation in letter D.O.No. 0001/11/55 from Ali Yavar Jung, Embassy of India, Cairo, 10 January 1955, File No. 1(9)—AAC/55, NAI.

91 See record of conversation in letter D.O.No. 0001/9/55 from Ali Yavar Jung, Embassy of India, Cairo, 13 January 1955, File No. 1(9)—AAC/55, NAI.

92 Letter from C. S. Jha, Joint Secretary, Indian Ministry of External Affairs, New Delhi, to Ali Yavar Jung, Embassy of India, Cairo, 17 January 1955, File No. 1(9)—AAC/55, NAI.

93 *Ibid.*

94 Mohamed Heikal, *Nasser: The Cairo Documents* (London: New English Library, 1973), pp. 224–5.

95 See Monthly Report No. F.20 (3)/54 (16 January–15 February 1955) by Embassy of India, Cairo, File No. 23—R&I/55, INA. On the meeting see also, Jean Lacouture, *Nasser Veyorshav* (Tel Aviv: 'Am-Oved, 1972), pp. 139–41 [Hebrew]. Robert St. John, *The Boss, The Story of Jamal 'Abd al-Nasser* (Tel Aviv: Ma'arkhot, 1962), pp. 238–9 [Hebrew].

96 Monthly Report No. F.20 (3)/54.

97 Monthly Report No. F.20 (3)/54.

98 See Monthly Report No. F.14 (2)/55 (16 February–15 March 1955) by Embassy of India, Cairo, File No. 23—R&I/55, NAI.

99 Heikal, *Nasser the Cairo Documents*, p. 245.

100 *Ibid*, pp. 245–8.

101 Monthly Report No. F. 14 (2)/55.

102 See dispatch 1622 from G. Lewis Jones, Chargé d'Affaires, US Embassy, Cairo, 19 February 1955, RG 59, 774.00/2-1955, Reel 1, M5812, SOAS Library.

103 Dispatch 1622.

104 On the agreement see dispatch 1962 from US Embassy, Cairo, 14 April 1955, RG 59, 674.911/4-1455. Dispatch 1921, *idem*, 8 April 1955, RG 59, 674.911/4-855. See also Monthly Report No. 14 (2)/55 (16 March–15 April 1955), from Embassy of India, Cairo, File No. 23—R&I/55, NAI, New Delhi.

105 See full text of the report attached to letter D.O. No. 0001/60/55 from Ali Yavar Jung, Embassy of India, Cairo, 28 February 1955, File No. 1(11)—AAC/55, NAI. See also letter No. 0001/79/55, 10 March 1955, *ibid.*

106 *Ibid.*

107 *Ibid.*

108 *Ibid.*

109 Department of State, Intelligence Report entitled "Developments Relating to the Bandung Conference," 18 March 1955, R&A Reports, IR No. 6830.3, National Archives, Washington.

110 Department of State, Intelligence Report entitled "Developments Relating to the Bandung Conference," 1 April 1955, R&A Reports, IR No. 6830.4, NA.

111 Intelligence Report No. 6830.4.
112 Department of State, Intelligence Report entitled "Developments Relating to the Bandung Conference," 15 April 1955, R&A Reports, IR No. 6830.5, NA.
113 Ginat, *The Soviet Union and Egypt*, p. 191. On Nasser's inter-bloc and inter-Arab policies in the period preceded the Bandung Conference, see *idem*, pp. 176–94. Podeh, *The Quest for Hegemony in the Arab World*, pp. 56–98.
114 Intelligence Report No. 6830.3.
115 See "Final Communiqué of the Asian-African Conference Held at Bandung from 18th to 24th April, 1955," 24 April 1955, File No. 1(37)—AAC/55, NAI.
116 For its special geographic location Egypt was considered both Asian and African.
117 See Secret telegram No. 3971/3972 from the Indian delegation, Bandung, 27 April 1955, File No. 1(37)—AAC/55, NAI.
118 Department of State, Intelligence Report entitled "Results of the Bandung Conference: A Preliminary Analysis," 27 April 1955, R&A Reports, IR No. 6903, NA.
119 Quoted from "Final Communiqué of the Asian-African Conference . . . ", *ibid*. See also Intelligence Report No. 6903.
120 See a copy of a note entitled "West Asia at the Asian-African Conference," recorded by C. S. Jha, Joint Secretary to the Government of India, Ministry of External Affairs, New Delhi, attached to letter No. 2662-AWT/55 from Ministry of External Affairs, New Delhi, to all Heads of Missions in the Middle East, 11 May 1955, File No. 1(37)—AAC/55, NAI.
121 Note from Nehru to Chief Ministers, New Delhi, 28 April 1955, in *Selected Works of Jawaharlal Nehru*, 2nd Series, Vol. 28, p. 131.
122 Intelligence Report No. 6903.
123 Telegram No. 3971/3972. See also letter 339/945:37/RN from David Hacohen, Israel Minister to Rangoon, to Daniel Levin, Asian Department, Israel Foreign Ministry, 4 May 1955, ISA, FM2564/8.
124 Telegram No. 3971/3972.
125 The following countries may be considered Middle Eastern: Afghanistan, Iran, Iraq, Jordan, Lebanon, Saudi Arabia, Syria, Turkey, Egypt, Yemen, Sudan and Libya.
126 "West Asia at the Asian-African Conference," letter No. 2662-AWT/55. See also similar analysis in Weekly Survey No. 123, "The Arabs in Bandung," by the Research Department, Israeli Foreign Ministry, 25 April 1955, Records of Israel Foreign Ministry (FM)2564/8. Ginzakh Hamedina, Jerusalem (hereafter cited as ISA, FM with appropriate filing reference).
127 See letter No. 2/10/CO/55/1598 from B.F.H.B. Tyabji, Indian ambassador to Djakarta, Indonesia, 28 April 1955, File No. 1(37)—AAC/55, NAI. Tyabji was also a member of the Joint Secretariat in the Bandung Conference. See also telegram 3971/3972.
128 Letter No. 2/10/CO/55/1598. See also telegram No. 3971/3972.
129 Letter No. 2/10/CO/55/1598.
130 Telegram No. 3971/3972.
131 "Final Communiqué of the Asian-African Conference . . . ," *ibid*.
132 "West Asia at the Asian-African Conference," letter No. 2662-AWT/55.

133 See letter 339/945:37/RN from David Hacohen, Israel Minister to Rangoon, to Daniel Levin, Asian Department, Israel Foreign Ministry, 4 May 1955, ISA, FM2564/8.

134 "Final Communiqué of the Asian-African Conference," *ibid.*

135 See a report from Cairo of the celebrations in Cairo on Nasser's arrival from Bandung, in "Hero's Welcome in Cairo," *Manchester Guardian* (Manchester), 3 May 1955.

136 *Ibid.*

137 Monthly Report No. 14(2)/55 (16 April–15 May, 1955) from Embassy of India, Cairo, 19 May 1955, File No. 23—R&I/55, NAI.

138 Monthly Report (16 April–15 May 1955), *ibid.*

139 See record of conversation between W. Pankowski, Polish Chargé d'Affaires, Cairo and 'Ali Sabri, Chief of the Office of Premier Nasser, in secret letter No. 2421/1/55 from W. Pankowski to Stanisław Skrzeszewski, Polish Minister of Foreign Affairs, Warsaw, 25 September 1955, z. 12, w. 6, t. 120, Arkhivum Ministerstva Sprav Zagranitshnykh, Warsaw (hereafter cited as AMSZ with appropriate filing reference).

140 Rawle Knox, "Voices of Asia," *The Observer* (London), 30 April 1955.

141 Knox, *ibid.*

142 Note from Nehru to Chief Ministers, New Delhi, 28 April 1955, in *Selected Works of Jawaharlal Nehru*, 2nd Series, Vol. 28, pp. 129–38.

143 See note from Nehru to Secretary-General, MEA, 14 April 1955, in *Selected Works of Jawaharlal Nehru*, 2nd Series, Vol. 28, pp. 216–17, NMM&L, New Delhi.

144 On Egypt's arms deals with the Soviet bloc, see Rami Ginat, "The Origins of the Czech–Egyptian Arms Deal: A Reappraisal," in David Tal (ed.), *The 1956 War, Collusion and Rivalry in the Middle East* (London: Frank Cass, 2001), pp. 145–167.

145 Minutes of talks held in New Delhi on 1 May 1955 and recorded by Nehru on 2 May 1955, in, *Selected works of Jawaharlal Nehru*, 2nd Series, Vol. 28, pp. 219–22.

146 Minutes of talks held in New Delhi on 1 May 1955, *ibid.*

147 Minutes of talks held in New Delhi on 1 May 1955, *ibid.*

148 Minutes of talks held in New Delhi on 1 May 1955, *ibid.*, p. 222, fn 2.

149 Monthly Report No. 14(2)/55 (16 March–15 April, 1955), from Embassy of India, Cairo, 21 April 1955, File No. 23—R&I/55, NAI, New Delhi.

150 Monthly Report No. 14 (2)/55 (16 March–15 April, 1955), *ibid.*

151 Minutes of talks held in New Delhi on 30 April 1955, and recorded by Nehru on 2 May 1955, in *ibid.*, Vol. 28, pp. 217–19.

152 Minutes of talks held in New Delhi on 30 April 1955, *ibid.*

153 See record of Nehru's conversations with Faysal in note from Nehru to Secretary-General, MEA, 5 May 1955, in *ibid.*, Vol. 28, pp. 222–7.

154 Records of Nehru's conversation with Faysal, *ibid.* See also Note from Nehru to Secretary-General, MEA, 7 May 1955, Vol. 28, pp. 228–9.

155 Record of Nehru's conversation with Faysal, *ibid.*

156 Record of Nehru's conversation with Faysal, *ibid.*, p. 225.

157 Record of Nehru's conversation with Faysal, *ibid.*, p. 226.

158 Record of Nehru's conversation with Faysal, *ibid.*, p. 227.

159 Quoted from Ginat, *The Soviet Union and Egypt*, p. 177.

160 *Al-Ba'th* (Damascus), 29 June 1956. Michel Aflak, *Choice of Texts from the Ba'th Party Founder's Thought* (Firenze: Cooperative Lavoratori, 1977), p. 160.

161 Mischel 'Aflaq, "Fi al-Hiyad al-Ijabi," in *idem, Fi Sabil al-Ba'th* (Beirut: Manshurat Dar al-Tali'a, 1963), 3rd edition, p. 329.

162 'Aflaq, *Fi Sabil*, pp. 329–34.

163 'Aflaq, *Fi Sabil*, pp. 329–32.

164 On the Ba'th adverse view of the Baghdad Pact and the Western powers' use of the pact to act against Arab national interests, see an article published by the Ba'th Party in its paper *al-Ba'th* on 28 September 1956, a month before the outbreak of the Suez War; in Hizb al-Ba'th al-'Arabi al-Ishtiraki, *Nidal al-Ba'th*, Vol. III (Beirut: Dar al-Tali'a, 1964), pp. 223–8.

165 Hizb al-Ba'th, *Nidal al-Ba'th*, Vol. III (Beirut: Dar al-Tali'a, 1964), p. 71. The subject of Soviet–Syrian relations in the period 1954–58, Syria's policies toward the Baghdad Pact, and the Suez Crisis and the Eisenhower Doctrine are broadly discussed in the following chapters.

166 *Ibid.*, pp. 259–60.

167 *Ibid.*, p. 285.

168 *Ibid.*, p. 284.

169 See an interview between 'Aflaq and Patrick Seale, took place on 7 January 1961, in Seale, *The Struggle for Syria*, pp. 256–7.

170 'Aflaq, *Fi Sabil*, p. 97.

171 On Mahmud's visit see dispatch 62 from British Embassy, Damascus, 10 April 1956, FO371/121872, VY1061/1.

172 On Nehru's visit see dispatch 101 from British Embassy, Damascus, 22 June 1956, FO371/121872, VY1061/4.

173 Dispatch 101, *ibid.*

174 Department of State, Intelligence Report No. 7317, "Reactions to the Egyptian Crisis," 21 August 1956, M5618, reel 1, SOAS library.

175 On al-Quwatli's visit to India, see dispatch 14 from Acting United Kingdom High Commissioner in India, to Secretary of State for Commonwealth Relations, 26 February 1957, FO371/128247, VY10385/2.

176 Dispatch 14, *ibid.*

177 On the covering of the Indian press of al-Quwatli's visit, see dispatch 14, *ibid.*

178 See the text of the communiqué in telegram 8 from UK High Commissioner in India, to Commonwealth Relations Office, 22 January 1957, FO371/128247, VY10385/1.

179 On the visit see telegram 652 from British Embassy, Beirut, 17 June 1957, FO371/128247, VY10385/3.

180 Telegram 652, ibid. See also Pol.A.352 from S. J. Whithwell, Office of the High Commissioner for the UK, New Delhi, to W. G. Lamarque, Commonwealth Relations Office, London, 19 June 1957, FO371/128247, VY10385/3(A).

181 See more on the Indian press comments on Nehru's visit to Syria in telegram 652, *ibid.*

182 Telegram 652, *ibid.*

183 On al-Bitar visit, see letter 10334 from British Embassy, Belgrade, 20 July 1957, FO371/128248, VY10392/3.
184 See his interviews to the Yugoslav press, in letter 10334, *ibid.*
185 *Ibid.*
186 See letter from A. A. Stark, British Embassy, Belgrade, 20 July 1956, FO371/128248, VY10392.
187 The interview to *Review of International affairs* of 1 September is quoted in letter 10210 from British Embassy Belgrade, 13 September 1957, FO371/128248, VY10392/6.
188 See his interview in *Borba*, 2 September 1957, in letter 10334 from British Embassy, Belgrade, 7 September 1957, FO371/128248, VY10392/5.
189 See more on these articles in letter 10210, *ibid.*
190 A full text of the interview to *Nova Makedonija* is attached to letter 10210, *ibid.*
191 *Nova Makedonija, ibid.*
192 On the visit and the content of the discussions, see letter 10334 from British Embassy, Belgrade, 29 November 1957, FO371/128248, VY10392/8.
193 See letter 10334, *ibid.*
194 *Borba* (Belgrade), 24 November 1957.
195 *Ibid.*
196 On Nasser's Arab socialism—its ideological sources and theoretical tenets, the differences between it and Marxism-communism—see Rami Ginat, *Egypt's Incomplete Revolution*, pp. 9–29, 35–4.

4 Communism, Syria, and Neutralist Trends

1 See letter 10305/3/54 from British Embassy, Damascus, 6 May 1954, FO371/111146, VY1023/2.
2 On the development of political events in Syria following the overthrow of Shishakli and the elections of 1954, see "Review of Political events in Syria for the Year 1954," attached to dispatch 19 from British Embassy, Damascus, 4 February 1955, FO371/115942, VY1011/1. See also Nabil M. Kaylani, "The Rise of the Syrian Ba'th, 1940–1958," *IJMES* (1972), Vol. 3, pp. 3–23. Gordon H. Torrey, "The Ba'th—Ideology and Practice," *Middle East Journal* (Autumn 1969), Vol. 23, pp. 445–57. John F. Devlin, *The Ba'th Party A History from its Origin to 1966* (Stanford: Hoover Institution, 1976), pp. 99–114. Seale, *The Struggle for Syria*, pp. 164–85. A certain degree of underground cooperation between left-wing parties who acted as opposition to al-Shishakli had already existed in the early 1950s. In his last year in power al-Shishakli allowed a certain amount of freedom to the press and opposition. This development was exploited by left-wing parties and organizations that incited the anti-al-Shishakli student demonstrations in December 1953—demonstrations which were the first disturbances of their kind for a long time and provoked trouble and unrest which had far-reaching consequences. On the opposition to al-Shishakli see "Report on Political events in Syria for the year 1953," attached to dispatch 31 from British Embassy, Damascus, 12 February 1954, VY1011/1 FO371/111137.
3 In his memoirs, al-'Azm described the weekly meetings which used to take place in his house between him, Khalid Bakdash, the communist leader, and

Akram al-Hawrani and Salah al-Din al-Bitar, the Ba'th leaders. See *Mudhakkirat Khalid al-'Azm*, Vol. III (Beirut: Dar al-Mutaharir lil-nashr, 1973), p. 121.

4 On the foreign policy of al-Khuri's government, see letter 1028/4/160/54, from British Embassy, Beirut, 16 November 1954, FO371/111146, VY1023/7.

5 "Review of Political events in Syria for the year 1954," *ibid.*

6 Letter 21902/11/54 from British Embassy, Damascus, 15 July 1954, FO371/111144, VY1019/1.

7 Letter 21902/11/54, *ibid.*

8 Letter 21905/4/54 from British Embassy, Damascus, 3 August 1954, FO371/111144, VY1019/3.

9 Letter 21902/12/54 from British Embassy, Damascus, 21 July 1954, FO371/111144, VY1019/2.

10 Letter 21902/12/54, *ibid.*

11 "Review of Political events in Syria for the year 1954," *ibid.*

12 On the Soviet stand on the Syrian–Israeli dispute over the "Benot Yaacov Project," see Yaacov Ro'i, *Soviet Decision Making in Practice* (New Brunswick and London: Transaction Books, 1980), pp. 484–8. "Review of Political events in Syria for the year 1954," *ibid.* "Review of Political events in Syria for the year 1953," attached to dispatch 31 from British Embassy, Damascus, FO371/111137, VY1011/1.

13 V. Medvedev, "Turetsko-Irakskii voennyii sgovor," *Pravda*, 19 January 1955.

14 On the Cairo Conference with its various stages, see in detail, Elie Podeh, *The Quest for Hegemony in the Arab World, The Struggle for the Baghdad Pact* (Tel Aviv: Ministry of Defense Publishing House, 1996), pp. 83–8. See also Seale, *The Struggle for Syria*, pp. 213–26. See also conclusions on and evaluation of the conference in a report prepared by Gid'on Rephael, of the Israeli Foreign Ministry, 9 February 1955, FM2603/8, 9531/3. See also FO371/115484, 115486/7, 115489.

15 The National Party was divided into two groups. One was represented by Sabri al-'Asali who was anti-Iraqi and also objected to the Baghdad Pact, and the other was represented by Lutfi al-Haffar who was pro-Iraqi. During the Cairo Conference, the Leftist bloc represented by Khalid al-'Azm (he led the Democratic Bloc—a group of some 30 independent politicians, the Ba'th Party with its 16 representatives, one communist and other independents), who was not pleased with al-Khuri's stand and performance at the conference, approached Sabri al-'Asali with an offer to form and head a new government. Al-'Asali agreed and formed his government on 13 February 1955. On the development of events which led to the overthrown of al-Khuri's government, see Seale, *ibid.*, pp. 214–20.

16 See Note from Nehru to the Secretary General, MEA, 28 March 1955, in *Selected Works of Jawaharlal Nehru*, 2nd Series, Vol. 28, pp. 215–16, Nehru Memorial Museum & Library, The Murti House, New Delhi.

17 *Ibid.*

18 *Ibid.*

19 V. Medvedev, "Naglye Domogatel'stva SSHA v Sirii," *Pravda*, 9 January 1955. See also S. Losev, "Dlia chego Menderes posetil Irak," *Izvestiia*, 14 January 1955.

20   *Izvestiia*, 15 February 1955.
21   "Iraksko-Turetskii voennyii sgovor," *Izvestiia*, 15 February 1955.
22   Seale, *The Struggle for Syria*, p. 218.
23   On the motives behind al-'Azm's pro-Soviet approach see *Mudhakkirat Khalid al-'Azm*, Vol. II, pp. 48–9, 427–33, and Vol. III, pp. 28–30. See also Seale, *The Struggle for Syria*, pp. 219–20.
24   Al-'Azm is quoted by Seale, *ibid.*, pp. 219–20.
25   Al-'Azm, *Mudhakkirat Khalid al-'Azm*, Vol. II, pp. 48–9.
26   *Ibid.*, Vol. III, pp. 28–30.
27   See record of conversation between al-'Azm and the British Ambassador to Damascus, took place on 21 February 1955, in dispatch 26 from British Embassy, Damascus, 22 February 1955, FO371/115950, VY1022/1.
28   Dispatch 26, *ibid.*
29   See, for instance, V. Osipov, "Ne myt'em tak katan'em, novyii nazhim SSHA na Siriiu," *Izvestiia*, 2 March 1955. V. Bogoslovskii, "Proiski imperialistov na Blizhnem Vostoke," *Trud*, 30 March 1955. M. Afonin, "Vdokhnoviteli I ispolniteli," *Pravda*, 31 March 1955.
30   This communiqué was based on an earlier communiqué issued in Damascus by Syria and Egypt on 2 March. See the full texts of both communiqué in Khalil, *The Arab States and the Arab League*, Vol. II, pp. 239–40. On the consolidation of the anti-Iraqi Arab axis, see Podeh, *The Quest for Hegemony in the Arab World*, pp. 99–115.
31   Seale, *The Struggle for Syria*, pp. 233–4. On the Turkish note and the deterioration in relations between the two countries, see FO371/115501, V1073/560.
32   See telegram 286 from British Embassy, Moscow, 24 March 1955, FO371/115501, V1073/566. Dispatch 523 from American Embassy, Damascus, 25 March 1955, RG 59, 661.83/3-2555. See also *al-Ra'i al-'Amm* (Damascus), 24 March 1955. *Al-Nasr* (Damascus), 24 March 1955. *Barada* (Damascus), 25 March 1955.
33   See telegrams 127, 128 and 135 from British Embassy, Damascus, 25 and 28 March 1955, FO371/115502, V1073/576, 578, 590.
34   On the meeting and on the exchange of notes between Turkey and Syria, see telegram 123 from British Embassy, Damascus, 23 March 1955, FO371/115501/V1073/560.
35   Department of State, "US Policy in the Near East, South Asia, and Africa—1955," in Papers of Harry N. Howard, File Subject—Near East South Asia—1945–1955, box No. 3, Harry S. Truman Library, Independence, Missouri, pp. 21, 30.
36   *Radio Moscow*, 16 April 1955, SWB, USSR, pp. 8–9.
37   Ministerstvo Inostrannykh del SSSR, *SSSR I Arabskie Strany, 1917–1960, Dokumenty I Materialy* (Moskva: Gosudarstvennoe Izdatel'stvo Politicheskoii Literatury, 1961), pp. 116–20. See also enclosure to letter 2231/18/55 from British Embassy, Moscow, 22 April 1955, FO371/115508, V1073/733A.
38   On the meeting see telegram 400 from British Embassy, Moscow, 24 April 1955, F0371/115509, V1073/753. Dispatches 1902 and 424 from US Embassy, Moscow, 25 and 28 April 1955, RG 59, 661.83/4-2555 and 661.83/4-2855.

39 On the reaction of the Syrian press, see dispatch 1 from British Embassy, Damascus, 20 April 1955, FO371/115509, V1073/759.

40 See the content of al-'Azm's interview to *al-Jumhur* in letter 11901/762/55 from British Embasy, Damascus, 15 June 1955, FO371/115513, V1073/876.

41 See al-'Azm's full speech in The Ministry of Foreign Affairs, Republic of Indonesia, *Asia-Africa Speaks from Bandung*, Cl. No. U4: IPN55 J52, Library of Indian Council of World Affairs, New Delhi, pp. 125–8. See also a summery of the conference in *First Asian African Conference Held at Bandung Indonesia, April 18–24, 1955*, Cl. No. V4: IPN55ig, J53, *ibid.*

42 See intelligence report "Developments relating to Bandung Conference," 21 February 1955, R & A Reports, IR 6830.1, National Archives, Washington.

43 See, for instance, "Otkrylas Konferentsiia Stran Azii I Afriki," *Izvestiia*, 19 April 1955. *Radio Moscow*, 21 and 22 April 1955, SWB, USSR, pp. 29–30. On the resolutions and their implications from the Soviet and Western blocs' viewpoints, see intelligence report "Results of the Bandung Conference: a Preliminary Analysis," 27 April 1955, R & A Reports, IR 6903, National Archives, Washington.

44 David Dallin, *Soviet Foreign Policy after Stalin* (Philadelphia: Lippincott, 1961), pp. 301–2.

45 See letter No. 11901/758/55 from British Embassy, Damascus, 13 June 1955, FO371/115950, VY1022/2.

46 *Al-Nasr* (Damascus), 22 June 1955.

47 Department of State, Intelligence Report No. 7134, "Jordan, the Baghdad Pact and the Arab Legion," 10 January 1956, M5618, Reel 3, SOAS Library.

48 See Appendix I to Monthly Report No. F.14(2)/55 (16 February–15 March 1955) from Embassy of India, Cairo, File No. 23—R&I/55, NAI, New Delhi. On al-'Azm's and Salim's visit to Jordan, see also, Seale, *The Struggle for Syria*, p. 224.

49 See Memorandum of conversation between W. Pankowski, Polish Chargé d'Affaires, Cairo, and Ali Sabri, Cairo, "Sytuacja w Jordanii," 9 January 1956, z.12, w.6, t. 135, AMSZ.

50 See political report on the situation in the Middle East by the Polish Legation in Cairo for the period 1 February to 1 March 1956, "Polityka zagraniczna," z. 12, w. 6, t. 135, AMSZ.

51 See the content of these messages in Khalil, *The Arab States and the Arab League*, Vol. II, pp. 245–9.

52 Political report on the situation in the Middle East, z. 12, w. 6, t. 135, *ibid.* On Glubb's ouster and its aftermath, see Uriel Dann, *King Hussein and the Challenge of Arab Radicalism, Jordan, 1955–1967* (New York and Oxford: Oxford University Press, 1989), pp. 31–8.

53 See the full text of the treaty, in Khalil, *The Arab States and the Arab League*, Vol. II, pp. 287–9.

54 See the full texts of the exchange of notes terminating the treaty of alliance of March 1948, in Khalil, *The Arab States and the Arab League*, Vol. II, pp. 390–5.

55 See the text of their statement in Khalil, *The Arab States and the Arab League*, Vol. II, pp. 921–2.

56 Khalil, *ibid.*, pp. 916–19.
57 Department of State, Intelligence Report No. 7477, "Approaching Showdown in Jordan," 2 April 1957, M5618, Reel 3, SOAS Library.
58 On the development of events with regard to Jordan in the period 1955–7, see Podeh, *The Quest for Hegemony in the Arab World*, pp. 149–72, 224–6, 246. Seale, *The Struggle for Syria*, pp. 220–30, 264, 282. C. Johnston, *The Brink of Jordan* (London: 1972), pp. 34–74. See also Mohammed Heikal, *The Sphinx and the Commissar* (New York and London: Harper & Row, 1978), pp. 65–7. The Eisenhower Doctrine, which was announced in January 1957, will be discussed later on in the next chapter.
59 For instance, Hasan al-Hakim, the former Syrian Prime Minister published an article in *al-Hayat* on 14 January, in which he declared that the Arabs should side with the West on certain conditions: the settlement of the Arab's pending problems including the Palestine problem. Al-Hakim explained that neutralism was impossible for small weak nations like the Arab nation. In his view, India could allow itself to be neutralist because it was vast and strong, and neighbored Communist China. India, unlike the Arabs, possessed oil resources, for which the Soviets had many ambitions.
60 See Appendix I to Monthly Report No. F.14(2)/55 (16 February–15 March 1955) from Embassy of India, Cairo, File No. 23—R&I/55; and Monthly Report No. 14(2)/55 (16 April–15 May 1955), *idem*, NAI, New Delhi.
61 On the Syrian new government policy statement to the Parliament, see telegram 356 from British Embassy, Damascus, 21 September 1955, FO371/115950, VY1022/4. Following al-'Azm's failure to win the presidential elections of August 1955 (he was defeated by Shukri al-Quwatli), he resigned office as Foreign Minister on 18 August, and the Ba'th Party left 'Asali's government. On 6 September al-'Asali submitted his resignation. As for al-'Azm, soon after his defeat he had a heart attack and had to give up politics for a short period of time.
62 See the full texts of the pacts in: Khalil, *The Arab States and the Arab League*, Vol. II, pp. 242–5.
63 Monthly Report No. 14 (2)/55 (16 October–31 October, 1955) from Embassy of India, Cairo, File No. 23—R&I/55, NAI.
64 Department of State, Intelligence Report No. 7074, "The outlook for US interests in the Middle East," 14 November 1955, M5618, Reel 1, SOAS Library.
65 Department of State, Intelligence Report No. 7144, "Saudi Arabia: A Disruptive force in Western-Arab Relations," 18 January 1956, M5618, Reel 2, SOAS Library.
66 Seale, *The Struggle for Syria*, pp. 255–7.
67 Review of political events in Syria for the year 1955, in dispatch 16 from British Embassy, Damascus, FO371/121856, VY1011/1. Intelligence Report No. 7282, *ibid.*
68 See "Syria: Annual Review for 1956," in: letter (20256) from Gardener (former Ambassador to Damascus), London, to Selwyn Lloyd, the British Foreign Secretary, 13 November 1957, FO371/128219, VY1011/2. Sir Gardener was asked to leave Damascus on 2 November 1956 following the Syrian government's decision to break off diplomatic relations with Britain, because of its military action against Egypt.

69 Seale, *The Struggle for Syria*, pp. 258, 282.
70 Department of State, "Forces Shaping Syrian Policy," Intelligence Report No. 7595, 18 October 1957, Reel 2, M5618, SOAS Library.
71 Intelligence Report No. 7282.
72 See, Intelligence Reports No. 7282 and 7595 by the Department of State, 2 July 1956 and 18 October 1957, in OSS/State Department Intelligence and Research Reports, 12, the Middle East 1950–1961, Reel 2, M5618, SOAS Library. See also review of political events in Syria for the year 1955.
73 Review of political events in Syria for the year 1955, *ibid.*
74 Letter No. 2193/11/56 from British Embassy, Damascus, 24 March 1956, FO371/121860, VY1016/1.
75 Letter 2193/11/56. See also letter 2193/13/56 from British Consulate, Aleppo, 30 March 1956, FO371/121860, 6011 G.
76 See dispatch 59 from British Embassy, Damascus, 6 April 1956, FO371/121860, VY1016/2.
77 Dispatch 59.
78 Letter 1031/96/56 from British Embassy, Damascus, 3 April 1956, FO371/121862, VY1022/2.
79 See a detailed description and analysis of Shepilov's visit to Syria in dispatch 103 S. from John Gardener, Damascus, 27 June 1956, FO371/121867, VY10338/4.
80 Dispatch 103 S.
81 Dispatch 103 S.
82 Dispatch 103 S.
83 Department of State, "Syrian Vulnerability to Sino-Soviet Bloc Activities," Intelligence Report No. 7368, 1 November 1956, Reel 2, M5618, SOAS Library.
84 Intelligence Report No. 7368. Reports on the increase in the activities of the communist missions in Syria were also received by the Turkish Ministry of Foreign Affairs from its legation in Damascus. See letter 10613/41/56G from British Embassy, Ankara, 26 September 1956, FO371/121867, VY10338/8.
85 Intelligence Report No. 7368.
86 Intelligence Report No. 7368.
87 Intelligence Report No. 7368. See also "Syria: Annual Review for 1956". See also Letter No. 1074/10/57S from C. H. Johnston, British Embassy, Amman, 3 April 1957, FO371/128222, VY1015/42.
88 Dispatch 103 S.
89 Intelligence Report No. 7368.
90 On the visit and a copy of Chou En-Lai's letter, see letter 10625/12/56S from British Embassy, Damascus, 29 August 1956, FO371/121863, VY10310/3.
91 Letter 10625/12/56S.
92 See, "Syria: Annual Review for 1956."
93 Letter 1053/238/56 from British Embassy Damascus, 5 September 1956, FO371/121862, VY1022/8.
94 On the visit see dispatch 146S from Gardener, Damascus, 18 September 1956, FO371/121867, VY10338/7.
95 Dispatch 146S.

96 Dispatch 146S.
97 Dispatch 590 from Gardener, Damascus, 28 September 1956, FO371/121862, VY1022/12.
98 See dispatch 146S from Gardener, Damascus, 18 September 1956, FO371/121867, VY10338/7.
99 Dispatch 590.
100 Letter S10624/95/56 from British Embassy, Damascus, 9 October 1956, FO371/121867, VY10338/10.
101 Letter 10624/94/56 from British Embassy, Damascus, 6 October 1956, FO371/121867, VY10338/9.
102 Letter S10624/95/56.
103 "Syria: Annual Review for 1956.
104 Letter S10624/95/56.
105 Telegram 646 from Gardener, Damascus, 25 October 1956, FO371/121862, VY1022/15.
106 Telegram 646.
107 On the development of events in Hungary and their connection to the Suez crisis, see Laurent Rucker, "The Soviet Union and the Suez Crisis," in David Tal (ed.), *The 1956 War, Collusion and Rivalry in the Middle East* (London: Frank Cass, 2001), pp. 83–5.
108 On the Syrian press reaction to the events in Eastern Europe, see letter 10624/96/56 from British Embassy, Damascus, 27 October 1956.
109 Letter 10624/96/56.
110 See, "Syria: Annual Review for 1956."
111 See a full and thorough account on al-Quwatli's visit to Moscow in dispatch 246 from British Embassy, Moscow, 12 November 1956, FO371/121867, VY10338/20.
112 Dispatch 246.
113 Dispatch 246. An account of al-Quwatli's talks with the Soviet leaders is given by Heikal, *The Sphinx and the Commissar*, pp. 70–1.
114 Dispatch 246.
115 See telegram 203 from Foreign Office to certain British Representatives in the Middle East, 16 November 1956, FO371/121862.
116 Telegram 203.
117 On the Soviet threats throughout the crisis see documents No. 45–49, in Ro'i, *From Encroachment to Involvement*, pp. 182–99. See also Laurent Rucker, "The Soviet Union and the Suez Crisis," pp. 79–85.
118 Letter from British Embassy, Moscow, 7 December 1956, FO371/121867, VY10338/37.
119 See "Syria: Annual Review for 1956."
120 See record of their conversation in telegram 1362 from M. Wright, British Ambassador to Baghdad, 12 November 1956, FO371/121867, VY103338/17.
121 Telegram 1362.
122 Telegram 2063 from Foreign Office to British Embassy, Ankara, 14 November 1956, FO371/121867, VY10338/17G.
123 Telegram 2651 from Foreign Office to British Embassy, Baghdad, 14 November 1956, FO371/121867, VY10338/17G. See also a minute by E. M. Rose, Foreign Office, 14 November 1056, FO371/121867, VY10338/7

124 Letter 1061/23/56 from British Embassy, Moscow, 15 November 1956, FO371/121867, VY10338/23.
125 Letter 1061/23/56. Although British and American diplomats regarded the Turkish Air Attaché as not very reliable, they considered the above-mentioned information to be in line with the development of events in Soviet–Syrian relations.
126 See "Review of the International Situation: Syria," a paper prepared by the Soviet Section of the Foreign Office Research Department, attached to telegram 28 from Sir I. Mallet, Madrid, to Foreign Office, 15 February 1957, FO371/121867, VY10338/33(A).
127 See Intelligence report from T. Brimelow, Foreign Office, to Sir William Mayter, Moscow, 26 November 1956, FO371/121867, VY10338/32. Telegram 1251 from Middleton, British Embassy, Beirut, FO371/121867, VY10338/25. Telegram 2088 from Foreign Office to British Embassy, Moscow, FO371/121867. Telegram 215 C. Steel (NATO) to Foreign Office, 28 November 1956, FO371/121867, VY10338/29. Telegram 667 from Foreign Office to UK Permanent Delegation, Paris (NATO), 27 November 1956, FO371/121867. See also report on Soviet relations with Syria by the Foreign Office Research Department, Soviet Section, 6 December 1956, FO371/121867, VY10338/33.
128 See letter from the British Embassy, Moscow, to T. Brimelow, Northern Department Foreign Office, 7 December 1956, FO371/121867, VY10338/37.
129 See report of Colonel Marian Wałuchowski of the Polish Ministry of Foreign Trade on supplying arms to Syria, "w sprawie dostaw uzbrojenia przez P.R.L. do Syrii," AAN KC PZPR 2530, gP/0036, Warsaw.
130 See a full text of speech in FO371/128236, VY/1022/2.
131 Letter from the British Embassy, Moscow, to T. Brimelow, 7 December 1956.
132 See "Review of the International Situation: Syria," telegram 28.
133 "Review of the International Situation: Syria," telegram 28.
134 "Review of the International Situation: Syria," telegram 28.
135 See record of conversation in letter 1028/109/56 from British Embassy, Beirut, 10 December 1956, FO371/121862, VY1022/25.
136 Letter 1028/109/56.
137 Letter from F. G. K. Gallagher, Foreign Office, to Sir William Hayter, Moscow, FO371/121867, VY10338/32G.
138 Telegram 2541 from British Embassy, Washington, 24 December 1956, FO371/121867, VY10338/38.
139 On the new government and its composition see minute by E. M. Rose, Foreign Office, 1 January 1957, FO371/128220, VY1028/4.
140 "Note on Soviet Relations with Syria," FO371/121867, VY10338/33.

5 Syria's Rival Schools of Neutralism and the Road to Union

1 Letter 10217/9/57 "S" from I. D. Scott, British embassy, Beirut, 15 February 1957, FO371/128221, VY1015/20.
2 See the full text of Eisenhower's message to the Congress, in Khalil, *The Arab States and the Arab League*, Vol. II, pp. 909–15.
3 Letter 10217/9/57 "S".

4   Letter 10217/9/57 "S".
5   Ro'i, *From Encroachment to Involvement*, p. 227.
6   Letter 10217/9/57 "S".
7   Letter 10217/9/57 "S".
8   Letter 1074/10/57S from C. H. Johnston, British Embassy, Amman, 3 April 1957, FO371/128222, VY1015/42.
9   This information was given to the US ambassador to Damascus by Prime Minister 'Asali on 10 June during a conversation between them. See, telegram 26 from Johnston, British Embassy, Amman, 12 June 1957, FO371/128241, VY10338/3.
10 Letter 10717/67/57 "S" from I. D. Scott, British Embassy, Beirut, 28 June 1957, FO371/128241, VY10338/4.
11 Letter 10717/67/57 "S".
12 Ro'i, *From Encroachment to Involvement*, p. 228.
13 Ro'i, *From Encroachment to Involvement*, pp. 228–9.
14 The quotation was taken from Ro'i, *ibid.*, p. 230.
15 *Ibid.*, p. 232.
16 Telegram 866 from Scott, Beirut, 17 August 1957, FO371/128241, VY10338/8.
17 See a report on "Soviet–Syrian Relations" in dispatch 22 from T. E. Evans, British Embassy, Damascus, 22 July 1966, FO371/186904, EY103138/9.
18 See the US response to these allegations in Muhammad Khalil, *The Arab States and the Arab League, A Documentary Record* (Beirut: Khayats, 1962), p. 347. See also Salah al-Din's statement made in a press conference on 23 August, 1957, as quoted by *al-Ba'th* in *Nidal al-Ba'th*, Vol. III, pp. 287–91. *Al-Ra'i al-'Amm*, 15 and 16 August 1958. For a detailed discussion of US–Syrian relations at the time, see David W. Lesch, *Syria and the United States: Eisenhower's Cold War in the Middle East* (Boulder, CO: Westview Press, 1992), pp. 38–209.
19 On the changes of personals in the Syrian Chief of Staff, see *al-Ra'i al-'Amm*, 17 August 1957. See also Seale, *The Struggle for Syria*, pp. 291–6.
20 On Henderson's visit through Syrian's viewpoint, see *al-Ra'i al-'Amm*, 27 and 31 August 1957. See also Seale, *ibid.*, p. 296.
21 Letter 10217/71/57 "S" from British Embassy, Beirut, 10 September 1957, FO371/128228, VY1015/211.
22 *Al-Ra'i al-'Amm* is quoted in letter 10217/71/57"S".
23 See annex to letter 10217/71/57 "S".
24 Letter 10217/71/57 "S".
25 See "Weekly Economic and Commercial Report," annex to letter 10217/71/57 "S".
26 *Ulus* (Ankara), 3 September 1957, in letter 10212/44 "S" from British Embassy, Ankara, 6 September 1957, FO371/128226, VY1015/182.
27 See minute of report of Nemchina, Soviet ambassador to Syria, entitled, "ctenogramma soveshchaniya poslov v stranakh blizhnego I srednego vostoka," 8 October 1957, Fond 89, Opis' 17, Delo II. 1–18, Rossiskii goasudarstvennyi arkhiv sotsial'no- politicheskoi istorii, Moscow (hereafter cited as RGASPI-R.Ts.Kh.D.N.I).
28 "Ctenogramma soveshchaniya poslov v stranakh blizhnego I srednego vostoka," *ibid.*

29 See personal telegram No. T387/57 from Nehru to Macmillan, 18 September 1957, FO371/128230, VY1015/278.

30 Personal telegram No. T387/57.

31 Al-Bitar was quoted in "Weekly letter on Syria," No. 10217/79/57 "S" from British Embassy, Beirut, 24 September 1957, FO371/128229, VY1015/263.

32 "Weekly letter on Syria," No. 10217/79/57"S". On al-Bitar's anti-American statements, see al-Ra'i al-'Amm, 18 September 1957.

33 Al-Bizri was quoted in "Weekly letter on Syria," No. 10217/79/57 "S". See more on his anti-Western statements and declarations in favor of positive neutralism, in al-Ra'i al-'Amm, 14 and 17 September 1957.

34 President al-Quwatli was quoted in "Weekly letter on Syria," No. 10217/83/57 "S" from British Embassy, Beirut, 1 October 1957, FO371/128230, VY1015/297.

35 Al-Dawalibi was quoted in "Weekly letter on Syria," No. 10217/83/57 "S". See his speech of 28 September in Arab News Agency in Arabic, BBC, SWB, Part IV, The Arab World.

36 Bakdash was quoted in "Weekly letter on Syria," No. 10217/83/57 "S".

37 "Weekly letter on Syria," No. 10217/79/57 "S".

38 "Weekly letter on Syria," No. 10217/83/57 "S".

39 "Weekly letter on Syria," No. 10217/83/57 "S".

40 "Weekly letter on Syria," No. 10217/83/57 "S".

41 See Secret Report No. D5SYR.2421/6/57, "Sytuacja Syrii na Dzień 17.10.57" (The Situation in Syria 17/10/57), prepared by F. Mliczek, Polish Legation, Damascus, 19 October 1957, z. 12, w. 22, t. 538, AMSZ, pp. 1–4.

42 Report No. D5SYR.2421/6/57, ibid., pp. 4–6.

43 D5SYR.2421/6/57, ibid., pp. 7–8. On the arrival of Egyptian troops in Syria on 13 October 1957, and the Syrian and Egyptian press reaction to this development, see Voice of the Arabs (Cairo) and Radio Cairo, 14 October 1957, BBC, SWB, the Arab World, Part IV. Radio Damascus, 14 October 1957. See also al-Ahram and al-Jumhuriyya (Cairo), 15 October 1957. The Syrian press and politicians declared that the Egyptian troops came to defend Syria's independence. Radio Damascus declared that "in pursuance of the Joint Defense agreement between the Republic of Egypt and Syria, an implementation of the joint plans . . . the Egyptian armed forces began in mid-September to send basic elements to Syria for the purpose of augmenting Syria's forces and strengthening its defense potentialities". Radio Damascus, 13 October 1957. According to al-'Azm, the presence of Egyptian troops in Syria during "this delicate period through which Arab nationalism in Arab Syria is now passing has fostered our hopes and strengthened our belief that we are not alone in this respect . . . I believe that a unified Arab army will realize the aspirations of the Arab nation." See his speech at a Luncheon for the Egyptian Naval forces, in Radio Damascus, 16 October 1957.

44 See a copy of the full letter in Khalil, The Arab States and the Arab League, A Documentary Record, document No. 187, pp. 342–3. On Syria's complaint and al-Bitar's performance in the UN, see al-Ra'i al-'Amm, 18 and 31 October 1957.

45 See a full text of Gromyko's letter in Khalil, document No. 188, pp. 344–5.

46 See a full text of his statement in Khalil, document No. 189, pp. 345–6.
47 See a full text of his statement in Khalil, document No. 190, pp. 246–350.
48 Telegram 43 from D. P. Reilly, Moscow, 23 October 1957, FO371/128241, VY10338.
49 See weekly letters on Syria No. 10217/99/57 "S", 10217/102/57 "S" and 10217/106/57 "S" from British Embassy, Beirut, 14, 21 and 28 November 1957, FO371/128233, VY1015/356, VY1015/359 and VY1015/362.
50 See letter 10217/106/57 "S".
51 *Al-Ra'i al-'Amm* was quoted in weekly letter on Syria, No. 10217/111/57 "S", FO371/128233, VY1015/307.
52 Some studies have suggested that there was a communist conspiracy to takeover Syria. See, for instance, Ayyub Suhail, *al-Hizb al-Shuyu'i fi Suriyya wa Lubnan, 1922–58* (Beirut: Dar al-Nashr, 1959), pp. 180–1. Harris Jonathan, *Communist Strategy toward the "National Bourgeoisie" in Asia and the Middle East* (Michigan: University Microfilms, 1996), p. 275. Seale, although not clearly accepting the theory of communist conspiracy, writes: "By mid-1957 the communists came to believe that still further political advantage could be drawn from their great popularity with the public. Men were then flocking to the party less out of ideological conviction than because it was thought to represent, with Soviet support, the trend of the future. At the same time the confident bearing of the [communist] party leaders and the activities of the popular resistance forces led by Salah al-Bizri, the Chief of Staff's brother, seemed to suggest that the ground was being prepared for a classic bid for power." Quoted from Seale, *The Struggle for Syria*, p. 316. See similar but more detailed version in Gordon Torrey, *Syrian Politics and the Military, 1945–1958* (Ohio: Ohio State University Press, 1964), pp. 370–81. See also Muhammad Hasanain Haikal, *Ma alladhi Jara fi Suriyya* (Cairo: Dar al-Qawmiyya lil-taba'aha wa-al-Nashr, 1962).
53 See "Weekly letter on Syria," No. 10217/106/57 "S" from British Embassy, Beirut, 28 November 1957, FO371/128233, VY1015/362.
54 *Al-Ra'i al-'Amm* was quoted in letter 10217/99/57 "S".
55 Letter 10217/99/57 "S".
56 al-Hawrani, Kallas and al-'Asali were quoted in letter 10217/99/57 "S".
57 On his visit, see letter 10217/99/57 "S".
58 See "Stenogramma Soveshchaniya Poslov v Stranakh Blizhnego I Srednego Vostoka," 8 October 1957, *ibid.*
59 On the conference, see letter 10217/99/57 "S".
60 See letter 10217/102/57 "S".
61 See, "al-Wahda al-'Arabiyya dimanat al-Hiyad al-Ijabi," *al-Ba'th*, 13 December 1957.
62 See Monthly Report No. 14(2)/55 (16 April–15 May, 1955) from Embassy of India, Cairo, 19 May 1955, File No. 23—R&I/55, NAI.
63 Monthly Report (16 Apri–15 May, 1955), *ibid.* On the fact that Egypt favored and supported al-Quwatli *vis-à-vis* al-'Azm, see also the record of conversation between W. Pankowski, Polish Chargé d'Affaires to Cairo and 'Ali Sabri, Chief of the Office of Premier Nasser, in secret letter No. 2421/1/55 from W. Pankowski to Stanislaw Skrzeszewski, Minister of Foreign Affairs, Warsaw, z. 12, w. 6, t. 120, AMSZ.

64 On al-'Azm's visit to Moscow, see letter 10217/111/57 "S". See also weekly letter on Syria No. 10217/112/57 "S" from British Embassy, Beirut, 19 December 1957, FO371/128233, VY1015/372.
65 See quotation in letter 10217/111/57 "S".
66 Letter 10217/112/57 "S".
67 See a copy of the communiqué attached to telegram 1507 from British Embassy, Moscow, 21 December 1957, FO371/128241, VY10338/24.
68 Weekly letter on Syria No. 10217/114/57 "S" from British Embassy, Beirut, 23 December 1957, FO371/128233, VY1015/374.
69 Letter 10217/102/57 "S".
70 Letter 10217/102/57 "S".
71 See record of conversation with Jansen, in letter 10217/111/57 "S".
72 See record of conversation with Lalovic, in letter 10217/111/57 "S". See also letter 10611/421/57 from British Embassy, Beirut, to J. H. Lambert, British Embassy, Belgrade, 13 December 1957, FO371/134393, VY10392/1.
73 See telegram 631 from British Embassy, Washington, 13 December 1957, FO371/128233, VY1015.
74 Telegram 631, *ibid.*
75 See the record of the conversation between them in letter 10217/112/57 "S".
76 Letter 10217/112/57 "S".
77 See letter 10217/114/57 "S".
78 Ro'i, *From Encroachment to Involvement*, p. 204.
79 Khrushchev's words were uttered during his conversation in Moscow with the Prime Minister of Burma, on 3 December 1957. See quotation of his words in letter NS1072/123 from T. Brimelow, Levant Department, Foreign Office, London, 27 February 1958, FO371/134391, VY10338/3.
80 Elie Podeh, *The Decline of Arab Unity* (Brighton & Portland: Sussex Academic Press, 1999), pp. 44–5.

6 Nasserite "Positive Neutralism" and the United Arab Republic

1 Podeh, *The Decline of Arab Unity*, pp. 176–7.
2 *Ibid.*, pp. 36–42, 177–8.
3 See memorandum by the Polish Embassy in Cairo entitled (Polityka Polska na Bliskim Wschodzie [Polish policy in the Middle East]), 18 August 1958, z.12, w.7, t. 170, AMSZ.
4 On the communist factor and its role in bringing Egypt and Syria closer in late 1957 and early 1958, see the previous chapter. See also Podeh, *The Decline of Arab Unity*, pp. 34–48; Torrey, *Syrian Politics and the Military*, pp. 360–81.
5 Ismael, *The Communist Movement in Syria and Lebanon*, p. 50.
6 *Ibid.*
7 *Ibid.*
8 Department of State, Intelligence Report No. 7848, "Soviet–UAR Differences and Related Developments in Syria and Iraq," 22 October 1958, in OSS/State Department Intelligence and Research Reports, 12, The Middle East 1950–1961, Reel 2, M5618, SOAS Library.
9 Intelligence Report No. 7848, "Soviet–UAR Differences and Related Developments in Syria and Iraq."

10 The new communist international journal.

11 Intelligence Report No. 7848, by the Department of State, 22 October 1958.

12 *Ibid.*

13 On Nasser's visit, see: Department of State, Intelligence Report No. 7738, "UAR President Nasser's Trip to the USSR," 16 June 1958, in *ibid.* Department of State, Intelligence Report No. 7848, "Soviet–UAR Differences and Related Developments in Syria and Iraq," 22 October 1958, Reel 2, M5618, SOAS Library.

14 See: Dispatch 105 from D. P. Reilly, British Embassy, Moscow, 24 May 1958, FO371/131336, JE10338/26.

15 Dispatch 105, *ibid.*

16 Intelligence Report No. 7848 by the Department of State, 22 October 1958.

17 "Polish Policy in the Middle East," z. 12, w. 7, t. 170, AMSZ.

18 *Ibid.*

19 *Ibid.*

20 Intelligence Report No. 7848.

21 On this regard, see Podeh, *The Decline of Arab Unity*, pp. 60–4.

22 Department of State, Intelligence Report No. 7961, "Nasir and the Pan-Arab Conflict with Communism," 2 March 1959, Reel 3, M5618.

23 Intelligence Report No. 7961.

24 Intelligence Report No. 7848.

25 Department of State, Intelligence Report No. 7851, "The Kurdish Problem and its Implications for Future Trends in Iraq," 22 October 1958, *ibid.*, Reel 3.

26 *Ibid.*

27 *Ibid.*

28 See the record of conversation between Mukhitdinov and Nasser in Intelligence Report No. 7848, by the Department of State, 22 October 1958.

29 *Al-Akhbar* (Beirut), 14 December 1958.

30 See more on Bakdash's speech in: *The Times* (London), 17 March 1959.

31 Intelligence Report No. 7961.

32 Intelligence Report No. 7961.

33 Department of State, Intelligence Report No. 7921, "Iraq: The Crisis in Leadership and the Communist Advance," 16 January 1959, Reel 3, M5618, SOAS Library.

34 Intelligence Report No. 7848.

35 *Izvestiia* (Moscow), 1 January 1959. See further attacks on Nasser and his confidant Hasanain Haykal, in *Pravda* (Moscow), 19 February 1959.

36 See the content of Khrushchev's speech in Intelligence Report No. 7961. See also Central Intelligence Agency (CIA) report SC No. 00618/61A, "The Soviet Union and Egypt," 8 May 1964, Reel 2, M5617.

37 Department of State, Intelligence Report No. 7979, "Soviet–UAR Relations since the Iraqi Coup Attempt (March 8, 1959)," 24 March 1959, Reel 3, M5618, SOAS Library.

38 On the Shawwaf revolt, see Uriel Dann, *Iraq Under Qassem* (Jerusalem: Israel University Press, 1969), pp. 164–77.

39 See the content of Nasser's speech in Intelligence Report No. 7979.

40 Letter 10342/26/3 from Patrick Reilly, British Embassy, Moscow, 26 March 1959, FO371/141914, VG10338/3.
41 "Polish Policy in the Middle East, z. 12, w. 7, t. 170, AMSZ.
42 *The Sunday Times*, Magazine Section, 17 June 1962.
43 Intelligence Report No. 7961.
44 Ro'i, *From Encroachment to Involvement*, pp. 258–9.
45 Intelligence Report No. 7961.
46 Letter 10620/3/9/59 from British Embassy, Washington, 13 May 1959, FO371/141898, VG1016/7. See also "Review of Development in the UAR in 1959" by C. T. Crowe, British Diplomatic Mission, Cairo, 31 January 1960, FO371/15896, VG1011/1.
47 "Review of Development in the UAR in 1959," *ibid*.
48 Intelligence Report No. 7961.
49 See report No. Nr. 242/6/59/TpvDV ZRA 2421/13/59 by Władysław Domagała, Polish Consulate General, Damascus, Kilka uwag natemat aktualnej polityki Nassera w stosunku do prowincji syryjskiej ZRA," 28 May 1959, z 12 w 44 t 1089, AMSZ. On the deterioration of relations between Nasser and his former Ba'thist allies, see "O sytuacji w prowincji syryjskiej ZRA" (Information Note on the situation in the Syrian Province of the UAR), by the Polish Ministry of the Interior, Warsaw, 10 March 1960, z 12, w 44, t 1097, AMSZ. See also report No. 221/13/60 Tjn, Dep V ZRA 2421/23/60, by Władysław Domagała, Damascus, "Kilka uwag na temat aktualnej sytuacji gospodarczej i politycznej w prowincji połnocnej ZRA," 16 July 1960, z 12, w 44, t. 1097, AMSZ.
50 See report No. 221/7/60/tin, 2421/8/60 concerning Nasser's visit to the Syrian province of the UAR, by Władysław Domagała, Damascus, "dot. poby tu Nassera w prowincji syryjskiej ZRA," 17 March 1960, z. 12, w. 44, t. 1097, AMSZ. On the rise of Sarraj and the role he played in the Syrian province, see Podeh, *The Decline of Arab Unity*, pp. 126–9.
51 On "Amir's visit, see dispatch 66 from Sir F. Roberts, British Embassy, Moscow, 14 December 1960, FO371/150917, VG10338/6. Letter 10312/60 from British Diplomatic Mission, Cairo, 20 December 1960, FO371/158799, VG103138/1.
52 Central Intelligence Agency (CIA) report SC No. 00618/61A, "The Soviet Union and Egypt," 8 May 1964, Reel 2, M5617.
53 *Ibid.*
54 See quotation in Rami Ginat, *Egypt's Incomplete Revolution: Lutfi al-Khuli and Nasser's Socialism in the 1960s* (London: Frank Cass, 1997), p. 41.
55 *Ibid.*
56 *Ibid.*, pp. 40–1.
57 See record of Nasser–Ford's conversation in telegram 329 from R. A. D. Ford, Canadian ambassador, Cairo, 12 June 1961, in FO371/158800, VG103138/32.
58 Telegram 329, *ibid.*
59 Telegram 329, *ibid.* One of the African countries in which both Egypt and the USSR were vying for influence was Guinea led by Sékou Touré. Nasser, according to 'Ali Sabri, had convinced the Guinean leader to put an end to the infiltration of communists and communism to the Guinean government and

administration. He also persuaded Sékou Touré to follow the policy of non-alignment. See more on the Soviet–UAR crisis in record of conversation between Ford and 'Ali Sabri took place in Cairo on 23 June, in telegram 353 from Ford, Cairo, 23 June 1961, FO371/158800, VG103138/34.
60 Telegram 343 from Ford, Cairo, 16 June 1961, in FO371/158800, VG103138/32. See also similar analysis made at a speech of the Turkish representative at the meeting of the CENTO on 15 June 1961, in letter 22590/45, from British Embassy, Ankara, 16 June 1961, FO371/158800, VG103138/28.
61 Letter 22590/45, *ibid.*
62 Letter No. POL. 499/72/1 from C. M. Anderson, Office of the High Commissioner for the UK, New Delhi, 25 August 1959, FO371/153402.
63 On Sukarno's visit and the joint communiqué published at the end of the visit, see telegram 24 from British Diplomatic Mission, Cairo, 28 April 1960, FO371/150920, VG10362/2.
64 On Nasser's visit, see dispatch 63 from British Embassy, Belgrade, 29 June 1960, FO371/141918, RY10316/3.
65 On the ambassadors conversation of 28 June, see dispatch 63.
66 See the full text of the communiqué in *Borba* (Belgrade), 21 June 1960.
67 On Kardelj's visit, see letter 1038/60 from British Diplomatic Mission, Cairo, 23 December 1960, FO371/141918, RY10316/5 (c). See also Ginat, *Egypt's Incomplete Revolution*, p. 16.
68 On the Nasser's shift to socialism and the origins of his socio-economic ideology, particularly the Yugoslav influence, see Ginat, *Egypt's Incomplete Revolution,* pp. 68–9, 132–60.
69 On Tito's visit, see dispatch 42 from British Embassy, Cairo, 25 April 1961, FO371/160837, CY103116/2.
70 Central Intelligence Agency, Office of Current Intelligence, memorandum entitled "The Nonaligned Nations Conference," 7 August 1961, CIA Research Reports: Middle East, 1946–1976, M5617, Reel 2.
71 *Al-Ahram* (Cairo), 5 May 1961.
72 Letter 10717/61 from British Embassy, Cairo, 13 May 1961, FO371/158874, VG2231/6.
73 *Al-Akhbar* (Cairo), 13 May 1961.
74 Letter 10717/61, *ibid.* CIA, "The Nonaligned Nations Conference," *ibid.*
75 CIA, "The Nonaligned Nations Conference," *ibid.*
76 D. N. Mallik, "Belgrade New Phase," in Karunakaran, *Outside the Contest*, p. 189.
77 Both are quoted in Karunakaran, *ibid.*
78 Sukarno is quoted in Mohamad El Sayed Selim, *Non-Alignment in a Changing World* (Cairo: The American University of Cairo, 1983), p. 25.
79 Kimche, *The Afro-Asian Movement*, p. 224.
80 Bimal Prasad, "The Evolution of Non-alignment," in Uma Vasudev (ed.), *Issues before Non-Alignment Past & Future* (New Delhi: Indian Council of World Affairs, 1983), p. 41.
81 *Ibid.*, pp. 41–2.
82 On the shift toward socialism, see Ginat, *Egypt's Incomplete Revolution*; *ibid.*
83 See, e.g., Dispatch 537 from British Embassy, Cairo, 3 August 1961, FO371/158822, VG1102/83.

84　On Nasser's route to socialism, see: Ginat, *Egypt's Incomplete Revolution*, chapters 1–3, 8–10.

85　On the Soviet view of the July 1961 Laws, see record of conversation between R. A. Ford and Vladimir Erofeev, the Soviet Ambassador in Cairo, in Dispatch 537 from British Embassy, Cairo, 3 August 1961, FO371/158822, VG1102/83.

86　On Nasser's Arab Socialism—its ideological sources and theoretical tenets, the differences between it and Marxism–communism—see Rami Ginat, *Egypt's Incomplete Revolution*, pp. 9–29, 35–40.

87　In his analysis of the reasons for the break-up of the UAR, Podeh divided them into four groups: political errors committed by Egypt; ideological factors; external factors; and socioeconomic factors. See Podeh, *The Decline of Arab Unity*, pp. 179–90.

88　Rabinovich, *Syria Under the Ba'th*, pp. 18–20. See also Podeh, *The Decline of Arab Unity*, pp. 178–9.

Conclusion: The Rise of the Neo-Ba'th and the Gradual Demise of Neutralism

1　On the Syrian political scene in the period 1961–1963, see Devlin, *The Ba'th Party: A History from its Origins to 1966*, pp. 195–202. Rabinovich, *Syria Under the Ba'th*, pp. 26–48. Eliezer Be'eri, *Army Officers in Arab Politics and Society* (Jerusalem: Israel University Press, 1969), pp. 141–51. Yaacov Bar-Siman-Tov, *Linkage Politics in the Middle East: Syria between Domestic and External Conflict, 1961–1970* (Boulder, CO: Westview Press, 1983). Akram al-Hawrani, *Mudhakkirat Akram al-Hawrani* (Cairo: Maktabat Madbuli, 1999).

2　Ro'i, *From Encroachment to Involvement*, p. 359.

3　al-'Azma is quoted in Ro'i, *ibid.*, p. 360.

4　Parts of the information related to footnotes 4–26 is based on my article "The Soviet Union and the Syrian Ba'th Regime: From Hesitation to Rapprochement," *Middle Eastern Studies*, Vol. 36, No. 2 (2000), pp. 150–71, and includes some additions to the original. See also "Syria: Annual Review for 1963," by T. E. Bromley, British Embassy, Damascus, 8 January 1964, FO371/175857, EY1011/1. See more specifically on the coup: the Cairo talks and the Tripartite Charter, and the development of events in Syria at the time, in Rabinovich, *Syria Under the Ba'th, 1963–66*, pp. 43–74. Devlin, *The Ba'th Party A History from its Origins to 1966*, pp. 236–51. Munif al-Razzaz, *Al-Tajrriba al-Murra* (Beirut: Dar-Ghandur, 1967), pp. 89–98. Kamel S. Abu Jaber, *The Arab Ba'th Socialist Party* (New York: Syracuse University Press, 1966), pp. 67–74. Yasin al-Hafiz (ed.), *Fi al-Fikr al-Siyasi* (Damascus: Dar al-Dimashq, 1963), pp. 203–8. Be'eri, *Army Officers in Arab Politics and Society*, pp. 150–6. Malcolm Kerr, *The Arab Cold War, 1958–1964* (London, New York: Oxford University Press, 1965), pp. 56–101. Patrick Seale, *Asad of Syria* (Tel Aviv: Ma'rkhot, 1988), pp. 83–95 [Hebrew]. Elie Podeh, "To Unite or Not Unite That is Not the Question: The 1963 Tripartite Unity Talks Reassessed," *Middle Eastern Studies*, Vol. 39, No. 1 (2003), pp. 150–85.

5　"Syria: Annual Review for 1963," *ibid*. On the relations between the Iraqi and

Syrian Ba'th until the overthrown of the Iraqi Ba'th regime, see Abu Jaber, *The Arab Ba'th Socialist Party*, pp. 75–95.

6 *Ibid.* On the revision of the Ba'th ideology, see Rabinovich, *Syria Under the Ba'th*, pp. 84–91. Yaacov Ro'i, *From Encroachment to Involvement*, p. 400.

7 Amin al-Hafiz attended two Arab conferences (in January and September) as well as the conference of the non-aligned countries (October 1964). His participation in these conferences as Syria's head of state could be considered as an Arab, including Egyptian, de facto recognition of the Ba'th regime. Diplomatic relations with countries such as Algeria, Tunisia, Jordan, Lebanon, Saudi Arabia and Kuwait were improved during the year. See "Syria: Annual Review for 1964," *ibid.*

8 Relations with the conservative regimes of Jordan and Saudi Arabia were good. Tunisia's attitude toward Israel led to the severance of relations with Syria. The overthrow in Algeria of Ben-Bella—Nasser's ally—led temporarily to deterioration in relations between the two countries. The Syrians seized that opportunity to improve relations with Algeria in order to limit Nasser's influence. See "Syria: Annual Review for 1965," *ibid.*

9 See "Syria Annual Review for 1964," *ibid.*, and "Syria Annual Review for 1965," *ibid.*

10 See excerpt from "Ba'd al-Muntalaqat al-Nazariyya," quoted in Rabinovich, *Syria Under the Ba'th*, p. 245.

11 See excerpt from *"Ba'd al-muntalaqat al-nazariyya"*—the ideological report approved by the Sixth Congress, and quoted in Rabinovich, *Syria Under the Ba'th*, p. 253.

12 *Ibid.*, p. 255. It is noteworthy that the bulk of these ideas had been executed by the outset of 1965.

13 "Syria: Annual Review for 1964," *ibid.* See also Ziad Keilany, "Socialism and Economic Change in Syria," *Middle Eastern Studies*, Vol. 9, No. 1 (1973), pp. 67–9.

14 See *Radio Damascus*, 23 February 1966. See also dispatch 8 from T. E. Evans, Damascus, FO371/186896, EY1015/21. "al-Mu'tamar ta'bir 'an Iradat al-Qa'ida," *al-Ba'th* (Damascus), 28 February 1966. "Dawafi' Ta'ammur al-Quwan al-Mu'adiniyya," *al-Ba'th* (Damascus), 4 March 1966.

15 Dispatch 8, *ibid.* See also Rabinovich, *Syria Under the Ba'th*, p. 203.

16 See letter from W. Morris, FO, to T. E. Evans, British Embassy, Damascus, 9 March 1966, FO371/186896, EY1015/11.

17 See a report on "Soviet–Syrian Relations" in dispatch 22 from T. E. Evans, British Embassy, Damascus, 22 July 1966, FO371/186904, EY103138/9.

18 Ro'i, *From Encroachment to Involvement*, p. 419.

19 Dispatch 22, EY103138/9, FO371/186904, *ibid.* See also minute by W. Morris, FO, 4 May 1966, FO371/186899, EY1017/2. Minute by Roger Allen, FO, 6 May 1966, FO371/186899, EY1017/2. "Top Arab Communist Returns Home," *The Scotsman*, 6 May 1966.

20 *Ibid.*

21 Letter 1011/66, FO371/186897, EY1015/42, *ibid.* "Danger of class and confessional war in Syria" was one of the many headlines which dominated the Lebanese press of September 1966. The reports dealt with the increasing chaos in Syria and described and analyzed the struggle for survival of the new Ba'th

regime dominated by military officers of 'Alawi minority origin. See *The Guardian*, 12 September 1966. See also *The Times*, 10 September 1966.

22 See on this subject, Ginat, *Egypt's Incomplete Revolution,* pp. 15–29, 40–5, 58, 182–3.

23 See dispatch 22, FO371/186904, EY103138/9, *ibid.* Minute by W. Morris, FO, 23 August 1966, FO371/186904, EY103138/9.

24 See the joint Soviet–Syrian communiqué entitled: "In the Interests of Strengthening Peace and Mutual Cooperation," *Pravda*, 26 April 1966.

25 On *wahdat al-hadaf*, see in detail, Ginat, *Egypt's Incomplete* Revolution, pp. 84–5. On "the meeting point of the revolutions," see Salah al-Jadid's words in *al-Ba'th* (Damascus), 26 November 1966. Avraham Sela, *Unity Within Conflict in the Inter-Arab System* (Jerusalem: Magnes Press, 1983), pp. 3–63 [Hebrew]. Albert Sudai, "From the Rank's Unity to the Meeting Point of Revolutions," in Shimon Shamir (ed.), *The Decline of Nasserism 1965–1970* (Tel Aviv: Mif'alim Universitayim, 1978), pp. 253–68 [Hebrew].

26 On the Road to the June 1967 War and its aftermath from Syria's viewpoint, see Ma'oz, *Syria and Israel*, pp. 79–111.

27 Ro'i, *From Encroachment to Involvement*, pp. 490–1.

28 On this subject see, for instance, Ephraim Karsh, "Marriage of Comfort: The Soviet Union and Syria," in: Avner Yaniv, Moshe Ma'oz and Avi Kober (eds.), *Syria and Israel's National Security* (Tel Aviv: Ministry of Defense Publishing House, 1991), p. 254 [Hebrew]. On Soviet–Syrian relations during Hafiz al-Asad's period in power, see Ephraim Karsh, *The Soviet Union and Syria: The Asad Years* (London: Royal Institute of International Affairs, Routledge, 1988). On Hafiz al-Asad's period in power, see Eyal Ziser, *Asad's Legacy: Syria in Transition* (New York: New York University Press, 2001).

29 See more on Gorbachev's Middle-Eastern policy in Talal Nizameddin, *Russia and the Middle East Towards a New Foreign Policy* (London: Hurst & Co., 1999), pp. 44–70.

30 Nizameddin, *Russia and the Middle East*, pp. 179–80.

Bibliography

Primary Sources

I ARCHIVES (unpublished and official)

GREAT BRITAIN

Public Record Office, London
Foreign Office:
FO141—Embassy and Consular Archives, Egypt: Correspondence.
FO371—Political Correspondence of the Foreign Office.
FO501—Confidential Print Syria, 1947–1956.
FO1018—Embassy, Consulate and Legation, Lebanon Central Correspondence,
    1946–1968.

Library of London School of Economics and Political Science, London
US Declassified Documents Reference System, US, 1975, 1976, 1978, 1979, 1986

Library of School of Oriental and Asian Studies (SOAS), London
Confidential US State Department Files:
Syria, 1950–1954 (M5680).
Egypt, 1955–1959 (M5812).
Saudi Arabia, 1945–1949 (M5681), 1950–1954 (M5682), 1955–1959 (M5834).
Lebanon, 1945–1949 (M5683), 1950–1954 (M5684).
Iraq, 1945–1949 (M5685), 1950–1954 (M5686).
US Central Intelligence Reports: Middle East, 1946–1976 (M5617).
OSS/State Department Intelligence and Research Reports, 12, The Middle East,
    1950–1961 (M5618).
OSS/State Department Intelligence and Research Reports, 7, The Middle East
    (M5619).

INDIA

Department of Archives, Government of Maharashtra, Mumbai
Political Department Files "P" & S, 1922–1930.
Political and Services Department, S.32/39–A, S.131/19223–B, S.131/18698–B and
    S.131/8307–B.

National Archives of India, Janpath, New Delhi
Ministry of External Affairs, 1946–1955.

Nehru Memorial Museum & Library, Teen Mutri House, New Delhi
Selected Works of Jawaharlal Nehru, 1941–1955.

Library of Indian Council of World Affairs. Sapru House, New Delhi
Documents and Protocols of the meetings of the Afro-Asian and Non-Aligned
    Movements, 1954–1970.

ISRAEL

Israel State Archives, Jerusalem
Records of Israel Foreign Ministry.

Archive of the Dayan Center, Tel Aviv University.

Library of the Hebrew University, Jerusalem.

POLAND

Arkhivum Ministerstva Sprav Zagranitshnykh, Warsaw (AMSZ)
Documents of the Polish Foreign Ministry—Damascus and Cairo.

RUSSIAN FEDERATION—(FORMER SOVIET UNION)

Rossiiskii goasudarstvennyi arkhiv noveishei istorii—RGANI-Ts.Kh.S.D, Moscow
Documents of the Communist Party of the USSR.

Rossiiskii goasudarstvennyi arkhiv sotsial'no-politichskoi istorii RGASPI-R.Ts.Kh.D.N.I., Moscow
Documents of the Soviet foreign Ministry—Damascus and Cairo.

UNITED STATES

Dwight D. Eisenhower Library, Abilene, Kansas
Dulles, John Foster, Papers, 1951–1959.
Eisenhower, Dwight D., Papers as President of the USA 1953–1961:
Cabinet series, Diaries series, Dulles-Herter series, International Cabinet series,
    International Meetings series, National Security Council series.
Eisenhower, Dwight D., Records as President, White House Central Files:
    Confidential Files, General File, Official File.
White House Office: National Security Council Staff: Papers 1948–1961.
Papers of Clarence Francis, 1933–1973.

National Archives, Washington DC
General Records of the Department of State, RG 59.
R & A Reports.
Records of Charles Bohlen, 1942–1952.
Records of the Joint Chiefs of Staff, RG 218.
Records of the National Security Council, RG 273.
Records of the Policy Planning Staff, 1947–1953.

Princeton University, Princeton, New Jersey
John Foster Dulles Papers.

Harry S. Truman Library, Independence, Missouri
Papers of Dean G. Acheson.
Papers of George McGhee.
Truman, Harry S. Papers as President of the USA, National Security Council Files, 1947–1953.
Truman, Harry S. Papers as President of the USA, President's Secretary's Files, 1945–1953: Intelligence File, Subject File, National Security Council— Meetings, White House File.

Washington National Records Center, Suitland, Maryland
Foreign Office Posts of the Department of State, RG 84.

II OFFICIAL PUBLISHED MATERIAL

Foreign Relations of the United States, Diplomatic Papers, 1944. Vol. 5. Washington: US Government Printing Office, 1967.
Foreign Relations of the United States, Diplomatic Papers, The Berlin Conference, Vol. 1. Washington: US Government Printing Office, 1955.
United Nations Security Council, Official Records, 1st Year, 1st series, No.1, 21st Meeting.
"Tripartite Declaration regarding Security in the Near East," *Department of State Bulletin*, XXII, 5 June 1950.
US Department of State, *Foreign Relations of the United States, 1947–1955*. Washington D.C.: Government Printing Office, 1971–1989.
Watson, R. J. *History of the Joint Chiefs of Staff*, Vol. V. Washington D.C.: Historical Division Joint Chiefs of Staff, 1986.

III NEWSPAPERS, JOURNALS AND MONITORING SERVICES

Arabic Syria—*al-'Alam, al-Ayyam, al-Ba'th, al-Balad, al-Barada, al-Fayha', al-Insha', al-Ishtirakiyya, al-Jil al-Jadid, al-Jumhur, al-Kifah, al-Manar, al-Masa', al-Nasr, al-Qabas, al-Ra'i al-'Amm, al-Salam, al-Sha'b, al-Shabab, al-Tali'a.* Egypt—*al-Ahram, al-Akhbar, al-Jumhuriyya, al-Misri, al-Musawwar, Akhir Sa'ah.* Lebanon—*al-Akhbar, al-Anba', al-Hadaf, al-Hayat, al-Jarida, al-Nur, Sawt al-Sha'b.*

Other Languages *Summary of World Broadcast* (The USSR, Eastern Europe, Egypt and the Arab World), British Broadcasting Corporation, Written Archives Centre, Reading. *The Bharat Jyoti* (Bombay), *The Burman* (Rangoon), *Borba* (Belgrade), *Izvestiia* (Moscow), *Jhoghovourti Tzain* (Beirut), *Nova Makedonija, L'Orient* (Beirut), *Pravda* (Moscow), *Review of International affairs* (Belgrade), *The Guardian* (London), *The Nation* (Rangoon), *The Pilot* (New Delhi), *People's Struggle* (Beirut), *The Observer* (London), *The Sunday Times* (London), *The Times* (London), *Trud* (Moscow), *Ulus* (Ankara).

Primary and Secondary Published Sources

Abu Jaber, Kamel S. *The Arab Ba'th Socialist Party.* New York: Syracuse University Press, 1966.

Afonin, M. "Vdokhnoviteli I ispolniteli," *Pravda,* 31 March 1955.

'Aflak, Michel. *Choice of Texts from the Ba'th Party Founder's Thought.* Firenze: Cooperation Lavoratori, 1977.

———. *Fi Sabil al-Ba'th.* Beirut: Dar al-Tali'a, 1963.

———. *Ma'rakat al-Masir al-Wahid.* Beirut: Dar al-Adab, 1963.

———. *Mukhtarat min aqwal mu'assis al-Ba'th.* Beirut: al-Mu'assasa al-'Arabiyya lil-Dirasat, 1975.

"al-Mu'tamar ta'bir 'an Iradat al-Qa'ida," *al-Ba'th* (Damascus), 28 February 1966.

"al-Wahda al-'Arabiyya dimanat al-Hiyad al-Ijabi," *al-Ba'th,* 13 December 1957.

Allen, Richard. *Imperialism and Nationalism in the Fertile Crescent* (London, New York: Oxford University Press, 1974),

'Atiyyallah, Ahmad. *al-Qamus al-Siyasi.* Beirut: Dar al-Nahda al-'Arabiyya, 1980.

'Azm, Khalid al-. *Mudhakkirat Khalid al-'Azm,* Vol. I–III. Beirut: al-Dar al-Mutaharir lil-nashr, 1973.

Bakdash, Khalid. *Khalid Bakdash, Kalimat, ahadith, maqalat, 1974–1984.* Damascus: Dar al-Tali'a al-Jadida, 1997.

———. *Khalid Bakdash, Kalimat, ahadith, maqalat, 1984–1994.* Damascus: Dar al-Tali'a al-Jadida, 1994.

———. "For the Successful Struggle for Peace, National Independence, and Democracy We Must Resolutely Turn toward the Workers and the Peasants," *Middle East Journal,* Vol. 7, No. 2 (Spring 1953).

Banerjee, Malabika. *The Nonaligned Movement.* Calcutta: Firma KLM Private Limited, 1982.

Bar-Siman-Tov, Yaacov. *Linkage Politics in the Middle East: Syria Between Domestic and External Conflict, 1961–1970.* Boulder, CO: Westview Press, 1983.

Bashear, Suliman. *Communism in the Arab East, 1918–1928.* London: Ithaca Press, 1980.

Be'eri, Eliezer. *Army Officers in Arab Politics and Society.* Jerusalem: Israel University Press, 1969.

Bialer, Uri. *Between East and West, Israel's Foreign Policy Orientation 1948–1956.* Cambridge: Cambridge University Press, 1990.

Bitar, Salah al-Din al- and 'Aflaq, Michel. *al-Ba'th wa-al-hizb al-Shuyu'i.* Damascus: 1944.

Black, Cyril E., Falk Richard A., Knorr Klaus and Young Oran R. *Neutralization and World Politics.* Princeton, NJ: Princeton University Press, 1968.

Bogoslovskii, V. "Proiski imperialistov na Blizhnem Vostoke," *Trud,* 30 March 1955.

Brecher, Michael. *Nehru: A Political Biography.* London: Oxford University Press, 1969.

———. *The New States of Asia: A Political Analysis.* London: Oxford University Press, 1964.

———. *The Foreign Policy System of Israel.* London: Oxford University Press, 1972.

"The constitution of the Arab Resurrection," *The Middle East Journal,* Vol. 13, No. 2, Spring 1959, pp. 195–200.

Dallin, David. *Soviet Foreign Policy after Stalin* (Philadelphia: Lippincott, 1961).

Damodaran, A. K. *Jawaharlal Nehru: A Communicator and Democratic Leader.* New Delhi: Sangam Books, 1997.

Dann, Uriel. *Iraq Under Qassem.* Jerusalem: Israel University Press, 1969.

—— (ed.). *The Great Powers in the Middle East 1919–1939.* London, New York: Holmes & Meier, 1988.

——. *King Hussein and the Challenge of Arab Radicalism, Jordan, 1955–1967.* New York and Oxford: Oxford University Press, 1989.

"Dawafi' Ta'ammur al-Quwan al-Mu'adiniyya," *al-Ba'th* (Damascus), 4 March 1966.

Devlin, John F. *The Ba'th Party A History from its Origin to 1966.* Stanford: Hoover Institution, 1976.

El Sayed Selim, Mohamad. *Non-Alignment in a Changing World.* Cairo: The American University of Cairo, 1983.

Erlich, Haggai. *Introduction to the Modern History of the Middle East,* Vol. V. Tel Aviv: Open University Press, 1989.

Fromkin, David. *A Peace to end all Peace, Creating the Modern Middle East 1914–1922.* Tel Aviv: Dvir, 1994 [Hebrew].

Ghalib, Kiyyali. *Nazariyyat al-Thaura fi al-'Alam al-Thalith.* Beirut: Mu'asasat al-Ibhath al-'Alamiyya al-'Arabiyya al-'Ulya, 1973.

Ginat, Rami. "British Concoction or Bilateral Decision?: Revisiting the Genesis of Soviet–Egyptian Diplomatic Relations," *International Journal of Middle East Studies,* Vol. 31 (1999), pp. 39–60.

——. "Nasser and the Soviets: A Reassessment," in Elie Podeh and Onn Winckler (eds.), *Rethinking Nasserism: Revolution and Historical Memory in Modern Egypt.* Gainesville: University Press of Florida, 2004, pp. 230–50.

——. "The Egyptian Left and the Roots of Neutralism in pre-Nasserite Era," *British Journal of Middle Eastern Studies,* Vol. 30, No. 1 (2003), pp. 5–24.

——. "The Origins of the Czech-Egyptian Arms Deal: A Reappraisal," in David Tal (ed.), *The 1956 War, Collusion and Rivalry in the Middle East.* London: Frank Cass, 2001, pp. 145–67.

——. "The Soviet Union and the Syrian Ba'th Regime: From Hesitation to Rapprochement," *Middle Eastern Studies,* Vol. 36, No. 2 (2000), pp. 150–71.

——. *The Soviet Union and Egypt, 1945–55.* London: Frank Cass, 1993.

Gould, Julios and Kolb William L. (eds.). *A Dictionary of the Social Sciences.* London: Tavistock, 1964.

Hafiz, Yasin al- (ed.). *Fi al-Fikr al-Siyasi.* Damascus: Dar al-Dimashq, 1963.

Haikal, Muhammad Hasanain. *Milaffat al-Suways.* Cairo: Markaz al-Ahram, 1986.

——. *Ma alladhi Jara fi Suriyya.* Cairo: Dar al-Qawmiyya lil-taba'aha wa-al-Nashr, 1962.

Hamrush, Ahmad. *Qissat Thawrat 23 Yuliyu,* Vol. 1. Cairo: Maktabat Madbuli, 1983.

Hann, P. L. *Strategy and Diplomacy in the Early Cold War: United States Policy toward Egypt, 1945–1956.* Unpublished Ph.D. dissertation, Vanderbilt University, 1987.

Harris, Jonathan. *Communist Strategy toward the "National Bourgeoisie" in Asia and the Middle East.* Michigan: University Microfilms, 1996.

Hawrani, Akram al-. *Mudhakkirat Akram al-Hawrani*. Cairo: Maktabat Madbuli, 1999.

Heikal, Mohamed. *Nasser: The Cairo Documents*. London: New English Library, 1973.

——. *The Sphinx and the Commissar*. New York and London: Harper & Row, Publishers, 1978.

Hizb al-Ba'th al-'Arabi, "Ra'y al-Hizb fi al-itifaq al-Britani—al-Faransi," in *Nidal al-Ba'th*, Vol. I. Beirut: Dar al-Tali'a, 1963.

Hizb al-Ba'th al-'Arabi al-Ishtiraki. *Nidal al-Ba'th*, Vol. II. Beirut: Dar al-Tali'a, 1963.

——. *Nidal al- Ba'th*, Vol. III. Beirut: Dar al-Tali'a, 1964.

Hizb al-Ba'th al-'Arabi, "al-Sha'b al-'Arabi Yuridu Hiyadan Haqiqiyyan min al-Sira' baina al-Mu'askarin wa-yahdhiru al-Jami'a al-'Arabiyya min al-Indimam ila al-Kutla al-Gharbiyya al-'Isti'amariyya," 25 January 1951, Reel 3 M5680, SOAS Library.

Hourani, Albert. *A History of the Arab Peoples*. Cambridge, MA: Harvard University Press, 1991.

Hurewitz, J. C. *Diplomacy in the Near and Middle East A Documentary Record: 1914–1956*, Vol. II. London & New York: D. Van Nostrand Co., 1956.

"Iraksko-Turetskii voennyii sgovor," *Izvestiia*, 15 February 1955.

Ismael, Tareq Y. and Ismael, Jacqueline S. *The Communist Movement in Syria and Lebanon*. Gainesville: University Press of Florida, 1998.

Jackson, Richard L. *The Non-Aligned, the UN and the Superpowers*. New York: Praeger, 1983.

Jadirji, Kamil al-. *Mudhakarat Kamil al-Jadirji wa-Ta'arikh al-Hizb al-Watani al-Dimuqrati*. Köln: Al-Kamel Verlag, 2002.

Jaipal, Rikhi. *Non-Alignment*. Ahmedabad, Bombay: Allied Publishers, 1983.

Johnston, Charles. *The Brink of Jordan*. London: Hamilton, 1972.

Karsh, Ephraim. "Marriage of Comfort: The Soviet Union and Syria," in Yaniv Avner, Moshe Ma'oz and Avi kober (eds.). *Syria and Israel's National Security*. Tel Aviv: Ministry of Defense Publishing House, 1991 [Hebrew].

Karsh, Ephraim. *The Soviet Union and Syria: The Asad Years*. London: Royal Institute of International Affairs, Routledge, 1988.

Karunakaran, K. P. (ed.). *Outside the Contest: A Study of Nonalignment and the Foreign Policies of some Nonaligned Countries*. New Delhi: People's Publishing House, 1963.

Kaylani, Nabil M. "The Rise of the Syrian Ba'th, 1940–1958," *International Journal of Middle East Studies* (1972), Vol. 3, pp. 3–23.

Kedourie, Elie. *England and the Middle East*. London and Boulder, CO: Mansell Publishing and Westview Press, 1987.

——. *The Chatham House Version and other Middle Eastern Studies*. Hanover and London: University Press of New England, 1984.

——. "The Transition from a British to an American Era in the Middle East," in Shaked Haim and Rabinovich Itamar (eds.). *The Middle East and the United States*. New Brunswick and London: Transaction Books, 1980.

Keilany, Ziad. "Socialism and Economic Change in Syria," *Middle Eastern Studies*, Vol. 9, No. 1 (1973).

Kerr, Malcolm. *The Arab Cold War, 1958–1964*. London, New York: Oxford University Press, 1965.

Khalil, Muhammad. *The Arab States and the Arab League, A Documentary Record*. Beirut: Khayats, 1962.

Khoury, Philip S. *Urban Notables and Arab Nationalism, The Politics of Damascus 1860–1920*. London, New York: Cambridge University Press, 1983.

——. "Syrian Political Culture: A Historical Perspective," in R. G. Antoun R. J. and Quataert Donald (eds). *Syria: Society, Culture and Polity*. New York: State University of New York Press, 1991.

Khuli, Lutfi al-. *'Am al-Inkisar fi al-'Alam al-Thalith*. Cairo: al-Qahira lil-thaqafa al-'Arabiyya, 1975.

Kimche, David. *The Afro-Asian Movement*. Jerusalem:Israel University Press, 1973.

Korany, Bahgat. *Social Change, Charisma and International Behaviour: Towards a Theory of Foreign Policy-Making in the Third World*. Leiden: Institut Universitaire de Hautes Etudes Internationales, 1976.

Lacouture, Jean. *Nasser Veyorshav*. Tel Aviv: 'Am-Oved, 1972 [Hebrew].

Laqueur, Walter.*The Soviet Union and the Middle East*. London: Routledge & Kegan Paul, 1959.

Laqueur, Walter and Rubin, Barry (eds.). *The Israeli Arab Reader*. New York and Middlesex: Penguin Books, 1984

Lenczowski, George. *The Middle East in World Affairs*. Ithaca and London: Cornell University Press, 1980, 4th edition.

Lesch, David W. *Syria and the United States: Eisenhower's Cold War in the Middle East*. Boulder, CO: Westview Press, 1992.

Losev, S. "Dlia chego Menderes posetil Irak," *Izvestiia*, 14 January 1955.

Mansfield, Peter. *The Arabs*. London: Penguin Books, 1978.

Mansur, Sami. *Intiqasat al-Thawra fi al-'Alam al-Thalith*. Beirut: al-Mu'assasa al-'Arabiyya lil-Dirasat wa-al-Nashr, 1972.

Ma'oz, Moshe. *Syria and Israel From War to Peacemaking*. Oxford: Clarendon Press, 1995.

Maqsud, Clovis. *Ma' na al-Hiyad al-Ijabi.* Beirut: Dar al- 'Ilm lil-Malayin, 1960.

Martin, Laurence W. (ed.). *Neutralism and Nonalignment: The New States in World Affairs*. New York: Praeger, 1962.

Medvedev, V. "Naglye Domogatel'stva SSHA v Sirii," *Pravda*, 9 January 1955.

——. "Turetsko-Irakskii voennyii sgovor," *Pravda*, 19 January 1955.

Ministerstvo Inostrannykh del SSSR. *SSSR I Arabskie Strany, 1917–1960, Dokumenty I Materialy*. Moskva: Gosudarstvennoe Izdatel'stvo Politicheskoii Literatury, 1961.

Murqis, Ilyas. *Ta'arikh al-Ahzab al-Shuyu'iyya fi al-Watan al-'Arabi*. Beirut: Dar al-Tali'a, 1964.

Mustafa, Fahmi Husain. *Siyasat 'Adam al-Inhiyaz fi al-Majal al-Duwali*. Cairo: Dar al-Qawmiyya, 1962.

Nair, N. Parameshwaran, "Non-Alignment, History, Ideology, Prospects," in K. P. Karunakaran (ed.), *Outside the Contest*. New Delhi: People's Publishing House, 1963.

Nehru, Jawaharlal. *India's Foreign Policy, Selected Speeches, September 1946–April 1961*. Delhi: The Publication Division, Government of India, 1961.

Nehru, Pandit Jawaharlal *Toward Freedom: The Autobiography of Jawaharlal Nehru.* New York: John Day, 1941.

Nizameddin, Talal. *Russia and the Middle East Towards a New Foreign Policy.* London: Hurst & Co., 1999.

Novikov, N. V. *Vospominaniya Diplomata Zapiski 1938–1947.* Moskva: IPL, 1989.

Nyerere, Julius K. "Non-Alignment and its Future Prospects," in Uma Vasudev (ed.). *Issues before Non-Alignment Past & Future.* New Delhi: Indian Council of World Affairs, 1983.

Ogley, Roderick. *The Theory and Practice of Neutrality in the Twentieth Century.* London: Routledge & Kegan Paul, 1970.

Osipov, V. "Ne myt'em tak katan'em, novyii nazhim SSHA na Siriiu," *Izvestiia*, 2 March 1955.

"Otkrylas Konferentsiia Stran Azii I Afriki," *Izvestiia*, 19 April 1955.

Podeh, Elie. *The Decline of Arab Unity.* Brighton & Portland: Sussex Academic Press, 1999.

——. *The Quest for Hegemony in the Arab World, The Struggle for the Baghdad Pact.* Tel Aviv: Ministry of Defence Publishing House, 1996 [Hebrew].

——. "To Unite or Not Unite That is Not the Question: The 1963 Tripartite Unity Talks Reassessed," *Middle Eastern Studies*, Vol. 39, No. 1 (2003), pp. 150–85.

Polk, William R. *The United States and the Arab World.* Cambridge, MA: Harvard University Press, 1965.

Prasad, Bimal. "The Evolution of Non-alignment," in Uma Vasudev (ed.), *Issues before Non-Alignment: Past & Future.* New Delhi: Indian Council of World Affairs, 1983.

The Programme of the League of Communists of Yugoslavia (1958). Merhavya: Mapam, 1959 [Hebrew].

Rabinovich, Itamar. *Syria under the Ba'th.* Jerusalem: Israel University Press, 1972.

Razzaz Munif al-. *Al-Tajrriba al-Murra.* Beirut: Dar-Ghandur, 1967.

Robertson, David. *A Dictionary of Modern Politics.* London: Europa Publications, 1985.

——. *The Penguin Dictionary of Politics.* London: Penguin Books, 1993.

Ro'i, Yaacov. *From Encroachment to Involvement.* Jerusalem: Israel University Press, 1974.

——. *Soviet Decision Making in Practice.* New Brunswick and London: Transaction Books, 1980.

Rucker, Laurent. "The Soviet Union and the Suez Crisis," in Tal David (ed.), *The 1956 War, Collusion and Rivalry in the Middle East.* London: Frank Cass, 2001.

Safran, Nadav. *The United States and Israel.* Cambridge, MA: Harvard University Press, 1963.

Salem-Babikian, Norma. "Michel 'Aflaq, a Biographic Outline . . . ," *Arab Studies Quarterly* (Spring 1980), Vol. 2, No. 2, pp. 162–79.

Salibi, Kamal S. *The Modern History of Lebanon.* Delmar, New York: Caravan Books, 1990.

Sayegh, Fayez al- (ed.). *The Dynamic of Neutralism in the Arab World.* San Francisco: Chandler Publishing House, 1964.

Seale, Patrick. *Asad of Syria.* Tel Aviv: Ma'arkhot, 1988 [Hebrew].

——. *The Struggle for Syria.* London: Oxford University Press, 1965.

Sela, Avraham. *Unity Within Conflict in the Inter-Arab System*. Jerusalem: Magnes Press, 1983.

Seligman, Edwin R.A. (ed.). *Encyclopedia of the Social Sciences*, Vol. 11. New York: Macmillan, 1949.

Selim, Mohamad El-Sayed. *Non-Alignment in a Changing World*. Cairo: The American University of Cairo, 1983.

Shamir, Shimon (ed.). *The Decline of Nasserism 1965–1970*. Tel Aviv: Mif'alim Universitayim, 1978 [Hebrew].

Sills, David L. (ed.), *International Encyclopedia of the Social Sciences*, Vol. 11. New York: Macmillan Company, and the Free Press, 1968.

Singham A. W. and Hune Shirley. *Non-Alignment in an Age of Alignments*. London: Zed Books, 1986.

St. John, Robert. *The Boss, The Story of Jamal 'Abd al-Nasser*. Tel Aviv: Ma'arkhot, 1962 [Hebrew].

Suhail, Ayyub. *al-Hizb al-Shuyu'i fi Suriyya wa Lubnan, 1922–58*. Beirut: Dar al-Nashr, 1959.

Thomson, David. *Europe since Napoleon*. Tel Aviv: Zmora-Bitan, 1984 [Hebrew], original English version was published in 1962).

Torrey, Gordon H. "The Ba'th—Ideology and Practice," *Middle East Journal* (Autumn 1969), Vol. 23, pp. 445–57.

——. *Syrian Politics and the Military, 1945–1958*. Ohio: Ohio State University Press, 1964.

Van-Dam, Nikolas. *The Struggle for Power in Syria*. London: Croom Helm, 1979.

Vazeh, Pinhas. *Hamesimah-Rekhesh* (The Mission—Arms Acquisition). Tel Aviv: Ma'arkhot, 1966.

Wright, Gordon. "Contemporary History in the Contemporary Age," in Charles F. Delzell, *The Future of History*. Nashville, TN: Vanderbilt University Press, 1977.

Wunsche Renate, Linder Marion, and Voigtlander Roswitha, *The Struggle of the Movement of Non-Aligned Nations for Peace, Disarmament and Development— An Important Factor of Modern International Relations*. Berlin: Akademie-Verlag, 1985.

Zamir, Meir. *The Formation of Modern Lebanon*. Ithaca and London: Cornell University Press, 1985.

Ziser, Eyal. *Asad's Legacy: Syria in Transition*. New York: New York University Press, 2001.

Index